LAST SUBWAY

LAST SUBWAY

The Long Wait

for the Next Train

in New York City

Philip Mark Plotch

⋙ **THREE** HILLS

AN IMPRINT OF CORNELL UNIVERSITY PRESS

ITHACA AND LONDON

First published 2020 by Cornell University Press
Printed in the United States of America

Library of Congress Cataloging-in-Publication Data
Names: Plotch, Philip Mark, 1961– author.
Title: Last subway : the long wait for the next train in New York City /
   Philip Mark Plotch.
Description: Ithaca [New York] : Three Hills, an imprint of Cornell
   University Press, 2020. | Includes bibliographical references and index.
Identifiers: LCCN 2019019068 (print) | LCCN 2019021840 (ebook) | ISBN
   9780801453663 (cloth ; alk. paper)
Subjects: LCSH: Subways—New York (State)—New York—History. |
   Subways—Economic aspects—New York (State)—New York. |
   Subways—Political aspects—New York (State)—New York. | New York City
   Transit Authority. | Transportation and state—New York (State)—New York.
Classification: LCC HE4491.N65 P58 2020 (print) | LCC HE4491.N65 (ebook) |
   DDC 388.4/2097471—dc23
LC record available at https://lccn.loc.gov/2019019068
LC ebook record available at https://lccn.loc.gov/2019021840

ISBN 978-1-5017-4502-7 (epub/mobi ebook)
ISBN 978-1-5017-4503-4 (pdf ebook)

To Amy—for keeping me happy and healthy while giving me the confidence and support I need to pursue my dreams.

Also, to two strong, smart, and bold young adults, Cynthia and Andrew, who have given us such joy.

CONTENTS

Introduction: A Long Wait for a Train   1

1. From a Compact City into a Metropolis   10

2. An Empty Promise   27

3. The Billionaire's Ambitions   49

4. Construction Begins and Construction Ends   73

5. Saving the Subway   96

6. Planning from the Bottom Up   124

7. A Twenty-First-Century Subway   157

8. Building a Subway and Unleashing the Plagues   192

9. Andrew Cuomo's Finish Line   221

Conclusion: Delays Ahead   247

Acknowledgments   271

Key Dates in the Second Avenue Subway Saga   273

Notes   277

Index   341

A Long Wait for a Train

I had an epiphany in February 2005, across the street from a gaping hole in the ground where the World Trade Center towers once soared. I was interviewing for a position at the Lower Manhattan Development Corporation, a State of New York agency set up after the September 11 terrorist attacks. The agency's senior vice president, Stefan Pryor, liked my background. At the time, I was manager of planning at the Metropolitan Transportation Authority (MTA), working on plans to extend a subway line to Manhattan's far west side, expand New York City's convention center, build a new NFL football stadium, and lure the Olympics to the city in 2012.

Pryor asked me what I thought about the proposal to build a rail link connecting the World Trade Center in Lower Manhattan with Long Island and Kennedy International Airport. This project was a high priority for George Pataki, the governor of New York, who wanted Lower Manhattan to be more convenient for air travelers and suburban commuters, as part of his revitalization plan to keep the world's largest financial institutions from fleeing to Jersey City, Chicago, London, or Frankfurt.

I thought about telling Pryor that I had the skills and experience he needed to finalize the rail link's plan and help secure the $6 billion needed to build it. But I knew the rail link was unlikely to be built, because it was not a high-enough priority for the transportation agencies that were expected to finance and construct it. As my mind raced through other possible answers to his question, I realized for the first time that the planning and politics of transportation megaprojects were divorced from reality. So, I answered Pryor, "it doesn't matter whether or not the rail link gets built." As I pointed out his window to nearby office towers, I continued, "The important thing is that Goldman Sachs and Merrill Lynch and American Express all think we are going to build it."

Pryor smiled broadly, banged his fist on the table, and exclaimed, "You're the only one who gets it." A few weeks later, I was hired to serve as his director of transportation policy. For the next nine years, I contributed to the redevelopment of the World Trade Center and the renaissance of Lower Manhattan, while the rail link proposal quietly faded away.

Ever since that interview, I have discovered many other instances when elected officials raised false expectations about transportation improvements. Sometimes politicians are simply too optimistic about completing a project. Other times they lack an understanding of the enormous obstacles involved in constructing and financing large transportation projects. Most troubling are those occasions when politicians simply do not care about the truth, because their announcements about grand projects garner them so much favorable publicity.

THE NEAR-MYTHICAL SUBWAY LINE

New York once had the world's greatest subway system, but for decades elected officials have not fulfilled their promises to improve facilities and expand routes. False promises have led to unreliable service, obvious neglect, and abandoned tunnels. One of the best ways to understand why New York's subways have so many problems and what can be done about them is by learning about New York's near-mythical subway under Second Avenue.

Every city has its own fanciful project. In the nineteenth century, a London architect proposed building a ninety-four-story pyramid to accommodate more than five million dead bodies, a bold solution to the problem of overcrowded graveyards. When Frank Lloyd Wright was eighty-nine years old, he unveiled plans for a mile-high Chicago skyscraper, 528 stories tall, with parking for fifteen thousand cars and one hundred helicopters. Although construction never started on the London and Chicago towers, the Soviet Union did begin erecting steel for the world's tallest building in the 1930s. The Palace of the Soviets was designed to be a symbol of a new country and a thriving socialist economy. With twenty-one thousand seats in the main hall and a three-hundred-foot-tall bronze statue of Vladimir Lenin above, the palace would have been Moscow's version of the Statue of Liberty standing on top of the Empire State Building resting above Madison Square Garden.[1]

In the capital of capitalism, New Yorkers have been talking since 1903 about building a subway under Second Avenue, on Manhattan's East Side.

When the Second Avenue subway has not been a main character in the debates about improving transportation in New York City, it has been an ambitious understudy waiting to take its place center stage. Since the 1930s, the line has symbolized New York's inability to modernize its infrastructure and accommodate its residents. While the number of people living and working in New York City has grown, its rapid transit system of underground and elevated rail lines has shrunk. Train lines above Second and Third Avenues were torn down in the 1940s and 1950s, in anticipation of the Second Avenue subway. With less capacity to accommodate even more passengers, overcrowding would eventually become one of the leading causes of subway delays.[2]

While two subway lines run the length of Manhattan's West Side, only the Lexington Avenue line trains (numbers 4, 5, and 6) operate along the entire East Side. That is why the East Side's trains are the most crowded in the country, with ridership rivaling the number of passengers who ride San Francisco's, Chicago's, and Boston's entire transit systems combined. During peak periods, passengers crowd the subway cars, platforms, and stairwells—which slows down trains at stations, reduces the frequency of service, and exacerbates the crowded conditions.

New York's leaders blame external forces for their repeated failures to build the Second Avenue subway. After all, the project was delayed by the Great Depression, World War II, and the city's fiscal crisis in the 1970s. Although those were contributing factors, promises of improved subway services have always exceeded available resources. While politicians have repeatedly promised a Second Avenue subway to help advance their own careers, they have failed to acknowledge the enormous challenges involved in paying for it. The media have been complicit in raising false expectations and misleading the public into thinking unrealistic plans are achievable.

After decades of promises, New York actually started building the new subway line under the streets of East Harlem, the East Village, and Chinatown in the early 1970s. But to pay for the new subway, the city diverted resources from more critical work. As a result, the infrastructure on the existing system deteriorated and riders experienced frequent service delays.

In 1989, the Second Avenue subway was resurrected. Planners agonized over its exact route, engineers designed thousands of components, civic activists mobilized support, and elected officials allocated billions of dollars for the project. Thanks to thousands of workers who toiled underground in difficult and oftentimes dangerous conditions, the first three of sixteen planned Second Avenue subway stations opened to the public on New Year's Day in 2017. This 1.5-mile-long rail line was the subway's first major service expansion in more than fifty years, and has alleviated some subway crowding and reduced travel time for tens of thousands of New Yorkers. The spacious new stations, featuring dramatic works of art, have been widely acclaimed.[3]

CONCERN FOR THE FUTURE

Time will tell whether these stations were worth their $4.6 billion cost. The section of the Second Avenue subway in service has been disparagingly dubbed a "stubway," and a New York City deputy mayor, Dan Doctoroff, referred to it as "a silly little spur that doesn't generate anything other than some convenience for people who are perfectly happy to live where they lived before." Moreover, accelerating the construction schedule to meet a politically imposed deadline contributed to a subway crisis several months after its 2017 opening.[4]

On a per-mile basis, the completed section of the Second Avenue subway was the most expensive subway extension ever built anywhere in the world. Costs were high because of inefficient phasing and high real estate costs, powerful unions earning high wages and dictating costly work rules, and extensive regulations and environmental sensitivities. If the Second Avenue subway's thirteen other planned stations are ever completed, the 8.5-mile line would be one of the world's most expensive infrastructure projects, surpassing the $21 billion rail tunnel between England and France. Given the extraordinary cost and lengthy construction period, the Second Avenue subway will more than likely be the last subway line built in New York for generations to come.

The modern stations draw attention to the dirt, noise, and cramped conditions in the rest of the city's subway stations. In even more dire need of improvement are the vital subway components that passengers neither see nor appreciate, such as train signals that prevent trains from crashing, ventilation systems that keep smoke from asphyxiating riders, and pumping equipment that protects sensitive equipment from water damage. For most of the subway's history, politicians have preferred postponing upgrades to this critical equipment rather than raising fares.

New York's high costs and slow progress rebuilding and expanding its transit system are worrisome for New York's future. There is no guarantee that New York will always be able to attract the people and businesses that have made it a global center for business, media, and the arts. Throughout human history, once-great cities have lost out to competitors that were more nimble, farsighted, and aggressive. New York's competitors around the world are not satisfied with the status quo, or with relying on hundred-year-old transit facilities. For instance, while New York was constructing its 1.5-mile-long Second Avenue subway line, Beijing added more than 250 miles of new subway lines between 2007 and 2017.

New York's leading business organization, the Partnership for New York City, recognizes that safety, affordability, and livability are essential to New York City's global competitiveness. Many of New York's elected officials have long understood this. Scott Stringer, Manhattan's borough president in 2011, warned, "We cannot build a 21st-century city and compete globally if we continue to spend five, even seven times as much on construction projects as compared to our competitors."[5]

Just as skyscrapers need working elevators, New York City depends on a reliable and safe subway system that can accommodate more than five and a half million riders per day. Apartment buildings, office towers, hotels, universities, hospitals, and entertainment centers have been built around its 472 subway stations. The subway system is so extensive that laid end to end, its tracks would stretch from Times Square to Atlanta.

MTA officials justifiably take great pride in all the improvements they have made to the subways since the 1980s, when every station and subway car was covered with graffiti. New Yorkers, though, no longer use the 1980s as a benchmark. Instead, subway riders want something done about overcrowding, unreliable service, and noisy stations with narrow passageways, cracked tiles, and peeling paint. To see what a modern subway looks like, they do not need to get on an airplane. Anyone in Manhattan or Brooklyn can simply take the Q train and get off at one of the three new spacious, clean, and quiet stations on Second Avenue.

TRADE-OFFS AND TOUGH DECISIONS

Despite what most New Yorkers think, the subway system does not generate a profit that can be used for improvements. In fact, fares barely cover the salaries of the men and women who operate and maintain it. Annual multibillion-dollar subsidies from taxes and tolls are used to pay for employee benefits, electric power, fuel, supplies, insurance, maintenance, and growing debt payments.

Even with the introduction of New York's congestion pricing program, the MTA will have difficulty borrowing enough for future expansion projects because it already has more outstanding debt than dozens of US states. Asking passengers to pay more is also problematic because fares in recent years have been rising faster than inflation, and New York's subway riders already pay a higher share of operating expenses than transit riders in nearly every other US city.[6]

Given its limited resources, New York has to make tough decisions about prioritizing subway improvements. Powerful players in the government, business, and civic sectors constantly battle over how much the MTA should get to operate and maintain its transportation network. They also fight over which large transportation projects will get funded, and how resources should be allocated between existing systems and expansion projects. The stakes are high in terms of careers, jobs, money, property values, and prestige.

Some transportation projects are needed to enhance the subway system's safety, resiliency, and reliability, while others are important for passenger comfort, travel time, and accessibility. The Second Avenue subway is an unusual project because it provides numerous benefits. It alleviates crowding, improves reliability, reduces travel time, and improves accessibility. Compared to the rest of the city's subway lines, it was also built to a much higher standard of safety. Moreover, completing the Second Avenue subway would provide critical redundancy because eventually the century-old Lexington Avenue line will have to be shut down for an extended period of time for repairs and upgrades.

Because the public tends to ignore the needs of aging facilities they cannot see, obtaining sufficient funds to upgrade hidden infrastructure can be just as challenging as funding major expansion projects. Subway riders care when their trains are delayed or dirty, not whether the train signals are from 1920 or 2020. Likewise, New Yorkers can be complacent about the risks to the city's infrastructure associated with climate change and another terrorist attack. Subway riders are usually more interested in customer amenities like Wi-Fi service and electronic signs with real-time information. Since the media report on stories that interest the public, most people do not understand the importance of upgrading signals, pumps, and ventilation systems. Those issues and images are simply not sexy.

Because neither the public nor the media pay much attention to modernizing the subway's hidden infrastructure, politicians usually do not make it a high-enough priority. Voters are more likely to reward elected officials for preventing a fare hike. Many infrastructure improvements are actually unpopular among riders because they disrupt regular subway services. While the media tend to ignore announcements about basic infrastructure improvements, reporters and newspaper editorial boards usually praise the vision and foresight of politicians who announce grandiose transportation initiatives such as trains to airports, and subways under Second Avenue. Politicians get media coverage at groundbreaking events and ribbon-cutting ceremonies for new subway stations, not when pumping equipment is installed below the city's streets.

Obtaining sufficient funds to complete the Second Avenue subway has its own set of challenges. Compared to the first phase, which was built on the Upper East Side, each of the next three phases will cost more to build and will carry fewer passengers. Thus, subsequent phases will be less cost effective and not as likely to secure federal funding. Furthermore, the people who live and work in East Harlem, where the second phase will be built, have less political clout and have made the project less of a priority than their wealthier neighbors to the south.[7]

Securing enough funding to complete the Second Avenue subway will also be difficult given the slow progress on the first phase. In previous generations, transportation officials promised a relatively quick construction period for new subway lines, but now it appears that the Second Avenue subway's three remaining phases will each take about ten years to complete. The project has become an investment that may be needed to help the region's long-term prosperity, but not an improvement from which most current riders will benefit.

VISIONARY LEADERS OR SELF-SERVING ONES

New York can successfully both upgrade and expand its subway system to meet the public's needs and expectations, if elected officials are willing to look past the next election cycle and if they are convinced that the transit system's shortcomings threaten the region's long-term prosperity. Anything is possible. After all, since the Second Avenue subway was first proposed, the city has bounced back, stronger than ever, from the Great Depression, the loss of manufacturing jobs, middle-class flight to the suburbs, a fiscal crisis, high crime rates, the September 11 terrorist attack, and a financial crisis.

Generating and maintaining support for ambitious multibillion-dollar expansion projects is a formidable challenge, though, because elected officials come and go, public opinion shifts, fiscal conditions change, and the economy has its ups and downs. The lengthy process of reviewing environmental conditions, obtaining necessary sign-offs, designing projects, purchasing property, and moving utilities makes modernizing and expanding the subway vulnerable to all sorts of unexpected events.

The Second Avenue subway story reveals how rebuilding and expanding the subway requires visionary leaders. Transportation officials must develop comprehensive plans, civic and business leaders need to generate public support, and elected officials must champion improvements and secure resources. The story of the Second Avenue subway also reveals what has happened without that leadership. Repeatedly, uninformed and self-serving individuals have fostered false expectations about New York's ability to adequately maintain and significantly expand the transit system. The subway and its millions of beleaguered passengers are continuing to deal with the repercussions of those false expectations, every single day.

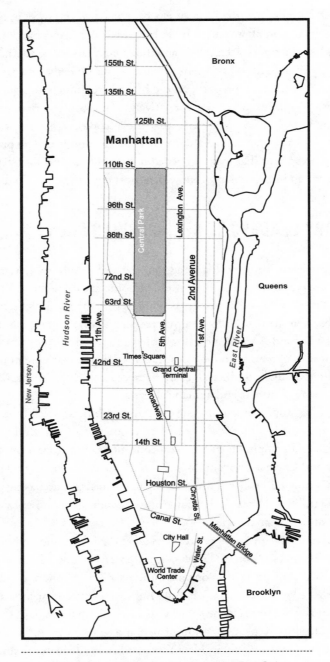

Map I.1. Manhattan (Second Avenue is on the East Side between 128th Street and Houston Street)

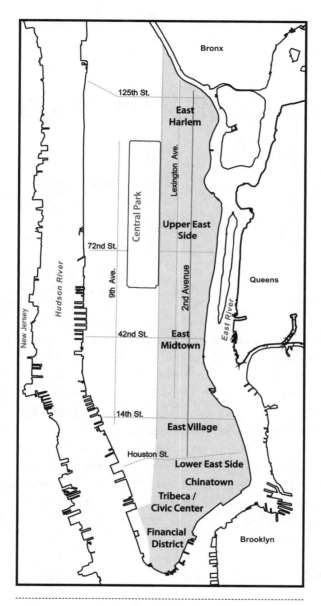

Map I.2. Neighborhoods that would be served by a Second Avenue subway running from 125th Street to Lower Manhattan

1

From a Compact City into a Metropolis

Cities compete with each other; they always have and always will. They vie to build the tallest buildings, largest convention centers, grandest boulevards, biggest stadiums, and hippest neighborhoods. In the nineteenth century, New York City created the world's largest urban transportation system, with ferries, bridges, and horse-drawn streetcars. After private railroad companies built tracks for elevated railroads (Els) above the city's streets in the 1870s, the city's population spread out and grew rapidly from Lower Manhattan.

The Els were one of New York City's most popular tourist attractions. For five cents, passengers could peer directly into homes and marvel at the city's elegant buildings, massive warehouses, tall churches, and ethnic enclaves. New Yorkers, however, complained about the deafening noise from the trains and the dark tunnels under the structures. Until the lines were electrified in the 1890s, people also had to deal with the stench from the passing locomotives and the hot ashes that dripped onto the sidewalks below.[1]

Manhattan's East Side had Els on Second and Third Avenues, while the West Side had Els on Sixth and Ninth Avenues. Workers could build railroads remarkably fast before today's environmental, safety, and labor regulations were instituted. For instance, the 7.5-mile-long Second Avenue El, with twenty-eight stations between 127th Street and Lower Manhattan, was built in less than eighteen months.[2]

Because the Els typically traveled twice as fast as horse-drawn streetcars, New Yorkers could commute from much greater distances to Lower

Manhattan's factories, warehouses, offices, and shops. A streetcar trip between 59th Street (in Midtown Manhattan) and City Hall (in Lower Manhattan) took at least forty-five minutes when the streets were clear and the weather ideal. A ride on the El covered that ground in twenty-eight minutes, and it was unaffected by traffic and less susceptible to inclement weather. As a result, after the Els were built, semirural parts of northern Manhattan were transformed into new residential neighborhoods. By the early twentieth century, the Els carried about seven hundred thousand daily riders every day, and over 80 percent of the city's inhabitants lived within walking distance of the stations.[3]

In the late nineteenth century, the mayor of New York City, Abram Hewitt, proclaimed that New York was destined to be the greatest city in the world. To continue growing, the city would need to build electric-powered rail lines, underground, that would travel faster and further and would accommodate even more people than the Els.[4]

STARVING THE SUBWAYS

Private companies paid for the construction and operation of the elevated lines, but no firm could finance an underground rail line because it was about four times as expensive per mile to build. The City of New York paid the construction costs for its first subway and in 1900 entered into a long-term lease with the Interborough Rapid Transit Company (IRT) to build and operate it.[5]

Subway service began with a grand celebration in October 1904 when trains first ran from City Hall up Manhattan's East Side on what is now known as the Lexington Avenue line. When trains reached the Grand Central subway station at 42nd Street, they traveled west to what is now known as Times Square, and then north to West Harlem. Although the early 1900s are sometimes cast as a genteel era, that was certainly not the case under the city's streets on the day the subways opened. The *New York Tribune* reported on the spectacle in an article titled "Birth of a Subway Crush": "Indescribable scenes of crowding and confusion, never before paralleled in this city, marked the throwing open of the subway to the general public last night. . . . Men fought, kicked and pummeled one another in their mad desire to reach the subway ticket offices or to ride on the trains. Women were dragged out, either screaming in hysterics or in a swooning condition; gray haired men pleaded for mercy; boys were knocked down, and only escaped by a miracle being trampled under foot."[6]

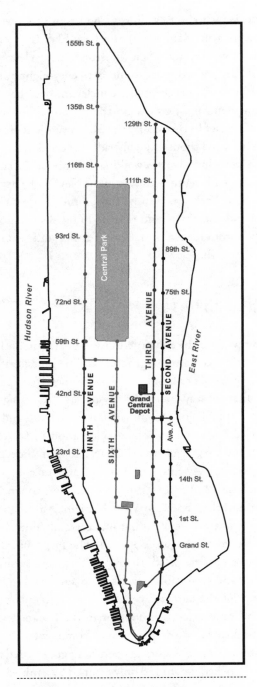

Map 1.1. Elevated railroads in Manhattan, 1881

In 1913, after years of acrimonious debate and tense negotiations, the City of New York entered into contracts with two companies—the IRT and the Brooklyn Rapid Transit Company (BRT)—to build more lines in Manhattan, Brooklyn, Queens, and the Bronx. Although a subway under Second Avenue had been under consideration as far back as 1903, the contracts did not include one. But the IRT was allowed to build additional tracks on its Second and Third Avenue Els, and to extend the Lexington Avenue line. A ride on the Lexington Avenue line's express train between 59th Street and City Hall would take only fourteen minutes, twice as fast as riding the El.[7]

Both the elevated lines and the subways spurred the population growth that city officials had anticipated and promoted. The number of people living in New York City's five boroughs rose from 1.5 million in 1870 to 3.4 million in 1900, and to nearly 7 million in 1930. The transit lines also enabled the city to grow upward because they could carry enough workers and visitors to make skyscrapers financially feasible. Before the El was built, Trinity Church on Broadway was the city's tallest building. In the 1890s, skyscrapers twenty to thirty stories tall towered over the church. In 1913, less than ten years after the first subway opened, the first office workers moved into the fifty-seven-story Woolworth Building on Broadway.

The IRT and the BRT expected to reap enormous profits, a portion of which they would share with the city. But their contracts with the city contained one provision that would affect the transit system's financial viability and the potential for further expansion: the fare had to be kept at five cents per trip for the duration of their forty-nine-year lease agreements.[8]

New York has long regulated the fees that privately owned monopolies, like the early twentieth-century railroads, were allowed to charge customers. For example, today, the utility company Con Edison cannot raise its electric rates without approval from New York State's Public Service Commission. The regulators know that limiting rate hikes might be politically popular, but if Con Edison did not have sufficient revenue, it would not be able to properly maintain its equipment and expand its electricity-generating capacity. As a result, residents and businesses would face brownouts and longer waits for new services and repairs.

In the early twentieth century, New York's politicians took a shortsighted approach to the transit system. Instead of raising fares, they raised false expectations that New Yorkers could have high-quality subway service with low fares. The repercussions would last for generations.

The financial health of the IRT and BRT deteriorated after they built their new lines. Passengers traveled longer distances, but the railroads could not recoup their increased operating expenses by charging higher fares. Moreover, in the twentieth century's second decade, automobile use soared and inflation surged. In 1919, the BRT declared bankruptcy, and in 1923 it would become the Brooklyn–Manhattan Transit Corporation (BMT). To deal with their red ink, the railroads replaced ticket takers with coin turnstiles, eliminated the gatekeepers who opened doors two cars at a time, reduced salaries, deferred investments, and cut back on station and train cleaning. As a result of their cost-cutting moves, service became less reliable and the system began to deteriorate.[9]

John Hylan, New York City's mayor between 1918 and 1925, had little sympathy for the firms' financial plight and no interest in bailing them out. He reportedly had a personal vendetta against the BRT because he felt the railroad had unjustifiably fired him as a motorman years earlier. Hylan first rose to citywide prominence when he led protests against awarding the initial contracts to the BRT and the IRT. His attacks on the private railroads earned him the support of the media mogul William Randolph Hearst, who advocated municipal ownership of the subway system.[10]

During his 1917 campaign for mayor, Hylan attacked the IRT and the BRT with missionary zeal. As mayor, he made mass transit his leading issue and referred to the two firms as "greedy, power-mad behemoths that double-crossed the public at every turn." One of the railroad heads accused Hylan of ruining the transit system and using it as a "political escalator." Hylan considered the nickel fare "as sacred and binding as any contracts ever drawn in the history of financial transactions the world over." With the fare as the centerpiece of his 1921 reelection campaign, Hylan trounced his Republican, Socialist, Labor, and Prohibition Party opponents, winning more than 64 percent of the vote.[11]

Hylan's rhetoric against the IRT and BRT struck a nerve with the city's voters, who were fed up with deteriorating transit services and increasingly crowded trains. During Hylan's term in office, ridership on the rapid transit system (subways and elevated trains) increased from 1.1 billion to 1.7 billion per year. The novelty of traveling underground had worn off long ago. LeRoy T. Harkness, a member of the state agency responsible for regulating the subways and elevated lines, admitted that crowding had "long passed the point of acute suffering."[12]

Although the subways were crowded during peak periods, they were still the envy of the world. In a 1920 visitors' guide to New York, Henry Collins

Brown wrote, "Taxis while comfortable are not absolutely necessary. The subway will take you within a few blocks of anywhere, and the fare is only a few cents, even if you ride to the end of its fifteen miles. There is no city in the world where transportation is so good, and between ten and four the cars are not uncomfortably crowded."[13]

Brown described the wide variety of people, shops, and buildings found on the East Side in 1920. One of the most densely populated neighborhoods in the history of the world, the Lower East Side, was full of seething masses, pushcarts, and open-air markets. Brown warned tourists about the Bowery, the "sordid" neighborhood north of Chinatown. Many of the city's most prominent residents, including the Carnegies, Rockefellers, and Roosevelts, lived farther north in what is now known as East Midtown and the Upper East Side. A must-see for all visitors to the city, Brown wrote, was a ride to the top of one of the city's new Lower Manhattan skyscrapers: "a veritable aeroplane trip with none of the dangers of the real thing." He also offered a tip about the locals: "Don't gape at women smoking cigarettes in restaurants. They are harmless and respectable."[14]

CITY BUILDS ITS OWN SUBWAY

In 1919, New York's state legislature established the Office of Transit Construction Commissioner to coordinate the planning of future subway lines. The next year, Daniel Turner, the office's chief engineer, proposed adding 830 miles of track to the existing 616 miles of elevated and subway lines over the next twenty-five years. Turner's plan envisioned every New York City resident living within half a mile of a rapid transit line. Like many of his contemporaries, he wanted New Yorkers to spread out from overcrowded Manhattan neighborhoods into the "open country" in the Bronx, Queens, and Brooklyn, where they could live in their own homes. His new subway lines would precede the population growth, not follow it. Turner argued that developing new neighborhoods without rapid transit would be like building a forty-story office tower without an elevator.[15]

Turner said that the existing subway system was unable to meet the future transit requirements of the East Side because the Lexington Avenue subway was "heavily overcrowded" and new offices and hotels were going up near Grand Central Terminal. His plan included two new north–south lines in Manhattan (one on the East Side and one on the West Side). Engineers referred to the subway lines in Manhattan as trunk lines because they had express and local tracks in Manhattan, with branches for local service in other parts of the city. These trunk lines were vital for the entire city because subway lines could not be extended into the Bronx, Queens, and Brooklyn unless the subway had sufficient capacity to accommodate passengers traveling into and through Manhattan.[16]

Although Turner's work would influence future plans, Mayor Hylan had his own vision for the subways that involved neither state oversight nor private railroad companies. In 1922, Hylan released a plan for a city-owned and city-operated "Independent" (IND) subway system that included a new East Side subway. Hylan's IND plan offered a more appealing, although unrealistic, alternative to the state's plan. The mayor promised that a consolidated, municipally owned transit system would earn a profit that could be used to fund new schools, parks, and highways. Passengers would no longer need to pay a second fare when they transferred between BRT and IRT trains, and there would be no strikes or labor disturbances because the city would always offer equitable salaries. All of this, he claimed, would happen without even having to increase the nickel fare.[17]

The fact that politicians and bureaucrats at the state capital in Albany were making decisions about new subways was a touchy subject in the city. The City of New York had only the powers that the state delegated to it. The state designated the city's boundaries, defined its governance structure, and then limited its ability to tax and spend. The relationship between city and state leaders constantly changed as elections shuffled the people and parties in power. In the early twentieth century, the state's top leaders (including the governor, assembly Speaker, and senate majority leader) were usually Republicans from rural parts of the state. They had very different interests than New York City's politicians, who were mostly Democrats.

In 1924, the mayor won his years-long battle with state regulators when the state agreed to give the city control over building future subway lines. Hylan's ally in the governor's office, Al Smith, had grown up on the Lower East Side and campaigned for governor on a platform of giving the city the power to build its own subways. Hylan subsequently set up a Board of Transportation, and his appointees put together an expansion program whose first phase included new lines on Sixth and Eighth Avenues. The board began mapping out the second phase of an IND system that would include a subway on the East Side. Since transit usage was higher near Sixth and Eighth Avenues, those living and working on the East Side would have to wait.[18]

Hylan continued excoriating the private transit railroads for political purposes. He pressured the private railroads to sell their lines to the city, while
accusing them of paying extravagant salaries and corrupting legislators to retain
their monopolies. At the 1925 groundbreaking for the IND system, he said, "It
means the beginning of the emancipation of the people of the City of New
York from the serfdom inflicted upon them by the most powerful financial and
traction dictatorship ever encountered."[19]

Construction for Hylan's new subway lines coincided with a booming New
York City economy. Skyscrapers were rising in Midtown Manhattan, while
new apartment buildings and single-family homes sprouted up near subway
stations all across the city. In the 1920s, one out of every five new apartments
and homes in the entire country was built in New York City.[20]

As in today's economy, the area in Manhattan below 59th Street was
the nation's center for finance, law, media, entertainment, and fashion. But the
city's economy was much more diversified, with about 14 percent of the nation's
manufacturing facilities located in New York City. Remarkably, approximately
three-quarters of all the women's clothes made in the United States were manufactured in New York City, nearly all of it south of 59th Street. Merchandise
buyers arrived into New York via the city's passenger ship terminals and its
two railroad stations, Penn Station and Grand Central Terminal. They stayed
at nearby hotels, dined in well-known restaurants, and attended Broadway
shows.[21]

The city's garment industry thrived on cheap immigrant labor and inex-
pensive transit services. But the combination of rapidly increasing ridership
and insufficient funding for the subways created a problem that raised the ire of
numerous civic groups in the mid-1920s. A leader of the Metropolitan Housewives' League pointed out "the inhuman, indecent, and dangerous crowding
and jamming of passengers, the unclean trains and platforms, and especially the
conditions of the public waiting and toilet rooms which are filthy, unsanitary
and disease breeding." Likewise, the City Club of New York told city officials,
"We do not get a civilized ride for a nickel today. We get instead a chance to
hang on, like a chimpanzee, to a flying ring suspended from the roof of the car
while we are crushed to the point of indecency by our fellow sufferers."[22]

In the 1920s, New Yorkers were also complaining about something right
outside their front doors—traffic jams caused by a rapid increase in automobile ownership. In 1922, the city's police commissioner wanted to tear down
the Second Avenue El and replace it with a Second Avenue subway so that the
street could accommodate more cars and trucks.[23]

In August 1929, with construction underway on the first phase of the IND system, the city's Board of Transportation announced that the centerpiece of the next phase would be a Second Avenue subway between Lower Manhattan and the Bronx. Construction of the Second Avenue subway was expected to begin the following year. The line would start at Water Street in Lower Manhattan and then go up Pearl Street, Chrystie Street, and Second Avenue. Nearly a century later, the plans for a Second Avenue subway follow a similar route in Manhattan.[24] Unlike twenty-first-century plans, however, the 1929 plan called for both express and local services in tunnels at least four tracks wide for most of their length. With connections to other proposed and existing lines, the 1929 plan for the Second Avenue subway was expected to primarily benefit passengers from the Bronx, Queens, and Brooklyn—not residents of Manhattan.[25]

Within weeks of the board's announcement, real estate brokers reported that owners selling property on Second Avenue raised their asking prices by about 50 percent and developers started assembling parcels of land for new apartment buildings by purchasing old five-story tenement apartment buildings that lined the avenue. The president of the Bronx Board of Trade was thrilled that a Second Avenue subway would be built. He called the plan "one of the greatest projects in years for encouraging the growth of the Bronx," and one in line with proposals that Bronx business leaders had been making for the past fifteen years.[26]

In 1930, about twelve thousand men were forming tunnels, building stations, and installing equipment for the IND's first phase. In preparation for the second phase, engineers surveyed the Second Avenue subway route and drilled holes to determine conditions below the street. They considered various options for the horizontal and vertical alignments, the location of express and local tracks, the connection to the Williamsburg Bridge, and the methods of construction. Construction was turning out to be much more expensive and time consuming in Manhattan than in the rest of the city because of Manhattan's extensive network of underground pipes, wires, and conduits.[27]

As construction and planning work proceeded, the new mayor, Jimmy Walker, struggled to obtain sufficient funds to operate the new IND lines. State legislation required the new subway service to be self-supporting within three years of opening. When the IND's Eighth Avenue subway line was ready to open in 1931, the stations remained closed for a year until immense pressure forced the city to begin service.[28]

In 1931, with the Great Depression devastating the city's finances, the city comptroller wanted to raise transit fares, but Walker refused to support him. Instead city leaders decided to cut the annual capital budget for new transit lines from $100 million to $70 million, and delay construction of the Sixth Avenue subway. By 1932, the city had amassed a debt that was nearly equal to that of all forty-eight states combined. Subways were the single biggest contributor to the city's debt burden, in part because the actual cost to build the IND system was more than twice the estimated cost. Operating losses were equally problematic. Although the fare was a nickel, every IND trip cost the city about fourteen cents. At the same time, transit ridership was falling because of high unemployment and rising levels of car ownership.[29]

The city cut back on its plans for the second phase in 1932 by slashing the number of new miles outside Manhattan. City officials said that the Second Avenue subway would have to be delayed for another two to three years. Two and a half years later, city officials acknowledged that it would have to be postponed indefinitely.[30]

The city could not borrow enough money to build the IND's second phase for several reasons: the state constitution limited the amount of money the city could borrow at no more than 10 percent of the city's total assessed property value, the Depression had lowered the value of the city's real estate, and the city wanted to borrow money to pay for new roads and parks. New York City never did allocate enough money to construct the second phase. Rather than creating a city where all residents would be within walking distance of rapid transit services, officials built one where all residents would be a short drive from a highway.

GOODBYE TO STREETCARS AND ELEVATED LINES

In 1934, the city's new mayor, Fiorello La Guardia, was in a bind about the subways. With the city in dire financial straits, he was unable to borrow enough money to finish construction of the IND's Sixth Avenue subway line, let alone start construction on Second Avenue. For political reasons, he would not raise the fare, but even if he could triple it, the expected drop in ridership levels would still make the city's new lines unprofitable. The other problem with raising the IND's fares was that it would increase the value of the IRT and BMT companies, because they would be able to increase their own transit fares.

Since La Guardia thought unifying all three subway lines would save the city money and improve the quality of transit services, he wanted to purchase the private railroad companies while their stock prices were low. In 1934, his administration even considered lowering the fare to four cents in hopes that it would force the railroads to sell their transit lines. La Guardia, a Republican in a heavily Democratic city, served as mayor from the depth of the Depression until the end of World War II. Thanks to help from both parties in the state capital, he was able to generate sufficient funds to preserve the five-cent fare, complete the Sixth Avenue line, and consolidate the subway system.[31]

In June 1940, the city purchased the properties of the IRT and the BMT for $326 million. The Board of Transportation, a city agency reporting to the mayor, was now responsible for operating and maintaining the most heavily used rapid transit system in the world. Today, the trains on the IND system are identified with the letters A through G, the IRT lines are all of the numbered trains, and the BMT lines are the letters J through Z.[32]

Building the Second Avenue subway was not one of La Guardia's priorities. While ships and trains had propelled the city's economy in the nineteenth century, La Guardia expected that modern cities would have to rely on cars, trucks, and airplanes. He heard from voters, businesses, property owners, city planners, civic groups, and other elected officials who clamored for highway improvements so that New York City would remain livable and economically viable.

When planners first considered building a second East Side subway line, few people could have predicted how automobiles would transform the metropolitan area. Motor vehicles were rare in the first decade of the twentieth century, but nearly a quarter of a million motor vehicles were registered in New York City by 1920. Five years later that number had more than doubled, and by 1941 the number of vehicles doubled once again.[33]

The mayor drew his vision for a new highway network from the Regional Plan Association, a group of leading business and civic professionals. In 1929, the association developed a plan for the New York/New Jersey/Connecticut metropolitan area that included an extensive highway and bridge network that would integrate the city with its growing suburbs. In the 1930s, La Guardia used state and federal funds to build new highways as well as parks all across the city. His close relationship with President Franklin D. Roosevelt and the leaders of the federal New Deal programs helped New York City receive a disproportionate share of federal funds during the Depression. Within months of La Guardia taking office, the city had captured one-seventh of the federal outlay for relief.[34]

Robert Moses, La Guardia's popular parks commissioner, helped the mayor obtain state and federal funding by identifying projects, acquiring necessary property, completing design, and then finishing construction—all in a timely and cost-effective manner. Under La Guardia, Moses increased the number of city playgrounds from 119 to 492. He also constructed seventeen large outdoor swimming pools, doubled the number of tennis courts, and tripled the number of golf courses. Furthermore, as chair of the Triborough Bridge Authority in the 1930s, Moses opened the Triborough, Henry Hudson, and Bronx-Whitestone Bridges. During La Guardia's tenure, New York also built the Kosciuszko Bridge, the Grand Central Parkway, the Henry Hudson Parkway, the Interboro Parkway (now the Jackie Robinson Parkway), the Moshulu Parkway, and the FDR Drive (East River Drive). By the end of the 1930s, La Guardia and Moses had built the greatest network of urban parks, bridges, and highways in the world.[35]

La Guardia's vision for the city did not include the electric-powered streetcars (trolleys) that operated on nearly every major avenue and street in Manhattan. He made it clear that streetcar lines should be converted to buses, saying that "trolleys are as dead as sailing ships." He then used New Deal funds to rip up tracks all over the city.[36]

La Guardia was not a fan of elevated lines either. When he first took office, New Yorkers traveling on the East Side could take the Lexington Avenue subway line as well as the Second and Third Avenue Els. The Second Avenue El ran from East Harlem to the southern tip of Manhattan, with a branch over the Queensboro Bridge to Queens, while the Third Avenue El connected the Bronx with Lower Manhattan. The Els carried fewer passengers than the subway, though. For example, in 1936, on Manhattan's East Side north of 64th Street, twice as many people used the Lexington Avenue line's stations as used all the elevated stations combined.[37]

No matter their usefulness, La Guardia called the elevated lines "old, unsightly and noisy." He wanted to demolish the vestiges of a nineteenth-century transportation system and replace them with buses so that cars would move faster and real estate values would increase. The Second and Third Avenue Els were getting in the way of what today would be called gentrification on the East Side. In the 1930s, Manhattan's Upper East Side, between 59th and 96th Street, had both extreme wealth and deep poverty. It was home to two hundred thousand people, which was more than any city in Florida or Connecticut at the time. Over one thousand apartments were in old tenement buildings where families lived in three-room apartments that offered little natural light and no central heat—most of the tenants used makeshift wood-burning stoves.[38]

The streets west of Third Avenue—Fifth, Madison, Park, and Lexington Avenues—had long been home to wealthy New Yorkers. In the 1920s, new apartment buildings, some of them with units featuring two floors and thirteen rooms, were built to house even more of the city's elite. The streets east of Second Avenue were also starting to attract wealthier residents. High-end apartment buildings and townhouses were replacing breweries, warehouses, coal yards, and old tenement buildings on First, York, and East End Avenues.[39]

Scions of New York's most prominent families were moving to Sutton Place, just east of First Avenue. In 1936, J. P. Morgan's daughter (Louisa Pierpont Satterlee) urged the mayor to remove the Second Avenue El because it "would increase use of Second Avenue for automobile traffic and help the rush congestion on First Avenue." Anne Vanderbilt told the mayor, "We are all, I feel sure, anxious to have this structure removed as soon as possible."[40]

The members of the First Avenue Association also lobbied city officials to demolish the Second Avenue El; they wanted to remove the noisy eyesore because it would increase their real estate values. The association, dominated by the owners of property east of Second Avenue between 23rd and 96th Streets, accurately predicted that demolishing the line would help accelerate the East Side's conversion into a large-scale apartment and hospital center. Property owners flooded the mayor's mailbox urging him to support state legislation that would allow the city to remove the El. They said it would increase real estate values, promote slum clearance, increase light and air, reduce noise, and increase city revenue. Improving traffic was a key motivator since they expected that removing the El's "pillars" would relieve the overburdened First Avenue and turn Second Avenue into an East Side highway.[41]

Real estate interests were among the city's most powerful players. Politicians coveted new development because it created jobs and homes. New buildings also allowed elected officials to expand municipal services and borrow more money, since the city's budget relied on property taxes. Furthermore, property owners had the ears of influential newspaper publishers because real estate ads were one of the biggest revenue sources for the newspaper industry.

In the 1930s and into the fall of 1941, state legislators from Queens thwarted La Guardia's efforts to tear down the Second Avenue El because so many of their constituents relied on it. The debate changed, though, after the Japanese attacked Pearl Harbor on December 7, 1941. Advocates for keeping the El were labeled unpatriotic when the nation's War Production Board urged city officials to demolish it because "scrap metal was so urgently needed." In the summer of 1942, La Guardia, wearing an iron worker's helmet and wielding a spike-pulling bar, ceremoniously began the demolition of the elevated line. He told the crowd at 23rd Street that they would now have more sunlight and fresh air than ever before. The elevated line did indeed help the war effort since thousands of its steel girders were used to build a defense factory on Long Island where the Hellcat fighter planes were built. When these navy planes landed on aircraft carriers, the crewmen would often yell, "Here comes another piece of the Second Avenue El!"[42]

The Els were also removed on the West Side, with service terminating on Sixth Avenue in 1938 and on Ninth Avenue in 1940. The new Eighth Avenue subway accommodated riders from the Ninth Avenue El, while the new Sixth Avenue subway replaced the Sixth Avenue El. But a new East Side subway did not replace the Second Avenue El. Likewise, the city did not build a new subway on the East Side after the Third Avenue El was demolished in the 1950s. The gains for East Side property owners came at the expense of working-class New Yorkers from East Harlem, the Lower East Side, Brooklyn, and the Bronx, as well as passengers traveling over the Queensboro Bridge and down Second Avenue. These train riders had less political clout than the First Avenue Association's wealthy members.

Lawrence Stelter, a city planner who has written extensively about New York's elevated lines, wrote in 1990, "What is blight to some, is charm to another. What is disdained as an eyesore in one era, may be revered in the next. Elevated noise and gloom may be unacceptable for one part of town, but tolerable elsewhere. There is, and has never been, one fixed ideal of urban living in our pluralistic culture."[43]

In retrospect, city officials made a mistake by demolishing both of the elevated lines. They encouraged new development on the East Side without adding to the transit system's capacity to serve a growing number of residents and workers. Inevitably, the East Side's only subway—the Lexington Avenue line—would bear the burden. Furthermore, removing the Third Avenue El made parts of the South Bronx more difficult to reach and less desirable to live in. Eliminating the transit service was one of the contributing factors that caused the South Bronx's population to drop from 247,000 to 92,000 in the 1970s and the area to become known as the worst slum in the United States.[44]

When the Second Avenue El was demolished in 1942, New Yorkers were still expecting the city to build a subway on Second Avenue. In a 1944 speech to the city council, La Guardia said, "The preparation of engineering plans for the construction of the Second Avenue subway has not been interrupted." He added, "Engineering plans will be available and ready at the propitious moment and when financial conditions permit."[45]

Despite decades of promises about imminent expansion, the rapid transit system has shrunk rather than grown since the unification of the transit system in 1940. Several elevated lines were demolished in Queens, Brooklyn, and the Bronx, along with Manhattan's four Els. The total number of track miles has decreased from 781 to 665, while the number of stations has decreased from 539 to 472. Moreover, all 437 miles of the city's streetcar lines are long gone.[46]

Figure 1.1. *Second Avenue with elevated line and tenements, looking north from 72nd Street in the 1930s. Source: The La Guardia and Wagner Archives, LaGuardia Community College/The City University of New York. Copyright: New York City Housing Authority.*

Figure 1.2. *Steam-powered elevated train with horse-drawn streetcar below. Source: Wood engraving by J. R. Brown. Wellcome Library, London. Copyrighted work available under Creative Commons Attribution only license CC BY 4.0.*

Figure 1.3. *Construction of four-track Lexington Avenue line at 97th Street in 1913. Source: Pierre P. Pullis and G. W. Pullis/ Museum of the City of New York. 2000.52.51.*

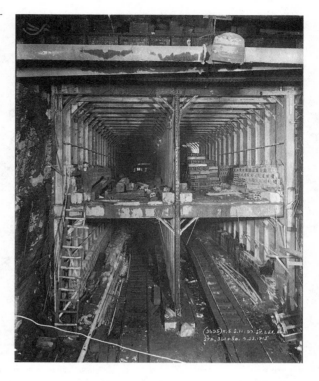

Figure 1.4. *Construction of Times Square station in 1903. Source: Identifier mac_2454, Municipal Archives Collection. Courtesy: NYC Municipal Archives.*

Figure 1.5. Robert Moses (left), Grover Whalen (center, president of World's Fair Corporation), and Mayor Fiorello La Guardia (right). Source: The La Guardia and Wagner Archives, LaGuardia Community College/The City University of New York.

2

An Empty Promise

During World War II, New York City was the nation's principal war port and the home to troops, European refugees, and wartime industries. Although the city halted large-scale construction projects unrelated to the war effort, building a Second Avenue subway remained one of its highest priorities. The new line would connect with two existing subway lines in the Bronx, run south to Lower Manhattan's financial district, and eventually extend all the way to Brooklyn via a new tunnel that would be built under the East River.[1]

But paying for the Second Avenue subway would be problematic, even after the anticipated end of the war. A 1944 study prepared for the city concluded that building the Second Avenue line would not produce any additional fare revenue, but would merely divert passengers from existing lines. That meant the city could not afford to operate the new line unless it raised fares and/or increased taxes.[2]

In 1945, the subways were still considered among the titanic engineering feats of science. Mayor La Guardia liked to say that "New York didn't build the subways; the subways built New York." In a *Saturday Evening Post* article titled "Manhattan's Daily Riot," Maurice Zolotow wrote, "The subways do an almost impossible job, and do it speedily and safely." He described the subway as a bewildering experience for a visitor, where "his eyes will be confused by the murky yellow dimness; his ears will be racked by the crashing, clashing, grating cacophony of the trains grinding against the tracks," and the "stale and heavy air will offend his nostrils." The visitor, Zolotow observed, will wonder "how New

Figure 2.1. *Crowded subway in 1946. Source: Stanley Kubrick for* Look *magazine. X2011.4.11107.105F ©SK Film Archives and Museum of the City of New York.*

Yorkers can read their newspapers during the rush hour, how lady shoppers can manage to carry armfuls of bundles, how mothers can carry their infants, how delivery boys can maneuver themselves and their large packages."[3]

While the subways were crowded, dimly lit, and poorly ventilated, New York's magnificent new parkways were the envy of the world. After World War II, engineers from all across the country came to New York to learn more about these highways, with their ribbons of green space that connected the city with beaches, lakes, and mountains. New York City, not Los Angeles, had more highway miles within its borders than any other city in the nation. Traffic congestion was getting worse, however, and it was not just affecting commuters. Heavy traffic slowed down emergency vehicles and increased delivery times and costs for the city's factories, wholesalers, and shops. Retailers threatened to move to the suburbs if the city did not build more parking to accommodate their customers.[4]

Elected officials would have to make a choice. They could not afford to build the Second Avenue subway, upgrade the existing transit system, and build all the highways on the drawing boards.

MAYORS GIVE MOSES CONTROL

In 1945, La Guardia decided not to seek a fourth term, due to his failing health. Through the Depression and the war, the Republican mayor had battled widespread corruption associated with the Democratic Party bosses who had long run the city. His parks commissioner, Robert Moses, had also developed a reputation as an honest reformer by efficiently building world-class parkways and parks.

Moses simultaneously held multiple public-sector positions that gave him enormous power over public works projects in the New York metropolitan area. In addition to leading the city's parks department, he was also president of the Long Island State Park Commission, chair of the New York State Council of Parks, president of the Jones Beach Parkway Authority, president of the Bethpage State Park Authority, chair of the Triborough Bridge and Tunnel Authority, and a member of the New York City Planning Commission. Moses told a group of highway officials, "There is a curious notion that I collect jobs as others collect stamps or marbles. Nothing could be further from the facts. I hold several jobs in related fields in order to overcome jurisdictional and geographical boundaries and get things done on a metropolitan and in some instances a wider scale."[5]

All of these roles enabled Moses to obtain the support of the numerous institutions and bureaucracies that were involved in proposing, approving, and funding new highway projects. He was the conduit for federal and state highway funds, and he controlled the Triborough Bridge and Tunnel Authority's resources, which were integral to the city's highway plans. He used the authority's toll revenues to finance new river crossings and construct new approaches to the existing ones.

In the 1945 mayoral race, the Democrats nominated William O'Dwyer. Brawny and blue-eyed with a radio announcer's voice and a wonderful grin, O'Dwyer was an immigrant who had arrived from Ireland thirty-five years earlier with only twenty-five dollars in his pocket. He had worked as a day laborer and a police officer before achieving prominence as a Brooklyn district attorney who successfully prosecuted organized crime figures. Four days before the election, O'Dwyer disclosed that if he won the race, he would create a new position for Moses, as the construction coordinator for new schools, hospitals, health centers, housing, parks, playgrounds, highways, and many other needed public improvements.[6]

Since O'Dwyer was the choice of the Democratic political bosses whom Moses had repeatedly castigated, many of Moses's friends and supporters were surprised that Moses would take a position in an O'Dwyer administration. They did not realize that Moses coveted power more than reform. His tacit support for O'Dwyer helped the Democrat overcome voter concerns about the influence of corrupt party bosses, and in January 1946, O'Dwyer was sworn in as the city's one-hundredth mayor.

Under La Guardia, numerous agencies and governing bodies coordinated the city's capital program, which consisted of projects to build and rehabilitate the city's infrastructure, such as renovating stations, purchasing new subway cars, and building new schools, parks, and libraries. Under O'Dwyer, Moses personally coordinated the program. He became the dominant player on the City Planning Commission, the body that recommended capital projects. Because he controlled so many resources, Moses held enormous sway over the city's Board of Estimate, whose eight members—the mayor, city comptroller, city council president, and five borough presidents—selected capital projects.[7]

Moses served as construction coordinator, while men loyal to him took on key City Hall positions, including deputy mayor. O'Dwyer allowed Moses to name all the board members of a new airport authority. He also appointed Moses to serve as chair of his emergency committee on housing, and then allowed him to name almost all of the other committee members.[8]

O'Dwyer served for only a little more than one term. During those four years and eight months, O'Dwyer and Moses convinced New Yorkers, the media, and even state legislators that the city would soon begin building a Second Avenue subway.

When O'Dwyer took office in 1946, La Guardia told him he was inheriting a perpetual headache. O'Dwyer laughed at the time, although he later admitted, "I had no idea what a headache it really was and how perpetual it was going to be." The city's facilities were in much worse shape than he expected because during the war, construction had been brought to a near standstill and public facilities were minimally maintained. Every city department and service cried out for essential and long-overdue repairs, replacements, improvements, and additions. At the same time, O'Dwyer thought that pay raises were long overdue for thousands of city employees.[9]

The mayor was surprised that the city had almost no money to carry out the public works he coveted. After the war ended, New York City was seemingly more prosperous than ever, far eclipsing the war-ravaged cities in Europe and Asia. With a population of nearly eight million—larger than those of forty-five of the nation's forty-eight states—New York City was the global center for finance and manufacturing, as well as home to the world's busiest port. Furthermore, the new United Nations headquarters rising on Manhattan's East Side would make it the diplomatic capital of the world.[10]

But the world's most prosperous city was in a precarious financial situation. Federal funds had paid for more than 30 percent of New York's municipal expenses at the height of the New Deal, but when O'Dwyer took office, federal support covered only about 5 percent. New York had less influence in Washington after President Franklin D. Roosevelt died, because the former governor of New York was succeeded by Missouri's Harry Truman.[11]

As mayor, O'Dwyer was head of the largest passenger railroad in the world. Although he thought that rehabilitation of the "obsolete and decrepit railroad" would be his administration's most important job, the mayor relied on Moses to identify and prioritize projects. O'Dwyer was awed and intimidated by Moses. The mayor admired Moses's extraordinary achievements, ability to cut through red tape, and reputation for honesty. But he was infuriated by Moses's steamrolling personality and tendency to put his own vision ahead of the mayor's wishes.[12]

Moses had an ambitious plan for the city's highways and he was anxious to implement it. The tree-lined parkways that Moses had built before the war were designed to bring New Yorkers to his new parks. Now he wanted to build a highway network with expressways for both passenger and commercial vehicles that would connect the city's five boroughs with the suburbs in Long Island, Westchester County, and New Jersey. He told a group of state highway officials that modern arterials were urgently needed, "as commerce and travel have more and more taken to the roads, as cars multiply and our entire civilization runs on wheels." He argued that delays to the city's ambitious highway program "would be an inexcusable civic and official blunder."[13]

In 1946, new highways were a far higher priority than new subway lines. The Board of Transportation chair, Charles Gross, announced plans to modernize the rapid transit system by lengthening platforms, buying new trains, installing escalators, and improving lighting. Due to funding constraints and the city's other priorities, the board's plan no longer included a Second Avenue subway.[14]

Not only was New York City getting less federal aid, but it was also reaching the maximum amount of money it could borrow, a level defined in the New York State constitution. Even if the city were allowed to issue more bonds, it would have trouble paying them off because the annual cost of paying off the city's existing debt, much of it incurred to support the subways and Moses's public works projects, was eating up a rising portion of the city's operating budget. While the city's capital budget included infrastructure projects such as modernizing subway facilities, the operating budget included day-to-day expenses such as salaries, fuel, and debt payments.[15]

The city's subway system had become a financial and political albatross. Politicians had long promised New Yorkers that the city could operate a more efficient transit system once it purchased the privately held IRT and BMT. A consolidated system was supposed to decrease costs and improve service. Things did not work out that way.

Since the city never allowed the IRT and BMT to raise fares, the railroads cut back on their maintenance costs, causing facilities and equipment to deteriorate in the 1920s and 1930s. Due to war restrictions, the city was unable to make significant improvements to the subway lines after purchasing them in 1940. After the war, the subway did not earn a profit that could pay for either capital improvements or the debt associated with building the subway and purchasing the private railroads.[16]

By the end of 1945, for the first time, a nickel fare could not even cover the cost of operating transit services. Operating expenses and deficits were growing rapidly, in part because war veterans returned to their old jobs on the transit system. While a private company might have laid off employees or not hired returning veterans, city leaders rehired the veterans and kept their existing employees. When O'Dwyer took office in 1946, the annual subway deficit was more than $50 million a year. A year later it rose to $78 million.[17]

The city's need to continuously subsidize the subway system was threatening Moses's ability to build more highways and bridges. To expand the roadway network and also properly maintain the subways, he needed to increase the fare. Even though the price of flour, eggs, potatoes, and milk had more than doubled since the subway opened in 1904, the fare had not changed. When La Guardia had refused to raise the fare, the *Saturday Evening Post* found it amusing that New York's transit fares were lower than those of almost every other city, considering that "people from Dubuque and Amarillo think of New York as a city of lavish spenders who give dollar tips to bell captains," a city "where a nickel wouldn't pay for the match to touch off the brandy on the black cherries." Most New Yorkers, though, did not realize that the subway system was losing money. The Citizens Transit Committee, a group of business leaders who advocated improving the subway system, conducted a survey in 1945 that revealed that almost three-quarters of the city's residents opposed an increase.[18]

In O'Dwyer's first week as mayor, instead of a fare hike, he called for temporarily doubling the city's sales tax from 1 percent to 2 percent. He vowed, "If anyone gets a nickel out of it for any other purpose than for the rehabilitation of the rapid transit system, it will be over my dead body." O'Dwyer's plan to generate new levies and taxes hit a wall, however, because the city could not raise the sales tax without state authorization. Governor Thomas Dewey and the leaders of the New York State Assembly and Senate, all of whom were

Republicans, were up for reelection in 1946. They were more interested in embarrassing the Democratic mayor than in helping him.[19]

O'Dwyer turned to the only person on the city's payroll who could help him obtain the support he needed in Albany. Robert Moses became the broker between the mayor and governor, and between the key factions in the state legislature: downstate and upstate, suburbs and city, Democrats and Republicans. Moses cut a new deal. The revenues from doubling the sales tax would be made available for general city purposes instead of being earmarked for transit rehabilitation.[20]

In March 1946, O'Dwyer said that subway rehabilitation would proceed at the same speed and to the same extent even without the dedicated 1 percent sales tax. That was not true, however, because the transit system had to compete with highways, schools, hospitals, parks, and other needs. The transit system would not win that competition while Robert Moses was prioritizing projects.[21]

To build his new highways, Moses still needed to increase the subway fare, for two reasons. First, the fare would generate more revenue for the city and allow the city to borrow more money. Second, when calculating the maximum amount of debt that the city could incur, the state did not include borrowing money for self-supporting projects. So if subways could break even, then $425 million of subway-related debt could be lifted out of the constitutional debt limit and the city could borrow another $425 million for public works projects.

Moses warned that keeping the fare at a nickel would mean deferring four hundred public works projects. Yet no single person—not a mayor, a governor, or a Robert Moses—could raise the fare on his own. Under state law, the city's Board of Estimate had the power to increase the fare. Since the transit system was so widely used—over 6.2 million nickels were collected on an average day—the eight elected officials who composed the board had little political appetite to raise it. To complicate matters, according to state law, if the board did vote to raise the fare, the city council could order a citywide referendum on the issue. The mayor knew that passing a fare increase through a referendum would be problematic, and that repudiation by the voters would weaken him and the Democratic Party.[22]

O'Dwyer was unable to build support for increasing the fare among the members of the Board of Estimate, those on the city council, or the state legislators representing the city. He did not want to publicly support raising the fare unless he gained the backing of the party leaders; however, he was unable to secure that either. O'Dwyer also failed to obtain support from New York's powerful labor unions. Even Michael Quill, the head of the city's largest transit union, stood with the other unions, despite the fact that raising the fare would have generated more money for the transit system.[23]

In early 1946, the mayor neither publicly supported nor opposed raising the fare. He indicated that if a fare hike was deemed necessary, he would support a citywide referendum to decide the issue. But he would not allow a referendum to be held on the same day as a citywide or statewide election, because he knew that if the Democratic leaders came out in support of a fare increase, it would hurt their party's chances in a November election.[24]

THE BUCK STOPS THERE

In April 1946, the Second Avenue subway became linked to a fare increase when Robert Moses claimed that doubling the fare would allow the city to borrow an additional $425 million and make it possible to begin building the Second Avenue subway. That might have been politically shrewd, but it was not forthright, since Moses expected to allocate no more than $38 million of the additional proceeds to the subway project, less than 10 percent of its estimated cost.[25]

The prospect of building the Second Avenue subway anytime soon appeared to be bleak. In July 1946, the Board of Transportation reported that a ten-cent fare would generate enough revenue to pay for the subway's operating expenses, but it would fall far short of paying for much-needed rehabilitation work and expansion. The board's spokesman admitted that even if the city borrowed an additional $450 million, those funds were unlikely to be used for a new Second Avenue subway line because of the city's many other urgent demands.[26]

The Second Avenue subway did not generate the same level of support as it had two decades earlier. The real estate industry had once been the biggest proponent of expanding the subways because new stations could transform farmland into new neighborhoods with apartment buildings, single-family homes, and commercial properties. By the late 1940s, however, new highways could also spur development, and they could be built faster and cheaper than subways. Moreover, a new highway would benefit many more property owners than just the few who owned land near stations.

Another reason to be pessimistic about the Second Avenue subway's prospects was that during O'Dwyer's first term as mayor, the financial situation of the subway system worsened. After the Transport Workers Union hired the mayor's brother as its new counsel and threatened a subway strike, O'Dwyer gave raises to thirty-five thousand transit workers. He said that the raises were "in the interests of good management and the protection of people." But they were costly. In 1940, labor costs were 54 percent of the system's passenger revenue; by 1946 they had increased to 72 percent.[27]

In 1947, the Board of Transportation estimated that it would need $92 million to purchase new cars, rehabilitate power facilities, extend platforms, and modernize the system. But Moses allocated only $43 million for transit improvements. He knew that the amount of money the city provided was little more than a fraction of what was really needed to improve service. He told the mayor that the system was in a "deplorable condition due to years of receivership under private ownership" and the city's decision to delay and defer adequate maintenance during the war.[28]

After the Board of Transportation asked Moses to allocate $400 million for a Second Avenue subway that would connect to a subway in the Bronx and the IND's Houston Street line in Lower Manhattan, Moses told O'Dwyer that the urgency of the rehabilitation program and the limited capital funds prevented major extensions of the subway system. Moses recognized the importance of rapid transit to the city's economy, just as he understood the need for the city to have decent schools, hospitals, and sewerage facilities. There was simply not enough money to satisfy everyone's needs, and his quest to reshape the city's landscape to accommodate the growing number of automobiles and trucks remained his priority.[29]

Moses explained to the mayor that although the Second Avenue subway extension would ease pressure on the other "presently overburdened lines," the new line's expenses would exceed its revenue because it would not induce sufficient demand to cover its costs. He realized that the entire subway system, not just the Second Avenue subway, needed ongoing subsidies. Moses told O'Dwyer that if the nation's largest railroads could not make a profit on their commuter service into the city, it was too much to expect the Board of Transportation to carry commuters with more frequent service at a lower rate of fare.[30]

When previous New York mayors were first sworn in, they could blame the IRT and the BMT for the subway's fiscal problems and inferior service. O'Dwyer had no one else to blame in the late 1940s. He was responsible for what one commentator referred to as a "mobile torture chamber," with passengers jammed as tight as matches in a box, speeding through dingy, noisy, foul-smelling dungeons that were too hot in summer and too cold in winter. A leading business official told the mayor that "the filthy, revolting and disgusting conditions in our subways at rush hours are a crying shame on our city." After interviewing several dozen subway passengers in 1946, a *New York Times* reporter concluded that New Yorkers favored increasing the fare as long as the additional revenue would be used to make the system more attractive, comfortable, and efficient. The reporter thought passengers should be "entitled to enough room to look at their wrist watches and button coats without risking a disorderly conduct charge."[31]

Charles Gross, the Board of Transportation chair, said that increasing the fare to ten cents was the only practicable way to pay for adequate service and fair wages. The drumbeat for raising the fare grew louder from business leaders, real estate interests, and fiscal watchdogs, who did not like the alternatives to a fare hike: either raising real estate taxes or reducing subway services.[32]

In private, O'Dwyer went to great lengths to generate support for a higher transit fare, including pressuring Albany legislators, pleading with party officials, cutting deals with union officials, and appointing an expert committee. He tried passing responsibility for raising the fare to the borough presidents, the party leaders, the state legislators, and the voters, but he could not find anyone who would take it. The mayor's approach to this issue was the opposite of the president's approach to controversial matters: Harry Truman's Oval Office desk sported a thirteen-inch sign with the words, "The Buck Stops Here."[33]

In 1947, O'Dwyer suggested that the legislature amend the rapid transit law to give his appointees on the Board of Transportation the power and duty to increase fares. The mayor and the other Board of Estimate members were hoping to avoid voting on a fare hike themselves. But the legislature was not receptive to his proposal. Raising the fare had become one of the most controversial issues the city had faced in years. After the mayor asked Democratic Party leaders to poll its members about raising the fare, he was told that people were four to one against raising it.[34]

In February 1947, pressure from the civic and business communities to raise the fare spurred O'Dwyer to hold a special Board of Estimate hearing about the issue. It was expected to be great political theater.

The Communist Party reportedly handed out a quarter of a million leaflets at subway stations urging opposition to the fare hike. The powerful American Federation of Labor, which had close ties to the Democratic Party, pledged an all-out fight against the fare increase. To handle the crowds at the hearings, city officials assigned more than fifty foot patrolmen and mounted police to City Hall, and they set up a small hospital in the basement, with doctors, nurses, cots, and medical supplies. Loudspeakers were installed outside City Hall so that people could listen to the hearings inside, and eight radio stations furnished facilities to carry the hearings. WNYC, the city-owned radio station, aired every word of the proceedings and even received special permission from the Federal Communications Commission to broadcast beyond its allotted evening time slot.[35]

The hearings started on a Monday morning and continued for two days and nights. Although at the beginning of the proceedings the mayor said he was open minded, he really wanted to use widespread opposition to a fare hike as a way to pressure state legislators to provide transit funding. O'Dwyer hoped the hearings would motivate real estate industry leaders to help him in Albany. Since the city relied on real estate taxes for most of its revenue, the mayor knew that property owners would rather the state provide transit funding than the city raise property taxes.[36]

Paul Windels, president of the highly regarded Regional Plan Association, was the first speaker at Monday's hearing. He acknowledged that if a citywide referendum were held that day, the voters would certainly say no to raising the fare unless they were given something for their extra nickel. With his voice rising, he argued that New Yorkers deserved adequate transportation services as a matter of comfort, health, decency, and safety.[37]

Windels explained that the subways did not have sufficient funds to run properly or keep equipment and structures up to date because the fares had long been a political football. He said that successive administrations allowed the city's transit system to fall more and more behind other railroads in both subway service and conditions. "So far as the IRT and BMT are concerned," he added, "the cars are a disgrace, the ventilation system is a joke, the sanitary facilities are a menace, and the station's entrances and exits are totally inadequate." He argued that while "we should have the finest subway cars and stations in the world, those now in use on the IRT and BMT are about the worst."[38]

The Board of Estimate's widely publicized hearings did not attract unruly and sizable crowds. In fact, only a few hundred spectators attended. A Cornell University public health professor, Wilson Smiley, was one of the sixty-nine people who testified. He warned that overcrowded subway cars were increasing the dangers of spreading influenza and pneumonia. When the mayor asked him, "Wouldn't that apply to people going to churches?" Smiley responded to great laughter, "Our churches are commodious and well-ventilated, but very seldom overcrowded."[39]

The mayor did not argue with those who claimed the subway was losing money or that it needed more investment. But he repeatedly interrupted those who supported raising the fare, while patiently listening to those opposing it. He reminded the crowds that he was going to Albany on Thursday in hopes of obtaining additional funds. In a radio speech after the hearings concluded, O'Dwyer denounced any fare increase as a harsh and unbearable tax on the city's low-income families, and criticized landlords for wanting to raise the fare on the backs of the city's working class. In a city where three-quarters of the residents rented apartments, the mayor found that landlords were a convenient group to demonize.[40]

Although O'Dwyer received eleven thousand letters praising his position, neither the fare hike opponents nor the real estate interests were powerful enough to help him obtain transit funding from Albany. So he continued passing the buck, stating, "I welcome a referendum, provided it places before the people directly the real question without first requiring the Board of Estimate to raise the fare." Accordingly, in June, O'Dwyer called for a November 1947 referendum to increase the fare to seven and a half cents. Democratic Party leaders nixed the idea, however, because the November ballot already included a measure that would eliminate the proportional representation voting system that had been enabling members of the Communist, American Labor, and Liberal Parties to win seats on the city council. Since these three smaller parties had pledged to fight a fare hike, they would have had strong support in November, and the Democrats would have had a difficult time convincing voters to eliminate proportional representation.[41]

On November 4, 1947, voters abolished proportional representation, and three days later, the mayor announced that he would ask the state legislature to permit a fare rise without the possibility of a public referendum. The Republican-controlled legislature, however, had no incentive to act on O'Dwyer's request.[42]

PROMISING A SECOND AVENUE SUBWAY

In December 1947, O'Dwyer finally admitted that he wanted to raise the fare. With letters pouring into his office at a rate of fifty-two to one against a subway fare increase, the mayor had to be creative. He knew that New Yorkers would need something extraordinary in exchange for raising the fare, so he raised their hopes and promised to build something that the city could not afford even with the fare increase.[43]

In a half-hour radio speech broadcast live from City Hall, O'Dwyer told New Yorkers that he had decided that the fare had to be raised to eight cents. "Reluctantly," he said, "I have come to the conclusion that, at this time, whether we like it or not, we must not let our transit operating deficit upset and stand in the way of the city's other vital needs." By raising the fare and issuing more bonds, he claimed, the city would be able to build a $400 million Second Avenue subway between 149th Street in the Bronx and Grand Street on Manhattan's Lower East Side, with connections to both Queens and Brooklyn.[44]

The newspapers lavished praise on the mayor for proposing to build the Second Avenue subway. The *Herald Tribune* said the new line would help relieve the city's "shocking transit congestion." The *Daily News* said it was "long needed," and the *New York Times* argued that "the intolerable, indecent crowding in the subways will not be relieved until we have another trunk line."[45]

Building a subway would be expensive, complicated, and disruptive. Construction workers would have to dig up the streets and then move utilities including sewer, gas, electricity, telephone, and steam. They would have to build deep trenches, lay tracks, and install signal systems. New stations would be needed along with stairs and mezzanines. O'Dwyer's proposed subway had an extra cost and complexity because portions of the line would be six tracks wide. South of Houston Street, where the streets were narrow, construction would have to occur under sidewalks and fragile nineteenth-century buildings.

The mayor's Second Avenue subway plan had another complication: the state's constitution had to be amended so that the city could borrow enough money to pay for it. This meant that the legislature would have to approve increasing the city's debt ceiling in two separate legislative sessions, and then the state's voters would have to approve the amendment in a referendum.

To generate support for raising fares and building the new subway, O'Dwyer's team lied. They claimed the Second Avenue subway would be self-sufficient and that the fare increase would create a financially sustainable and growing subway system. The mayor said he wanted the earliest possible construction of the Second Avenue subway line as insurance against any further fare rise. The O'Dwyer administration completely contradicted previous reports that concluded that building the Second Avenue line would not produce any additional revenue for the transit system, but would merely divert passengers from existing lines.[46]

The administration claimed that the city could keep the fare at eight cents or even possibly reduce the fare because the Second Avenue subway would improve the efficiency of the entire subway system. Apparently, the public had forgotten previous mayors' unrealistic promises about the costs and benefits of taking over the IRT and the BMT and building the IND line. But public officials were not the only ones who raised false expectations. In December 1947, the *New York Times* editors expected that fares on the Second Avenue subway would cover operating expenses and replacement costs. They even wanted to see fares cover debt service.[47]

In March 1948, O'Dwyer asked the legislature to repeal the law that permitted the city council to order a referendum on any fare rise. He still wanted the legislature to give the Board of Transportation the sole power to change fares, so that none of the elected officials would be required to approve an increase. The Republicans who controlled the assembly and senate had their own devious idea. They passed a bill that allowed the Board of Transportation to change the subway fare with the proviso that the mayor had to approve any fare hike. The Democratic mayor urged the Republican governor to veto that bill. But Dewey relished putting the onus on the mayor, so when he signed the bill he issued an unusually long memorandum that emphasized the responsibility that now rested with O'Dwyer.[48]

O'Dwyer bought union support by giving the transit workers another generous raise, and in April the Board of Transportation approved a resolution doubling the subway fare from a nickel to a dime. After the mayor approved the increase, he was applauded for his courage by major newspapers, real estate groups, and civic organizations. The next year, his grudging acceptance of the fare increase did not stop him from handily winning reelection.[49]

In 1949, the Board of Transportation's chair, William Reid, updated the mayor on the need for the Second Avenue subway. He explained that four different Bronx lines were feeding into the Lexington Avenue line at or near 125th Street, and that a similar bottleneck was occurring on northbound trains coming in from Brooklyn. The Lexington Avenue line could not add any more trains since it was already operating express trains and local trains every two minutes during peak periods.[50]

O'Dwyer had more pressing matters to worry about, however. In August 1950, he resigned from office after getting caught up in a police corruption scandal. President Truman gave his fellow Democrat an opportunity to get away from the investigation by naming him ambassador to Mexico. O'Dwyer later said, "My doctor told me I would not live through another spring if

I tried to stick it out for my second term. The problems of highways, bridges, traffic and housing alone would stagger a man." But O'Dwyer's promise of a Second Avenue subway did not disappear along with the mayor. It had a life of its own.[51]

Upon the mayor's resignation, the city council president, Vincent Impellitteri, became the acting mayor. He won a special election in November to fill the remaining three years of O'Dwyer's four-year term. Impellitteri was not known for his intellect or his political acumen. A story often told, which may or may not be true, is that he rose to power when the Democratic Party bosses needed to find someone with an Italian surname to balance the ticket with William O'Dwyer (the Irish candidate for mayor) and Lazarus Joseph (the Jewish candidate for comptroller). The party leaders reportedly found the name Impellitteri by flipping through a directory of city officials and selecting the one with the longest Italian surname.[52]

The historian Robert Caro describes how Robert Moses had been a powerful player in La Guardia's administration and a dominant force under O'Dwyer. In Impellitteri's administration, Moses was arguably more powerful than the mayor himself. According to Caro, within weeks of Impellitteri's inauguration, the new mayor was consulting with Moses before making any important decisions, and he filled the upper echelons of city government with Moses's men. Moses told Impellitteri whom to appoint to the City Planning Commission, and then Moses determined the commission's priorities. Since Moses controlled so many city, state, federal, and transportation authority resources, he was often able to intimidate the Board of Estimate's members to get his city projects funded and approved. He was also able to exert his influence in Albany.[53]

In 1950 and 1951, the state legislature authorized a constitutional amendment that would allow the city to borrow an additional $500 million over and beyond its constitutional debt limit. City officials, state legislators, civic institutions, and newspapers all said that these funds would be used to build the Second Avenue subway. To ratify the amendment, voters would have to approve it in a statewide referendum in November 1951.[54] City officials made two underhanded moves to make sure that voters would support the amendment. First, they claimed that $500 million was enough to expand the subway all across the city. Second, they kept under wraps a report that showed that the subway system was facing a financial crisis and that it was far from an opportune time to begin any expansion program.

In September, the city unveiled the construction program it would undertake if voters approved the amendment. In reality, the program was just a wish list of projects that would never get built, including a Second Avenue subway to the Bronx and two new Brooklyn lines. In 1929, the Board of Transportation had estimated that the cost to build the Second Avenue subway would be $500 million, and now, twenty-two years later, the board was pretending that $500 million could finance a much more ambitious set of expansion projects.[55]

The city's public relations efforts—including speeches, press releases, and posters in the subways touting the program's projects—generated support for the amendment. For example, the *Brooklyn Daily Eagle* told its readers that the $500 million would mean the realization of the borough's most urgent needs. In October, the Board of Transportation placed posters in every subway car, station, and bus promoting the citywide benefits of passing the amendment.[56]

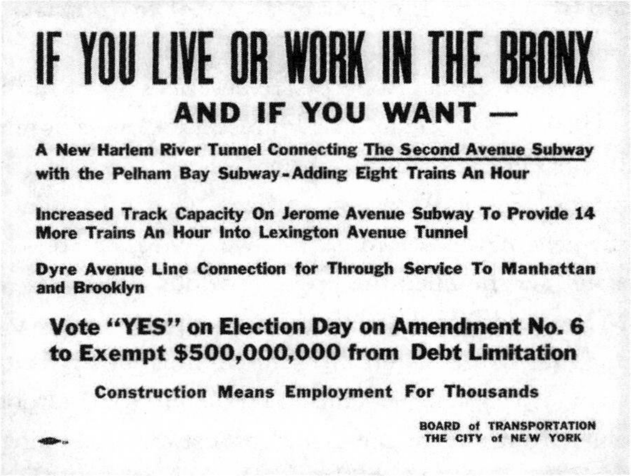

Figure 2.2. *Bronx poster urging transit riders to support the amendment. Source: Courtesy of New York Transit Museum.*

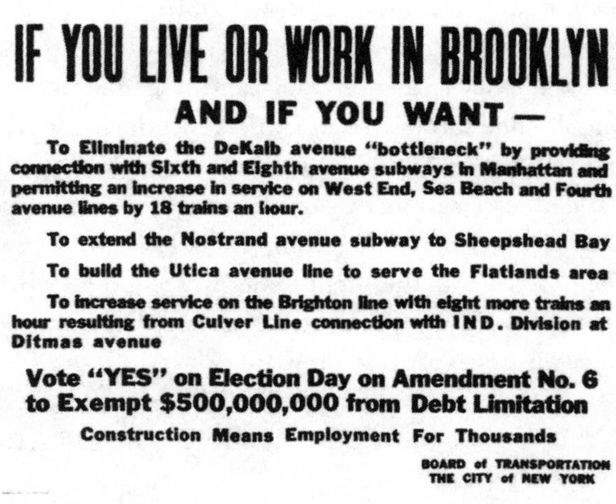

IF YOU LIVE OR WORK IN THE BRONX
AND IF YOU WANT —

A New Harlem River Tunnel Connecting The Second Avenue Subway with the Pelham Bay Subway - Adding Eight Trains An Hour

Increased Track Capacity On Jerome Avenue Subway To Provide 14 More Trains An Hour Into Lexington Avenue Tunnel

Dyre Avenue Line Connection for Through Service To Manhattan and Brooklyn

Vote "YES" on Election Day on Amendment No. 6 to Exempt $500,000,000 from Debt Limitation

Construction Means Employment For Thousands

BOARD of TRANSPORTATION
THE CITY of NEW YORK

Figure 2.3. *Brooklyn poster promoting the amendment's benefits. Source: State of New York, Senate Committee on the Affairs of the City of New York, First Interim Report on the Inquiry into the Public Transit System of NYC including Minority Report, May 15, 1957, Exhibit D.*

IF YOU LIVE OR WORK IN BROOKLYN
AND IF YOU WANT —

To Eliminate the DeKalb avenue "bottleneck" by providing connection with Sixth and Eighth avenue subways in Manhattan and permitting an increase in service on West End, Sea Beach and Fourth avenue lines by 18 trains an hour.

To extend the Nostrand avenue subway to Sheepshead Bay

To build the Utica avenue line to serve the Flatlands area

To increase service on the Brighton line with eight more trains an hour resulting from Culver Line connection with IND. Division at Ditmas avenue

Vote "YES" on Election Day on Amendment No. 6 to Exempt $500,000,000 from Debt Limitation

Construction Means Employment For Thousands

BOARD of TRANSPORTATION
THE CITY of NEW YORK

The amendment placed before voters was more than five hundred words long and virtually incomprehensible because it included complex changes to the state's system of school financing. Newspapers explained to their readers that the legalistic wording of the proposed constitutional amendment boiled down to something simple: a "yes" vote was a vote for a new Second Avenue subway. All of the major newspapers in the metropolitan area urged their readers to vote for the amendment, and in November the voters overwhelmingly supported it by a margin of 74 percent to 26 percent.[57]

The report that had been suppressed until after the amendment passed was a detailed evaluation of the subway system's condition, organization, and finances. Consultants hired by the Board of Transportation found that the city was not spending nearly enough money on capital improvements. As a result, many of the structures and stations were in "deplorable" condition. Out of 6,957 subway cars, only 760 were modern and up to date, and only 1,790 others were considered "reasonably adequate."[58]

The subway's financial situation was troublesome because, although the fare had doubled to ten cents in 1948, revenue was not keeping up with skyrocketing costs. Since the city took over the subway lines, workers were making more money and working fewer hours. Salaries and wages for the thirty-two thousand rapid transit employees rose from $60 million in 1941 to $152 million in 1950.[59]

Because of increased automobile use, the subways and elevated rail lines were carrying the fewest number of passengers since 1925. The Board of Transportation was trying to maintain equipment and employ enough workers to accommodate millions of people who used the system only a few hours a day, five days a week. While ridership decreased slightly during weekday peak periods, it plummeted on weekends. In 1944, on a typical weekend, the subway carried 70 percent of the number of weekday riders. By 1950, weekend ridership was less than half of weekday ridership.[60]

NEW YORKERS HAD BEEN DUPED

After the amendment passed, city officials knew that the city could not afford to proceed with the Second Avenue subway. Four years later, New Yorkers would learn that they had been duped.

In March 1952, George Spargo, one of Moses's trusted advisers, told Moses that the transit system was slowly deteriorating because the city was not spending enough on cars and equipment. The city needed to modernize all of the transit system's components, maintain them properly, and periodically replace them. But the city had never done that. Spargo explained that since the 7,000 subway cars had a useful life of fifty years, approximately 140 of them should be replaced each year. Likewise, the city needed to replace 250 of its 2,500 buses every year. Subway cars and buses were the most obvious needs, but the transit system also had to spend $325 million in the next six years just to modernize the power plants and equipment that provided electricity to run the subways.[61]

In the summer of 1952, the Board of Transportation raised its cost estimate for the Second Avenue subway and the other expansion projects from $500 million to $900 million. City Comptroller Lazarus Joseph warned Mayor Impellitteri that building the new line would imperil the city's credit ratings and force it to pay much higher interest rates on its bonds. The members of the private watchdog group the Citizens Budget Commission rang their own alarm bells. In a confidential report to the mayor, they warned him that moving ahead with the new subway line could leave the city with a series of gaping holes underground and a grossly dilapidated transit system. They realized that the Board of Transportation was exaggerating the Second Avenue subway's benefits and underestimating its costs. The commission members urged the mayor to focus on rehabilitating the existing system since the board's resources were already overextended, in part because Moses had added projects not in its capital program, such as taking over a railroad line to beaches in the Rockaways.[62]

Impellitteri disregarded these warnings, and in September 1952 he told city officials to proceed with the Second Avenue subway. Not so coincidentally, he surprised his aides and the city that very same day by indicating his interest in running for a full term as mayor in 1953.[63] Robert Moses ignored the mayor's wishes, however. A few weeks after Impellitteri's announcement, Moses told his fellow City Planning commissioners that there was a serious shortage of funds for all capital projects, and that it was quite obvious that the $500 million bond proceeds would not be adequate to build the Second Avenue subway and the other extensions as planned. In October, the commission eliminated funding for the Second Avenue subway from the city's 1953 capital budget. The commission did not cancel the subway project, but rather recommended that it be delayed until "the entire city transit situation, including its relation to the transportation problems of the metropolitan area," were reviewed.[64]

By 1953, the city's business leaders and their allies in the state capital had lost faith in the city's ability to manage the transit system. Concerned about both the subway's physical deterioration and its fiscal condition, they wanted the system to be modernized and operated more efficiently. Only thirteen years after the city took direct control of a unified transit system, the state took it away. Governor Dewey and the Republican-led legislature established the New York City Transit Authority to operate the subways and buses. The authority, a public-benefit corporation, would be managed by a board of directors, with members appointed by the governor and mayor. The mayor grudgingly complied with the new law, while leading New York City Democrats denounced the governor as a dictator.[65]

The state had previously set up similar authorities to build and operate parkways, bridges, tunnels, and other infrastructure. Advocates for the Transit Authority claimed that the board, buffered from day-to-day politics, would be able to operate transit services more efficiently than the city by eliminating unnecessary services, taking a harder line on unions, reducing political patronage, and setting an appropriate fare. The Republicans had high hopes that the authority could manage the system like a private enterprise and eliminate the need for public subsidies. But the Transit Authority was put in an impossible situation: its revenues could not cover the system's operating costs, let alone pay the cost to replace equipment and pay off the debt associated with building and consolidating the subways.

Postwar suburbanization, the rise in automobile use, and the public sector's investments in roads, bridges, and highways would necessitate ongoing transit subsidies. Even after the fare was raised to ten cents, the subways continued to deteriorate. Brakes, signals, and other equipment were replaced less frequently than necessary. The authority still ran 2,500 subway cars purchased before 1920, including 279 purchased between 1904 and 1905. The older equipment frequently malfunctioned and was extremely expensive to operate and maintain. Subway riders knew that trains and stations were old and crowded, but they did not realize that the roadbed supporting the track was deteriorating, the rails were out of alignment, and the repair shops lacked necessary tools.[66]

Instead of using the $500 million in bond proceeds to build a new Second Avenue subway and expand other portions of the subway, in 1953 the Transit Authority decided to use those funds to replace aging cars, modernize the electrical system, and replace obsolete equipment. It had no other choice, because the City of New York diverted funding from the authority's capital program toward new highways and other capital projects. In the first few years of the O'Dwyer administration, the city had allocated about $45 million per year for transit capital improvements. After the referendum, the city's budget director, Abe Beame, told the Transit Authority that ongoing rehabilitation work would have to be funded using the $500 million. Aside from the bond proceeds, the city would not supply any other capital funds for transit purposes. Two decades later, as the city's mayor, Beame would play another prominent role in defunding the Second Avenue subway.[67]

Hard as it may be to believe, it was another three years before many elected officials realized that none of the $500 million would be used for the Second Avenue subway. Transit Authority officials were not being deceptive, but they certainly never issued a press release or held a news conference to announce that the project was dead. By 1956, $378 million of the bond proceeds had already been spent or allocated for other uses. One city council member accused Mayor Robert F. Wagner Jr., who succeeded Impellitteri, of a "disgraceful double cross." A committee headed by a state senator and state assemblyman called the disappearance of the $500 million a mystery. They said, "Mayor Wagner cannot escape responsibility for participating in what turned out to be a fraud on the people both upstate and in the city."[68]

Apparently, many of the legislators had not paid attention to the wording on the bond amendment, though they did not have to dig very far to find it. Article VIII of New York's state constitution still says today that proceeds from the $500 million bond could be used "for the construction and equipment of new rapid transit railroads" and/or the "reconstruction and equipment of existing rapid transit railroads."[69]

By the time the public realized that the city was not going to build a Second Avenue subway, it was too late to save the Third Avenue El. Property owners on the East Side had targeted the Third Avenue El, claiming it was a menace to health, comfort, and peaceable home life. The line had opened in 1878 and was still running wooden cars before Manhattan service ended in 1955. Transit officials knew that overcrowding on the Lexington Avenue line was only going to get worse after the El was torn down and all the new office buildings proposed and under construction around Grand Central Terminal were completed. They could only hope that some of the crowding would be alleviated by rehabilitating signals and lengthening platforms to accommodate trains with ten cars (rather than eight).[70]

The Transit Authority could consider only relatively minor improvements because of factors far beyond its control. After World War II, political support had shifted from building new subway lines to expanding the highway network. New Yorkers wanted their piece of the American Dream—a single-family home with new appliances and a new car. Between 1945 and 1955, the number of registered vehicles in the state nearly doubled, from 2.45 million to 4.8 million. The head of New York State's Public Works Department in the 1950s said that "passenger vehicles are no longer luxuries" and that "our whole economy has become entirely dependent on the motor vehicle and the highways over which it rolls." The American way of life, he noted, "is irrevocably geared to the motor vehicle."[71]

During Impellitteri's three years as mayor, the city started building a remarkable eleven new highways. City leaders would have liked to build the Second Avenue subway; Moses himself said in 1947 that it was "the sole and only answer to major rapid transit improvements." But it was a simple fact that the city could build many highways for the cost of a new subway line. In 1956, the city estimated that for $363 million, it could design and construct the Van Wyck Expressway, Brooklyn-Queens Expressway, Cross-Bronx Expressway, Major Deegan Expressway, New England Thruway, Horace Harding Expressway, Sheridan Expressway, Bronx River Parkway, Bruckner Expressway, Prospect Expressway, and Nassau Expressway. All of these highways combined would cost less than one new subway line on Manhattan's East Side.[72]

Moreover, the City of New York was getting help to pay for its new highways. Between 1946 and 1955, state and federal funds provided over $200 million to build new highways in the city. At the time, the federal government did not provide cities and states with a single penny to expand their transit systems. A Second Avenue subway, less than ten miles long, would have cost about $500 million in the 1950s. For only twice that amount, the state acquired land and built the New York State Thruway, a highway more than five hundred miles long, from one end of the state to the other. The Second Avenue subway would have lost money, year after year, while the Thruway would generate more than enough money in tolls to pay off the debt incurred for its construction as well as its ongoing expenses.[73]

As New York City's traffic engineers looked to cities such as Detroit and New Haven for innovative solutions to its transportation problems, New York dedicated more and more of its public spaces for cars and trucks. While the Upper East Side remained home to many of America's wealthiest families, with what one journalist called their "be-furred matrons, pampered dogs, chauffeur-driven limousines and expensive restaurants," many other neighborhoods became less desirable to live in when the city demolished homes and businesses to build new highways. The new roads also made it easier for the growing middle class to move to the city's outskirts and suburbs. Federal and state policies encouraged this road building and middle-class flight from urban centers.[74]

In 1957, Transit Authority chair Charles Patterson said, "We cannot embark on the construction of new lines or extensions of existing lines without much more careful and searching investigation of their effects on the operating revenues and expenses of the system." He added, "It would have been the height of folly to have embarked on a transit construction program which the $500 million would be insufficient to complete, while at the same time permitting the existing system to continue its deterioration for lack of funds, perhaps to the point of breakdown of essential elements."[75]

Unfortunately his successors a decade later did not heed his warning.

Figure 2.4. *Dismantling of the Second Avenue El. Source: Identifier bpm_1654-43, Borough President Manhattan Collection. Courtesy: NYC Municipal Archives.*

Figure 2.5. *Grand Central subway station in 1946. Source: Stanley Kubrick for* Look *magazine. X2011.4.11107.9 ©SK Film Archives and Museum of the City of New York.*

The Billionaire's Ambitions

In the early 1960s, nineteen million people lived in the thirteen-thousand-square-mile New York metropolitan area. The economic future of hundreds of municipalities in New York, New Jersey, and Connecticut depended on the continued economic vitality of one relatively small portion of the region—Manhattan's central business district (CBD)—a nine-square-mile area south of 60th Street where one-third of the region's jobs were located. As Manhattan's manufacturing sector eroded in the 1950s and early 1960s, its employment became tied to the expanding fields of advertising, communications, and finance.[1]

New York City in the early 1960s had twice as much office space as the next nine largest US cities combined. National and international corporations established their headquarters in Manhattan so their executives could work with other corporate leaders and tap into readily available resources such as financial, legal, and marketing services. Much of the construction boom occurred on the East Side near Grand Central Terminal, which was accessible via the subway for office workers who lived in the Bronx, Brooklyn, and Queens. It was also convenient for residents of the Westchester County and Connecticut suburbs, since the terminal was served by the privately owned New Haven and New York Central Railroads.[2]

After the Second and Third Avenue Els were torn down, East Side property owners had prospered as brownstones, loft buildings, and tenements were replaced by high-rise offices and apartment buildings. The area east of Central

Park between 59th and 96th Streets, known as the Upper East Side, became home to fashionable boutiques, luxury restaurants, and expensive furniture houses. With thousands of well-educated young professionals moving there, the neighborhood contained the greatest concentration of single people in the entire country.[3]

Even though the number of cars registered in the United States grew by 47 percent in the 1950s, New York City's economy still relied on the subway in the early 1960s. During the 8:00 to 9:00 a.m. rush hour, 72 percent of the people entering the CBD traveled by subway, which could move people far more efficiently than automobiles. Each subway car could carry approximately one hundred people, and a ten-car train could accommodate a thousand. Since trains could operate every two minutes, each track could carry thirty thousand people per hour. By comparison, one lane of a highway could carry only about two thousand cars in an hour.[4]

Although Manhattan and the region were dependent on the rail transit system, 750,000 cars and trucks were entering the CBD on a typical weekday, three times more than had been the case thirty years earlier. Many New Yorkers expected the city to accommodate the growing number of cars. For example, the Greater New York Safety Council's transportation division claimed that Americans had a fundamental freedom to drive, and that it was the city's obligation to accommodate drivers by building more parking spaces in Manhattan. The members argued that without more parking, Manhattan would not be able to continue its role as the region's CBD because a growing number of suburbanites were so highly conditioned to using their cars.[5]

In the early 1960s, New York City had the most modern, extensive urban highway system in the world, with ambitious plans to expand it. Robert Moses, as head of the Triborough Bridge and Tunnel Authority (TBTA), was building the world's longest suspension bridge to connect Staten Island and Brooklyn. He was also trying to build two elevated expressways right through the heart of the city: a Mid-Manhattan Expressway above 30th Street and a Lower Manhattan Expressway that would cut a wide swath through SoHo and Little Italy. The two new highways were expected to alleviate traffic, but they would require destroying historic neighborhoods and displacing approximately two thousand families and a thousand businesses.[6]

By contrast, most of the Transit Authority's improvements to the subway since World War II had been relatively modest, such as installing new lighting and escalators. In the 1960s, the authority finished extending platforms on the Lexington Avenue line to accommodate ten-car trains; however, the new capacity could not keep up with growing demand on the East Side or make up for the loss of the Second and Third Avenue Els. The East Side had nearly half of Midtown Manhattan's jobs, but only one subway line, the Lexington Avenue line, ran along its length. When asked about the prospects for a new East Side subway in 1962, the Transit Authority's public relations director responded, "The Second Avenue subway project has not been entirely abandoned. However, the completed and planned improvements which have and will continue to provide additional service on the existing routes do not justify the expense of a new subway route at this time. Such a new route does not only involve construction along Second Avenue but additional routes must also be considered in the Bronx, Queens and Brooklyn in order to have a proper outlet for such a route."[7]

The Transit Authority's only major expansion initiative was facing difficulties in the mid-1960s. Underneath Chrystie Street on the Lower East Side, workers were building a new tunnel segment to connect an IND line and a BMT line. When construction began, it was expected to take three years; instead it would take ten. Those delays should have been a clear warning sign to the advocates of a Second Avenue subway about the complexity and cost of building a new subway in Manhattan.

In 1966, the typical rush-hour subway rider traveling into the CBD had an average of 3.7 square feet of floor space. That was not even enough space for passengers to comfortably read their newspapers. Riders on the Lexington Avenue line's express trains had even less room to stand—2.9 square feet of floor space during rush hour. Most passengers could experience that level of crowding only for a short period of time without enduring some physical and psychological discomfort. Subway riders on the East Side were not the only ones dealing with severely overcrowded trains. The problem was particularly acute for commuters from Queens and Long Island, where the population grew more than in the other nineteen counties in the region combined during the 1950s.[8]

Starting in the early 1960s, improving transit services for Queens and Long Island residents would be tied to adding new subway service on the East Side. Adding more transit riders from Queens would overwhelm the capacity of the Lexington Avenue line, which is why transit expansion plans developed by both the Transit Authority and Mayor Wagner included a new East Side subway with connections to Queens. An influential group of business leaders led by David Rockefeller created the Downtown-Lower Manhattan Association, and promoted a new line under Water Street in Lower Manhattan, as either a spur or part of a new East Side subway.[9]

None of the ideas to expand the subway system were financially feasible, however. The city could expand its highway network because it could tap into federal and state funding, and tolls from the TBTA's bridges and tunnels. Federal grants and TBTA revenue, however, could not be used for transit improvements. After Congress passed the Urban Mass Transportation Act of 1964, city officials were hoping that the federal government could pay for an expansion of the transit system. The amount of funding available through this law was limited, though: only $375 million for three years, and no state could get more than 12.5 percent ($47 million) of the total.

THREE UPPER EAST SIDERS

In 1965, after several years of intensive study, the City Planning Commission released a comprehensive transportation plan. The planners said that the city needed to build a new East Side subway and also what they referred to as a "super subway" between Queens and Manhattan that would operate on both existing Long Island Rail Road tracks and new transit lines. Super-subway riders would be expected to pay a higher fare, but their trains would go about 50 percent faster and would have more seats and less standing room.[10]

The Planning Commission also recommended that the city go ahead with the Lower Manhattan Expressway because it would help free up local traffic on surface streets. But the planners said that the city should no longer build highways or parking facilities that would attract more traffic into and through the Manhattan CBD. They were concerned that additional parking would encourage more people to drive, overwhelming the local streets and putting even more political pressure on city officials to expand highway capacity into Manhattan. The commission was sending a clear message to the major department stores that were clamoring for more parking spots: you need to face the fact that your future is dependent on customers who are workers, visitors, and residents in Manhattan, rather than futilely trying to accommodate people driving in from the suburbs.[11]

The Regional Plan Association (RPA), an influential civic organization, was spreading a similar message. In 1929, the RPA's first regional plan served as an early blueprint for decentralizing the metropolitan area and building a vast network of highways, bridges, and tunnels. With the resulting suburbanization threatening the region's vitality, in 1966 the RPA was developing plans to rein in the sprawl by reinvigorating the region's downtowns and expanding public transportation. The civic association still supported the Lower Manhattan Expressway, but argued that the only way to end traffic jams in Manhattan was by making public transportation faster and more comfortable than driving. Even though the average speeds on the expressways into Manhattan were as low as fifteen miles per hour in many places, driving was still faster than the average door-to-door speed for train commuters.[12]

In 1966, two liberal Republicans with presidential aspirations—New York governor Nelson Rockefeller and New York City mayor John Lindsay—were poised to radically transform the region's transportation system. Lindsay called his job the "second toughest in America."[13] Rockefeller had even more political power, as well as a personal fortune that he used to obtain political support, and a younger brother (David) who controlled one of the world's largest banks. Lindsay and Rockefeller would serve during an era of urban unrest, with middle-class flight to the suburbs and a rapid deterioration of city services.

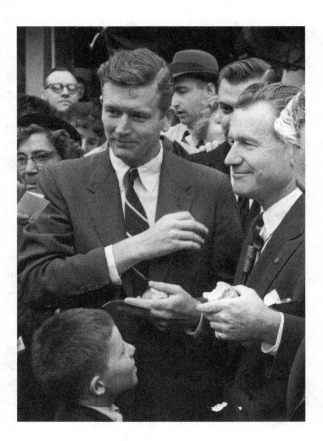

Figure 3.1. *John Lindsay and Nelson Rockefeller in the early 1960s. Source: The La Guardia and Wagner Archives, LaGuardia Community College/ The City University of New York. Copyright: Thomas K.*

First elected governor in 1958, Rockefeller was known for having an "edifice complex." Inspired by a visit to the Dalai Lama's soaring palace in Tibet, he had the state purchase 1,150 buildings in downtown Albany, and then replace them with marble state office towers, a performing arts center, and reflecting pools. Rockefeller relied on the advice of William Ronan, a former dean at New York University. Ronan, Rockefeller, and Lindsay all realized that improving public transportation was critical to strengthening the economy of the city and the region. They were also well aware of the benefits of a Second Avenue subway, since all three of them lived on the Upper East Side.[14]

Ronan came to public prominence in the mid-1950s when he directed the staff of a special state commission investigating the growing powers of public authorities. He found that public authorities controlled by an independent board of directors could manage many government functions (such as building and operating new bridges) more efficiently than agencies that reported directly to elected officials. Although Ronan's commission praised the use of authorities, he openly challenged the practices of Robert Moses and called for stricter supervision of the state's authorities.[15]

Rockefeller appreciated Ronan's intellect, loyalty, and bulldozing style. As secretary to the governor between 1959 and 1966, Ronan was in effect the state's general manager. He took the lessons he learned about authorities and applied them in Rockefeller's administration. For instance, in 1961, after voters rejected a $500 million bond issue earmarked for a vast expansion of the State University of New York, Rockefeller and Ronan established a public authority to construct new schools with the debt serviced by student tuition and other fees. Within five years, the authority had either completed or had under design $600 million in projects to accommodate more students. Unlike state agencies, the state's public authorities did not need voter approval to issue bonds.[16]

Rockefeller entrusted Ronan with all of his transportation policy issues, including the deteriorating financial condition of the privately owned Long Island, New Haven, and New York Central railroads. The Republican governor's reelection bids relied on continued support from tens of thousands of Long Island and Westchester County residents who commuted to New York City on the three railroads. Ronan helped settle a 1960 Long Island Rail Road strike and prevented the New Haven Railroad from terminating all of its train services. One of Rockefeller's top aides, Bob Douglass, said that when it came to transportation issues, if Ronan told Rockefeller that "the moon was made of green cheese," he would believe it.[17]

During his first five years in office, Rockefeller was not interested in having the state take over the struggling private railroads. Instead he supported tax relief that would allow them to remain fiscally solvent. In early 1965, however, Rockefeller decided that the state had no choice but to purchase the Long Island Rail Road and operate its services. The alternative, he said, would be "pretty grim." The railroad carried 260,000 passengers a day, and if services were shut down, the entire region's economy would have suffered. He and Ronan succeeded in gaining legislative support to establish a Metropolitan Commuter Transportation Authority (MCTA) that would take over the Long Island Rail Road. The legislation was written so that the MCTA could one day take on a more regional role by incorporating other mass transit systems.[18]

As Rockefeller's right-hand man, Ronan began to amass the kind of power that Moses had possessed, controlling both the planning and the operations of transportation systems. Rockefeller appointed Ronan chair of the MCTA and the Long Island Rail Road, a commissioner of the Port Authority of New York and New Jersey, and chair of a tri-state committee that addressed the region's overall transportation issues. Like Moses, Ronan was known for his cunningness and arrogance. Unlike many other officials, Ronan was not afraid of Moses. After Rockefeller's inauguration, a Ronan-led committee tasked with reorganizing the state government developed a plan to take the state parks away from Moses's purview.[19]

In 1965, while state officials focused on suburban commuters, mayoral candidate John Lindsay laid out a far more ambitious transportation plan than Rockefeller or Ronan had ever developed. Lindsay argued that every facet of the transportation system was inadequate. The subways were inconvenient, poorly maintained, slow, and subject to frequent delays, and the subway cars, platforms, and entrances were filthy and poorly lit. The city's highways were hopelessly clogged, buses were moving at a snail's pace, trucks wasted hours of valuable time, and emergency equipment was frequently delayed. Lindsay's deputy mayor would later say that "cities are for people, not automobiles."[20]

Lindsay bemoaned the lack of a coordinated citywide transportation policy. Transportation in the city was the responsibility of three public authorities, four city agencies, three state agencies, six commuter railroads, and numerous private and municipal bus lines. Lindsay said, "On policy and operations we can no longer afford the ineffectiveness, the quarrels and the waste which characterize the hydra-headed and fragmented monstrosity of the city's transportation structure today."[21]

He supported proposals by the RPA to expand the public transportation system. Although the city's elected officials were under pressure to expand the highway network and build more parking, the association explained that those strategies would not solve the city's transportation problems. The only way to relieve traffic on the roads was to enhance public transportation's speed and attractiveness. New York City's economy relied on a concentration of business activities, and that required a successful transit system. New Yorkers might want to drive to work, but it was more important for them to have jobs.[22]

Lindsay understood that the different transportation modes were inextricably related and mutually dependent. For example, because the commuter railroads and the Transit Authority provided inferior train service, more people drove to work, which increased roadway traffic and increased the cost to operate buses. Before the 1965 election, Lindsay developed a "program of action." The city, he said, needed to establish a unified transportation agency to integrate planning and policy making, and to coordinate operations. Rather than paving the city over with asphalt or turning its heart into a vast parking garage, transit services needed to be faster as well as more comfortable, convenient, and affordable.[23]

During Lindsay's mayoral campaign, he issued a series of announcements touting his transit proposals. He told Queens residents about his plan to build a new rail tunnel under the East River and he told Brooklyn residents about his plan to extend subway lines to Sheepshead Bay and the Flatlands area. In the Bronx and Manhattan, residents heard about his plan for a new East Side subway that would provide express service from the Bronx to Lower Manhattan and also connect with lines coming in from Queens.[24] To help finance his proposed improvements, Lindsay's campaign plan recommended using the annual $14 million in surplus revenues from the TBTA, issuing another $500 million transportation bond, changing the federal law so that New York State could obtain more than 12.5 percent of federal transit funds, and increasing revenues from other sources such as tolls and parking.[25]

After beating the Democratic candidate, Abe Beame, to succeed Robert F. Wagner Jr. as mayor, Lindsay had New York City's shortest-ever mayoral honeymoon. Five hours after taking office, on January 1, 1966, the Transit Authority's bus and subway workers went on strike. One New Yorker trying to enter a subway station quipped, "My God, Wagner left and took all the trains with him." The twelve-day strike that crippled the city ended with the unions winning higher pensions and wages that far exceeded inflation.[26]

Lindsay inherited a transit system with both rising expenses and serious unfunded needs. His own urban design task force referred to the subways as "the most squalid public environment of the United States: dank, dingily lit, fetid, raucous with screeching clatter, one of the world's meanest transit facilities." To fulfill his campaign pledge to reorganize the region's transportation agencies and tap into the lucrative tolls from the city's bridges and tunnels, he needed the state legislature to act.[27] For help obtaining obtain support in Albany, Lindsay turned to Roswell Perkins, who had served as Rockefeller's counsel during the governor's first year in office. Perkins confidently told the mayor that Rockefeller was willing to offer his full cooperation, subject to one condition: that it be announced jointly and promoted jointly. But the mayor's plan was thwarted once Ronan got involved. Perkins later told the mayor, "The proposed regional transportation agency is obviously Bill Ronan's baby, which he is bound and determined to get. It took me until February to catch on to the fact that it was Bill who was killing us with the governor and solely because he became fearful that once the city had its own transportation house in order, the MCTA could never take over the whole structure."[28]

Likewise, Robert Moses, chair of the TBTA, had no intention of giving up his power and resources. When Lindsay first took office, he assumed Moses would go along with his plan to consolidate transportation agencies, but the new mayor underestimated both Moses's influence and his determination. Only three weeks after the mayor's inauguration, Moses and other TBTA board members publicly denounced Lindsay's plan to consolidate the TBTA with the Transit Authority, claiming that it would destroy bondholders' rights, discriminate against automobile users, jeopardize federal and state funds, and hold the entire region hostage to a potential strike against a unified transportation system.[29]

At a legislative public hearing in Albany, Moses and his friends in the legislature humiliated Lindsay by bringing in two former governors, a former mayor, union leaders, bankers, bond attorneys, and a slew of other powerful representatives to ridicule the mayor's plan. Chase Manhattan Bank, acting as the trustee for the TBTA bondholders, said it would challenge the constitutionality of the legislation. When the TBTA issued more than $379 million in outstanding bonds, the bank had been given the responsibility to protect the rights of the bondholders.[30]

Lindsay's plan died in 1966 after Ronan sabotaged the mayor in the governor's office and the seventy-seven-year-old Moses blocked him in the legislature. Nevertheless, the stars were beginning to align for transforming the transportation system, including the resurrection of the mythical Second Avenue subway.

ROCKEFELLER RUNS WITH LINDSAY'S PLANS

Megaprojects (i.e., very large public infrastructure projects) typically get started when a city's population is rising, its economy is booming, resources appear to be available, and the project has widespread support from voters, elected officials, business leaders, and the media. In 1966 and 1967, that seemed to be the case for a new East Side subway. The RPA was estimating that the metropolitan area's population would rise by the end of the century from nineteen million to thirty million, and employment from eight million to thirteen million.[31]

After Lindsay failed to reorganize the transportation agencies, Rockefeller and Ronan developed their own grand vision for the region's transportation network, and in December 1966, Ronan stepped down from his post as secretary to begin implementing their plan. At the beginning of the state's 1967 legislative session, Rockefeller and Ronan announced their two-pronged approach. First, they proposed integrating the Transit Authority and the TBTA into the MCTA. To signify the MCTA's broader mandate, the word "commuter" would be dropped from the name of the transportation authority, which would be known as the Metropolitan Transportation Authority (MTA).[32]

In addition, Rockefeller and Ronan would seek voter approval to borrow $2.5 billion that would be dedicated for roadway and public transportation improvements across the state. Rockefeller said that the expansion would put New York State out in front of the nation in meeting transportation challenges. Not incidentally, the proposal would also enhance his reputation in preparation for a 1968 presidential bid. Rockefeller's team identified a long list of potential improvements they would undertake with the $2.5 billion. They developed the most ambitious transit expansion plan since the second phase of the IND plan was proposed in 1929, and as with that plan, a Second Avenue subway would be its most important element.[33]

The governor led a campaign to generate support for the November voter referendum, the largest single authorization ever sought by a state. He championed the ballot initiative with almost as much energy as he devoted to his own campaign for governor. Rockefeller encouraged the formation of a well-funded advocacy group, personally campaigned around the state, and made sure that the initiative was prominently placed on the ballot far from a controversial voter referendum. Commercials, newspaper advertisements, signs, speeches, meetings with editorial boards, and millions of handbills urged voters to vote yes. The bond proposal received support from a wide range of civic groups, unions, and business organizations, and nearly every elected official in the state.[34]

Ronan overpromised, as city leaders had done in the 1910s, 1920s, 1930s, 1940s, and 1950s. His team told the press that consolidating the transportation agencies would help keep fares down. State officials said that the Long Island Rail Road would break even, the city's buses would make a profit, and the TBTA's surpluses would cover the Transit Authority's deficit. Newspaper reporters did not realize that Ronan's numbers were no more realistic than Mayor O'Dwyer's and Mayor Hylan's promises had been, years earlier.[35]

Two astute elected officials privately warned the governor that he was setting false expectations. Assemblyman Robert Abrams, from the Bronx, was concerned that the state's 1967 bond referendum would have the same results as the 1951 referendum because state officials were promising a Second Avenue subway that they would not be able to deliver. Likewise, the president of the New York City Council thought the governor was misleading the public about his ability to complete the Second Avenue subway and other projects.[36]

The proposal put together by Ronan appealed to just about every constituency in the state: better subways in the city, commuter rail improvements in the suburbs, new rural highways, a bridge across the Long Island Sound between Westchester County and Long Island, and plenty of construction jobs for unions. Rockefeller won Lindsay's support by promising to use the TBTA surplus to subsidize the subway and bus system. The governor also promised the mayor that he could nominate three people to serve on the nine-seat board of the MTA. Not only did Lindsay support Rockefeller's bond referendum, but the mayor even told every one of his commissioners, administrators, agency heads, assistants, and deputies to promote the initiative wherever they could and to seek out opportunities to address civic, fraternal, and religious groups about the referendum's importance.[37]

If Rockefeller wanted to tap into TBTA's annual surplus, he would have to overcome two obstacles that had thwarted Lindsay: the TBTA's Robert Moses and Chase Manhattan Bank. The governor overcame Moses's reluctance to support the creation of the MTA by linking it with the $2.5 billion bond proposal and by assuring Moses that he would have a leading role at the MTA, planning and building the new Long Island Sound crossing. Rockefeller lived up to his word to support the bridge even when his sister became furious at him because the bridge's right of way would infringe on her Long Island estate. The governor neutralized opposition from the TBTA's bondholders because he was born into the right family: David Rockefeller was the chair of Chase Manhattan Bank—the trustee of TBTA's bonds.[38]

In 1967, the governor and Ronan obtained the support they needed to transform the transportation network, a feat that Lindsay had not been able to accomplish. In the spring, the state assembly and state senate overwhelmingly passed a bill supporting the creation of the MTA. One assemblyman said, "You've got to hand it to the Governor. He really put this transportation thing on the road." In the fall, the statewide transportation bond proposal easily passed with 58 percent of the vote, thanks to overwhelming support in New York City, where 69 percent supported it.[39]

The MTA would soon be responsible for the city's subways and buses as well as the Long Island Rail Road, two airports, seven bridges, and two tunnels. As MTA chair, Ronan would be the state's highest-paid public official and would have so much power that some critics began referring to the MTA as the "Wholly Ronan Empire." One politician said that compared to Ronan, Robert Moses looked like a "schoolboy with a small allowance."[40]

There was a key difference between the institutions controlled by the two men. As chair of the TBTA, Moses had controlled money-making bridges and tunnels that allowed him to continuously expand his empire. In contrast, Ronan's empire consisted mostly of public transportation services that needed ongoing public subsidies. Ronan would later refer to the transit agencies as "the biggest collection of losers ever collected under one roof."[41]

MAKING UP FOR THIRTY YEARS OF DO-NOTHINGISM

After New York's voters approved the November 1967 proposal, Rockefeller gave the MTA ninety days to develop a regional transportation plan. Ronan and his planning director, Bob Olmsted, took the lead and worked with the Lindsay administration for ideas and support. Olmsted, who had grown up near the Third Avenue Elevated line, had been thinking about a Second Avenue subway for a very long time.[42]

When Olmsted was twenty years old and stationed in the Philippines during World War II, his parents sent him a newspaper article about a proposal by the New York City Board of Transportation. The army soldier wrote back to his parents, "First of all, I found the two clippings about potential subway construction very interesting. The plans for the Second Ave line have changed a bit since I last studied them. I note that they incorporate a modification of one of my 'proposals,' namely a spur from the Sixth Ave line (two tracks) under 57 St to Second Ave." Only after offering his own suggestions to improve the latest subway proposal did Olmsted mention in his 1945 letter that three days earlier, the Japanese general in the Philippines had surrendered to the US Army.[43]

Olmsted started his career as a civil engineer at the TBTA, working for Robert Moses on the Brooklyn–Battery Tunnel, and he was the first person to walk from Manhattan toward Brooklyn in the tunnel. In his mind, Olmsted could picture the city's entire subway system: its stations, tunnels, elevated lines, tracks, and switches. He also liked to build things, a trait he might have inherited from one of his nineteenth-century ancestors, Frederick Law Olmsted, the designer of New York City's Central Park.[44]

Olmsted expanded on a March 1967 proposal developed by Transit Authority engineers for a four-track Second Avenue subway line along with a planned 63rd Street tunnel that together would provide train service between Manhattan, Queens, Brooklyn, and the Bronx. The Transit Authority's proposal was more ambitious than the 1950s proposal because it would run further south, all the way to Lower Manhattan's financial district. The Downtown-Lower Manhattan Association had pushed for a subway under Water Street along with the construction of a World Trade Center as a way to revitalize the area. Transit Authority engineers estimated that the cost for the Second Avenue subway, including connections to existing subway lines, would be $538 million. The cost to expand service to Queens, including the construction of a 63rd Street tunnel, would be an additional $391 million. On top of that, purchasing additional cars and expanding storage facilities to provide these services would add another $253 million.[45]

By Christmas, Olmsted and Ronan struck a deal with the mayor and the city's planners that pleased the governor's brother and did not backtrack on the expectations raised in the 1967 bond act. The MTA would build new subway lines in all five boroughs, including a Second Avenue subway between the Bronx and the financial district. Lindsay agreed to allocate $200 million for the MTA's expansion program, with the state and federal government paying for the rest. Lindsay was delighted. In the early 1950s, the city had been poised to spend much more for subway expansions. Moreover, Ronan agreed that the city would be part of the decision-making process about construction schedules, station locations, frequency of service, and fares.[46]

In February 1968, the governor and the transportation authority released their program for system-wide improvements, in a report titled *Metropolitan Transportation: A Program for Action.* The MTA said the program was "big" but "do-able." When Olmsted recommended that the MTA expand the subway in short, functional segments, Ronan told him that "that was not how great builders built things." Ronan was not interested in making incremental changes to the region's transportation network, and over the next two months, his plan became even more grandiose.[47]

Ronan said, "We're making up for 30 years of do-nothingism in mass transportation," and claimed that the New York metropolitan area was facing a transportation crisis because it had not built any new subways in thirty years, nor made any significant improvements to the commuter railroads since Grand Central Terminal was built in 1913. Rockefeller said that it was the first time in the nation's history that there had been a total regional approach to mass transportation. *New York Times* editorial writers proclaimed that "a brighter day for metropolitan transportation is dawning" and called the plan "an epic step forward." Even though Ronan took many of Lindsay's ideas and even the title *A Program for Action*, the governor, not the mayor, received all of the praise and credit.[48]

Rockefeller was hoping to generate national publicity for his efforts. At the time, his senior advisers were holding regular strategy sessions about entering the 1968 presidential race. Rockefeller told his aides that the things he was trying to do in New York State would set a pattern for domestic issues in the rest of the country.[49]

Ronan split the MTA's expansion program into two phases. The first phase included the Second Avenue subway between the Bronx and 34th Street, as well as a new 63rd Street bi-level tunnel between Manhattan and Queens with tracks for the subway and the Long Island Rail Road. Like Lindsay's 1965 campaign proposal, Ronan's first phase benefited a wide range of constituencies. The Transit Authority, now controlled by the MTA's board of directors, would buy air-conditioned subway cars, build new high-speed express tracks for the Queens Boulevard line, and extend subway service in Brooklyn and Queens. The new subway lines promised to be a dramatic leap forward compared to the existing system. The subway cars, signals, power supply, and tracks would be designed to safely operate trains at speeds up to eighty miles per hour; the existing lines operated between only twenty-five and fifty-five miles per hour. Moreover, the new trains would accelerate 28 percent faster than the existing ones.[50]

The first phase was estimated to cost $1.6 billion and be completed within ten years. It would be financed with state transportation bonds, local contributions, public authority contributions, and federal aid. But much of Ronan's plan was simply a fantasy. Even more remarkable is that Ronan had another set of major initiatives.[51]

The $1.3 billion second phase of the MTA's program comprised even more unrealistic projects, such as additional Queens and Bronx subway lines and an extension of the Long Island Rail Road service to lower Manhattan. This phase also included a southern extension of the Second Avenue subway from 34th Street to Lower Manhattan that would be built deep enough below Water Street so that one day it could be extended to Brooklyn or Staten Island. Not one of the subway and commuter rail expansion projects from the second phase would be completed within the next fifty years. Nor, for that matter, would any from the first phase.[52]

Ronan's two-phase plan was quite popular with New Yorkers because he and the governor did not disclose the fact that the MTA would have to raise fares and tolls to pay off billions of dollars in new debt. Instead the two men talked about their efforts to maintain the fare and claimed that the federal government would be a generous benefactor to the MTA's expansion program.[53]

Similarly, the MTA deceived the public by lowballing the projects' costs. The cost estimates for the Second Avenue subway were lower than those prepared the previous year by Transit Authority engineers. Ronan said it would cost only $335 million to build a new subway from 138th Street in the Bronx to Whitehall Street in Lower Manhattan, plus an additional $79 million to connect with the Dyre Avenue and Upper Pelham lines in the Bronx. It was a delusional figure given that transit officials had used higher cost estimates in the 1950s.[54]

Ronan deliberately failed to adjust the cost estimates for anticipated inflation. When the Downtown-Lower Manhattan Association's engineers estimated costs for the Lower Manhattan portion, they assumed an inflation rate of at least 6 percent per year. Likewise, the city's consultant who reviewed the Second Avenue subway's cost estimates reported that construction costs were escalating at 7 percent a year. Although Lower Manhattan's financial leaders and the city believed in using realistic cost assumptions, the state's transportation leader did not.[55]

Ronan knew he had created a house of cards. Within weeks of releasing his plan, he told the governor that the MTA did not have sufficient funds to carry out its responsibilities and get its improvement program underway. The MTA needed additional sources of continuing and reliable funds. The city's Planning Department also realized that a serious shortfall existed. With $600 million from the state's transportation bond issue and $200 million from the city's capital budget, the planners estimated that the MTA would be approximately $500 million short of funding the first phase. When making their determination, the city planners were not even aware that Ronan's cost estimates were fatally flawed.[56]

Although the MTA had taken over the Transit Authority, the city still played an important role. Under state law at the time, the Transit Authority could operate, but not build, a new subway line on its own. The city owned the subway system and it held the power to finance and construct a new route. The Transit Authority could act only as the city's agent. Before any construction could begin, Ronan would need to obtain approval from the city's Board of Estimate, the eight-member body consisting of the five borough presidents, the mayor, the city council president, and the comptroller.[57]

When Ronan submitted his proposed new routes to the Board of Estimate, he told them, "For almost 40 years, we've been forced to ask citizens of this city and great metropolitan region to make do with a transportation system which has not been able to adapt to changing times, and with transportation facilities that are obsolete and inadequate to meet modern travel demands." He talked about New York City's recent successes: Manhattan's CBD had experienced the greatest office building boom in US history and become the job magnet for the entire region. The metropolitan area had the nation's greatest ocean port and served as the nation's international air gateway. But Ronan warned the board that the city's "advantage is seriously threatened because of inadequate ground transportation." He explained that cities across the globe, including London, Paris, Leningrad, Montreal, San Francisco, and Washington, DC, were creating sleek, modern subway systems.[58]

The Board of Estimate members did not understand the complexity and the real costs of improving the existing system and building new subway lines because the MTA chair told them that the plan was "practical, doable, and meets present and future needs." Since New York City had built a vast and integrated network of highways, bridges, and tunnels in the past few decades, it did not seem far-fetched that the public transportation system could also be dramatically improved. In fact, they thought Ronan's plan was long overdue.[59]

The board members did not want Ronan to scale back his plans; instead they wanted him to be even more aggressive. They had their own ideas that were not in the MTA's proposal, such as improving rail service between Brooklyn and Kennedy International Airport. Regarding the Second Avenue subway, they did not want to wait another decade before construction began on the southern section. The Manhattan borough president and prominent civil rights leader Percy Sutton had his own concerns. He referred to the line as the "the snob express" because many Lower East Side residents would have longer walks to the subway than the wealthy residents on the Upper East Side. Ronan and Olmsted were not discriminating based on race or class; Lower East Side residents were simply at a geographical disadvantage because their neighborhood had more streets and avenues east of Second Avenue than any other East Side neighborhood.[60]

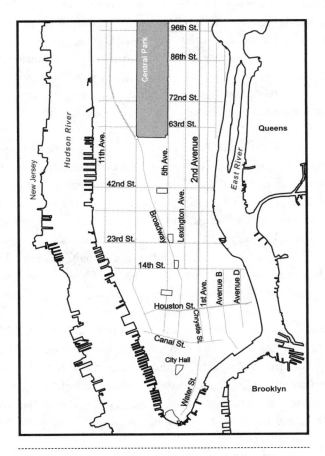

Map 3.1. The Lower East Side has more streets and avenues east of Second Avenue than other East Side neighborhoods.

To obtain the Board of Estimate's approval, Ronan agreed to accelerate the southern section of the Second Avenue subway so that it would be built in the program's first phase. He also agreed to add a future Lower East Side loop, known as the "cuphandle," that would swing east from Second Avenue along 14th Street to Avenue C. Bob Olmsted warned Ronan that this loop would be a fiasco because it would cost an additional $60 million, require taking more private property, miss an important transfer point at Grand Street, and lead to slower travel times. Ronan, though, was more concerned with obtaining approval from the Board of Estimate and starting construction as soon as possible.[61]

The Board of Estimate did offer one recommendation to reduce costs. In 1952, the board had approved a Second Avenue subway that would be six tracks wide along much of its length. In 1968, the MTA proposed a four-track-wide tunnel that would initially be equipped with only two tracks. City officials in the Planning, Transportation, and Budget Departments, as well as the RPA, all recommended against spending the extra money on a four-track line because they thought two tracks would provide sufficient capacity. Ronan acquiesced to reducing the number of tracks, saying that a two-track subway was preferable to building no subway at all.[62]

In September 1968, the Board of Estimate approved the Second Avenue subway and eleven other new routes. The board and the mayor agreed to contribute an additional $300 million, for a total of $500 million, toward the MTA's program. The board's costly changes made the plan even less financially viable, despite the city's additional contribution. Although Ronan needed the board's approval, he was able to resist requests from other prominent organizations. For instance, the RPA did not think Ronan's plan would meet the needs of the future, the chair of the City Planning Commission wanted better east–west service in Midtown Manhattan, and the *New York Times* called for better access to Times Square, not coincidentally the home of its headquarters.[63]

The following year, Congress added another hurdle for the MTA. States seeking federal funds for transportation projects would need to identify their potential environmental impacts and incorporate public participation into the planning process. Environmental awareness and community opposition would not stop the Second Avenue subway, although it did kill three planned highway projects: the Long Island Sound crossing, the Lower Manhattan Expressway, and the Mid-Manhattan Expressway.

As required by the 1969 federal environmental law, the MTA held a public hearing in 1971 to solicit public input about the new subway line. The Upper

East Side's state senator, Roy Goodman, was delighted that transit officials were even listening to the public. Remembering when Robert Moses started his projects during the La Guardia era, Goodman said, "One day an earth moving piece of equipment would arrive and a project would unfold, to the wonderment and distress of the uninformed public." Assemblyman Antonio Olivieri was not in a very friendly mood toward MTA officials when he walked in late for the hearing on East 68th Street. Olivieri said he had just seen a cockroach "attack" a subway passenger on the Lexington Avenue train. Then the train stalled at 42nd Street and passengers were advised to take other means of transportation.[64]

The MTA told the attendees that the two-track Second Avenue subway would include five stations north of 50th Street, at 57th, 72nd, 86th, 106th, and 125th Streets. The number of tracks and stations was the most controversial issue at the time. Because of intense political pressure, the MTA had added the 72nd Street station right before the hearing. Olmsted's team had wanted to minimize the number of stations because they were costly to build and each additional one increased subway travel times by about forty seconds. Meanwhile, residents, business leaders, local civic groups, and elected officials at the Upper East Side hearing were calling for more stations and tracks. Those two features were tied together. If four tracks were built, then the Transit Authority could offer express service to a few stations and local service to many more.[65]

Only the RPA supported the MTA's efforts to limit the number of stations. The civic group's transportation planners, Boris Pushkarev and Jeff Zupan, calculated that in the aggregate, New Yorkers would have shorter travel times if only four Manhattan stations were built north of 50th Street. The optimal distance between subway stations, they determined, was approximately one mile. The Upper East Side residents might not like that, but most of the passengers traveling on the Second Avenue subway were expected to start in the Bronx and Queens.[66]

The RPA was particularly concerned about the Bronx because the borough was having trouble attracting and retaining middle-income families. If subway service from the Bronx was slow and the MTA implemented plans that would speed up commuter rail services from Westchester County and Connecticut, the Bronx's future would be jeopardized.[67]

Many East Siders pushed the MTA to add a station at 96th Street. Metropolitan Hospital, a city-owned facility located at 97th Street, sent about one hundred doctors, nurses, and other employees to the hearing. One of its directors charged the MTA with "brutal insensitivity toward the sick poor" and said it was not a coincidence that Rockefeller University and New York Hospital, where the governor was a major benefactor, would have much more convenient access. After the hearing, which lasted four hours and fifteen minutes, the MTA board subsequently voted to add a new station at 96th Street. The Bronx did not have as much political clout as the Upper East Side.[68]

ON A DOWNWARD SPIRAL

The MTA's cost estimates for its expansion projects rapidly escalated. In 1968, Ronan said that the cost to build the Second Avenue subway line between the Bronx and 34th Street would be $220 million. By 1971, his estimate for an even shorter segment, between 126th and 34th Streets, was $371 million, and that did not even include engineering expenses and the cost to purchase subway cars for the new service.[69]

MTA officials were also not forthright about their ability to pay for the new subway. The state did allocate $99 million from its bond proceeds, the first time it had ever made a direct financial contribution to the city's subway system. The MTA was hoping the federal government would pay for about two-thirds of the cost and the city would cover the rest, but that was simply wishful thinking.[70]

In 1970, President Richard Nixon signed a law that authorized $10 billion over a twelve-year period for public transportation improvements. Although it vastly expanded the federal government's role in public transportation, it continued the proviso that no state could receive more than 12.5 percent of total transit funding. New York State's share would not even provide enough funding to rehabilitate the Long Island Rail Road, let alone expand the New York City subway system. Meanwhile, city budget officials told Mayor Lindsay that they did not know how the city could possibly generate sufficient funds to pay for its share of the subway expansion program.[71]

The MTA had even bigger problems than financing the Second Avenue subway. In 1971, a Wall Street bond specialist said that working together, the Mad Hatter (a wacky *Alice in Wonderland* character) and Mr. Micawber (an ever-hopeful Charles Dickens character who landed in debtors' prison) could never have dreamed up anything as strange as the Transit Authority's finances. Fares, tolls, taxes, and federal funds have never been able to keep up with the MTA's needs. At times, the state has tried to solve the problem by levying fees and taxes that most people would not notice. For example, only a year after the MTA was formed, the state legislature increased the tax that homebuyers pay when they take out a mortgage, and dedicated the additional revenue to the MTA.[72]

The mortgage tax and the surplus revenue from the TBTA were simply not enough to deal with the MTA's structural deficit, as expenses continued to outpace inflation. After the 1966 transit strike, the unions had received generous salary and benefit increases. Transit Authority salaries, wages, pensions, and other costs increased 77 percent between 1965 and 1970, from $284.4 million to $504.1 million.[73]

In the 1950s and 1960s, the subway system experienced a spiraling cycle of decline. After a fare increase, the number of riders decreased, which led the Transit Authority to cut train service. Cutting back service led to lower ridership, and as the Transit Authority's deficits grew, another round of fare increases, ridership declines, and service cuts ensued. The nickel fare, which increased in 1948 to a dime, rose to fifteen cents in 1953, twenty cents in 1966, and thirty cents in January 1970. Another fare hike to thirty-five cents in 1972 did not help stem the Transit Authority's operating losses, which increased from $74 million in 1970 to $153 million in 1972. Beginning in 1969, subway ridership fell every single year for the next nine years.[74]

The MTA had limited flexibility to cut its expenses. The subways had very high fixed costs and the Transit Authority needed to provide enough services for the four-hour peak commuting period. While a private business would have tried to replace full-time workers with part-time workers or scaled back salaries and benefits, those were not feasible options for a state-run enterprise whose workers were politically influential. Instead, a new union contract in 1968 allowed transit workers to retire with half pay after twenty years of work, exacerbating the MTA's financial problems and affecting service quality after most of the car maintenance workers and 40 percent of the electrical workers retired in the next two years.[75]

With cost estimates for the Second Avenue subway rising and funds from the 1967 bond running dry, Rockefeller proposed another $2.5 billion transportation referendum in 1971. State officials identified even more expansion projects to generate support for the measure, such as an underground people mover across 48th Street where passengers would either sit or stand on a conveyer belt. Although the proposed bond issue received widespread support from city officials, civic groups, labor unions, and the leaders of both major parties, voters were suspicious of yet another bond referendum and turned down the proposal by nine hundred thousand votes out of four million cast.[76]

While Ronan and elected officials focused on expanding the system and avoiding another fare increase, service on the long-maligned subways rapidly deteriorated. Between 1968 and 1970, on-time performance dropped from 95 percent to 85 percent, and the number of times that passengers had to be evacuated from trains doubled. Inexperienced personnel at maintenance facilities with archaic equipment tried to maintain outdated subway cars that were increasingly being vandalized.[77]

Three fundamental organizational changes had failed to stem the decline of subway services and facilities. The city's purchase of the IRT and BMT in 1940 did not improve overall conditions for passengers. Service continued to deteriorate after the New York City Transit Authority was established in 1953. Now the creation of New York State's MTA in 1968 did not appear to be helping either. Subway cars were not getting cleaned, inspected, or overhauled in a timely manner. Trains experienced more breakdowns, accidents, and fires, while the number of service interruptions rose from approximately fourteen thousand in 1967 to twenty-one thousand in 1971.[78]

The mayor said that the subways were "going through the worst period of performance, safety and public confidence in its history," which was threatening the city's economic and social vitality. In the 1940s, 1950s, and 1960s, the subway did not have one single accident with a fatality. In 1970, it had two. Furthermore, by October 1972, virtually every one of the 7,100 subway cars was covered with graffiti.[79]

New York City's fiscal health was no better than the state of its subways. Lindsay and the city comptroller, Abe Beame, were engaging in a series of fiscal gimmicks to keep the city's operating and capital budgets afloat. They were trying to satisfy too many constituents by undertaking ambitious capital projects, minimizing fare increases, and providing some of the most generous pension benefits in the nation to municipal employees.

Government agencies have two types of budgets: operating budgets and capital budgets. The operating budget pays for day-to-day expenses such as salaries, pensions, and office supplies, as well as ongoing maintenance and basic repairs, such as cleaning buses and filling potholes. The capital budget funds the construction and rehabilitation of the city's infrastructure and facilities.

Like other cities across the nation, New York City paid for its operating expenses with taxes, grants, and user fees. To finance its capital projects, the city usually issued long-term bonds. Since infrastructure and facilities, such as schools and sewers, last for decades, it is appropriate to pay off the cost of building and rehabilitating them over twenty or thirty years, just as homeowners take out thirty-year mortgages to purchase a home. The city, though, was spending beyond its means, as it recklessly borrowed money not only for its capital projects but also to balance its annual operating budgets. In 1970 the city had a $542 million deficit in its $8 billion budget; in 1971 it had a $779 million deficit in a $9 billion budget; and in 1972 it had a $618 million deficit in a $10 billion budget.[80]

To show that each new budget would be balanced, a requirement under state law, Lindsay and Beame deferred payments, borrowed money in anticipation of revenues that never materialized, and depleted contingency reserves. They also underfunded pension funds and borrowed against those funds to pay for the transit system's operating deficits. In addition, they irresponsibly used money earmarked for the city's capital budget to pay for operating expenses—the equivalent of taking out a loan to buy a car and then putting the minimum monthly payments on a credit card. In 1972, one-quarter of the city's total capital budget was used to pay for operating expenses, and that number would rise to one-third the following year. As a result, between 1962 and 1972, the city's long-term debt grew from $3.5 billion to $5.5 billion, and the annual payments on its debt rose from less than $500 million to more than $1 billion.[81]

Unaware of New York City's budget shenanigans, taxpayers expected city officials to keep the transit fare low and expand the city's already generous municipal services. Making matters worse, the city had fewer middle-income taxpayers to pay for rising government expenses. New York City's loss of manufacturing jobs meant fewer employment opportunities for the low-skilled, poorly educated workers who were attracted to the city. While middle-class taxpayers moved from the city out to the suburbs, the poor people who moved in required more expensive city services. In the early 1970s, the city had more than one million residents receiving welfare benefits, nearly a tenth of the nations' recipients. More than three-quarters of the city's welfare recipients had not even been born in New York City. Although the state and federal government paid for three-quarters of the welfare costs, the city's share created a huge burden on its budget.[82]

Prior to the 1960s, the city had relied on real estate taxes to fund its services, but the city's tax base shrank as residents and employers left the city for greener pastures, lower taxes, and better schools. Meanwhile, property values and property taxes in the city were kept artificially low because of New York City's strict rent regulations. To generate new revenue and provide more generous services between 1959 and 1971, a slew of new municipal taxes were implemented: the real property transfer tax, the commercial rent tax, the general corporation tax, the unincorporated business tax, the bank tax, the personal income tax, and the mortgage recording tax.[83]

In October 1972, the city sat on the edge of a fiscal crisis, and if it continued to lose private-sector jobs, it might not be able to pay its bills. The MTA was facing lower ridership and deteriorating facilities, as well as rapidly escalating cost estimates on its expansion projects. Unbelievably, after nearly fifty years of promises, it was now time to begin building the Second Avenue subway.

Figure 3.2. *Rockefeller campaigning in Lower Manhattan for the 1968 Republican presidential nomination. Source: W. K. Leffler (photographer),* U.S. News & World Report *magazine photograph collection, Library of Congress.*

Construction Begins and Construction Ends

Politicians love ribbon-cutting ceremonies. They can brag about their accomplishments, celebrate with their cronies, hobnob with local celebrities, and get their pictures in the newspapers. After Mayor George McClellan cut the ribbon for New York's first subway on October 27, 1904, he was so excited that he took over the motorman's duties on the subway's maiden trip and refused to relinquish the controls until he reached West Harlem.[1]

Groundbreaking ceremonies can be just as appealing. Elected officials take credit for getting construction underway, extoll the virtues of a new project, and then pose for photographs with their ceremonial shovels. In 1900, thousands of people attended the ceremony to mark the beginning of the first subway line's construction. The mayor scooped up some "official dirt" with his silver spade, poured it into his new silk hat, and proudly carried it back to his office.[2]

In October 1972, exactly sixty-eight years to the day after McClellan's wild subway ride, Governor Nelson Rockefeller and Mayor John Lindsay presided over the Second Avenue subway's groundbreaking ceremony at Second Avenue and 103rd Street. Tongue in cheek, Lindsay told the crowd that some people in the 1920s had suggested a transit facility along Second Avenue, "and it was such a good idea that I decided to follow up on it immediately." Rockefeller proudly proclaimed, "Ladies and gentlemen, the talking and the planning and the promising stages are over." He credited three historic events: voter approval of the 1967 transportation bond issue, the state's creation of the MTA, and the willingness of the federal government to assume a substantial share of the project's cost. Rockefeller said, "The federal government is making a grant of $25 million as an initial step on the city's application for $254 million."[3]

The MTA chair, William Ronan, declared that the Second Avenue Subway "is no longer a planner's dream or an unfulfilled political promise. It is now being built and should carry its first passengers in 1980 thanks to the firm commitment of the federal government, State of New York, and City of New York to supply the funds necessary for completion." Ronan was dishonest about both the timeline and the funding. The federal government's contribution of $25 million and the state's $99 million grant were enough to pay only a small fraction of the costs. MTA officials added to the deception by saying that the "city had committed itself to pay all construction costs not covered by state and federal funds."[4]

In fact, the city had agreed in 1968 to provide a total of $500 million for all of the MTA's expansion projects, across all five boroughs. Now Ronan was apparently expecting the mayor to contribute at least $650 million just for the Second Avenue subway. At the groundbreaking, the mayor was not even aware that the MTA's latest cost estimate for the project had reached $1 billion, three times as much as Ronan's original 1968 estimate. When Ronan and Lindsay discussed who would pay for cost overruns, they could only agree to disagree. The mayor told Ronan that he would consider providing additional funds for the MTA's expansion projects on a case-by-case basis, depending on how much funding was available and the nature and urgency of the work.[5]

While Ronan raised false expectations about the city's contribution, the governor misled people about the federal government's contribution. Rockefeller told the crowd at the groundbreaking that he had gone to Washington, DC, earlier in the year to speak with President Richard Nixon about the Second Avenue subway. He said he told Nixon, "Look, it's now or never. You can do it, if the federal government steps in with some money right now. We can build it. If we lose this opportunity, it will never be done." The governor said the president "pledged right then and there—the initial $25 million on the $250 million from the federal government which is going to make it possible."[6] Rockefeller later backtracked somewhat, when he told a group of students, "President Nixon said—well, he didn't say 'okay' but that's what it was. That is what I was interested in hearing. He said 'all right. The federal government will do it and I will make a commitment.'"[7]

Rockefeller heard what he wanted to hear and he told the public what they wanted to hear. But we now know exactly what was said at the June 21 White House meeting, because Nixon had secretly installed an audio recording system in the Oval Office. When Rockefeller walked into the White House, he did not need to give the president a detailed presentation about New York politics, the importance of the subways, or the need for a new line on Second Avenue. When the two of them had competed with each other for the Republican Party's presidential nomination in 1968, they lived in the very same Upper East Side building. After the election, Nixon gave up his spacious twelve-room apartment for the White House, while Rockefeller held on to his thirty-room apartment on the top three floors.[8]

The audio tape from their meeting, stored at Nixon's presidential library in California, reveals that Nixon gave Rockefeller and Ronan a warm welcome but did not promise to support any additional funding. He did say that the Second Avenue subway would happen only "when the leaders of the city, the establishment if I may pardon the term, get off their butts." He added that business leaders "can't just bitch about everything, they've got to help run that city. They've really got to do it." Referring to the city's future, he said, "Unless what we call the business establishment in New York takes a hell of a lot greater interest in sound decent government for the city . . . it's had it. It's going to be finished."[9]

Nixon was clearly preoccupied by other matters as he steered the conversation toward pressing global affairs, including the security of Israel, the economies of Latin America, and the need for a credible threat against the Soviet Union. The president, who had periodically taken the Lexington Avenue line between his Upper East Side apartment and his Wall Street office, also lauded the palatial subway stations he had seen in Moscow.[10]

THE WORLD'S MOST MODERN, FUTURISTIC SUBWAY

Although Second Avenue subway stations would not be lined with marble or adorned with chandeliers like those in Moscow, the MTA's New York City Transit Authority proudly declared that it was building "the most modern, futuristic subway in the world." Rather than walking down narrow stairways directly to crowded platforms, passengers would be whisked down escalators to mezzanines lined with shops. The stations would be cooled in the summer, and train rides would be quiet, spacious, and smooth. In addition to five stations on the Upper East Side and East Harlem, the Transit Authority would build five stations between 14th and 57th Streets, two stations on the Lower East Side (Houston Street and Grand Street), a station in Chinatown (Chatham Square), and two in the Financial District (Wall Street and Whitehall Street).[11]

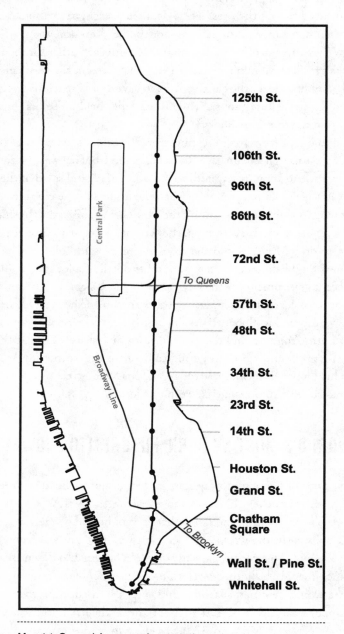

Map 4.1. Second Avenue subway stations

Construction would be costly and complex for many reasons. For example, to avoid excavating under the financial district's skyscrapers, the engineers designed the Whitehall Street station with one level under the street for Bronx-bound trains and a second level for the trains traveling to Queens via the 63rd Street tunnel. The subway also had to be built deep enough so that trains would pass below the east–west subway lines crossing Water Street and under the Brooklyn Bridge's timber foundation, which would weaken if exposed to air.[12]

The engineers took advantage of plans that went all the way back to the 1920s. For instance, when the Sixth Avenue IND line was built on the Lower East Side, the station at the intersection of Houston Street and Second Avenue was designed so that one day Second Avenue subway trains running north–south could run directly above the platforms of the IND trains traveling east–west between Manhattan and Brooklyn.

Although elected officials and the public wanted the Transit Authority to minimize construction impacts, New Yorkers would have to endure major inconveniences and disruptions. The Transit Authority needed to purchase private properties for new stations and ventilation shafts. Workers would close off streets and sidewalks during construction, and excavate and remove over five million cubic yards of rock and soil (the equivalent of a pile of dirt half a mile high, sitting on top of a football field). Manhattan's soil conditions and geology dictated which one of two construction methods would be used: tunneling or "cut and cover."[13]

Where solid rock was located close to the surface, tunnels could be built by drilling through the rock and then using explosives to create larger holes. At the time, the city was using this tunneling technique to build a water tunnel from a Westchester County reservoir to Queens. Since the water tunnel was nearly three hundred feet below ground, its construction had a minimal effect on the residents and businesses above. But a subway could not run three hundred feet below the surface, the equivalent of thirty floors below ground, because moving thousands of people every hour between a station at that depth and the street was impractical. New York's subway stations are typically only twenty to fifty feet below ground. Even the deepest station in the Washington, DC, Metro system would not be much more than one hundred feet below the surface. The Second Avenue subway stations were designed to be less than forty-five feet below street level.[14]

Although tunneling was preferred, it was not feasible at station areas that required train platforms and mezzanines. Likewise, tunneling was not feasible where soil, not solid rock, was near street level. Along the 14.3-mile route, most of the subway would have to be built using a method known as "cut and cover." First, construction workers would reinforce the foundations of fragile buildings, open up the street, excavate rock and soil, and relocate all the utility pipes and cables in the way. Then, steel beams would be driven down to the depth of the future tracks, and a temporary wooden roadway laid over the tops of the beams to accommodate cars, buses, and trucks. The next steps included pouring concrete for the tunnel's floor, walls, and ceilings. After the tunnel areas were waterproofed, workers would lay tracks and install systems for power, signals, communication, drainage, and ventilation.[15]

City Hall officials feared that protests in East Harlem's predominantly black and Puerto Rican community would halt construction before it even started. Bedrock was not close to the surface north of 92nd Street, although it was close to the surface on the Upper East Side. That meant construction workers would have to rip open Second Avenue in the poor neighborhood, but could tunnel under the avenue in the wealthy neighborhood. The mayor's top transportation official insisted that the Transit Authority carefully explain these geological differences to the East Harlem community and make sure that contractors made special efforts to hire its residents.[16]

Because New Yorkers had become much less tolerant of construction impacts since the last major subway expansion, the Transit Authority promised to take extensive precautions to minimize noise, dust, and obstacles to pedestrians and vehicles. Workers would provide access to building entrances and exits at all times during construction. They would also maintain traffic for cars and trucks, which was especially important to motorists because Second Avenue was the most heavily traveled one-way avenue in all of Manhattan. In addition to minimizing disruptions to the community, the MTA also would have to comply with new federal environmental and planning regulations relating to public participation, water, air, and other natural resources. Ronan's sensitivity to community and environmental issues helped him generate the support and approvals he needed; however, they did not help the engineers' efforts to contain costs.[17]

Moving utility lines and minimizing service disruptions were much more costly and time consuming than they had been in previous generations. Since the city did not maintain accurate utility maps, the construction crews did not know what they would find when they opened up the streets. Construction workers building the East Harlem subway tunnels found pipes and cables for gas, steam, water, oil, sewers, electricity, telephones, streetlights, fire alarms, and police call boxes. When they did uncover utility lines, they were not always sure whether the utilities were active or abandoned. They often had to dig by hand to avoid disrupting services to residents and businesses. The mayor's transportation administrator said, "The men may not be using spoons to dig, as some archeologists do, but they're being just as careful. It's like relocating a spider's web."[18]

To minimize noise during construction, the Transit Authority required its contractors to use equipment that muffled the sounds of pavement breakers, pile drivers, and rock drills. The authority also limited the number of hours that construction crews could work and required them to erect acoustic barriers. Since New Yorkers complained about dangerously high noise levels on the existing subway stations, Transit Authority officials agreed to build the new tunnels and stations with sound-absorbing materials. They also promised to weld the rails together rather than bolt them. Although welding rails would increase construction costs, it would significantly reduce the noise levels in trains and reduce long-term maintenance costs.[19]

Despite the Transit Authority's extensive precautions, building subways was inherently risky, dangerous, and disruptive. Underground streams bedeviled the engineers and construction workers in the 1970s because water created enormous pressure on the sides and bottoms of the tunnels. In East Harlem, a construction worker and two women were killed when a sidewalk collapsed, and several families and businesses had to evacuate their Second Avenue building when dangerous cracks in the walls created an imminent danger of collapse.[20]

THE HOUSE OF CARDS COLLAPSES

By 1973, the financial health of both the MTA and the city had become so dire that not only was the Second Avenue subway's future in jeopardy, but so was Ronan's entire expansion program.

The state law that established the Transit Authority explicitly stated that the transit system would be self-sustaining. The city was responsible for capital costs, but it was not allowed to subsidize the fare. With ridership falling to levels not seen since 1918 and expenses soaring, the city started indirectly subsidizing the fare by paying for transit police and student fare discounts. Then with Lindsay's support, the legislature revised the state law so that the city could directly subsidize operating costs.[21]

When the state first established the MTA in 1967, the city's transit services were running an annual deficit of $2 million; six years later it was $175 million. Ronan told Lindsay in 1973 that the city would have to budget almost $600 million over the next two years to avoid raising the fare from thirty-five cents to sixty cents. Since the city's entire annual budget was only $10.3 billion at the time, the mayor responded that it was impossible for the city "to accept this crushing burden." The mayor also told the MTA chair that the subways were now "properly the joint responsibility of the metropolitan region, the state, and the federal government."[22]

Ronan, not the mayor, had to take the brunt of complaints from riders and elected officials about dirty, unreliable, unsafe, and crowded transit services across the region. The media were increasingly depicting a graffiti-covered, lawless environment underground. In Woody Allen's movie *Bananas*, subway muggers assault a woman on crutches, and in John Godey's novel *The Taking of Pelham One Two Three*, four men hijack a subway car on the Lexington Avenue line and threaten to execute passengers, one by one, unless the police deliver $1 million. The MTA chair simply did not have enough resources to counteract the media's portrayal and the deterioration of New York's buses, subways, and commuter rail facilities. Only after Ronan created the MTA did he truly understand the enormous financial challenges he faced. He told a group of transportation professionals in 1972, "Until we can provide a major infusion of dollars, equipment, and skills to aid public transport operators, we can at best merely hold these beleaguered outposts against the relentless ravages of deterioration and financial erosion."[23]

Ronan tried to get more money by reaching out directly to elected officials all over the MTA region, including the state's congressional delegation, state legislative leaders, Board of Estimate members, city council members, county executives, and county legislators. Once he realized that the MTA could not afford to complete the first phase of his expansion plan, his only practical option was having the state borrow more money. So he and Rockefeller proposed a $3.5 billion transportation bond for the November 1973 ballot. They were taking a risk, since voters had turned down a $2.5 billion bond issue for transportation improvements two years earlier.[24]

Ronan and Rockefeller overpromised, just as they had done before voters went to the polls in 1967 and 1971. They laid out yet another list of new projects that would supposedly be funded with bond proceeds, including more new subway lines in the Bronx and Queens, upgrades to the commuter rail network, and the Avenue C loop of the Second Avenue subway. The New York State comptroller, Arthur Levitt, sharply criticized Ronan's plan because most of the new funds would pay for projects that should have already been funded from the 1967 bond. He was also worried about the MTA's escalating construction cost estimates and its soaring labor costs.[25]

Levitt was especially concerned about one particular aspect of the referendum. To obtain the support of Lindsay and City Comptroller Abe Beame, Rockefeller had agreed that $300 million of the proposed bond's proceeds would subsidize transit services for the next two years. The deal suited the governor's purposes because it allowed him to tell voters that their approval of the bond would allow the MTA to maintain the thirty-five-cent fare and avoid fare increases of up to 70 percent on the commuter rail lines. The state comptroller, however, thought Ronan's plan was a reckless fiscal maneuver and potentially a violation of a state law that prohibited using bond proceeds for ongoing operating expenses.[26]

To get around the statute, state officials said that the bond's proceeds would provide $300 million for "capital maintenance," a euphemism for work that should have been funded out of the operating budget. Rockefeller blurred the line between capital and operating expenses because borrowing more money was politically expedient. The other options (e.g., cutting expenses, paring back projects, raising fares, hiking tolls, and increasing taxes) were not very attractive for a politician. From the state comptroller's perspective, issuing long-term bonds to pay for ongoing expenses was like a homeowner taking out a second mortgage to pay for a year's worth of heating bills. It was irresponsible because after the first winter, the homeowner would have to pay for ongoing heating expenses in addition to making two mortgage payments.[27]

The shortfalls in the Transit Authority's operating and capital budgets were just one part of an even larger problem. In the early 1970s, New York City's economy rapidly deteriorated. The city lost a quarter of a million jobs between 1970 and 1973, even while employment levels increased in the rest of the metropolitan area. The subways were not the only part of the city that was languishing. Other sources of civic pride, such as Times Square, had become national embarrassments. The celebrated Broadway producer Alexander Cohen said that any visitor to the theater district could quickly "comprehend the swiftness of the area's relentless descent into squalor." Noting the massage parlors and pornographic bookstores, he said, "The decay is steady and inexorable."[28]

Few people outside of City Hall realized the extent to which the city government was deferring payments, depleting reserves, and borrowing money to pay for municipal services that New Yorkers had come to expect. Legislators and borough presidents did not express concerns about the city's fiscal stability; instead, they battled over how to spend the city's resources. The banks were happy because they profited from underwriting the city's bonds. Remarkably, in December 1972 and December 1973, the two most influential rating agencies, Moody's and Standard & Poor's, upgraded their rating of New York City's bonds to an A.[29]

Just twelve days before the 1973 bond referendum, Lindsay and Ronan broke ground for the section of the Second Avenue subway near the Manhattan Bridge in Chinatown. October groundbreakings had become an annual fall ritual. The previous year's ceremony in East Harlem had occurred eleven days before Election Day. Meanwhile, subway fires and other serious incidents were occurring more frequently. The evening after the Chinatown groundbreaking, 136 passengers were treated for smoke inhalation and other injuries after an electrical fire broke out on a train in the Bronx. While the passengers were waiting to be rescued from the smoke-filled darkness, their train was hit by the one traveling behind them.[30]

Despite Ronan and Rockefeller's efforts, the $3.5 billion bond proposal was soundly defeated in November 1973, with only 42 percent of the voters supporting the additional state debt for subways, buses, and commuter rail. That did not stop Ronan, however, from claiming that the MTA was still moving ahead with the greatest subway construction in the city's history, including the super-express train to Forest Hills, a subway line to southeast Queens, and an extension of the Long Island Rail Road to Third Avenue. Within a few months, construction would be underway simultaneously on four different segments of the Second Avenue subway, constituting 1.5 miles of the 14.3-mile line: 2nd to 9th Streets, 99th to 105th, 110th to 120th, and a seven-hundred-foot section in Chinatown.[31]

With contractors submitting bids much higher than expected, continuing construction on four separate segments was a risky strategy. If the MTA ran out of money, it would not be able to provide any new train service because none of the new segments under construction would connect with a storage yard, maintenance facility, or existing train service. Ronan was using a lesson he had learned from the master builder, Robert Moses: get the public excited about a project and find enough money to start construction, knowing that officials would not want to stop a project once work was underway. The strategy would not work for Ronan, though, because subway lines were so much more expensive to build than highways and parks.

The same day that the transportation referendum failed, the man who had been using accounting gimmicks to balance the city's budget was elected New York City's new mayor. During his 1973 mayoral campaign, Abe Beame promised New Yorkers that the subway fare would not increase. He had a different perspective about the subway fares than Rockefeller (one of America's wealthiest men) and Lindsay (whose father was a lawyer and investment banker). As a child on the Lower East Side, Beame had roller-skated to public school just to save a nickel, and now, as mayor, he hoped to get enough aid from Albany and Washington to save the thirty-five-cent fare. Although the state legislature and Congress had never been willing to subsidize transit services on an ongoing basis, the issues associated with New York's struggling public transportation system had become an even more important issue in the state legislature, and a critical economic and security concern at the national level.[32]

The Democratic state legislators from the city could get support for more transit funding from their suburban Republican counterparts because Ronan had brought the Long Island Rail Road and the New York City Transit Authority together under the MTA umbrella. In January 1974, the state assembly Speaker (a Long Island Republican) announced that he supported providing state subsidies to transit operators. Several days later, the governor signed a bill to help protect the thirty-five-cent fare by allowing the city to borrow $100 million from the state.[33]

When Beame took office in January 1974, the federal government also appeared to be willing to provide transit operating assistance for the first time. The country was in the midst of an energy crisis because the world's leading oil producers in the Middle East had stopped selling petroleum products to countries that supported Israel. With US gas prices quadrupling and motorists waiting in long lines to fill up their tanks, Beame and others argued that increasing train and bus ridership would help reduce the nation's dependence on Middle Eastern oil.

A transit advocate, Theodore Kheel, wrote in *New York* magazine that "for decades, New York City's subways were neglected by the people who managed them, despised by the people who worked them, and, God knows, unloved by the people who had to use them." Pointing to the prospects of the Second Avenue subway, gasoline rationing, stricter air quality controls, and more federal mass transportation aid, he claimed, "Thanks to an extraordinary accident of history, a coincidence of forces no one could have foreseen, all that seems now to be changing, literally before our eyes." Kheel was wrong about the subways having hit rock bottom and gasoline rationing being imminent, but he did predict that New York would beat out Los Angeles and other US cities because "the city with the best public transportation system is going to be the one most likely to thrive in the future."[34]

A month after Beame was sworn in as mayor, he met with Nixon in the White House. When Rockefeller had met with Nixon in the Oval Office only nineteen months earlier, he had sought the president's help in funding the Second Avenue subway. Beame had a much more short-term goal—obtaining federal funds to prevent a subway fare increase. While the Republican governor had seen public transportation as an important tool to promote economic development, the Democratic mayor was more concerned about protecting New York's poor and working-class residents who relied on the city's transit services.

Beame did not get all the help he sought, although a few days after the meeting, Nixon did propose doubling the federal government's annual commitment to mass transportation systems and, for the first time, allowing transit agencies to use federal funds to pay for operating expenses. Obtaining congressional approval for a transit operating assistance program would be one of Beame's top legislative priorities, and he recruited business, labor, and finance leaders to help him generate that support.[35]

As mayor, Beame used the same tricks to balance his budgets that he had employed as comptroller. He referred to them as "fiscal gymnastics." Beame did not want to raise taxes since New Yorkers were already paying the highest in the nation. Nor did he want to cut expenses by laying off workers, because the politically powerful municipal unions had helped him get elected. Instead he claimed savings that were not real, issued more short-term bonds, and tapped into funds that had been set aside for future pensions. Taking a page from City Hall's playbook, the MTA also deferred its own pension obligations to avoid a fare increase.[36]

Beame's capital budget did not provide sufficient funds to complete the Second Avenue subway, let alone to properly maintain the rest of its infrastructure, as he slashed spending on fire and police stations, schools, housing, hospitals, parks, and sewers. Meanwhile, Beame continued his fiscally irresponsible policy of allocating capital funds for operating expenses, such as $114 million for vocational education and $55 million for job training.[37]

The Arab nations' oil embargo exacerbated inflation and sent the US into a severe recession. With a shrinking economy and interest rates on short-term debt exceeding 7 percent, the city was borrowing money at an unsustainable pace. In 1974, the bond market became skittish about the city's ability to issue any new bonds. Little more than a decade earlier, New York had been one of the world's most prosperous cities. Now it would soon face the very real prospect of defaulting on its loans.[38] With the city teetering on the edge of a financial collapse, it was unclear whether a new subway line in Manhattan was even needed anymore. The East Side's existing subway line, the Lexington Avenue line, was still the city's busiest subway route, but ridership was plummeting all across the city.[39]

In 1974, few people questioned the wisdom of continuing work under Second Avenue. Construction was not facing any organized community opposition, in part because most of the work was taking place in East Harlem, which had fewer people, offices, and shops than the rest of the route. Many of the low-income housing projects that lined the avenue in East Harlem were set back from the street, which gave their residents a buffer from the cut-and-cover construction. The neighborhood was facing much more serious issues than subway construction impacts, including a persistently high unemployment rate, an increasing number of abandoned buildings, and a heroin epidemic.

One of the few Second Avenue subway opponents was Frank Lichtensteiger, who was either an Upper East Side community leader or a community agitator, depending on one's perspective. He had been fired from his city housing job after publicly testifying against plans to build a new housing complex (Ruppert Towers) on the site of an old brewery near Second Avenue and 91st Street. He also had been part of a lawsuit claiming that Bruce Gimbel had a conflict of interest when he was simultaneously serving as an MTA board member and building a new Gimbels department store at the corner of 86th Street and Lexington Avenue. Gimbel was excited about building a store on the Upper East Side, a neighborhood the retailer referred to as "the richest suburb in the world."[40]

In November 1974, Lichtensteiger wrote in *Our Town* (an East Side newspaper) that Ronan's arrogance and Rockefeller's support made the MTA chair "totally impervious to all suggestions for, and criticisms of, the transit empire he ruled." As a result, Lichtensteiger said, New York had "an antiquated 700 mile subway system that has received no major maintenance funds outside of superficial monies to paint the ugly stations." He accused MTA executives of lying and blamed them for a sudden increase in underground fires and accidents. Regarding the Second Avenue subway, he said that neither the funding nor the planning was "coherent." He asserted, "In the midst of this chaos, a few have stood as lone voices against the wind, calling for proper attention to the existing deteriorating system and pointing out such potential assets as costless bus-lanes on the avenues." Lichtensteiger argued that "planning boards and elected officials have been lethargic, falling all over themselves to pay homage to Dr. Ronan's plan for the vacuous Second Avenue subway."[41]

Construction continued on Second Avenue despite the city's economic and social problems. At this point, adding a new subway line made as much sense as a married couple pouring the foundation for an expensive vacation house while their permanent home was falling apart. But Ronan and Rockefeller were not ready to throw in the towel. They had invested so much time, money, and political capital into the Second Avenue subway that it would have been embarrassing for them to cancel the megaproject and admit they had made a mistake. Their legacies and national reputations were at stake. So they continued to pour money down four holes under Second Avenue because that was more appealing than telling voters they had wasted taxpayers' money. It was also a good time for the two men to look for new jobs.

A month after Abe Beame was elected mayor, Nelson Rockefeller resigned from office to lead two national commissions and test the waters for another presidential bid. Fleeing Albany before he had to face the repercussions of his careless spending certainly did not hurt Rockefeller's career. In August 1974, Nixon resigned from office after the Supreme Court ordered him to turn over White House recordings relating to the Watergate scandal. Nixon's successor, Gerald Ford, appointed Rockefeller to be his vice president.

New York's lieutenant governor, Malcolm Wilson, was sworn in to replace Rockefeller as governor, and several months later, Ronan resigned his position as MTA chair. Even on his way out, Ronan continued lowballing the cost estimates for the Second Avenue subway (now at $1.3 billion) and claiming the project would be completed by 1981. His successor at the MTA, David Yunich, would defend the project, arguing that "it would be stupid to stop construction; we might as well let this island sink. It's fundamental to the future development of New York if we want to entice business and manufacturers to come in." Yunich also called it a "gross injustice to refer to this as simply a Second Avenue subway line when in fact it is a new interborough system with connections to Queens, the Bronx, and Brooklyn."[42]

Yunich was more candid after Wilson lost the gubernatorial election to Hugh Carey in November 1974. Two days after the election—for the first time in six years—the MTA gave its first public update on the costs and schedules for all of its expansion projects. Yunich said that the new date for completing the Second Avenue subway would be 1988 rather than 1980 or 1981. And New Yorkers would have to wait until 1994 for the Second Avenue subway's Lower East Side cuphandle, the link to JFK Airport, and subway extensions in

Brooklyn and Queens. Yunich admitted that when one gives a completion date that far out, "It's a polite way of saying not in our lifetime."[43]

For the first time, an MTA chair finally acknowledged that the MTA did not have sufficient funds to pay for all of its planned expansion projects. The estimated cost of the MTA's priority projects approved by the city had already quadrupled. Yunich suggested that legislators consider a number of potential new revenue sources for transit, such as tolling the free East River bridges.[44]

How could the cost estimate for building the Second Avenue subway between the Bronx and Lower Manhattan rise in one decade from $335 million to $2.25 billion?[45] Ronan and other MTA officials were quick to blame high rates of inflation. Between 1960 and 1965, the US inflation rate ranged from 1 percent to 1.6 percent before it started rising dramatically. In 1973, when ground was broken for the subway in Chinatown, inflation was at 6.2 percent. The following year, it hit 11 percent due to the oil crisis. Ronan also blamed other factors beyond his control, including multiple reviews by local, state, and federal officials that exacerbated delays and added expenses to every stage of the planning, contracting, and construction processes.

Accommodating community concerns also took time and increased costs. Various stakeholders tacked on expensive elements to the Second Avenue subway, such as additional stations and the Lower East Side cuphandle. A Transit Authority official fondly recalled "When La Guardia built the Eighth Avenue subway, there was no nonsense about consulting the communities on where the stations were to be located. One day the jackhammers appeared and that's when you knew where the stations would be."[46]

But inflation and a more inclusive planning process only partly explain why Ronan's cost estimates were so flawed. The major problem with his 1968 estimates was that they were hastily put together with little concern for accuracy. Ronan and Rockefeller were trying to put together not a realistic plan, but rather a visionary concept that would generate widespread enthusiasm in the New York metropolitan area and help Rockefeller garner favorable national attention for his 1968 presidential ambitions.

The MTA's cost estimates were developed without an adequate engineering review and without knowing basic elements of the program, such as the exact number and location of stations. The MTA planners did not have detailed cost estimates for all of the necessary construction elements, including tunnels, stations, tracks, and signals. Ronan wanted to keep initial cost estimates as low as possible, so he deliberately left out hundreds of millions of dollars for new subway cars that would be needed to operate on the new lines. He also ignored standard cost-estimating practices by failing to incorporate inflation into cost estimates. At the time, another state authority set up by Rockefeller (the Urban Development Corporation) was using the same trick to estimate construction costs for new housing on Roosevelt Island.[47]

According to a scathing report issued by the state comptroller's office five years after Ronan resigned, the MTA's headquarters staff, with only about two dozen employees, had not attempted to verify their initial cost estimates by seeking input from the one thousand employees who worked in the Transit Authority's Engineering Department. Rather than reviewing existing New York City construction costs, the MTA planners used cost patterns and ratios experienced during the design and construction of the IND system in the 1930s. That approach was both sloppy and fundamentally flawed. The IND was built during the Great Depression, when unemployment was higher, the workday was longer, and unions had different work rules. Furthermore, the Second Avenue subway was designed with more costly features and had to be constructed in a way that would be less disruptive to businesses and residents.[48]

Since the MTA lacked many important details about its expansion projects, the cost estimates should have included a contingency amount that would cover unexpected conditions. Contingencies had long been standard practice in the construction industry. Typically, cost estimates start with a high contingency amount that is reduced as a project works its way through the design and construction phases.

Ronan might have been a brilliant strategist for the governor, but he was also ignorant, overly optimistic, and devious when he put together his 1968 plan. He did what the sponsors of large infrastructure projects typically do: they underestimate costs to gain the approvals and funding they need to move their plans along. Ronan, however, went a step further, by raising false expectations about how much money the government would provide for the project—claims that were repeated by the media and civic advocates. Ronan started lying to the public about the transit expansion projects on the MTA's very first day in existence, and he never bothered to set the record straight before he resigned as chair more than six years later.[49]

A BANKRUPT CITY

Upon taking office in January 1975, Governor Carey did not gloss over the state's economic problems. In his first State of the State message, he told New Yorkers, "This government and we as a people have been living far beyond our means. . . . The days of wine and roses are over." Carey's predecessor, Nelson Rockefeller, later said, "Poor Hugh, I drank the champagne and Hugh Carey got the hangover."[50]

Carey found Beame exasperating because the mayor did not face the city's fiscal crisis head-on. Beame told Carey, "You could always borrow more, tomorrow." Beame was neither a prudent comptroller nor a courageous leader, but his actions were not the only reason why the city was facing such a dire predicament. Some factors were beyond the city's control. The middle class had fled to the suburbs, along with the stores where they shopped and the corporate headquarters where they worked. Manufacturers moved to locations where they could build single-story facilities on cheaper land with lower labor costs. Federal policies exacerbated these shifts by encouraging investments in suburban areas and paying for new highways to access them.[51]

New York City's laudable policies designed to reduce the gap between the rich and the poor were simply not sustainable. On average, residents paid 10.2 percent of their incomes to the city in 1975, more than a third higher than a decade earlier. The city's elected officials (the mayor, comptroller, borough presidents, and city council members) provided services for its citizens and offered benefits to its municipal workers that the city could not afford.[52]

Mayor Robert F. Wagner Jr. set the tone in the 1960s. When submitting his last budget, he said, "I do not propose to permit our fiscal problems to set the limits of our commitments to meet the essential needs of the people of the city." In Lindsay's first term as mayor, the city's labor force grew from 250,000 to 350,000 and the city's budget rose almost 50 percent. The public university system eliminated all tuition charges and accepted any student with a high school diploma. State officials, including Rockefeller, enabled the city's profligate spending. At the federal level, President Lyndon B. Johnson's new programs to eradicate poverty passed along costly mandates to local governments.[53]

In early 1975, the City of New York literally ran out of cash. The city did not have enough money to meet its payroll, banks would no longer issue it loans, and the city was frozen out of the bond market. President Ford's blunt press secretary said that the situation was a "self-inflicted act by the people who have been running New York City." When Beame met with Ford about the city's fiscal plight, the president asked the mayor why the subway fare was only thirty-five cents and why tuition at the City University was free. Beame launched into a long explanation and concluded with, "Mr. President, if it weren't for free tuition at City University, I wouldn't be here with you today."[54]

The *Daily News* published its famous October 1975 front-page headline "Ford to City: Drop Dead" after the president threatened to veto any bill that would bail out the city. Although the newspaper riled up New Yorkers, Ford did not really say "drop dead." Rather, he said, "If we go on spending more than we have, providing more benefits and more services than we can pay for, then a day of reckoning will come to Washington and the whole country just as it has to New York City. . . . When that day of reckoning comes, who will bail out the United States of America?"[55]

New York's business leaders used their national and global connections to convince the Republican president to soften his position. The French president warned Ford that a New York bankruptcy could precipitate a financial crisis, and the German chancellor bluntly told Ford, "If you let New York go broke, the dollar is worth shit." Although Ford was not willing to write a blank check to New York, he did support subsequent legislation that allowed the city to borrow up to $2.3 billion.[56]

In 1953, the state had created a Transit Authority because it no longer trusted city officials to operate the subway system. In 1975, the state no longer trusted the city to manage any of its other services either. Governor Carey and the legislature set up a corporation to issue bonds on the city's behalf, and established an emergency financial control board with broad powers to control the city's finances. If the state had not done so, the city certainly would have gone bankrupt, along with possibly more than one hundred banks.[57]

DESPERATE TO PROTECT CITY AND FARE

After telling Yunich that he planned to reallocate funds that had been designated for the Second Avenue subway, Beame set up a transportation policy committee consisting of his deputy mayors and senior officials. The committee members mimicked the mayor's stand in March 1975, arguing in their seventy-page report that the city had much more important transit priorities than building a Second Avenue subway. "Clearly," they said, "our first responsibility is to do everything possible to protect the fare." Beame's six-year transit construction program would not include any more funds for the Second Avenue subway. A disappointed Yunich said that waiting another six years for funding might delay the project "to the turn of the century, when a lot of us will be playing harps instead of riding subways."[58]

Beame claimed that the four sections of the Second Avenue subway under construction would be completed and sealed off, while engineering and design work for the entire line would continue so that construction could resume when funds became available. He said, "We cannot abandon the Second Avenue subway; we must, however, defer it." Mayor La Guardia had said something very similar more than forty years earlier.[59]

The MTA did not have enough money to complete the sections under construction, let alone the entire Second Avenue subway, the subway extension to Queens, or the Long Island Rail Road connection to Manhattan's East Side. At the time, Yunich was warning state legislators that the MTA had "for all practical purposes, run out of money" and was "living almost from day-to-day on a hand-to-mouth basis." For the coming year, New York City Transit's operating deficit was expected to be nearly $600 million. When state and city leaders had first created the MTA, they thought that profits from the Triborough Bridge and Tunnel Authority would wipe out transit losses, but excess toll revenues were providing only $48 million in 1975 to fill the gap.[60]

The federal government was offering some flexibility to those who favored protecting the fare over construction projects. The previous year, as Congress was finalizing a new transportation law that would provide transit operating subsidies, Manhattan's congressman, Edward Koch, inserted an amendment that would later become known as the "Beame Shuffle." The provision, added at the mayor's request, allowed localities to use up to one-half of their federal capital funds for operating assistance, provided that the federal funds were replaced by state and local funds within two years.[61]

In a memo to Ford before the bill was signed, the director of the US Office of Management and Budget expressed his concern that New York would use the Beame Shuffle to "subvert sound financing principles" by issuing long-term debt for operating expenses. He told the president that if New York used this provision to excessively subsidize transit operations, it might not be able to fund needed capital investment. Despite White House reservations about the amendment, the president signed the National Mass Transportation Assistance Act. Afterward, a delighted Beame gave Ford gold-plated cufflinks made from subway tokens, a creation of Yunich's wife.[62]

Beame was the only mayor in the country who was desperate and short-sighted enough to take advantage of the Beame Shuffle. He used half of the remaining federal funds allocated for the Second Avenue subway to pay for transit operating expenses, and the other half to complete construction work underway in Queens. He also had another trick up his sleeve: he convinced

Albany's legislative leaders to amend a state law so that $170 million from the 1967 transportation bond monies could be used to repay the federal government for funds it advanced to finance the Transit Authority's operating deficit. The state comptroller later pointed out that if New York State had instead used those proceeds to pay for the local share of federally funded capital projects, the Transit Authority would have been eligible to receive hundreds of millions of dollars more in federal aid.[63]

East Siders seemed to be the victims of another hoax. In 1951, New York voters had approved a bond referendum for the Second Avenue subway, but the funds were used to fix up the existing system. Now, 1967 referendum funds that had been dedicated for subway expansion were being used to maintain the fare.

Bob Olmsted, MTA's planning director and the architect of Ronan's expansion program, reached out to the Regional Plan Association (RPA), hoping the civic organization could use its influence with city officials to save at least one portion of the Second Avenue subway. Olmsted had been working with Boris Pushkarev, the RPA's lead transportation researcher, for nearly a decade on the route and station locations.

Olmsted told the RPA that construction should continue between 125th Street and 63rd Street because it would tie into the rest of the subway system when the MTA finished building the east–west subway tunnel underneath 63rd Street. Trains heading uptown on the existing Broadway line could travel east under 63rd Street and then north on Second Avenue. The MTA would need to operate only a short extension of existing services on Second Avenue, which would add relatively little to the system's total operating costs. Olmsted reminded the RPA that construction was well underway in East Harlem, and that the MTA had already completed the federal planning requirements for this portion of the Second Avenue subway. The segment north of 63rd Street, he explained, would serve a large population and would relieve the Lexington Avenue line, which in spite of a decline in usage was still the most crowded line and well beyond any acceptable comfort standards.[64]

Using Olmsted's arguments, RPA president John Keith urged the mayor and his aides to prioritize the northern leg of the Second Avenue subway. He told Beame that canceling the entire subway line would add to the image and reality of New York City's economic decline, and would further erode business confidence at a time when corporations were moving out. But Keith could not change the mayor's mind. In 1975, Beame pared back the capital budget so much that there was not even enough money to build a single new school, police station, firehouse, or park.[65]

The Second Avenue subway would be kept alive thanks to the MTA's Olmsted and the RPA's Pushkarev. Olmsted's idea to focus on the section between 63rd and 125th Streets would be resurrected two decades later, when he advised the next generation of MTA planners. Pushkarev's protégé at the RPA, Jeff Zupan, would help generate the political support needed for Olmsted's idea.

Pushkarev was devastated by Beame's decision to suspend construction. He took the long view, though, figuring that the best way to improve transit in New York would be to expand the constituency for rail services outside the New York metropolitan area. So he and Zupan wrote a book titled *Urban Rail in America* that identified urban corridors where new rail lines would be cost effective. As Pushkarev hoped, the book helped spur the development of new passenger rail systems around the country, which in turn generated more support for transit in Congress. Forty years after Beame put the Second Avenue subway on hold, a new federal program would provide over $1 billion toward Olmsted's idea of extending an existing subway line up Second Avenue north of 63rd Street.[66]

Beame never did meet his commitment to complete the four sections of the Second Avenue subway. Only fourteen months after Beame and Wilson broke ground for the segment between Second and Ninth Streets, Beame told the Transit Authority to terminate its work there. The East Village would not be getting a new subway, just some nice new sidewalk curbs. Beame did not have a choice: Peter Goldmark, Governor Carey's brash young budget director, told the mayor that he was pulling state funding for the project and that the city needed to halt construction immediately. Goldmark had worked in Mayor Lindsay's budget office, where it had been obvious to him that the city did not have the resources to both adequately maintain and expand the transit system.[67]

The state budget director was using every tool at his disposal to prevent the city from declaring bankruptcy. Late one night, Goldmark was in his office as the state assembly debated legislation designed to avoid a municipal default the next morning. After he learned that the assembly had passed only nine of ten bills that needed to be approved, Goldmark tried to reach the governor but was unable to. So at two o'clock in the morning, Goldmark took matters into his own hands. He told the capitol police to lock the capitol building's doors, and he instructed the state police to bring every legislator found on the New York State Thruway back to Albany. Then Goldmark assembled his staff and told them, "Go to every bar in Albany. I want every legislator back in." After state officials retrieved enough of them (mostly from the bars), the assembly Speaker called the lawmakers to order at five o'clock in the morning. Although the assembly was able to get enough yeas for the tenth bill in a voice vote, no one bothered to check whether everyone who voted was actually a member of the assembly.[68]

The state's emergency financial control board put the City of New York on a road to fiscal recovery by forcing city officials to cut costs and raise revenues. Thousands of workers were laid off and several public hospitals closed. The city university started charging first-year students $750 per year in tuition, and the Transit Authority raised the cost of a subway token more than 40 percent, from thirty-five cents to fifty cents.[69]

Three years earlier, Nixon had told Rockefeller that the business leaders had to help run the city. Now it was actually happening. The seven-member emergency control board, which managed the city's revenues and expenditures, included the heads of the New York Telephone Company, American Airlines, and Colt Industries. Nixon also had said that "the business community is not going to invest if they have no confidence in the political leadership." That confidence and investment would come in time, along with the resurrected dream of a subway underneath Second Avenue.[70]

Figure 4.1. *White House meeting about the Second Avenue subway in June 1972. Left to right: MTA chair William Ronan, Senator Jacob Javits, Governor Nelson Rockefeller, President Richard Nixon, Secretary of Transportation John Volpe, and Senator James Buckley.* Source: File ID: WHP0-9433-03, *White House Photo Office, Richard Nixon Presidential Library and Museum, Yorba Linda, CA.*

Figure 4.2. *Groundbreaking at 103rd Street in East Harlem for the Second Avenue subway in October 1972. Wielding shovels and pickaxes, from left to right: Manhattan borough president Percy Sutton, Senator Jacob Javits, Secretary of Transportation John Volpe, Governor Nelson Rockefeller, and Mayor John Lindsay. Source: Courtesy of New York Transit Museum.*

Figure 4.3. *Subway car in 1973. Source: Identifier 553823, Records of the Environmental Protection Agency (1944–2006), National Archives.*

5

Saving the Subway

In 1980, the New York State Department of Transportation commissioner said that those who developed and encouraged William Ronan's 1968 plan to expand the region's transit network should not be faulted, "since it moved the state firmly into a position of national leadership in public transportation." He claimed the plan "was a massive bold new venture that excited everyone involved in transportation in the State."[1]

In fact, the plan by the first chair of the MTA nearly ruined New York City's public transportation system and the city that relied so heavily on it. New Yorkers would have been far better off if Rockefeller had taken the advice of New York City Transit Authority chair Charles Patterson, who said in 1957 that "it would have been the height of folly" to have built the Second Avenue subway line without sufficient funding in place while the existing system was deteriorating.[2]

Ronan wasted hundreds of millions of dollars. Starting construction on subway and Long Island Rail Road expansion projects resulted in abandoned, never-used tunnels. Purchasing new subway cars did little to improve service because Ronan did not provide the Transit Authority with adequate resources to clean, maintain, and repair them. Once he began his expansion program in 1968, Ronan started siphoning money away from rehabilitating the existing system. The Transit Authority spent more than three-quarters of its capital funds buying new cars and expanding the system, while annual expenditures to upgrade its existing infrastructure decreased by nearly 40 percent.[3]

Bob Olmsted, the architect of Ronan's expansion plan, had clearly been overly ambitious. Olmsted might have had an encyclopedic knowledge of the subway system, but he had never worked at the Transit Authority dealing with its aging infrastructure. Norm Silverman, one of Olmsted's former aides, later realized that Ronan's team "totally underestimated the needs of the subway system." He said, "We just didn't realize how many components of the system were approaching seventy years old and were quickly wearing out, like pump rooms, signal cabling, third rail, power cabling, tracks and ties, and station finishing." Years of vibration and water intrusion, he said, had taken their toll. He blamed the transportation authority's fiefdoms for not adequately communicating with each other about the system's requirements.[4]

Ronan and his team were not the only ones to blame for underfunding the existing system. To avoid a fare increase, Mayor Abe Beame shifted city funds from the Transit Authority's capital program to its operating budget. When Ronan first announced his expansion plan, the city was supposed to provide $100 million per year for transit capital improvements. In 1975, Beame's senior aides estimated that the transit system needed about $250 million annually for capital improvements. In 1978, however, the city contributed only $41 million. Adjusted for inflation, that was less than one-fourth of what Ronan had expected. As a result of budget cuts and shifting priorities, in the late 1970s the transit system was deteriorating nearly three times faster than it was being restored.[5]

The subways, once a source of national pride, had become a symbol of urban decay. After spending a week riding them, the New England travel writer Paul Theroux wrote, "People waiting for the bus have a special pitying gaze for people entering the dark hole in the sidewalk that is the subway entrance. It is sometimes not pity, but fear; often they look like miners' wives watching their menfolk going down the pit." Theroux was disgusted and horrified by the graffiti that marred every surface. It was so extensive that he said it was "hard to believe that the perpetrators are not the recipients of some enormous foundation grant." He also expressed his contempt for "smells so hideous, you want to put a clothespin on your nose" and for the trains that were so noisy they hurt his ears.[6]

Compared to other subway systems that he had visited, Theroux was impressed by some aspects of New York's subways. Trains ran twenty-four hours a day, unlike London's, which shut down at midnight. New York's subway routes were extensive, covering twice as many miles of tracks as the Paris Metro. Theroux thought that New York had the world's fairest and most sensible pricing system, because subway riders paid the same price whether they rode half a mile between Grand Central and Times Square or thirty-one miles from northern Manhattan to the last stop in Queens. After Theroux's week, he wrote, "The subway is New York City's best hope. The streets are impossible; the highways are a failure; there is nowhere to park. The private automobile has no future in this city whatsoever. This is plainest of all to the people who own and, frightened of the subway, use cars in the city; they know, better than anyone, that the car is the last desperate old-fangled fling of a badly planned transport system."[7]

DEFICITS, DECAY, AND DESPAIR

For the New York City subway system, the 1970s continued the downward spiral of fewer riders, budget cuts, and reduced service, which led to a loss of more riders, further budget cuts, and even worse service. As the city's population fell from 7.9 million to 7.1 million, the postwar decline in transit use accelerated as ridership dropped 21 percent on the subways and 24 percent on the buses.[8]

Despite carrying fewer passengers, the transit system's operating costs kept increasing. MTA officials did not want to reduce the number of subway cars or buses because the system was being fully utilized about twenty hours each week. The MTA had limited ability to reduce its biggest expense, labor costs, because the politically powerful unions made sure their members were well compensated and would not let the authority hire part-time employees.[9]

The MTA chair in the mid-1970s, David Yunich, urged lawmakers to raise taxes and place tolls on the free East River bridges, but his pleas fell on deaf ears. Yunich, who never got along well with Governor Hugh Carey, resigned in 1977 before he had finished his six-year term as chair. His successor, Harold Fisher, was a longtime Brooklyn Democratic Party leader whose first loyalty was to the governor, not to improving the transit system. Fisher failed to address the MTA's slide, although he claimed that his programs were making public transportation travel more efficient, comfortable, and safe.[10]

Fisher helped the governor promote his pet project, a new covered highway along the West Side of Manhattan, even though it had nothing to do with the public transportation system. The proposed project, known as Westway, involved adding more than two hundred acres of landfill in the Hudson River for parks and apartments. Dozens of business and labor groups supported the project, claiming that it was essential to Manhattan's economic survival.

Newspapers praised the highway's potential to take trucks off the streets, alleviate air pollution, open up the waterfront, and signal Manhattan's rebirth.[11]

Many environmental and transit advocates, however, opposed Westway and wanted to take the $798 million that the federal government had allocated for the new highway and use it for transit improvements instead. The law that allocated these funds included a provision allowing for such a trade. Carey put Fisher in the uncomfortable position of championing the ambitious highway project and extolling its benefits rather than seeking additional federal aid for the MTA. Fisher made the dubious claim that using the funds for Westway would create up to ten thousand more jobs than using them for major transit improvements and a modest highway improvement.[12]

Carey wanted to subdue Westway's critics, including New York City's newly elected mayor, Ed Koch. So in 1978, the governor pledged to provide more than $800 million for transit improvements. He claimed he had obtained a commitment from federal transportation officials for more than 80 percent of that amount, but that was not true. When the funding did not appear, Carey claimed the White House had reneged on its promise. In fact, the state had never sought these funds, nor were they ever available.[13]

Fisher was woefully short on funds at the MTA, and in a shortsighted move to reduce costs, he cut back on maintenance expenses. Before the MTA began pursuing Ronan's expansion program, a subway car did not leave a storage yard until it was deemed ready for service. In the late 1970s, workers waited until subway cars broke down before fixing them. As a result, trains broke down four times more often in 1980 than in 1968. The practice was also more costly in the long run because car components not maintained properly wore out faster.[14]

By 1980, New York City's subway riders had more to complain about than ever before. One-third of all the subway cars pulling into stations had broken doors, and nearly as many had lighting problems. Because of cutbacks in maintenance and cleaning, a subway car caught fire nearly seven times a day, usually a result of burning trash on the tracks or faulty electrical equipment. Upgrades that should have been made decades earlier continued to be deferred. For example, only 10 of the city's 459 subway stations had ever been modernized. In a citywide poll, half of the respondents cited filthy conditions and terrible smells as among the subway's biggest problems. When asked to compare various public services, the subways ranked at the very bottom, below sanitation, law enforcement, highways, and public education.[15]

Even though ridership had been declining, a shortage of subway cars and frequent delays were causing dangerously overcrowded conditions at some stations. On January 9, 1981, a Manhattan resident who typically took the sub-way from 79th Street to Midtown Manhattan lamented, "I have tried to ignore the pushing, shoving and crowding and, except for an occasional collision with people who stand directly in front of the opening doors when I get out, I have been successful. The graffiti and other facets of the deplorable conditions are so pervasive that I am not even aware of them anymore, except when I happen to travel to another city where they don't exist."[16]

Three days later, a train derailed in Brooklyn after a motor fell off a sub-way car. Transit officials diverted buses to carry stranded subway riders; how-ever, not enough buses were available because 637 of the buses in the fleet had potential cracks in their undercarriages. Subway riders on virtually every line were affected by crowding and delays because one-fifth of the subway cars were stalled in storage yards by mechanical failure. Extra maintenance workers were called in, but their repair work was hampered by a lack of spare parts.[17]

Psychiatrists were concerned about the mental and physical health con-sequences, such as fatigue and hypertension, associated with crowding and delays. The director of a center for stress-related disorders warned, "From a health point of view, chronic distress takes its toll." He added, "These people have to go right in to work. It's stress on top of stress." On January 16, John Simpson was appointed to one of the city's most stressful jobs, president of the Transit Authority. He later said about the beginning of his tenure, "We were clearly on the verge of collapse."[18]

The Transit Authority's problems were caused by numerous factors. For instance, the wooden ties that lay underneath the tracks were rotting away because transit workers did not inspect tracks as frequently or as extensively as necessary. Since a single subway car weighed up to forty tons, even slight distortions in the track resulted in rough, noisy rides that jarred passengers and harmed equipment. These track problems were causing new subway cars to break down four times as frequently as they should have. Subway workers were trying to maintain equipment, but they were short staffed and using obso-lete equipment in dilapidated maintenance facilities. Most of the repair shops still had only DC power, so the workers could not use AC-powered tools and equipment.[19]

The Transit Authority's long list of items that needed to be rehabilitated or replaced included eight hundred pumps that removed water pouring in from streets, underground streams, damaged water mains, and broken sewer pipes. Transit officials could not properly maintain all of its ten thousand aging sig-nals (the subway's version of traffic signals for cars) and the interconnected

2,400 track switches, 8,700 automatic train stops, 12,000 track circuits, and 111,000 relays. Since much of this equipment was obsolete and no longer manufactured, subway workers cannibalized old equipment, and at great time and expense built replacement parts themselves.[20]

New York City's subway system was not just unreliable, crowded, and filthy; it was also the most dangerous in the world, with an average of more than 250 felonies per week. Between 1970 and the early 1980s, the number of felonies in the city increased by approximately 20 percent, but tripled in the subways. A newspaper reporter observed that "violent crime is always frightening, but a special terror arises in the dirty, noisy, confining subway tunnels, where imagination turns every stranger into a potential enemy, where cries for help often go unheeded and escape seems impossible." With the city unable to afford more police officers, an anticrime private vigilante group known as the Guardian Angels took enforcement into its own hands and began patrolling the subways in 1979. The same year, a well-organized and influential subway riders' group, the Straphangers Campaign, was formed to advocate for improving the subways.[21]

When the travel writer Paul Theroux was riding the subway, police officers gave him the following suggestions for staying safe: Do not display jewelry. Avoid sitting next to the door, where a thief could quickly grab a purse or bag and run out. Sit in a car with a conductor and wait for a train near the token booth clerk. Stay with the crowds. Keep away from empty corridors and stairways. One officer shared what he called rule number one: "Don't ride the subway if you don't have to."[22]

The perception of crime magnified other subway problems. Delays seemed longer when trains were empty and graffiti marred every surface. The narrow, winding passageways and the long platforms with columns spaced fourteen feet apart were never charming, but now they were seen as menacing spaces where rapists and murderers hid. Navigating the complex and sprawling network of train lines had always been difficult for those unfamiliar with the system; now it seemed impossible, with so many signs and maps covered with spray paint. Theroux warned that learning the system "is very hard work and requires imagination and intelligence. It means navigating in four dimensions. No one can do it idly, and I doubt that many people take up subway riding in their middle years."[23]

For many New Yorkers, images of modern subways were no longer limited to those seen in travel magazines or conjured up in science fiction movies. After Washington, DC, opened its first subway in the late 1970s, visitors to the nation's capital took photos of the spacious stations with wide entrances that were easy to navigate. The trains were clean, quiet, and reliable. The New York architectural critic Paul Goldberger called the Washington Metro "a welcome change from the squalid environment of the New York subway system." In his book about the Metro, Zachary Schrag wrote that New York's subway system served as an inspiration for the Metro's designers. They used New York "as a model of what not to do."[24]

In New York, the ongoing deterioration of the subways was threatening the city's economy. In numerous surveys, business leaders expressed much more concern about transit than about highways and parking. The city needed its extensive transit services to compete with other cities since 90 percent of the commuters traveling into Manhattan's central business district during the peak period used public transportation. The area south of 59th Street could not readily accommodate any more cars; it already had the slowest automobile travel speeds of any major business district in the entire country. Poor subway service was encouraging more people to drive, which was exacerbating highway congestion. Residents and businesses—frustrated, frightened, and disgusted—were leaving the city for the suburbs and areas outside the region.[25]

Although the number of riders on the city's buses and subways was only half of what it had been after World War II, no other city in the nation still relied on public transportation as much as New York City did. Almost half the city's workers used public transportation; the next-closest city was Chicago, with 21 percent. The MTA carried one-third of the nation's public transit riders and two-thirds of its rail riders, and it operated more rail cars than all of the other transit systems, including Amtrak, combined.[26]

In the late 1970s, the MTA, the mayor, state legislators, and even the US president realized that New York City's subway system was in trouble. But none of them developed a realistic plan to address its underlying problems. In 1977, after the US Department of Transportation requested that transit systems across the country prepare ten-year capital needs assessments, Transit Authority officials hurriedly prepared a list that included $10 billion in work needed to improve its subways and buses. On top of that, the MTA identified $5.5 billion in expansion projects, including $2.2 billion for a Second Avenue subway line that would run from the Bronx to Lower Manhattan. MTA chair Fisher did not push to fund the projects in the plan; instead he focused on avoiding fare increases, forestalling union strikes, and promoting Westway. The legislators in Albany did not take the MTA's list of capital needs seriously either, because they saw it as a wish list, thrown together with little apparent thought as to what was actually possible to accomplish and with no indication of the relative importance of the projects listed.[27]

The MTA's failure to properly identify its needs and prioritize projects caught the attention of two young attorneys at the Natural Resources Defense Council, a New York–based environmental advocacy organization. Ross Sandler and David Schoenbrod were frustrated that New York was trying to build Westway while the subway system was collapsing. As they reviewed transportation-related documents, the men were surprised to find that the Transit Authority was undertaking projects on an ad hoc basis. They approached the City Planning Department (the agency responsible for preparing the city's capital program) about conducting a thorough study of the MTA's capital needs. The City Planning chair and then the Transit Authority president both agreed to help.[28]

The Natural Resources Defense Council paid for and cowrote with City Planning the first comprehensive review of the Transit Authority's capital needs. The report, titled *A New Direction in Transit*, clearly explained why the Transit Authority needed to triple its current capital expenditures to provide safe, efficient, and comfortable services. Bobby Wagner Jr., who served simultaneously as a deputy mayor, an MTA board member, and the City Planning chair, strongly supported the report's recommendations. The report was so important to the city that Mayor Koch personally revealed it at a December 1978 City Hall event. Koch knew from his days in Congress that the inadequacies of the city's public transportation system were causing corporations to leave the city, and he would later appoint Sandler to head the city's Department of Transportation.[29]

Although the report focused on basic infrastructure needs, it did include some overly ambitious proposals for the financially strapped transit system, such as moving walkways and light rail lines (a reincarnation of streetcars or trolley cars). The report had another shortcoming: it did not identify how to pay for its proposed $5.5 billion ten-year program. The environmental advocates and city officials hoped that the very existence of a plan would help attract state and federal money.[30]

A few months after the City of New York issued its report, the State of New York undertook its own assessment. Spurred on by another national energy crisis (this one precipitated by the Iranian Revolution), the legislature set up a commission to explore the state's transportation needs. Generating consensus in Albany on MTA issues would not be easy, though, because the assembly and the senate had very different priorities. While the assembly was controlled by New York City Democrats who were sympathetic to the Transit Authority's needs, the senate was led by upstate and suburban Republicans. The commission's chair, Republican state senator John D. Caemmerer, had to bridge the difference.

Born in Brooklyn and raised on Long Island, Caemmerer was an important advocate for improving public transportation in both the city and its suburbs. Growing up, he had taken the Long Island Rail Road to his high school in Manhattan, and as state senator he represented thousands of railroad riders. When Caemmerer first started calling for transit operating subsidies in the 1960s, his Republican colleagues were appalled by what they considered to be his "socialist" position. He emphasized the subway's importance by referring to it as the second-largest single public investment ever made by Americans, eclipsed only by the Panama Canal.[31]

Although the legislative commission's members wanted the MTA to modernize the subway system, they were confused about how much it would cost because widely diverging estimates had been prepared by the MTA, City Planning, the state Department of Transportation, and other public agencies. Moreover, Caemmerer could not get his members to agree on who should pay for the necessary work.[32]

Even the president of the United States, Jimmy Carter, realized the significance of the subway system's deterioration. Appearing at a 1979 convention of public transit professionals held in the New York Hilton, Carter said it was critical to improve public transportation because the nation was in "a crisis of dangerous overdependence on foreign oil." He argued that the US had made a mistake by letting its public transportation systems "fall prey to decay and to neglect," and called on Congress to dramatically increase aid for transit. Dubbing New York's seventy-five-year-old subway system the "senior citizen of underground rail travel," he prompted laughter from the crowd when he said, "When Ed Koch and Harold Fisher and I get through with it—with the tools we are fighting to get from the Congress—it's not going to look a day over Sweet 16."[33]

Less than two weeks later, Fisher resigned from his position as MTA chair. After numerous conflicts with the mayor, union leaders, other MTA board members, and his friend the governor, he said, "I've decided to leave because I've had it." Fisher stuck around just long enough so that he and his wife could greet the president at the Hilton.[34]

Carter was unable to secure the funds he sought from Congress, and the reports prepared by the MTA, City Planning, and the state legislature did not provide a financial blueprint for moving forward. There was some light at the end of the subway tunnel, however, because the reports revealed the importance of rehabilitating the transit system, and would eventually establish the basis for a multiyear MTA capital program.

RICHARD RAVITCH TO THE RESCUE

The governor, legislature, and mayor all avoided identifying funding sources to pay for the MTA's capital needs because they did not want to be associated with raising taxes, tolls, or fares. Although elected officials were sensitive to the system's physical deficiencies, they paid more attention to filling short-term gaps in the operating budget so that the MTA could avoid increasing the fare again. A ride on the city's subways and buses, which had cost fifteen cents in early 1966, had been raised three times in the 1970s, most recently to fifty cents in 1975.

No public consensus had emerged on who should pay for needed improvements. Transit advocates thought raising the fare would be counterproductive because it would just encourage more people to drive. Drivers did not want to pay higher tolls to help someone else's commute, and since most of the region's suburban residents did not use public transportation on a regular basis, they tended to think of the transit problems as an urban issue. While city and state officials pointed fingers at each other, transit users and the system itself suffered.[35]

In the fall of 1979, Governor Carey appointed Richard Ravitch, a forty-six-year-old housing developer, to serve as MTA chair. Several years earlier, as head of the state's near-bankrupt economic development agency, Ravitch had saved the struggling agency from defaulting on its financial obligations. Before taking over the MTA, Ravitch was somewhat familiar with the condition of the subway cars and stations since he took the subway to work every day. He was also acutely aware of the crime problem, which is why he would not let his teenage sons ride the subway. The real estate developer was the type of person whom Nixon had in mind when he told Rockefeller, "Unless what we call the business establishment in New York takes a hell of a lot greater interest in sound decent government for the city . . . it's had it. It's going to be finished."[36]

Ravitch's first year as chair was tumultuous. A labor strike shut down the Long Island Rail Road for eight days, and four months later another strike shut down the city's subways and buses for ten days. Ravitch ended the five-year-old practice of deferring maintenance, but to fund it, the MTA's board of directors eliminated popular half-fare programs for weekend and off-peak riders, and half-fare rides for the elderly during the morning rush hour. Taking away discounts for little old ladies certainly did not help the chairman's popularity. Ravitch, who wore a bulletproof vest after someone tried to shoot him at MTA headquarters, said, "It has become abundantly clear to us that the problems of the MTA system are real and have been ducked for too long."[37]

The MTA was providing services for a troubled city with thousands of abandoned buildings and declining school enrollment. In the 1970s, the number of New York City residents fell by more than 823,000, the equivalent of the entire population of Dallas or Washington, DC. In anticipation of a continued shrinking population, the City Planning Commission proposed closing two hundred schools and eliminating up to five thousand beds in city hospitals. The MTA could have eliminated underused subway lines and stations to reduce its operating and capital expenses. That is exactly what the city had done decades earlier, when it removed the Second and Third Avenue elevated lines. But Ravitch had no interest in scaling back the subway system. Eliminating transit services could have decimated entire neighborhoods, especially those that were experiencing the most dramatic population losses. It also would have splintered a coalition of potential transit supporters whom he needed to rebuild the transit network. So instead, he decided to protect every line and every station.[38]

Ravitch had no interest in restarting the Second Avenue subway, and the project was a low priority for many of the communities it would serve. During the 1970s, East Harlem lost more than 22 percent of its population, and one-quarter of those who remained were on welfare. In seven Bronx census tracts, more than 97 percent of the buildings were either burned down or abandoned, leaving block after block of rubble. On the Lower East Side, where the number of apartments fell by 7.5 percent, a nonprofit environmental group known as the Green Guerillas took over vacant lots and turned them into community gardens. The wealthy Upper East Side neighborhood was an exception. It weathered the decade relatively unscathed, with new apartment buildings rising near Second Avenue.[39]

Under Ravitch's leadership, the MTA took care of the abandoned tunnels below Second Avenue. Workers closed them up and built structural supports so that the streets above them would not cave in. More importantly for the future of the neighborhoods that the Second Avenue subway had been designed to serve, Ravitch rescued the existing subway system and the city along with it.[40]

When Ronan and Fisher led the MTA, their highest priorities had been helping their respective governors get reelected and positioning them for a possible run for president. That was not Ravitch's biggest concern. He took very seriously his fiduciary responsibility to act in the best interests of the nation's largest public authority. He understood that a public agency, just like a private real estate company, had an obligation to take care of its assets.[41]

Ravitch wanted the MTA to prepare its own capital plan. The *New Direction in Transit* report prepared under the auspices of City Planning was a useful starting point, but he needed much more detailed information. He wanted "unarguable, credibly presented facts about the gravity of the situation" before asking local, state, and federal officials for more funding. In the summer of 1980, Ravitch asked the MTA agencies to provide him with information that they had never calculated before—the replacement cost and useful life of every component of the system.[42]

He wanted to restore the system to what he called a "state of good repair." The MTA, he argued, should properly maintain all of its equipment and facilities, and replace them once they reached the end of their useful lives—the point at which they became much less reliable and typically more expensive to maintain than to replace. Meeting that standard, he would learn, meant that every subway car older than forty years would need to be replaced, track switches would be replaced every thirty years, and no bus would stay in service for longer than twelve years.[43]

While MTA officials were completing the assessment of their needs, they learned that President Carter was not going to be the system's savior. On November 4, he lost his reelection bid to Ronald Reagan, a California Republican who wanted to slash federal aid to urban areas. Three weeks after the election, the MTA board issued a detailed report proposing a ten-year, $14.4 billion capital program to restore the system to a state of good repair. Most importantly, the board suggested ways to pay for the capital program and new legislation that would streamline the process so that projects could be completed in a more cost-effective and timely manner.[44]

Ravitch said, "I will not cease for a minute petitioning the government to provide more capital funding. But on the other hand, we should not put our heads in the sand and think that we have fulfilled our responsibilities at the MTA merely by exhorting elected officials to provide funds which, as a practical matter, are simply not available." That is why Ravitch was prepared for the MTA to take on billions of dollars in new debt to pay for improvements. He suggested increasing the maximum amount of bonds that the MTA's Triborough Bridge and Tunnel Authority (TBTA) could issue, and allowing its bond proceeds to be used for transit improvements, something it had never done before. He also proposed that the MTA be able, for the first time, to issue bonds that would be paid back from future fares.[45]

The MTA's financial proposals purposely refrained from recommending ideas that Ravitch knew Albany would balk at, such as instituting tolls on the free East River bridges. Ravitch also proposed that the MTA, rather than the state, issue debt. The last two statewide referendums on borrowing money for transportation improvements had been rejected by the voters. As a public authority, the MTA did not need voter approval to issue bonds.

Ravitch had an ingenious idea (inspired by his former law professor) for a way to obtain hundreds of millions of dollars in assistance from the federal government. From his private-sector experience, Ravitch was familiar with various schemes that private corporations used to reduce their taxes. Although the MTA was a publicly owned corporation that did not pay any taxes, Ravitch proposed changing a federal tax law to benefit the MTA. He wanted private companies to purchase new rail cars and buses and then lease them to the MTA. If the federal government would consider those purchases as an investment, then corporations could claim an investment tax credit on their tax returns and pass the savings on to the MTA.[46]

Ravitch deliberately proposed changing US tax policy rather than its spending policies for two reasons. First, President Reagan was looking at ways to slash, not increase, spending. Second, when Congress allocated money to the nation's transit operators, New York received a disproportionately low share. At that time, the MTA received less than 20 percent of federal transit funds even though it carried more than one-third of the nation's riders. By using the tax code, the MTA region would benefit at the same rate as other parts of the country, which meant that more than one-third of the tax benefits would go to the MTA.[47]

Ravitch was hoping to change the public debate so that the media reported on the transportation network's long-term needs rather than just its short-term financial woes. That would help him generate support for his plan to restore and then perpetually maintain the MTA's physical network. Ravitch's detailed list of needs and financing ideas gave his plan credibility. Now all he had to do was gain approval from the governor, mayor, state assembly, state senate, US House of Representatives, US Senate, and US president. Not exactly a walk in the park.

UPSETTING THE NORMAL POLITICAL RHYTHMS

After the MTA released its $14.4 billion plan in November 1980, a governor's aide told Ravitch that Carey was not interested in entertaining a fare hike or a tax package for the MTA. Carey preferred holding down the fare rather than financing a multibillion-dollar capital program. The governor also saw Ravitch's proposal as a threat to Westway. A coalition of thirty-seven civic and environmental groups had filed suit in federal court to stop the highway project. They wanted the state to take the federal transportation funds designated for the project and use them for transit improvements instead. If Carey admitted that the transit system was underfunded and starved for capital, it would have played into the hands of the Westway opponents.[48]

Faced with resistance in Albany, Ravitch began a lobbying effort that no state official other than Robert Moses at the height of his powers could have undertaken. He started by pleading with the governor and his staff, explaining that without new sources of revenue he would have to dramatically raise the fare. Then he took his case directly to the public. Rather than minimizing the transit system's problems, Ravitch made sure that reporters learned about all the delays and breakdowns occurring in MTA facilities. He visited editorial boards and told them, "If you don't pay attention, the politicians won't." He talked to every reporter who called. Unlike his predecessors, he admitted that the MTA's services, particularly during peak hours, were "deteriorating at an accelerated rate." The newspapers, he said, were "my shield and my sword."[49]

As part of Ravitch's public relations campaign, he did not want New Yorkers to think they had only a mass transit problem; he wanted them to realize that it was a genuine crisis. The subway's performance measures were on his side because 1980 was a horrible year for the subways. Compared to the previous year, the number of fires increased by 40 percent and the number of trains abandoned during routes rose by 64 percent. In 1980, twenty people were murdered on the subway, four times more than in 1976. As more people decided to drive rather than take the subway, traffic conditions worsened in Midtown.[50]

By 1980, the state had already weathered the depths of the 1970s fiscal crisis with a growing economy and rising employment. Even so, the MTA's proposed capital program was an audacious request. The MTA was a highly unpopular agency seeking to increase its annual capital expenses from less than $300 million to more than $1.4 billion, almost five times the current level. Ravitch was asking the governor and legislature for authorization to spend more rehabilitating the transit system than the city of New York spent on its entire capital budget, which included schools, municipal buildings, sanitation trucks, streets, sewers, water mains, highways, and bridges.[51]

The intense public relations campaign orchestrated by Ravitch, along with his behind-the-scenes lobbying, created an outcry that put intense public pressure on state legislators and the governor. The media repeated Ravitch's declaration that the subway was in "a state of emergency." Reporters gave little coverage to the downside of Ravitch's plan, such as how bonds would have to be paid back. Those details were complicated and offered little drama. Derailments, delays, and fires made much better news stories.[52]

Ravitch created a groundswell of support by rallying the labor and business communities. He called on influential people to contact reporters, editorial boards, and elected officials and emphasize the importance of rebuilding the transit system. Thanks to Ravitch's phone calls, the Federal Reserve of New York initiated a study on the effects of train delays on worker productivity, the bond rating agencies expressed their concern that the deterioration of the transit system would harm the city's fiscal health, and influential business leaders declared that the city's economy depended on improving the transit infrastructure.[53]

While Ravitch had some success explaining the transit system's needs to Warren Anderson, the Republican leader of the state senate, his pitch was much more effective after he had David Rockefeller, the civic leader and Chase Manhattan Bank president, call the senator. Ravitch's campaign and lobbying also changed the governor's thinking. Unlike previous mayors and governors, Carey began to express more concern about repairing structures, signals, and tracks rather than preventing a fare hike and expanding the subway system.[54]

In March 1981, with pressure coming from all sides, Carey proposed a five-year, $5 billion capital program for the MTA, and he told the legislators to pass a bill and put it on his desk in forty-eight hours. But Carey had a stormy relationship with the legislative leaders, and they were not interested in moving at the governor's pace. One legislative staffer said about the MTA, "It's a Catch-22. The service is so bad nobody wants to say give them more money to spend—but if they don't get more money to spend, service will never get better." Not only did the assembly and senate need more than two days, but the Democratic leaders in both houses did exactly what Carey had feared would happen: they called on the governor to trade in the federal funds earmarked for Westway to help pay for the MTA's capital program.[55]

Mayor Koch, who had misgivings about a multibillion-dollar capital program, was causing trouble for the governor and the MTA chair. The mayor's support was crucial because he could influence public opinion and also put pressure on state legislators who represented New York City residents. Koch was one of the city's most popular and colorful characters, eminently quotable, with a larger-than-life personality. Neither Carey nor Ravitch, however, was in a strong position to get Koch's support. At the time, the governor and mayor were publicly sniping at one another, and Ravitch and the mayor were barely talking to each other due to bitterness over the previous year's transit strike.[56]

Unlike the governor and the state legislators, the mayor was up for reelection in 1981. Koch was concerned that the proposed capital program would lead to much higher transit fares because the MTA would have to pay interest and principal on its fare-backed bonds. Moreover, the TBTA would not be able to provide as much funding for transit operations. In 1980, the MTA used $150 million of the TBTA's toll revenue to subsidize the MTA's transit services, but if the TBTA issued bonds to pay for transit capital improvements, it would have to dedicate more of its toll revenue to paying off its debt. For these reasons, the Straphangers Campaign was calling the capital program proposal a "disaster for mass-transit riders."[57]

By the spring of 1981, the Straphangers Campaign had become an influential player in the transportation policy arena. The leaders of the riders group knew how to get their protests, studies, and recommendations covered in newspapers and on television. They hosted forums attended by hundreds of people, widely distributed their newsletters, and held well-publicized contests for the worst subway station and best subway poems. They also established effective collaborations with other civic groups to promote their legislative strategy. Ravitch was fortunate: the Straphangers were not able to thwart the MTA's efforts to issue more debt, but they did help Ravitch highlight the subway's woes and build support for increasing the state's transit operating subsidies.[58]

While Ravitch understood the Straphangers' concern about the risks associated with increased debt, he was hoping that increased transit ridership would generate additional revenues to offset future bond payments. Although he did not trust politicians to prioritize the long-term needs of the transit system, he did expect that they would find the resources to keep fares down.[59]

In March, Koch threatened to stop Westway if the state did not provide funding to protect the fare at the same time that it passed an MTA capital program. That was not an idle threat, since federal officials did not want to be caught in the middle of a local battle. The US Department of Transportation had clearly stated that federal funds for Westway would be awarded only if both state and city officials agreed that it should be built. In response, the governor told reporters that Westway would be built and that he was not planning on meeting with the mayor to discuss the issue. He said, "If the mayor wants to come to a meeting, tell him to bring money." Deputy Mayor Bobby Wagner pointed out that "traditionally the politics of mass transit brings out the worst in public officials."[60]

Carol Bellamy, the city council president, who also served on the MTA board, supported Ravitch and publicly feuded with the mayor over the MTA's capital program. In March, she said, "There is so much posturing. All the characters—the governor, the mayor, the MTA, the comptroller, the legislative leaders, the council president—trying to avoid responsibility, and meanwhile the system collapses around us." An exasperated Ravitch remarked, "There are always four factors involved in these types of decisions. They are personalities, political interests, geographic and economic interests, and substance. In this case, we have an excess of the first three."[61]

In the midst of this turmoil, Governor Carey had other things on his mind. The state was operating without a budget longer than it ever had before, because the governor and legislative leaders were unable to compromise on taxing and spending priorities. As a result, hospitals, nursing homes, and schools were borrowing money to meet their expenses, and the state had to issue IOUs rather than paychecks to its workers. At the same time, Reagan was trying to eliminate programs that New York relied on, such as the $150 million per year it received in operating assistance for public transportation.[62]

Carey was continuing to tout the benefits of Westway. In April 1981, he defended the project in front of a thousand people at a Midtown Manhattan event sponsored by the Regional Plan Association. He talked about how it would provide construction jobs and give New Yorkers access to the Hudson River, and he inexplicably argued, "To all those who are hissing, Westway is part of our mass-transit system." The governor was also at a turning point in his efforts to clean up Times Square, with its peep shows, massage parlors, and pornographic movies. *Rolling Stone* magazine referred to a stretch of 42nd Street as the "sleaziest block in America." The state was proposing to use its power of eminent domain to replace undesirable buildings and businesses with new office towers, restaurants, and restored theaters.[63]

Something else was distracting the governor and causing him to miss meetings. A widower with twelve children, he had fallen madly in love. On the night of Reagan's inauguration in January, Carey met Evangeline Gouletas, an attractive and charming multimillionaire. They had their first date in February, he proposed in March, and they were married in April. His friends said they had never seen Carey happier. Gouletas's official biography indicated that she was a widow, but before the wedding, she publicly revealed that she had divorced a second husband. Days after the wedding, Carey learned from reporters that his wife had actually been married three times before, and her first husband was still alive. A whirlwind romance gave way to a national embarrassment.[64]

In May, two months after the governor's forty-eight-hour deadline to the legislature had come and gone, Ravitch lost his patience. He told the governor and the legislative leaders that he realized he was asking for an immense amount of money, but that failing to act would "result in the continuing physical collapse of our system, catastrophic fare increases, and ultimately, economic strangulation of the metropolitan region." Ravitch's next move got the attention of the distracted governor, the state legislators, and just about every other New Yorker. On July 2, the MTA board voted to increase the transit fare from sixty cents to seventy-five cents and raise commuter railroad fares by 25 percent. Ravitch also announced that if the state legislature did not provide additional aid promptly, the board would authorize a second increase, raising the transit fare to one dollar and commuter railroad fares another 25 percent. In a bit of an understatement, Ravitch said, "I'm not the most popular man in Albany today."[65]

Because of the tense relationship between the governor and the legislative leaders, Ravitch decided to take matters into his own hands. He drafted legislation with the Democratic assembly Speaker and the Republican senate majority leader that would provide both capital and operating funds. He negotiated the bill's details directly with the legislators without telling the governor or his staff. The legislative leaders agreed to impose new taxes, including a sales tax increase in the city and in the suburban counties served by the MTA, as well as a temporary 18 percent surcharge on corporate taxes in the twelve-county region. (Although the legislature would reduce the "temporary" surcharge to 17 percent in 1983, it would stay in place permanently.)[66]

The proposed legislation had two important components that would affect future projects, including the Second Avenue subway. First, the approval process for the MTA's capital projects was streamlined by eliminating most of the requirements for preapproval by state and city agencies. In some instances, the number of approvals was cut from seventeen to two. Second, the legislation gave the legislative leaders as well as the mayor leverage over the MTA by setting up a capital program review board whose four members would be appointed by the governor, mayor, assembly, and senate. Each member was given the power to veto the MTA's capital programs.[67]

Ravitch developed a close working relationship with Warren Anderson, the senate majority leader. Although the senator represented a district more than a three-hour drive from the nearest subway station, he needed to support transit improvements in the New York metropolitan area. His leadership position depended on electing Republican senators in suburban communities where the MTA provided commuter rail services. The assembly Speaker, Stanley Fink, a Brooklyn Democrat, was a strong supporter of Ravitch's efforts, and later became a national figure in the fight to improve infrastructure. While Anderson and John Caemmerer twisted arms in the senate, the Speaker rounded up votes in the assembly.[68]

On July 10, the assembly and senate passed the legislation that would fund the five-year capital program, enact five new taxes, and keep the fare at seventy-five cents for the next two years, ending what a reporter called "an extraordinary, months-long political nightmare." With Carey signaling his support, the package passed by a single vote in the state assembly thanks to last-minute phone calls from Koch to New York City Republicans in the state assembly. The historical significance of the legislation was not lost on the lawmakers, one of whom called it "the most far-reaching and comprehensive transportation measure that has ever been dealt with on this floor."[69]

While Ravitch was fostering a sense of crisis and lobbying Albany's power brokers in 1981, he was also meeting with Wall Street investment bankers and bond rating agencies. In order to borrow billions of dollars, he would need to convince the financial community that transit fares were a reliable revenue source and that rebuilding the MTA's infrastructure would strengthen the MTA's financial condition as well as the region's economy. When investors were ready to purchase the MTA's new bonds, they would in effect be lending money to the MTA in return for receiving regular interest payments. If investors thought the bonds were a safe investment, they would be willing to accept lower interest payments. Bond rating agencies would play an important role in determining these interest rates because they would give the bonds a grade based on the MTA's finances as well as the economic conditions and prospects of the MTA region. Investment bankers were important players because they would underwrite bonds—that is, they would assume the risk of buying newly issued bonds and then reselling them. Ravitch's meetings were successful; he convinced investors to purchase MTA bonds backed by future fares and persuaded the agencies to rate them at investment-grade levels.[70]

In addition to meeting with government, business, and civic leaders in New York City and Albany, Ravitch also went down to Washington, DC, to meet with Reagan's secretary of transportation, budget director, and chief of staff. Ravitch made his case for federal legislation that would allow corporations to reduce their taxes by purchasing buses and subway cars and then leasing them to the MTA. When they asked him about trading in the federal funds programmed for Westway and using them for the MTA instead, he told them he thought it was a good idea. If the governor's aides had heard his answer, they would have considered it treasonous.[71]

At a meeting in the White House, Ravitch learned that the president was preparing to introduce a bill that would enhance the tax benefits associated with the depreciation of assets. Although Ravitch had been advocating for a bill related to investment tax credits, he immediately realized that he should try to revise Reagan's bill because it would provide very similar benefits. The MTA might be able to save hundreds of millions of dollars if private companies purchased new rail cars and buses and then leased them to the MTA.[72]

Ravitch and his special counsel, Steve Polan (who had been camped out in Washington for months), worked closely with New York's congressional delegation on potential legislation. They also used their contacts at other transit agencies to line up support on Capitol Hill. Just as Ravitch had urged business and union leaders to call key elected officials in Albany, he asked the Chicago Transit Authority to lobby the House Ways and Means Committee chair, Representative Dan Rostenkowski from Chicago. Only a few members of Congress actually understood the significance of the depreciation language when it was buried in a complex tax bill that passed in August 1981. Remarkably, the legislation would eventually provide more than $500 million for the MTA's capital program.[73]

In December 1981, the MTA finalized its five-year, $7.9 billion transit improvement program. Ravitch was now authorized to spend almost five times as much as Sears, the world's largest retailer, planned to spend refurbishing more than six hundred stores and building sixty-two new ones. And the MTA's capital program was eight times greater than New Jersey Transit's statewide program. The MTA's program did not, however, contain any money to resurrect the Second Avenue subway. In 1981, that project had reverted again to its near-mythical status.[74]

Ross Sandler, Koch's transportation commissioner and coauthor of the 1978 capital needs report, would later say that Ravitch was extremely smart, competent with numbers, politically shrewd, and fearless. "What Ravitch did was extraordinary," he said. "He's a hero, a true hero." Likewise, a reporter in the *New Yorker* wrote that Ravitch's accomplishment in overcoming "hostility, indifference, egotism, and confusion" was "one of those astonishing feats that every so often upset the normal, lackadaisical rhythms of politics and demonstrate that the great Rube Goldberg contraption of government can—with enough care, patience, oiling, and kicking—be made to deliver."[75]

Richard Ravitch never completed his six-year term. When Carey's successor, Mario Cuomo, moved into the governor's office in January 1983, he did not return Ravitch's phone calls. Although the MTA was an independent authority controlled by a board of directors, Cuomo wanted to manage it the same way that he did state agencies, and he wanted someone at the MTA whose loyalty was unquestionable. Ravitch did not fit that role because he was a well-respected public personality. His strong ties with legislative leaders, Washington officials, business leaders, and the press were threatening to the new governor. Ravitch could have made deals in Albany and Washington that jeopardized Cuomo's own priorities and his reelection chances. Moreover, Ravitch, not the governor, would have been given credit for improvements associated with the MTA's capital projects.[76]

Cuomo did not try to push Ravitch out, nor did he ask for Ravitch's resignation. Firing the MTA chair would have been problematic because the governor could remove an MTA board member only for inefficiency, neglect of duty, or misconduct. Instead Cuomo simply ignored him. The governor did not want to meet with Ravitch in January, February, March, April, or May 1983. In early June, Cuomo's top aide, Michael Del Giudice, told Ravitch that Cuomo would not see Ravitch unless he supported legislation that would give the governor more control over the MTA. Ravitch said to Del Giudice, "Go tell Mario to fuck himself."[77]

Although Cuomo could not get much support in the legislature for changing the MTA's structure, Ravitch decided to resign anyway. He was frustrated and exhausted after four years of intense pressure in a position that did not pay him anything. He gave Cuomo only an hour's notice before an August press conference announcing his resignation. The MTA chair did not want to give Cuomo an opportunity to say that he had pushed Ravitch out.[78]

In his autobiography, published in 2014, Ravitch wrote that both Carey and Koch had staffed their administrations with the highest-quality people they could find and did not try to micromanage them or begrudge them credit. Control, he said, "was not uppermost in their minds." Ravitch then took a dig at New York State's fifty-second and fifty-sixth governors (Mario Cuomo and his son, Andrew), saying, "This was not and is not the Cuomo style."[79]

TRANSFORMING THE ORGANIZATION

When he put together the MTA's first capital program, Ravitch said it would bring all of the MTA's equipment and facilities up to a state of good repair in ten years, and then the MTA could replace its assets as they approached the end of their useful lives. But he later admitted, "I exaggerated about the ten years. I was raising fares and imposing taxes. I couldn't say we'd still be in deep shit. That's not a very political thing to do." Moreover, his initial survey of assets did not reveal the extent of the Transit Authority's problems, in part because the authority did not have sufficient skills to understand all of the system's deficiencies, let alone how to overcome them. In 1984 the Transit Authority's senior vice president said, "We have track inspectors who just don't know what good and bad track is. There's a serious drought of management, technical and supervisory skills."[80]

After the capital program was approved, the MTA did not know how to spend its newfound wealth effectively because of numerous organizational and managerial problems. Transit officials had trouble defining project scopes, schedules, and budgets, and then they failed to effectively manage projects and coordinate them with other ongoing work. Rebuilding was more complex, time consuming, and costly than expected because of the need to minimize disruptions in a system that operated twenty-four hours a day, 365 days a year.[81]

The entire transit system was poorly managed. Managers of capital projects often failed to identify the amount of materials that would be required to complete necessary work, while in other instances, they had the space and materials they needed but the workforce was not available. Because of a barely functioning inventory system, the Transit Authority had a 27-year supply of radiator assemblies and a 144-year supply of snow chains for buses. Weekly track reports routinely took more than three months to reach top management.[82]

Ravitch's successor, Robert Kiley, said in 1984, "The subway system is having a nervous breakdown." David Gunn, his newly appointed Transit Authority president, quickly realized that certain aspects of the capital program had been hastily conceived and poorly laid out. Instead of speeding up the rebuilding effort, he decided to slow it down. Because of the system's overwhelming needs, Gunn had to say no to MTA board members who pushed projects he considered frivolous, such as replacing subway tokens with electronic fare cards. Gunn, who had previously managed Philadelphia's transit system, was bothered by the intense criticism that he received in the New York City media from board members and elected officials. He said, "If your public relationship with your superiors is awful, that sends a real strong message to your troops."[83]

Gunn's biggest frustration was that he could not control his own workforce. Of the approximately 40,000 people working under him, only 600 were exempt from union and civil service protection. For example, he found it nearly impossible to make any changes at the subway repair shop in Coney Island; the facility had 1,700 employees, 1,699 of whom were in a union. A few months after taking over the Transit Authority, he told a reporter, "I can issue orders till I'm blue in the face, but unless you have an effective chain of command translating the order into a meaningful program, it's not going to work."[84]

In 1985, after reviewing the progress of the capital program, the MTA's inspector general said that projects were running into delays and cost overruns "for the most basic of reasons. The left hand doesn't know what the right hand is doing." Upgrades to repair shops, stations, and other facilities were floundering or not functioning properly because of a total lack of communication between the Transit Authority departments that designed and constructed projects and the departments that would use them. Gunn, realizing that no one was taking responsibility for work, decided to restructure the Engineering Department and hire professional project managers who would manage projects from inception to completion. One of the Transit Authority's first professional managers was an engineer named Mysore Nagaraja, who would one day manage the design and construction of the Second Avenue subway's first phase.[85]

Gunn had few carrots to reward good performance and few sticks to punish shoddy work. Most of the Transit Authority's managers, even its senior ones, were compensated according to collective bargaining agreements, and their promotions were based on passing written exams, not on their job performance. Because of the union and civil service protections, the Transit Authority's executives often did not even bother disciplining workers who fixed their own cars at bus depots or spent half their days playing cards. MTA chair Kiley proposed legislation that would remove some managers from union protection, but the idea went nowhere in the legislature. Instead he made a deal with the unions—the MTA would contribute $1.8 million to the unions' health and welfare funds in return for the ability to hire 1,200 nonunionized middle managers. Productivity increased after managers were rewarded based on their performance and executives could dismiss Transit Authority workers for insubordination and inebriation.[86]

By 1988, the sense of lawlessness and neglect in the subways was fading, because fewer than 15 percent of the subway cars in service were defaced with graffiti. This accomplishment could be attributed to a concerted effort by both transit officials and the City of New York. The Transit Authority put up new fences with razor-ribbon wire around storage yards, the area where most of the trains were vandalized. Koch, who had run for office on a law-and-order platform, pressured Ravitch to deploy dogs around these yards to deter vandals. He said, "If I had my way, I wouldn't put in dogs, but wolves." The Transit Authority also removed trains from service as soon as they were defaced, so that "graffiti artists" would not get the satisfaction of seeing their handiwork. In addition, the mayor obtained city council support for legislation that banned the sale of spray paint to minors. When teenagers started stealing paint cans, the city passed another ordinance that required store owners to keep them out of the reach of customers.[87]

As the MTA rebuilt its infrastructure in the 1980s, the era of big projects in New York City appeared to be over and the prospects of ever seeing a Second Avenue subway seemed even dimmer. New highways and massive development projects were scrapped as historic preservation, community concerns, and environmental protection took on even greater importance.

Koch was never interested in restarting the Second Avenue subway. If he had the resources, he would have preferred building a high-speed rail link between Kennedy Airport and Manhattan. In 1982, however, he did ask one of his most trusted aides to look into renting out the fourteen-foot-high, twenty-eight-foot-wide abandoned tunnels under Second Avenue. After more than a year of negotiations between city, federal, and MTA officials, they finalized a plan whereby the MTA would manage a public bidding process and the city would dedicate all of the profits to transit uses. The mayor's office came up with several novel ideas for the tunnels, including wine cellars, restaurants, mushroom farms, and discos. After the MTA sought renters for two tunnel segments (99th to 105th Streets and 110th to 120th Streets), only one serious bidder materialized—a New Jersey businessman who wanted to build an automated storage facility with conveyor belts. He said it would be "the world's largest filing cabinet." He ultimately built a facility beneath the World Trade Center instead, because it had several features the Second Avenue tunnels did not, such as plumbing, ventilation, and easy access from the street. At the time, the only way to enter the Second Avenue subway tunnels was by opening up a manhole cover with a pair of pliers or a wrench.[88]

Regional Plan Association (RPA) officials, however, did not give up on expanding the transit system. In 1986, Boris Pushkarev tried to resurrect the Second Avenue subway and a Long Island Rail Road connection to Grand Central Terminal. He also had other expansion ideas, including extending the number 7 subway line to New Jersey. The RPA's plans in the 1920s had provided the blueprint for the metropolitan area's highway network, and the association's forecasts and plans in the 1960s had influenced the MTA's expansion plans. In the 1980s, though, the region had neither the resources nor the will to undertake ambitious expansion projects. The MTA's response to the RPA's proposed projects was, "Our primary concern is to just get the existing transit system working properly."[89]

Environmental advocates, not Koch or Ravitch, were responsible for killing Westway in the 1980s and ending an era of expanding New York City's highway network. A federal court ruled that the project's environmental impact statement did not adequately assess the impacts on striped-bass breeding along the Hudson River's piers. US senator Daniel Patrick Moynihan, who had secured funds to build Westway and also remove toxic chemicals from the river, lamented in 1989 that "you can't build Westway because of the fish, which you can't eat because of the PCB's, which you can't clean up because there's no place you may put them." The striped bass were not the only beneficiaries of the lawsuit. Most of the federal funds designated for Westway were reallocated for improving the city's transit system.[90]

In 1989, New York's congressional representatives were frustrated that they and their staffs were putting in countless hours trying to obtain federal funds for projects that were either getting canceled or subject to endless delays. Brooklyn congressman Chuck Schumer said that it seemed that almost anyone with "a cause and a lawyer" could stop a project. Likewise, US senator Alfonse D'Amato, from Long Island, lamented, "It is a sad commentary when the captains of the system become the captives of the system." New York City's deputy mayor, Robert Esnard, explained that "you just can't do things the way you used to" because the US was a "very litigious society," with New York City at the center of it all.[91]

In the 1980s, Ronan's overly ambitious 1968 plan still haunted elected officials. Senator D'Amato found it hard to obtain congressional funds because his colleagues would point to New York's failure to complete projects like the Second Avenue subway. In Washington and New York, the 63rd Street bi-level tunnel designed for subway and Long Island Rail Road service was dubbed the "tunnel to nowhere." The failure to build the Second Avenue subway discredited the MTA and the state. Elected officials found it harder to generate support for transportation referendums because voters remembered how previous bonds were wasted or diverted for other uses. At the end of 1986, when asked to make a prediction for the year 2000, D'Amato quipped, "Subway riders will be hoping that the Second Avenue subway may one day open."[92]

Although the politicians did not get as many chances to cut ribbons and attend groundbreakings in the 1980s, they could see a dramatic difference in the condition of the subway thanks to the ten-year capital program. By 1991, subway cars traveled, on average, four times farther before they had to be taken out of service for mechanical failure. Subway doors opened when they pulled into stations and stayed closed between them. The number of track fires decreased by a third and car-equipment fires fell by 80 percent. Most of the subway cars were new or overhauled and they were all graffiti free. The tracks were in good repair, and trains arrived on time more than 90 percent of the time, compared to less than 80 percent ten years earlier. The manager of the San Francisco Municipal Railway said that New York City's subway system had "gone from representing the worst in the transit industry to the best." Alan Altshuler, the director of Harvard's Center for State and Local Government, declared, "It's one of the great public management turnarounds of our time."[93]

While the MTA took enormous strides toward restoring its system, Ronan's expansion program had provided few benefits. In 1989, twenty years after construction began, a new 3.2-mile subway service under 63rd Street and the East River finally began operating. The new 63rd Street subway line had been part of Ronan's far more ambitious and aborted plan for new services to northeastern and southeastern Queens. But in 1989 the line still did not connect with any existing Queens subway lines and served only one sparsely populated Queens neighborhood. Manhattan congressman Bill Green called it an "enormous waste of money." While subway riders were getting some benefits, Long Island Rail Road riders were not so fortunate. The lower level of the East River tunnel, designed to connect the Long Island Rail Road with Manhattan's East Side, still remained unused.[94]

Dark clouds hung over the authority's prospects in the early 1990s. High crime levels (the city had more murders than at any time in its history) and a sense of social deterioration were keeping many New Yorkers off the subways, especially during weekends and evenings. Even though the Transit Authority spent more than $11 billion on capital improvements in its 1982–91 capital program, only its rail cars, tracks, and switches had reached a state of good repair. Most of the rest of the subway system still needed to be repaired, rehabilitated, and modernized, including tunnels, elevated structures, bridges, escalators, elevators, pumps, and power substations.[95]

Ravitch's ten-year program to rebuild the MTA's facilities and equipment had coincided with a surging stock market and an economic boom that added nearly six hundred thousand jobs to the region. Financially, though, the MTA was not in much better shape than it had been ten years earlier. Ravitch's plan marked both the beginning of the MTA's renaissance and the crushing debt load that would inhibit its ability to expand the system. At the start of the capital program, the MTA had less than $300 million in debt. Ten years later, its outstanding debt was thirty times higher—approximately $9 billion—and its annual principal and interest payments on this debt were approaching $250 million per year.[96]

In 1990, the MTA's planners estimated that the authority would need an astronomical $37 billion over the next ten years to finish modernizing the rest of its transportation properties. The Transit Authority alone would need $10.4 billion to bring the bus and subway system to a state of good repair, another $12.3 billion for normal replacement projects, and an additional $2.6 billion for system improvements. Undaunted by the system's extraordinary needs, the planners were confident enough about the future of New York City and the MTA that they were starting to think once again about expanding the subway system.[97]

Figure 5.1. *Mayor Ed Koch (center) riding the subway in August 1981. Source: Identifier eik_08.010.0655, Mayor Edward I. Koch Collection. Courtesy: NYC Municipal Archives.*

Figure 5.2. *Richard Ravitch,*
Stanley Fink, Hugh
Carey, and Ed Koch in
March 1981. Source: New
York State Archives. New
York (State). Governor.
Public information
photographs, 1910–1992.
Series 13703-83, box 10,
no. 020.

6

Planning from the Bottom Up

In 1988, the Second Avenue subway was resurrected—not by a mayor, a governor, or an MTA chair, but by four young men in a crumbling old office building on Lawrence Street in downtown Brooklyn. In the cubicle pod where they worked, these New York City Transit Authority rail service planners spent their days poring over statistics that measured travel time, ridership, crowding, and delays. Sharing just one phone and one computer, they analyzed how rerouting trains, skipping stations, and running overnight shuttle services could improve the performance and productivity of the subway system.

Subway riders might have thought that the Transit Authority was oblivious to their problems, but that was far from the truth. Peter Cafiero, Chuck Kirchner, Glenn Lunden, and Jon Melnick were not just government bureaucrats. As kids, they had enjoyed playing with model railroad sets and taking pictures of trains. Now they were subway aficionados who enjoyed riding the rails, visiting train depots, and talking about the arcane workings of public transportation systems. On September 27, 1988, they were given erasable markers and a whiteboard with six words written on it: "Brilliant Capital Ideas for the Future."[1]

Even though the Transit Authority was in the early stages of its 1987–91 capital program, the planners' bosses wanted to start getting ready for the next program, which would run from 1992 to 1996. The first step would be to create a document that assessed the authority's long-term needs and identified projects that would rehabilitate the subway system, increase ridership, improve productivity, and expand system capacity.[2]

Over a series of brainstorming sessions, the four men came up with over one hundred ideas to improve the rapid transit system, and then they ranked them. At the top of the list was eliminating what they called the "hell hole" conditions at Grand Central, Union Square, Times Square, and West 4th Street. These stations were dilapidated, crowded, difficult to navigate, and stiflingly hot in the summer. Another highly ranked idea was creating new pedestrian passageways between subway stations on different lines. The Transit Authority was still trying to improve connections between the IRT, BMT, and IND lines nearly half a century after the three transit systems were consolidated. The planners also considered ways the subway system could take advantage of unused capacity, especially during service disruptions. They identified locations where new switches and crossovers could be built so that trains could shift from one track to another, and from one subway line to another.[3]

Cafiero, a twenty-six-year-old civil engineer, and his three colleagues talked about how to address problems on the most crowded subway line, the number 4 and 5 trains on the Lexington Avenue line's express tracks. The Transit Authority's policy was to provide enough service so that all of its riders had at least three square feet of space to stand. Since subway ridership was higher in 1988 than it had been in the previous fourteen years, the Transit Authority now needed to operate thirty-seven trains per hour on the Lexington Avenue line's express tracks to meet this standard during the peak period. Using forecasts prepared by the Regional Plan Association (RPA), the planners determined that in 2005 the Transit Authority would have to operate forty-two trains per hour to provide three square feet of space.[4]

There were two fundamental problems with these numbers. First, three square feet did not give passengers much space to turn the page of a newspaper without poking someone in the eye. Second, the Lexington Avenue line had the capacity to operate, at the very most, only thirty express trains per hour.[5]

One proposal the planners wrote on the whiteboard to address the Lexington Avenue's problems received a relatively high ranking. It was an idea the MTA planner Bob Olmsted had first championed in 1975—a Second Avenue subway north of 63rd Street. Trains would operate northbound along the Broadway line's rarely used express tracks, connect with the new east–west 63rd Street tunnel, and then travel north on Second Avenue. The idea was timely because the Transit Authority was getting ready to operate trains in the 63rd Street tunnel, with a new station on Lexington Avenue. Thanks to Olmsted, this station was built with temporary walls, additional tracks, and an opening on its north side so that if a Second Avenue tunnel were ever to be constructed, trains could stop at 63rd Street and then travel north on Second Avenue. The planners agreed that the Second Avenue subway's first phase should start north of 63rd Street and a second phase should extend south to 34th Street.[6]

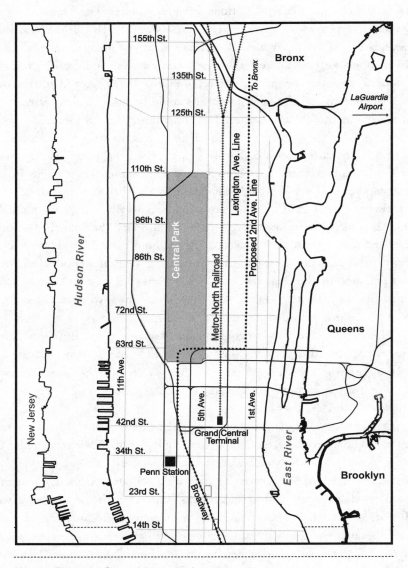

Map 6.1. Proposed Second Avenue subway

Figure 6.1. *"Temporary" brick wall hiding tracks for a future connection to a Second Avenue subway at the Lexington Avenue–63rd Street station. Source: Ben Heckscher/The Launch Box*

Figure 6.2. *Platform of the Lexington Avenue–63rd Street station after the "temporary" wall was removed and the station was renovated in 2016. This platform serves trains that travel on 63rd Street east to Queens and also those operating north along Second Avenue. Source: PrecipiceofDuck, Creative Commons.*

Norm Silverman, one of the planners' senior colleagues, learned an important lesson in the 1970s when he had worked for Olmsted. The Transit Authority, a subsidiary of the MTA, should never have started construction simultaneously on four different segments of the Second Avenue subway. The abandoned Second Avenue tunnels in East Harlem and Chinatown, hidden from the public, did not provide New Yorkers with any benefits. If the Transit Authority had an opportunity to build another subway expansion, it should do so incrementally, so that each segment, once completed, could provide useful services.

The young men were not optimistic about the Transit Authority's ability to build a Second Avenue subway. After all, they had come of age in an era of urban decay and graffiti-covered subway cars. They were now witnessing an increasing number of homeless people living in stations and on trains. The planners' instincts matched Silverman's experience: if we build something, Melnick said, "Let's do it as piecemeal and as incrementally as possible."[7]

As the Second Avenue subway proposal moved up the Transit Authority hierarchy, the authority's president, David Gunn, agreed that the time was right to begin thinking about expanding the subway system. Before he could devote significant resources to advancing the Second Avenue subway, however, it would have to compete with other potential megaprojects under discussion at the MTA's agencies.

THE BUREAUCRATIC HURDLES

In the early 1980s, MTA chair Richard Ravitch had obtained approvals for the MTA's first capital program by convincing the public and elected officials that the transit system was in a state of crisis. In the early 1990s, Robert Kiley could not make that same argument because Ravitch's ten-year, $16 billion program—the largest transportation rebuilding effort ever undertaken in the United States—had made significant improvements to the system.[8]

To kick off discussions with government officials about the MTA's next capital program, Kiley released a document in May 1990 that assessed the authority's long-term capital needs. The MTA calculated that it would need nearly $2 billion every single year for the next twenty years to attain a state of good repair, sustain it with normal replacements, and improve existing services. That did not even include the cost of expanding the transit system. While Ravitch's 1980 request to spend $1.4 billion per year had been considered extraordinary, Kiley indicated that the MTA would need multibillion-dollar capital programs in perpetuity.[9]

Kiley knew that he could not obtain billions of dollars a year by simply promising to fix up the existing transit system. Instead he needed to convince elected officials and the general public that strategic investments would allow the MTA to integrate its transportation services, improve traveler information, reduce traffic, and improve air quality. An important element of his vision was replacing the antiquated tokens with an automated fare-card system, which would provide convenient transfers between subways and buses and also allow the MTA to offer discounts for off-peak travel and multiple rides. Installing what would be known as the MetroCard system would be a massive project that involved replacing every subway farebox and bus turnstile, as well as upgrading the subway system's electrical and data communications network. It was expected to cost $672 million.[10]

Kiley argued that the MTA needed to expand its public transportation system to accommodate economic growth. The region had no other choice. In the 1980s, the number of cars in both the city and its suburbs had increased by more than 25 percent, a result of rising incomes and employment levels. Motor vehicles were not just choking the roads; they were also preventing the New York City region from meeting the federal government's minimum air-quality standards. There was no political appetite to build new highways even though the existing ones were carrying far more vehicles than they were designed to accommodate. The region's transportation agencies had come to the realization that building more highways in New York City would only encourage more people to drive, which would exacerbate, not alleviate, the region's traffic and air-pollution problems.[11]

Many of the ideas generated by the four Transit Authority planners, including a Second Avenue subway north of 63rd Street, were incorporated into Kiley's long-term capital needs document. Kiley was well aware of the conditions under Second Avenue. In 1990, he authorized $2 million to maintain and secure the abandoned tunnels. Every two weeks, Transit Authority inspectors walked through the tunnels to make sure they were dry and safe, and that the streets above were not in danger of collapsing. The inspectors made sure the electricity and water pumps were working properly, the steel girders were not rusting, and the locks and alarms kept out vandals and homeless people.[12]

As the components of the next capital program started taking shape, Cafiero prepared numerous documents related to the Second Avenue subway, including an initial scope of work that would be given to consultants. (Even though the Transit Authority had more than forty thousand employees, it typically hired outside consultants to perform highly technical and specialized planning and engineering work.) Cafiero estimated that the Transit Authority would need to spend approximately $6 million on a planning and environmental study that would begin after the capital program was approved. He expected that the study's final recommendation would be a new five-mile two-track subway line between 63rd Street and the Bronx. He told his supervisors that initial planning should be completed in early 1995 and that another $26 million would be needed in 1995 to begin preliminary design and engineering work.[13]

When the MTA's 1992–96 capital program was finalized, it included funds for Cafiero's planning study. But funding for the subsequent design and engineering stages of a Second Avenue subway was eliminated after the New York City mayor, Rudy Giuliani, cut back on the city's contribution to the MTA's capital program. Nevertheless, Cafiero's planning would proceed in the hopes that if the project proved worthwhile, additional funds would one day be made available. Since the MTA relied on the federal government to pay for about one-third of its capital program, the planners would follow the federally mandated planning process so that projects that came out of the study would be eligible for future federal funds.[14]

Obtaining federal funds for transportation projects had become much more onerous, however, because of the backlash that resulted from leaders such as Robert Moses and William Ronan. Between the 1920s and 1960s, Moses was able to build highways through the heart of New York City because the federal government did not require him to respond to public concerns, accommodate public transportation, or comply with strict environmental regulations. In the 1970s, the US Department of Transportation did not question the financial feasibility of Ronan's projects before giving the MTA chair hundreds of millions of dollars to start building train tunnels.

The rules changed after the public became aware of the urban decay and environmental degradation associated with new highways. Both Republicans and Democrats supported efforts to address community concerns, improve the nation's air and water quality, and protect open spaces and endangered species. As a result, Congress passed a series of laws in the 1970s and 1980s that required transportation agencies to solicit public input, conduct comprehensive planning, prepare environmental impact statements, and comply with new environmental regulations. Those hurdles made it much harder to build new highways (such as Westway), and as a result many cities in the 1980s turned toward other types of economic development initiatives, such as building new rail transit systems, convention centers, and sports stadiums.[15]

Congress also saw how Ronan and his contemporaries stretched the truth in order to obtain federal funding for their rail projects. In 1989, a US Department of Transportation researcher, Don Pickrell, meticulously compared project sponsors' initial forecasts with the actual costs and benefits of projects after they were completed. Pickrell found that transit agencies grossly overestimated the number of passengers their proposed rail lines would carry. In fact, nearly all recently built projects were carrying less than half the number of forecasted riders. Likewise, nearly all the projects cost more than expected. Because of this, the 1991 federal transportation law that authorized about $800 million per year for large transit projects mandated a rigorous review process to evaluate the cost effectiveness of proposed projects.[16]

Cafiero would have to navigate his study through a minefield of federal regulations and approvals before any subway construction could begin. First he needed to complete an "alternatives analysis study" that assessed the potential of every realistic transportation improvement along the East Side, including subways, buses, and ferries. This analysis would have to be transparent and comprehensive. After soliciting public comment and thoroughly evaluating all of the alternatives, Cafiero's consultants would then need to prepare an environmental impact statement that complied with federal as well as state and city environmental requirements. This impact statement would be subject to intense public scrutiny and numerous approvals before it could be finalized. The MTA would need to obtain additional resources and approvals before it could even begin preliminary engineering and final design.

The federal agency responsible for administering transit funds, the Federal Transit Administration (FTA), was not the only bureaucracy that slowed down Cafiero's study. In June 1993, MTA executives established an interagency task force to coordinate the long-term studies underway at three of its transit subsidiaries.[17] The MTA's largest agency, the New York City Transit Authority, operated buses and subways in the city (the authority would soon be renamed NYC Transit). The MTA also ran Long Island Rail Road train services from Long Island and Queens into Penn Station. The most recent addition to the MTA family was Metro-North Railroad, which was set up in 1983 to take over the private railroads that operated service from New York City's northern suburbs and Connecticut to 125th Street and Grand Central Terminal in Manhattan.

These three transit agencies were considering several other megaprojects in addition to a Second Avenue subway, including connecting the Long Island Rail Road with Grand Central Terminal via the unused lower level of the 63rd Street tunnel, a new subway line between Lower Manhattan and Brooklyn, a new east–west commuter rail line north of New York City, and a new rail tunnel between Manhattan and New Jersey. MTA executives wanted to make sure that all of the studies for these major projects were evaluated consistently so that the MTA board could choose the best projects to advance. Cafiero and other planners from the MTA agencies met regularly to develop a common set of regional forecasts along with evaluation criteria that would be used to assess and compare all the projects. They also explored potential clashes and overlaps, as well as how projects would relate to one another as part of a regional transit network. For example, they assessed how passengers taking a future Long Island Rail Road connection to Grand Central Terminal and then transferring to the adjacent subway station might exacerbate overcrowded conditions on the Lexington Avenue line.

Although the planning might have seemed comprehensive, the MTA did not integrate its planning efforts with broader regional efforts relating to housing, economic development, open space, and the environment. The New York region, sprawling across three states, had no government body that took on that role. The Regional Plan Association had created comprehensive visions in the 1920s and 1960s, but the association was simply a civic group that had no accountability to the public or any power to implement its plans.

EVALUATING PROBLEMS AND POTENTIAL SOLUTIONS

Peter Cafiero was an intense New Yorker, reserved, with an encyclopedic understanding of the nation's most complex transit network. His analytic skills and diligence were prized and rewarded with a series of promotions at the Transit Authority. As the director of rail service planning in early 1994, he was given authorization to retain a consulting team and hire Todd DiScala to manage the Second Avenue subway study. DiScala was someone who would complement rather than duplicate Cafiero's strengths. He was a native southwesterner, laid back, and outgoing, and he knew less about the subway system than most of its riders. Cafiero told DiScala, "We're trying to move away from over-the-top railroad enthusiasts and you're a good fit."[18]

In 1990, Cafiero had expected a Second Avenue subway study to be completed in early 1995. But he and DiScala first needed to obtain numerous approvals from Transit Authority officials, MTA management, the MTA board, and the FTA. They had to wait until June 1995 before all the approvals were granted to kick off the study.[19]

Before the planning study began, Cafiero decided to scale back its scope to focus on Manhattan because he did not want to "open up a can of worms" and overly complicate his planning and engineering efforts. Since the 1920s, a countless number of ideas had been considered for connecting the new line to existing lines in the Bronx as well as building new extensions in the borough. While the Second Avenue subway's route had been well defined in the 1970s, plans for the Bronx portion had never been finalized. By eliminating the Bronx component from his study, Cafiero could avoid the time and cost associated with analyzing potential Bronx transit improvements and collaborating with Bronx planners, community groups, and elected officials.[20]

Even without the Bronx, the planners were studying an area that was extraordinarily complicated. If the East Side and Lower Manhattan formed their own separate city, it would have had a larger population than Boston, Seattle, Denver, Cleveland, or Washington, DC. Nearly 700,000 people lived in its neighborhoods (30 percent on the Upper East Side, 28 percent on the Lower East Side, 22 percent in East Midtown, 16 percent in East Harlem, and 4 percent in Lower Manhattan). In addition, over 1.2 million people worked in the area, most of them in East Midtown and Lower Manhattan.[21]

Cafiero and DiScala decided to call their planning study the *Manhattan East Side Transit Alternatives Study*. NYC Transit had two reasons for not including the words "Second Avenue subway" in the title. First, federal officials did not want the study to identify a specific project before the planning efforts even began. It was quite possible that after the planners finished evaluating various alternatives, the study might simply recommend bus service improvements or minor subway changes. Second, Cafiero's boss, Norm Silverman, emphatically told DiScala, "You cannot under any circumstances make this a study about Second Avenue. You can't mention it and you can't allow people to think that it's a Second Avenue subway, because it's not." DiScala recalled that Silverman "didn't even want the study to recommend a new subway because he thought it was unlikely to ever get built. He didn't want us to waste our time talking about it. He wanted to get a benefit out of the study without a Second Avenue subway."[22]

Cafiero's study team included seven different consulting firms and more than a dozen NYC Transit employees. They started their work by analyzing problems that the Lexington Avenue line's riders were experiencing. During peak periods, passengers crowded the subway cars, platforms, and stairwells. In the mornings, Upper East Siders often watched three or four crowded express trains go by before they were able to squeeze on to one heading downtown. Trains were held up in stations because so many people tried to simultaneously exit and enter the subway cars. Consequently, travel time between 125th Street and Bowling Green in Lower Manhattan was nine minutes longer during the peak periods than during the off-peak. Because of station crowding, NYC Transit could not operate as many trains during the peak periods, which exacerbated the crowded conditions.[23]

The most severe crowding occurred at Grand Central, where thousands of people transferred between subway lines and Metro-North Railroad's Harlem,

Hudson, and New Haven lines. They poured in from some of the nation's most exclusive suburbs, including Greenwich, Scarsdale, and Bronxville. During the average weekday peak period, Metro-North carried more than seventy thousand southbound passengers; while most of them walked from Grand Central Terminal to their final destinations, about twenty thousand transferred to the subways. The Lexington Avenue line was their choice for destinations to Manhattan's East Side, Lower Manhattan, and Brooklyn.[24]

The lack of local subway service to the financial district in Lower Manhattan also caused problems. The Lexington Avenue express trains (numbers 4 and 5) stopped in the financial district; however, the tracks for the local train (number 6) did not extend that far south. Many passengers who lived or worked near a local train station added to station crowding when they switched between local and express trains at the express stops. With crowding leading to delays, and delays leading to more crowding, NYC Transit officials found themselves in a paradoxical situation. To reduce crowding, they needed to run more trains on the Lexington Avenue line, but they could not operate more trains unless they reduced the number of passengers.[25]

NYC Transit had similar capacity problems aboveground. The Manhattan buses that traveled on First and Second Avenues had more riders than any other bus route in the entire country. Although buses were scheduled to arrive every two minutes, they moved slowly and tended to come in bunches because of heavy street congestion, double-parked cars in the bus lanes, and the timing of traffic lights.[26]

The study team started with a list of more than two dozen potential alternatives that would help solve the East Side's transportation problems, including eight different subway routes, five improvements to Lexington Avenue subway service, four bus alternatives, and two potential light rail lines. Second Avenue was chosen early on as the most appropriate route for a new subway line for many of the same reasons it had been written on the planners' whiteboard in 1989. A Third Avenue subway would have been only a block away from the Lexington Avenue line, while First Avenue was ruled out because it would be too difficult to construct near the Queensboro Bridge, the United Nations, and the Queens–Midtown Tunnel. A route along Second Avenue also had a distinct advantage because it could use tunnel sections that had been built in the 1970s and directly connect with the east–west 63rd Street line. Moreover, the planners thought that Second Avenue would have fewer belowground utility lines to contend with because city officials had tried to minimize the number of them under Second Avenue. Although New Yorkers might have given up hope that a Second Avenue subway would ever be built, the City of New York's transportation and planning departments had not.[27]

In 1995, DiScala and Cafiero started meeting with numerous community organizations, elected officials, and subway riders to learn more about transportation problems on Manhattan's East Side. When they mentioned the possibility of a Second Avenue subway, the mythical project usually elicited laughter and disbelief from anyone who knew about its checkered history. Although Cafiero and DiScala found no groundswell of support for a new subway line, they did not encounter anyone against it either.[28]

Public skepticism was certainly warranted, because the MTA was sending mixed messages about its intentions. While Cafiero's team discussed a potential new multibillion-dollar subway line, the MTA was trying to accommodate a new governor, George Pataki, who wanted to scale back state spending. His MTA chair, Virgil Conway, proposed eliminating free student passes, raising fares 20 percent to $1.50, permanently closing a station, and reducing service on at least eleven subway lines and sixty bus lines. When Cafiero started talking about a Second Avenue subway, he recalled, "People looked at me like I was nuts."[29]

As the study moved along in 1996, New York City was thriving. Crime was rapidly falling with the end of the crack epidemic and more police officers deployed on the streets. Mayor Giuliani, a strong proponent of the broken-windows theory, had instructed the police force to more diligently enforce laws against minor violations, such as jumping over the subway turnstiles to avoid paying the fare, because he was convinced it would establish order and prevent suspects from committing more serious crimes. Giuliani boasted, "The crime declines in New York City that now reach 36 percent over a three-year period blows every stereotype that exists of New York City."[30]

In Times Square, new restaurants, hotels, and entertainment centers were set to open in 1996. Renters were in bidding wars for Manhattan apartments, with one real estate executive calling the rental market "frenzied." Although the number of jobs was growing only modestly, income growth was strong thanks to the booming financial industry and expanding technology sector. In the subways, ridership had increased every year for the past five years.[31]

Over the next three years, the team screened out impractical alternatives, such as extending the platforms of the Lexington Avenue line to accommodate twelve-car trains rather than ten-car trains. The team evaluated all of the remaining alternatives based on cost effectiveness, mobility improvements, and environmental benefits. Cafiero was thorough. With so many people at

NYC Transit, the MTA, and the FTA looking over his shoulder, he wanted to make sure that "things were just right." To do so, the study team developed the world's most sophisticated travel demand model for estimating future travel patterns. Using survey results and actual ridership levels, the computer model initially simulated the travel patterns of millions of people in the metropolitan area. Trips by foot, car, bus, taxi, subway, ferry, and commuter railroad were all included. Next, the modeling experts predicted future travel patterns by incorporating forecasts for future population and employment levels. Then the model determined how different East Side transportation alternatives would affect future travel patterns throughout the region.[32]

The model revealed both direct and indirect consequences associated with various alternatives. For example, a Second Avenue subway north of 63rd Street would reduce travel time from the Upper East Side to Times Square by fifteen minutes. That would encourage some people living and working on the Upper East Side to take the Second Avenue line instead of taxis, buses, and other subways. In turn, the Lexington Avenue trains would be less crowded, and travel times on trains from 125th Street to Lower Manhattan would be reduced by three minutes.[33]

The most complex part of the model, and the reason it took the planners' state-of-the-art computer about ten days to run a single scenario, related to the fact that travel behavior of people is interrelated. For example, if the Lexington Avenue line were to become a little less congested during the morning rush hour, some people who had been waking up early to avoid the crowds might start taking the subway at rush hour. Likewise, if some Upper East Siders started taking the Second Avenue subway instead of a taxi, others might decide to start taking a taxi because it would be easier to find one. Although the modeling experts used sophisticated software programs, they had to rely on thousands of assumptions that would affect their analysis. They did not have crystal balls that could predict where people would live and work, or how economic, social, and rapid technological changes would transform travel.

The planners debated where to locate the northernmost station of a Second Avenue subway. They considered 96th Street, but were sensitive to environmental justice issues because President Bill Clinton had focused attention on the disproportionate impacts that federal actions were having on minority and low-income populations. A subway line that terminated at 96th Street would include several new stations in the mostly white and affluent Upper East Side community while neglecting East Harlem, just to the north, where half the population lived below the poverty line.[34]

The planners considered terminating the line at the intersection of 125th Street and Second Avenue; however, the computer model indicated that a station near this corner would not generate much ridership. Bob Olmsted, the retired MTA planner, suggested that the Second Avenue tunnel instead curve toward the west and terminate on 125th Street at Lexington Avenue. The model confirmed that this location was preferable because thousands of riders every day would transfer at 125th Street between trains on the Second Avenue subway, the Lexington Avenue line, and Metro-North's 125th Street station.[35]

THE GOVERNOR'S PRIORITIES

The MTA's planners had been naive and idealistic in 1993 when they set up an interagency task force to evaluate, coordinate, and prioritize all of their megaproject studies. The agencies had expected to determine and compare the costs and benefits of their coordinated studies so that the MTA board could develop a unified program of regional transit expansion projects. Instead their efforts were usurped by three powerful Republicans—Governor George Pataki, Senator Alfonse D'Amato, and MTA chair Virgil Conway—who prioritized their suburban political base over the city's transit needs. Although elected officials from New York City and its suburbs often worked together to secure billions of dollars for the MTA, they battled over allocating the MTA's resources among NYC Transit, Metro-North, and the Long Island Rail Road.[36]

People perceive transportation problems differently and have different priorities for solving them depending on where they live and work. In the 1960s, the governor, MTA chair, and mayor all lived on the Upper East Side and all enthusiastically supported the Second Avenue subway. That was not the case during the Pataki administration. The Republican governor lived in Westchester County, near a Metro-North station an hour north of the city. Pataki owed his unexpected victory to D'Amato, from Long Island, the chair of the US Senate committee with jurisdiction over federal transit programs. Conway had a home in Westchester and summered on Long Island, where he had grown up. He had been an early supporter of Pataki's gubernatorial campaign and a member of the governor's self-described "kitchen cabinet."[37]

In early 1996, Pataki, inspired by a plan prepared by the RPA, decided the time was right to develop and announce his own vision for the metropolitan area's transportation system. In preparation for his speech to the New York City Building Congress, his senior staff went through a list of potential projects prepared by the RPA and the state's transportation agencies. They selected their favorite projects, packaged them, and gave them what one Pataki aide called a new "twist."[38]

The governor and his staff did not evaluate potential megaprojects the same way the MTA's interagency task force did. The MTA's planners used sophisticated computer models and considered numerous criteria including capital costs, operating costs, revenue, ridership, reductions in crowding, and travel time savings. Although the governor's team took into account whether a project was feasible and affordable, they also heavily weighed two criteria that had never entered the MTA's mix—whom the project would benefit and whether those beneficiaries had helped the governor get elected. Those criteria did not bode well for a new East Side subway. In the 1994 gubernatorial race, Pataki won the suburban counties where most Long Island Rail Road and Metro-North Railroad riders lived, but he received only 28 percent of the votes cast in New York City. Pataki performed especially poorly in Manhattan, winning only 16 percent of the votes there.[39]

The governor named his 1996 plan to improve public transportation all across the region "Master Links." His highest-priority MTA megaproject was the one that D'Amato also championed—connecting the Long Island Rail Road with Grand Central Terminal via the abandoned lower level of the 63rd Street tunnel. Pataki appreciated how the new connection would benefit Long Island commuters. When Long Islanders arrived in Penn Station on Manhattan's West Side, they needed to take two subways to reach office buildings on the East Side near Grand Central. The new Long Island Rail Road connection would save these commuters time, money, and stress. They would also be spared from going through Penn Station twice a day. Pataki was familiar with Penn Station after campaigning on its platforms while running for governor. His opinion of the station was shared by most New Yorkers who used it every day: it was "a dump."[40]

All of the MTA's other high-priority capital projects in Master Links were designed to benefit suburban residents, including bringing Metro-North to Penn Station and renovating commuter railroad stations in Manhattan, Brooklyn, and Queens. As part of Master Links, the MTA would study an improvement for East Side commuters that was not a Second Avenue subway. Instead, as part of a "Lower Manhattan Access Study," the MTA would evaluate extending Metro-North Railroad south of Grand Central Terminal. The politically influential Lower Manhattan business community had instigated this planning effort because they thought workers who lived in the northern suburbs would be more likely to work in Lower Manhattan if they could avoid the crowding and unreliability of the Lexington Avenue line.[41]

While Pataki thought a Second Avenue subway was a "nice idea," he did not think it was affordable. He relegated the Second Avenue subway to a list of long-term needs. The governor's priorities would be the MTA chair's priorities. After Pataki appointed him MTA chair, Conway said, "I don't see any need to separate myself from the governor."[42]

Under Conway's leadership, in 1996 the MTA board amended its five-year capital program to include $192 million for the Long Island Rail Road connection to Grand Central Terminal. The following year, when Congress debated a bill authorizing transit funds for the next six years, the Long Island Rail Road project was at the top of the New York congressional delegation's list of priorities. Thanks to D'Amato, the new law would include $353 million for the project. Meanwhile, the only funding in the law relating to the Second Avenue subway was $5 million for Peter Cafiero's study.[43]

Although the Second Avenue subway was not a priority of the governor's office, Cafiero and DiScala continued meeting with East Side residents and officials. They were able to address some of the community's transportation-related concerns by moving bus stops and modifying bus routes. Their work also led NYC Transit to adopt a "Step Aside, Speed Your Ride" program on the Lexington Avenue line. Workers wearing orange vests asked passengers on subway platforms to step aside from the car doors when crowded trains arrived at stations. The subway workers had limited effectiveness, though, because New Yorkers were not inclined to give up precious platform real estate at rush hour. One subway rider suggested that more effective slogans might be "Step Aside, Arrive Alive" or "Step Aside, Hot Hors D'oeuvres Inside."[44]

As DiScala and Cafiero evaluated long-term alternatives, their analysis indicated that a Second Avenue subway between 125th and 63rd Streets would provide the most bang for the buck. Building a new line all the way to Lower Manhattan would cost more than twice as much; however, it would not attract twice as many riders. Because the shorter segment was more cost effective, it would be more likely to qualify for FTA funds. DiScala said, "We wanted a project that could move forward and actually happen, not one that failed again because it was too expensive."[45]

At a January 1997 public meeting hosted by Manhattan borough president Ruth Messinger, Cafiero's team explained how they had narrowed down their initial list of more than two dozen potential ideas to just three alternatives that they would study in more depth. The first alternative involved relatively low-cost improvements, such as new bus lanes on First and Second Avenues. The second alternative was a two-track Second Avenue subway between 125th Street and 63rd Street. Trains would connect with the 63rd Street tunnel and operate on the Broadway line's express tracks, terminating in either Lower Manhattan or Brooklyn. The third alternative was the Second Avenue subway between 125th and 63rd Streets coupled with a light rail line on the Lower East Side. Light rail service was similar to the streetcars or trolley cars that operated on Manhattan streets until the 1930s when Mayor La Guardia ripped up all the tracks. In the 1990s, the light rail proposal was opposed by many East Siders, especially business owners, for the same reasons the tracks had been removed—because they slowed down cars and reduced the number of parking spots.[46]

Few East Siders complained when the study team dropped the subway alternative that would run along the full length of Manhattan. Instead, local groups and elected officials expressed their support for building a Second Avenue subway line between 63rd Street and 125th Street. Sheldon Silver, the Speaker of the New York State Assembly, was also supportive even though the subway would not reach his Lower East Side district. NYC Transit planners explained that the northern portion of a Second Avenue subway could be considered the first phase of an eventual longer line.[47]

The team's members were candid about the problems the Lexington Avenue line would face as it tried to accommodate increasing population and employment. They did not hide the fact that the subway would get more crowded after the Long Island Rail Road started providing service to Grand Central Terminal. Although the team was not trying to sabotage the Long Island Rail Road project, elected officials picked up on the issue. City Councilman Gifford Miller, who represented the Upper East Side, said that any additional commuters from Long Island at Grand Central would "push the [Lexington Avenue] line well beyond its capacity, creating a nightmare for subway users." Ruth Messinger said, "Clearly, these two projects are related and should be funded and developed in a coordinated manner." In response, officials at MTA headquarters claimed that the Long Island Rail Road project would have a minimal effect on East Side subway riders.[48]

After considering various factors such as travel time, convenience, and construction costs, Cafiero's team identified potential locations for subway stations approximately every ten blocks. The study team also developed hypothetical train schedules and conducted an analysis of the dust, noise, vibration, and other impacts that would be associated with construction and operations.

Because federal environmental analysis requirements had become so demanding, many of the individual chapters in their twenty-four-chapter draft environmental impact statement were longer than the entire impact statement produced for the Second Avenue subway in the 1970s.[49]

The team's members prepared what they considered to be conservative cost estimates. Norm Silverman's experience at the MTA in the 1970s had shown him the dangers of proposing a project with unrealistically low cost estimates. He had Cafiero combine two different cost estimates prepared by consultants with a third one prepared by NYC Transit engineers. Unlike the MTA's Second Avenue subway estimates from the late 1960s, the study team's included a contingency for unexpected costs, an inflationary component, and the cost of buying hundreds of new subway cars to operate on the new line.[50]

No one at the MTA or the governor's office pressured the planners to fudge their numbers. But that was not the case with all of the Second Avenue subway's competitors. After D'Amato told the head of the MTA Planning Department to use overly optimistic estimates, the MTA said that connecting the Long Island Rail Road with Grand Central would cost $2.1 billion and be completed in 2010. In fact, that megaproject is now expected to cost more than five times as much and take about twice as long to complete. Likewise, Metro-North's planning director told his staff and consultants studying a new rail line across the Hudson River north of New York City to lower their cost estimates and increase their ridership forecasts.[51]

Although the environmental impact statement was completed by January 1999, it could not be released until it received approvals from MTA executives. They were not in a hurry to provide them.[52]

ADVOCATES FILL THE VOID

In 1999, the transit system appeared to be ripe for expansion. Cafiero's East Side alternatives study had coincided with a transformative decade for New York City, much of it attributable to a booming stock market and a remarkable reduction of the city's crime rate. In the 1990s, the Dow Jones Industrial Average more than quadrupled. Violent crime in the city declined by more than 56 percent and property crimes fell 65 percent. Employment and tourism soared, and the subways were safer, cleaner, and more crowded.[53]

Although the large investment projects promoted by Pataki and Conway favored the suburbs over the city, the two men gave city residents a generous gift in 1997. When Conway was first appointed to the MTA, he wanted to be remembered for one day eliminating the two fares that customers paid when they transferred between buses and subways. He was thrilled when the MTA eliminated the two-fare zones on July 4, 1997, and the following year introduced a thirty-day unlimited-ride MetroCard for sixty-three dollars. The number of people using the Lexington Avenue line increased at every station between 1996 and 1999, although the increase was most dramatic in lower-income neighborhoods. For example, ridership increased 22 percent at 68th Street and 19 percent on 86th Street, while in East Harlem ridership increased 42 percent at 116th Street and 41 percent at 125th Street.[54]

In the 1990s, subway ridership across the city rose 34 percent, with about half of that increase occurring after the MTA began offering the unlimited-ride MetroCards and free transfers between buses and subways. Even though the discounts lowered the subway fare for most New Yorkers, the MTA was stronger financially because of increased revenues from the Triborough Bridge and Tunnel Authority and higher tax revenues dedicated to the MTA from real estate sales, mortgages, retail sales, business franchises, and petroleum.[55]

The downward spiral of cutting service and raising fares, and then cutting more services and raising fares again as ridership declined, had been replaced with an upward spiral. With people feeling safer on the subways, more people were riding them, which made riders feel safer and helped to attract even more riders. The Straphangers Campaign, the riders' advocacy group, rarely had kind words to say about MTA services. In February 1999, however, a spokesperson exclaimed, "It's a tremendous resurgence for the subways and buses, which have come from the abyss of the 1970s to the 1980s to this unbelievable comeback." Researchers could tell that New Yorkers were feeling safer and less anxious on the trains because after many years of having to stay alert while riding the subways, passengers were taking naps on the trains again.[56]

Despite all the positive news, the Second Avenue subway was in trouble in early 1999 because at the MTA's headquarters in Manhattan, Conway wanted to cancel Cafiero's study. The publicity about a Second Avenue subway was threatening the Long Island Rail Road's planned connection to Grand Central because it was raising concerns about conditions on the Lexington Avenue line, as well as raising the public's expectations about building a new subway line. The two projects would inevitably compete for limited federal resources, and Pataki was afraid that if the MTA went ahead with both of them, neither would be completed in a timely manner. At NYC Transit's headquarters in Brooklyn, Cafiero's team resented that MTA officials were trying to derail their study because they knew their project would benefit more people than the Long Island Rail Road's project.[57]

The MTA, by state law, was required to submit its 2000-2004 capital program by October 1, 1999, and Conway did not want the results of Cafiero's final report to recommend that the MTA allocate hundreds of millions of dollars for the Second Avenue subway in the next capital program. The study was saved, though, when the chair was told by his senior advisers that canceling it would damage the MTA's relationship with federal officials. Federal funds had been paying for the study, and federal officials had been working with MTA planners on it for nearly five years.[58]

In early 1999, Conway was not preparing for a five-year capital program the same way as his predecessors Richard Ravitch and Robert Kiley had. When Ravitch and Kiley were MTA chairs, they laid out visions for improving the transportation system and then advocated for funds to fulfill those visions. Conway did not give eloquent speeches, nor did he try to build coalitions to lobby the governor and legislature. Communication was not one of his strengths; he mumbled his words and came across as gruff, especially after suffering a stroke a year earlier. The executive director of the MTA, Marc Shaw, could have taken on the role of MTA champion, but he was even more uncomfortable in the limelight than Conway. But there was a more important reason why Conway was not interested in announcing grand plans or releasing details about the next capital program: he did not want to put any public pressure on his friend Pataki to raise taxes.[59]

Because Conway kept a low profile, he unwittingly allowed transit advocacy organizations to shape the next capital program and prioritize the MTA's megaprojects. By 1999, NYC Transit's study had taken on a life of its own. Cafiero, DiScala, and their consultants had held hundreds of meetings with stakeholders up and down the East Side, sometimes five or six in one week. By studying the transportation problems and evaluating potential solutions in a transparent manner, they had inadvertently created a constituency that would demand a Second Avenue subway. While DiScala and Cafiero were identifying the environmental impacts of potential East Side transportation improvements, a new transportation advocacy group would catapult their efforts and transform the MTA's priorities.[60]

In 1997, Lee Sander, an executive at a transportation consulting firm and the head of a transportation-related think tank at New York University, wanted to create a coalition to promote more transit spending in the metropolitan area. He was concerned that the MTA's progress on rebuilding the transit system was in jeopardy because Conway was expected to scale back the MTA's next capital program in line with the governor's fiscally conservative policies. As Mayor Giuliani's first transportation commissioner, Sander had seen how a coalition of housing stakeholders had shaped the city's policies on vacant buildings, affordable housing, and rezoning. He wanted to create his own coalition that would influence policy in the transportation arena.[61]

Sander reached out to stakeholders who had once lobbied him. When he asked Bob Yaro, the RPA's executive director, to join a coalition, Yaro agreed as long as he could cochair it. Sander was delighted because both Yaro and the RPA were highly regarded. Yaro understood the coalition's potential. He said, "The default mode in New York is nothing happens. You need a powerful coalition of interests that politicians and bureaucracies can't say no to." When Yaro told Sander that he wanted the coalition to make the Second Avenue subway a priority, Sander initially thought Yaro was joking, because it seemed so far-fetched. Sander was convinced of the project's viability only after talking with one of his colleagues, Sheldon Fialkoff, who had worked for Bob Olmsted at the MTA.[62]

In early 1998, RPA planners developed a multipronged strategy to generate political support for the Second Avenue subway. They wanted the private sector and advocacy organizations—not the MTA—to control the debate about expansion projects in the MTA's next capital program. Yaro and his team would appeal to New Yorkers' emotions by talking about the intolerable subway conditions on the East Side, and about how transportation funds were benefiting the suburbs over the city. They would develop a campaign to directly and indirectly persuade those political leaders who would determine the MTA's level of resources, while maintaining an ongoing dialogue with the MTA and neutralizing the authority's opposition.[63]

Lee Sander was a preeminent networker and a master at building coalitions. According to a former RPA planner, "Sander has a circle of friends, two hundred to three hundred people, who live, breathe, think, and do transportation. The venue and menu changes, but the conversation is ongoing." Sander and Yaro deliberately kept the alliance's goals flexible enough so that they could bring in new members who had somewhat different priorities.[64]

Although the coalition would focus on the MTA's capital program, Sander and Yaro gave their group a broader name, the Empire State Transportation Alliance. Many of the coalition's members benefited financially from the MTA's multibillion-dollar capital programs, including executives from engineering firms, construction contractors, and labor unions. Some of them, like Sander himself, moved between public-, private-, and civic-sector positions. Their close ties with public officials, including those in the governor's office, legislature, and MTA agencies, made them something akin to a transit-industrial complex.[65]

Yaro asked Gene Russianoff, a leader of the Straphangers Campaign, to join the alliance. Russianoff would be an important addition because his group had long-standing ties to the transit unions as well as local officials in minority communities. The Straphangers could call on their army of volunteer coordinators, including many college students, to distribute fliers and bring out crowds to hearings and events. Russianoff said that city council members "trusted us because we looked like them." Another contribution that Russianoff could make was his ability to get extensive newspaper coverage with his clever sound bites and the results of the Straphangers' ongoing studies and surveys. In 1998, Russianoff had told a reporter that with ridership growing rapidly, the MTA was going to have to rename its peak ridership period "crush hour."[66]

Russianoff had to convince the other Straphanger leaders and his fellow community activists that they should work with Yaro. The RPA was associated with corporate interests, and it had once been a leading advocate for new highways (including Westway) that Russianoff and his friends had spent countless hours fighting. The Straphangers' leaders also struggled with the question of whether they should support a Second Avenue subway. Russianoff was worried that it would take resources away from the MTA's efforts to improve reliability, customer information, and cleanliness in the rest of the subway system. But his colleagues argued, Why shouldn't New York have a new subway line when other cities were building new rail lines? They also reminded him that more riders would start using the Lexington Avenue line after the Long Island Rail Road came into Grand Central.[67]

Russianoff grudgingly went along with supporting the new subway. He hoped that a new line would create a political atmosphere where people would be more receptive to fixing up stations and improving services across the system. He also thought that if the Straphangers opposed the new subway line, it might tarnish their image of standing up for the powerless subway rider. Besides, he did not think that what he called the "damn thing" was going to get built anyway.[68]

The RPA staff took the lead in documenting the MTA's needs, and Yaro convinced the other coalition members that the MTA's next five-year capital program should repair and replace the transit system's components, as well as selectively expand the system to meet growing demand. The Empire State Transportation Alliance's members eventually included representatives from more than forty organizations representing a broad range of interests, including businesses, environmentalists, unions, transit riders, and even the Automobile Club of New York. Yaro called it a "coalition of unlikely partners." Together, the broad alliance had enormous influence with policy makers and the media. They turned the Second Avenue subway from a joke into a reality.[69]

Yaro assigned the RPA's Jeff Zupan to lead the alliance's research efforts. Zupan had worked for Boris Pushkarev in the late 1960s and early 1970s on MTA-related expansion projects. According to Zupan, "Transit operators think about running service day-to-day, politicians want to cut ribbons, and the business sector thinks about stock prices." The RPA, he says, is different: "We develop ideas whose time has not yet come." Since not all of the coalition's members shared the RPA's enthusiasm for expansion projects that could cost over $20 billion, the RPA led its own advocacy efforts that were distinct from those of the Empire State Transportation Alliance.[70]

The alliance used the RPA's research and its staff to generate both attention about the region's needs and support for transportation investments. The RPA team included Al Appleton, the city's former environmental commissioner, who had a close relationship with legislators, members of Congress, and their staffs. Zupan also had a great deal of help from Bob Olmsted, the retired MTA planner. Olmsted, who was hoping to live long enough to see the Second Avenue subway built, kept himself busy by offering invaluable advice to NYC Transit staff, the study's consultants, community board members, and the RPA.[71]

Yaro and Zupan realized they needed to develop a vision for improving transit and promoting economic development, one that would capture the imagination of the entire city. In January 1999, the RPA released a proposal called MetroLink that built on a regional plan that the RPA had issued several years earlier. MetroLink's concept for expanding the rail network centered on Olmsted's idea of building a Second Avenue subway that would connect the Bronx with Lower Manhattan and then go through a new tunnel to Brooklyn, where it would continue along an underused railroad line to downtown Jamaica and on to Kennedy International Airport in Queens. Zupan called it a "Second Avenue subway on steroids." In total, the RPA proposed nineteen miles of new tunnels, and new uses for fifty-three miles of existing tracks.[72]

The planners at the RPA and NYC Transit took very different approaches in the late 1990s. The RPA's Yaro and Zupan wanted to generate political support for a rail expansion plan that would help achieve broad economic and environmental benefits for the entire metropolitan area. The MTA's Cafiero and

DiScala, however, were insulated from the political environment and focused only on Manhattan's East Side. They followed the federal guidelines for conducting a transportation planning study, which involved identifying a specific problem (in this case, excessive crowding on the Lexington Avenue line) and then selecting several alternatives that could alleviate the problem most cost effectively. Zupan felt that the MTA was being shortsighted and was "lurching toward a piecemeal effort."[73]

The RPA's MetroLink plan filled a void left by Conway because it proposed a clear, coherent vision for expanding transit services, one that would end what the RPA called "intolerable conditions" on the subway's most crowded lines. Implementing the MetroLink plan would put hundreds of thousands more New Yorkers within walking distance of the subway.[74]

The RPA's proposal was met with some skepticism. The president of NYC Transit's engineers union dismissively said, "Unequivocally, the Second Avenue line will not be built because there is simply not enough money to go around." More ominously for the Second Avenue subway, Pataki, his economic development officials, and his transportation team were not interested in pursuing it. "They were totally opposed to it," Sander recalls. "We had a cold peace at best [with Conway]."[75]

In spite of the skepticism and the governor's cold shoulder, MetroLink sparked widespread media interest and support for the Second Avenue subway because of the public's frustration with overcrowded conditions and a desperate desire for a response to them. According to the RPA's Appleton, the MetroLink plan had a "catalytic impact" and New Yorkers took notice. Indeed, a few weeks before releasing MetroLink, one of the RPA team members presciently told a newspaper reporter, "Watching politics is like watching the grass grow. But one day you turn your head and everything has changed." A few weeks after the release, a Straphangers leader realized that the tide had already turned for a Second Avenue subway. He said, "It's really unheard of, but this might be a moment when elected officials follow the public on something instead of trying to lead. The public support is there for this, so politicians can't dismiss it with a knee-jerk reaction."[76]

The RPA team gained the support of Upper East Side congresswoman Carolyn Maloney, and in February one of her aides said, "There is a wonderful window of opportunity to get this done now." The RPA also successfully sold its plan to the Manhattan, Bronx, Brooklyn, and Queens borough presidents by targeting their key staff members first. The Straphangers presence helped assuage the fears of local officials and community activists who worried about the subway causing gentrification and displacing residents of public housing projects on the Lower East Side and in East Harlem.[77]

While the RPA reached out to members of Congress and borough presidents, its most important target was the Lower East Side's assemblyman, Sheldon Silver. As assembly Speaker, Silver controlled a vote on the four-member MTA Capital Program Review Board, whose unanimous support was needed to approve the MTA's capital programs. The RPA team expected that Silver would be especially sensitive to the claim that the MTA was prioritizing suburban commuters over New York City residents. They also knew that the Democratic Speaker was more than willing to fight the Republican governor. In recent years, Silver had held up the adoption of state budgets because he refused to acquiesce to the governor on fingerprinting welfare recipients, cutting taxes on the rich, and eliminating rent control laws. The RPA team and the other members of the Empire State Transportation Alliance cultivated a relationship with three key members of Silver's staff in an effort to get the Speaker's support.[78]

Obtaining Giuliani's support would be trickier because the mayor had other subway expansion preferences, including extending the Astoria subway line to LaGuardia Airport and extending the number 7 line that ran under 42nd Street to Manhattan's far West Side. Initially Giuliani called MetroLink a "pipe dream," but Zupan's team figured out how to soften him up by making friends inside City Hall who offered suggestions about crafting arguments that would persuade him. The mayor's stance on subway projects was critical because he too had a representative on the Capital Program Review Board who could veto the capital program. Moreover, the mayor had four representatives on the MTA's seventeen-member board of directors.[79]

Although the RPA's plan might have been visionary, it was not necessarily practical. The RPA woefully underestimated both costs and completion times, saying it would cost $13 billion and take thirteen years to build the MetroLink projects. Newspaper reporters and editorial writers repeated the RPA's cost estimates and its rough rule of thumb that every mile of subway would cost about $1 billion. It might have been an easy number to remember, but it greatly understated the MTA's actual cost of building tunnels and stations in Manhattan. Furthermore, most people who read about the RPA's plans did not understand the MTA's financial constraints. For example, when the *New York Times* editorial writers praised the plan, they pointed out that New York City spent far less on improving its transit system than Tokyo, London, or Paris. Although the *Times* was technically correct, those cities relied on much more generous contributions from their national governments.[80]

After the RPA's MetroLink proposal was released in January 1999, Manhattan's elected officials took on a more prominent role in advocating for the Second Avenue subway. In March, the Upper East Side's state senator, Roy Goodman, convened a hearing about the Second Avenue subway and whether it should be incorporated into the MTA's next five-year capital program. The senator had previously praised the MTA at a hearing for the Second Avenue subway—but that was twenty-seven years earlier. In 1999, he called the Second Avenue subway "one of the great civic fiascoes in our history." He said that it had truly been "a tunnel to nowhere and a project of broken dreams," and that "rush hour conditions on the Lexington Avenue subway had become so overcrowded that you not only can't get on the train when it comes, you often may have difficulty even getting on the platform."[81]

Goodman was not pleased with the MTA chair's position at the hearing because Conway would not say whether the Second Avenue subway would be included in the MTA's next capital program. Instead, Conway talked about how the ongoing study was considering a 125th-to-63rd-Street segment along with improvements to the Lexington Avenue line. Conway was a lonely voice at the hearing because Goodman had invited more than a dozen people to testify about the importance of the project. Thanks to lobbying by the RPA's team, Giuliani's deputy mayor testified that the mayor now supported allocating $400 million in the next capital program to cover engineering studies for a Second Avenue subway.[82]

Gene Russianoff from the Straphangers Campaign said that because New York had not built a new subway line in half a century, subway riders had to deal with "elbow-in-the-ribs crowding that would violate Department of Agriculture guidelines for shipping cattle." He argued, "If the region can raise $3.5 billion to spare tens of thousands of daily Long Island Rail Road commuters, we must find the resources to come to the rescue of the hundreds of thousands of New Yorkers suffering from grossly inadequate subway service on the East Side." Robert Paaswell, the director of City College's transportation research center, explained that overcrowding on platforms and stairways causes people to fall and get jammed up as they try to get on and off trains. He warned that the problem could be especially dangerous for the elderly and disabled. Then he brought up a question that had not yet received any attention in the Second Avenue subway discussion: what would happen if an overcrowded Lexington Avenue–line subway station needed to be suddenly evacuated in the event of a terrorist attack?[83]

Former MTA chair Richard Ravitch testified that "you don't have to be a rocket scientist to know how desperate the need is to build an alternative form of north/south mass transit for the East Side." But he qualified his support, arguing that the government needed to compare various capital improvements to demonstrate that the Second Avenue subway would have a positive economic return. He pointed out that the city had massive infrastructure needs; for instance, almost one-third of New York City's public schools were still using inefficient and highly polluting coal furnaces, some of them a century old, to heat their buildings.[84]

Unlike Ravitch, Goodman was not interested in conducting a cost-benefit analysis that compared various projects. He said, "To put the matter plainly, there is a competitive situation out here in which there are many demands being made upon the MTA for improvements of different sorts. And to a degree perhaps it's the old story that the squeaking wheel will get the grease." He told Conway and others, "Part of the purpose of this hearing this morning is to let the loudest possible squeak emerge from Room 400 of the State Office Building."[85]

Two weeks later, Representative Carolyn Maloney sponsored an Upper East Side forum titled "Making the Second Avenue Subway a Reality." Maloney had helped the MTA obtain federal funding for Cafiero's East Side alternatives study, and now she was whipping up support among her constituents and Manhattan's Democratic Party activists. Behind the scenes, she was also lobbying the rest of New York's congressional delegation and Speaker Silver. The congresswoman was confident that if the elected officials worked together, the MTA's next five-year capital program would include funding for a Second Avenue subway.[86]

Zupan and Maloney coined a new word at Maloney's forum that would solidify public support for a Second Avenue subway along the full length of Manhattan's East Side: they started referring to the 63rd-to-125th-Street segment that Cafiero's team had been studying as a "stubway." The pejorative nickname seemed to indicate that the MTA was considering a two-mile subway line rather than an extension of an existing line that would connect East Harlem and the Upper East Side with Lower Manhattan and Brooklyn. Even the editors of one of the most widely read newspapers in the region, *Newsday*, were confused once the word "stubway" became widely used. They called the segment between 63rd and 125th Streets "a joke," "laughingly inadequate," and the "weirdest part of the capital program."[87]

While Maloney's efforts were critical to getting legislative and congressional support, Manhattan borough president C. Virginia Fields organized an effective and important grassroots effort. In 1998, the longtime civil rights activist had told Cafiero's team that subway construction should begin at 125th Street; otherwise the tunnel might not ever reach East Harlem. In

1999, she was concerned that the subway would never reach the Lower East Side. At the time, the median household income of Upper East Side residents was about $81,000, while it was $24,000 on the Lower East Side and $22,000 in East Harlem.[88]

The borough president formed a Second Avenue subway task force, led weekly meetings with community leaders, and set up an education and awareness campaign that would tap into "rider rage" as a way to motivate people. Fields had mayoral ambitions, and once she realized how the issue was giving her extensive citywide media coverage, she put even more time into promoting a full-length Second Avenue subway. Borough presidents had held relatively little formal power ever since the Board of Estimate was eliminated in 1990. But Fields knew how to use her bully pulpit, and she could tap into an extensive network because the borough president appointed all six hundred members of Manhattan's community boards. She organized a lunchtime gathering where television cameras captured her eating sardine sandwiches to represent the crammed Lexington Avenue subway riders. Her office held town hall meetings, issued press releases, and with the Straphangers Campaign organized a postcard drive that collected over twenty-four thousand yellow postcards indicating support for a full-length subway. When Fields stood outside the subway stations collecting signatures on the postcards, she wore her matching yellow dress.[89]

When Cafiero and DiScala first began evaluating alternatives in their study, Silver and his staff had not objected to eliminating a full-length Second Avenue subway. By the spring of 1999, though, building a Second Avenue subway that would serve his Lower East Side district seemed much more feasible. The economy was stronger, subway ridership was booming, and the project had widespread support. After lobbying from transit advocates, Maloney, his fellow state legislators, and other elected officials, Silver became the full-length Second Avenue subway's most important supporter. By the summer, he and the city's other Democratic leaders were on a collision course with the Republican governor.

In June 1999, the MTA gave the FTA a list of capital projects that it wanted to build using federal funds. The MTA requested $580 million to connect the Long Island Rail Road with Grand Central Terminal, but it did not ask for any money to build a Second Avenue subway. Meanwhile, Manhattan assembly members publicly vowed to fight for a Second Avenue subway. Pete Grannis said, "The full-length Second Avenue subway must be addressed," and John Ravitz warned that "if it's not, we can't sit back and not raise holy hell." In July, Silver also indicated that he would reject any MTA capital program that did not include funding for a Second Avenue subway between East Harlem and Lower Manhattan.[90]

Under pressure from members of Congress, legislators, borough presidents, and the FTA, the MTA chair could not bury the final report of the Manhattan East Side alternatives study. In August 1999, eleven years after NYC Transit's planners picked up their markers and wrote "Second Avenue subway" on a whiteboard, the results of their work were finally released to the public.

Cafiero and DiScala had met all the federal requirements to study potential solutions for the East Side's transportation problems. They had done so in a comprehensive and transparent manner by soliciting input from other public agencies, two advisory committees, community boards, elected officials, community and civic groups, and the general public. After analyzing dozens of alternatives and subway configurations, their team identified the costs and benefits of three options. New bus lanes and some modest subway improvements would cost $119 million, a Second Avenue subway between 125th and 63rd Streets connecting with the Broadway express tracks via the 63rd Street tunnel would cost $3.6 billion, and the same subway segment along with a light rail line on the Lower East Side would cost $4.6 billion. The study did not recommend one option over another, nor did it evaluate a full-length subway alternative.[91]

By September 1999, a full-length Second Avenue subway had overwhelming support from the public, the media, and local elected officials. When the city council's transportation committee members looked into the Second Avenue subway issue in early September, they could not find one elected official or community group that was publicly opposed to its construction. Russianoff told the committee that since the MTA was considering a route only from 125th to 63rd Streets, "the MTA's approach to a Second Avenue subway is half-hearted, half-a-loaf thinking that's only half the answer." Moreover, many of Manhattan's business leaders and real estate moguls—two interest groups that Pataki liked to accommodate because they made generous political donations and could use their influence to help him in Washington, DC— were lobbying for the subway.[92]

The RPA and the other members of the Empire State Transportation Alliance used their media contacts to place stories supportive of a full-length Second Avenue subway. Yaro was especially influential; members of the *New York Times* editorial board had once told him, "Everyone else has an axe to grind except for you. You just care about the public interest." In August and September, the *New York Times* published two editorials supporting the full-length Second Avenue subway. "Once completed," the newspaper wrote, "the Second Avenue line could be the basis for a major expansion of the region's entire mass-transit system, as the Regional Plan Association demonstrated in an imaginative report released earlier this year." The editors argued that "New York has used up the transportation system built by its grandparents. It is time now to start constructing a route or two for the grandchildren."[93]

The *New York Post*, a conservative-leaning newspaper owned by Rupert Murdoch, had been instrumental in helping elect both Giuliani and Pataki. Its editors enjoyed publishing articles that made MTA officials look incompetent, out of touch, and shortsighted. In the fall of 1999, they kept up a steady drumbeat for the full-length Second Avenue subway, giving their articles and editorials provocative titles such as "Cheap 2nd. Av. Subway Ripped," "MTA's Own Study Disses Stubway," "Half-Measures Won't Do for a Project Critical to the Future of This City," "E. Siders on Track for Chaos," and "MTA OKs $700m for Stubway."

To wrap up the East Side alternatives study, the MTA held a public hearing on September 15. MTA officials told a very disappointed Peter Cafiero to stay away because they were afraid he might talk about the benefits of a Second Avenue subway line. But Cafiero's absence did not make a difference. While he was on the beach at Coney Island, nearly every single person at the hearing supported building a Second Avenue subway along the full length of Manhattan.[94]

In the last week of September, the MTA unveiled a $16.6 billion capital program that included $700 million for the Second Avenue subway's engineering and design work. In addition, the proposed program included approximately $650 million for a subway extension to LaGuardia Airport and $1.5 billion for the Long Island Rail Road connection with Grand Central. The transit advocates were disappointed that Conway included funds only for the Second Avenue Subway segment north of 63rd Street. Several years earlier, transit advocates might have celebrated, but they had much higher expectations in 1999.[95]

The media did not focus on the fact that the new capital program was $4 billion more than the previous five-year program. Nor did they pay much attention to the fact that the MTA did not have $16.6 billion to spend on capital improvements. Instead the focus was on a battle between an eight-and-a-half-mile subway along the full length of Manhattan and the MTA's proposed three-mile route. Conway said, "We're all in favor of a Second Avenue subway"; he just thought it had to be done in phases.[96]

Speaking on behalf of the RPA, Zupan responded that the MTA could describe the Upper East Side portion as a first step, but "they have no second or third step." He explained that when other cities, such as Washington, San

Francisco, and Atlanta, built their subway system in stages, they laid out the full network before breaking ground on the first segment. Using NYC Transit's own figures, he showed that even with the stubway, the Lexington Avenue express trains at Grand Central would be more crowded in twenty years than in 1999 because of expected ridership growth on the subways and the Long Island Rail Road's connection to Grand Central.[97]

The transit advocates continued their efforts. In November, they rented a trolley, decorated it with banners, and brought in a brass band for what was billed as a "whistle-stop tour" of the Bronx, Manhattan, and Brooklyn. Led by a woman in a cow costume, hundreds of protestors carrying cow masks glued to popsicle sticks called for a new line that would connect the three boroughs. New York City's public advocate, Mark Green, said, "We're here to say boo and moo to the MTA for not doing enough to stop the cattle-car crowding on the Lexington Avenue line." Congresswoman Maloney told the fired-up crowd, "We're here to support the subway, not the stubway."[98]

NYC Transit and MTA officials were frustrated by what they considered the RPA's disingenuous use of the word "stubway," but they did not come up with an effective way to counter it. An October 1999 Quinnipiac College poll found that 64 percent of registered voters in New York supported a full-length subway. Only 18 percent of the respondents, however, were willing to pay a higher fare to build it. That sentiment put the elected officials in a bind. If they wanted to get reelected they needed to support the subway, but they could not ask taxpayers or subway riders to pay for it.[99]

The decision about the initiatives in the MTA capital program and how they would be funded would come down to four people: the mayor, the governor, the state senate majority leader, and the assembly Speaker. Each controlled a vote on the MTA Capital Program Review Board, which had to unanimously approve the next capital program. Conway believed that "a good chairman is a mediator, a consensus builder," and his approach was to "make everyone feel part of a solution." The MTA's proposed capital program, though, satisfied only three of the four men.[100]

Giuliani was pleased because the program included funds for a subway extension to LaGuardia Airport. Conway, working closely with Pataki and his staff, protected the Long Island Rail Road's megaproject and did not call for any new taxes. The senate majority leader was onboard because the governor promised sufficient highway funding and the powerful Long Island Rail Road unions supported the MTA's capital program. The holdout was Silver. He wanted a full-length Second Avenue subway and he did not want the Long Island Rail Road connection to open years before the subway's first phase.

Silver also wanted additional state funds to protect the subway fare. He stood his ground and delayed not only the MTA's capital program, but approval of the entire state budget.[101]

In March 2000, the transit advocates outwitted Conway one last time. The RPA and the Straphangers Campaign raised half a million dollars to place advertisements in over two thousand subway cars. The subway posters featured a picture of passengers standing in a crowded subway car, with the words, "With livestock it's called animal cruelty. With people it's called a morning commute." Conway played into the transit advocates' publicity stunt by turning down the advertisement, claiming it was not in the MTA's commercial interests.

The RPA and the Straphangers promptly filed a suit in federal court, claiming that the MTA was denying them their First Amendment rights, an action that generated extensive and free media coverage for the full-length Second Avenue subway. The Straphangers' Gene Russianoff told reporters, "Essentially, their argument is that people will see the ad and realize for the first time in their lives that subways are crowded, that they will flee and the system will lose tons of revenue. It is an argument that does not pass the laugh test." After a federal judge, behind closed doors in his chambers, hinted to Conway that he was not likely to win, the MTA reversed course and announced that it would allow the advertisement to run. Assessing the winners and losers, the *New York Post* referred to the Straphangers Campaign as "New York's most polished band of self-promoters," and *Newsday* called the MTA's leaders "clueless" and "wooly mammoths."[102]

A few weeks later, the governor and the legislative leaders finally agreed on a state budget, and capital programs for both the MTA and state highways. The MTA would allocate $1.05 billion in its 2000–2004 capital program for the Second Avenue subway and prepare an environmental impact statement for the full-length route. The governor, assembly Speaker, and senate majority leader also agreed to support a $3.8 billion transportation bond act that would provide about $1.5 billion for the MTA. In May, the MTA Capital Program Review Board approved the capital program, and the Second Avenue subway was on its way.[103]

As the Second Avenue subway moved toward its engineering and design stages, many people could take credit for resurrecting the mythical project. Cafiero and his team at NYC Transit brought numerous stakeholders together to identify the best solution to a transportation problem. The RPA and the other members of the Empire State Transportation Alliance created a vision and generated a groundswell of support. And Manhattan's elected officials stopped the state-controlled transportation authority from prioritizing the transportation needs of suburban Republicans over those of city Democrats.

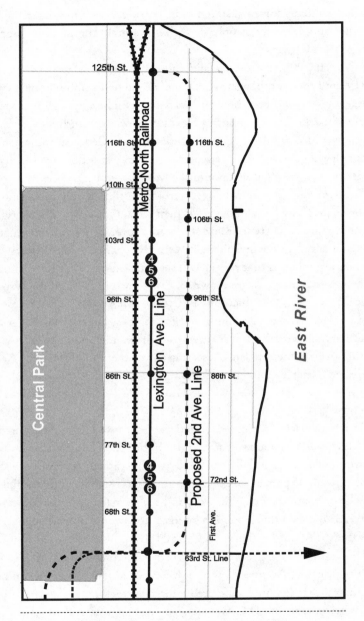

Map 6.2. The MTA's 1999 proposal for a Second Avenue subway, dubbed the "stubway"

A Twenty-First-Century Subway

When Governor George Pataki and Assembly Speaker Sheldon Silver agreed in 2000 to include a Second Avenue subway in the MTA's capital program, they did not have a plan to pay for the whole megaproject because the Republican governor would not increase taxes and the Democratic assembly leader did not want to raise fares.

Pataki had promised to cut taxes, not raise them, in his successful campaign over three-term governor Mario Cuomo. In fact, after Pataki was first elected, he took revenue dedicated to the MTA and used it to reduce state taxes. His MTA chair, Virgil Conway, did not lobby legislative leaders for additional resources because he prioritized Pataki's political ambitions ahead of his own agency's needs. Conway said, "We're part of a large team, which I would call the governor's team, with his philosophy, which is to do more with less." Silver, meanwhile, said, "I don't support a fare increase under any circumstances. Unequivocally, not two years from now, not four years from now."[1]

While Pataki railed against a liberal "tax and spend" ideology, he governed with a "borrow and spend" philosophy. To pay for its 2000–2004 capital program, the MTA undertook the largest sale of municipal bonds in US history, issuing more than $11 billion in new bonds and refinancing most of its existing $12 billion of debt. Its outstanding bonds, which had an average of thirteen years left before they would have been paid off, were replaced with new bonds that would not be fully paid off until after 2030. Overall, the MTA relied on debt to pay for 65 percent of its 2000–2004 capital program, compared to 37 percent in the previous program.[2]

The politicians liked the MTA's financing plan because it generated enough money to pay for popular projects without their having to raise tolls, fares, and taxes in the short term. Indeed, the new bonds were designed so that payments would be low in the first few years and then soar after that. The Wall Street investment bankers, the ones who concocted the financing scheme in the first place, liked it because they reaped about $85 million in bond underwriting fees. Former MTA chair Robert Kiley warned that the backloading of debt would "make it harder, if not impossible, to manage future capital plans." Gene Russianoff, the leader of the Straphangers Campaign, said that with the MTA mortgaging "every stick of furniture," the transportation authority would find it harder to build the Second Avenue subway."[3] Former MTA chair Richard Ravitch later explained why the state's elected officials put the authority in such a bind. "You have to understand," he said, "that politicians want to kick the can down the road. If it saves them from imposing a burden, they will do it. They will all do it."[4]

When negotiating the MTA's $17.1 billion five-year capital program, the governor and legislative leaders agreed to place a $3.8 billion bond referendum on the November 2000 ballot. Half the money would be used for the MTA capital program and the other half for state highway projects. Getting New Yorkers to approve a transportation bond act typically requires a well-coordinated statewide campaign. Elected officials need to collaborate with civic groups and transportation industry representatives, and then convince voters that they would directly benefit from the bond's proceeds. Since upstate voters are more fiscally conservative and tend to oppose bond proposals, a high voter turnout in New York City is usually needed to ensure passage.[5]

In 2000, supporters of the transportation bond were unable to put together an effective campaign because so many transportation advocates had serious misgivings about the state's plans. The Empire State Transportation Alliance sat on the sidelines even though the coalition of business, labor, and transportation organizations had persuaded state leaders to fund the Second Avenue subway in the first place. Many of the coalition's members were not comfortable with the MTA's level of borrowing, while some were concerned that the bond proceeds would be used to fund highway projects they considered to be environmentally harmful.[6]

The governor and the legislative leaders did not promote the benefits of the transportation bond act. Nor did they identify specific projects that would be funded by the bond's proceeds. Instead they simply said the money would help fund all of the projects in the highway and transit programs. Unlike with most previous bond referendums, the governor did not send out his agency heads to lobby newspaper editorial boards for endorsements. Pataki remained lukewarm toward the bond act because it did not help his carefully crafted image as a fiscal conservative. Nevertheless, the governor never backtracked on his support for the Second Avenue subway.[7]

He and other leading Republicans had another reason for sitting on the sidelines—they did not want to give New York City's Democrats another reason to go to the polls in 2000. A high turnout in New York City would have jeopardized Republican congressman Rick Lazio's chances of defeating the First Lady, Hillary Clinton, in the battle for a US Senate seat.[8]

A lobbyist for the state's highway contractors, A. J. Castelbuono, lamented the lack of support that state officials showed for the referendum. "Everybody seemed to be heading toward the witness protection program," he said, "and the Assembly was nowhere to be found. The Senate was nowhere to be found. The administration was nowhere to be found. The transit interests were nowhere to be found and a lot of the major unions were not all that supportive." On Election Day, even though nearly three-quarters of Manhattan's voters supported the transportation bond act, the state's voters defeated it by a vote of 52 percent to 48 percent. But transportation advocates learned some useful lessons that would come in handy five years later, when the fate of the Second Avenue subway would rest in the hands of the state's voters.[9]

THE WORLD TRADE CENTER

Three months after the referendum failed, the MTA's executive director, Marc Shaw, told legislators that the Second Avenue subway might be on the "chopping block." If the MTA had to reduce its capital program, he said, "it would obviously come out of the expansion projects." Rather than eliminating funding for the Second Avenue subway, Pataki wanted the Port Authority of New York and New Jersey to help pay for the new subway by selling off some of its extensive real estate holdings, most notably the World Trade Center in Lower Manhattan.[10]

At the same time, the governor was turning over the reins of the MTA from Virgil Conway to a real estate developer named Peter Kalikow. Kalikow would be the first MTA chair to champion the Second Avenue subway since William Ronan in the early 1970s. He appreciated its benefits, and his wealth was dependent on frequent, rapid, reliable, and affordable East Side subway service. Kalikow had purchased more than a dozen buildings on the Upper East Side, and his most valuable properties were only a two-minute walk from the Lexington Avenue line in Midtown and Lower Manhattan.[11]

As soon as Kalikow was appointed, he reached out to Lee Sander and Bob Yaro, the leaders of the Empire State Transportation Alliance, and he committed himself to working with them to advance the Second Avenue subway. Yaro said that Kalikow understood "viscerally the need to create redundancy and relieve congestion" on the Lexington Avenue line. Unlike Pataki and Conway, Kalikow grew up in New York City, not in the suburbs. He lived on the Upper East Side, the same neighborhood where Governor Nelson Rockefeller, Mayor John Lindsay, and MTA chair William Ronan all lived when they championed the Second Avenue subway.[12]

In early 2001, the MTA said it would begin construction on the Second Avenue subway in 2004. That was an optimistic schedule because Congress and the Federal Transit Administration (FTA) had set up numerous hurdles for transit agencies seeking federal funds for new transit lines. Congress had authorized spending about $1.2 billion annually for large new transit projects under a program it called New Starts. New York faced stiff competition for these funds from cities all across the country, including Charlotte, Dallas, Denver, Los Angeles, Louisville, Miami, New Orleans, Phoenix, Philadelphia, Raleigh, San Diego, and Seattle. The FTA determined which projects would obtain New Starts funds by comparing the benefits of proposed projects as well as the ability of transit agencies to build and operate them. The federal agency required extensive documentation and frequently changed the criteria it used to rate and rank projects. In the early 2000s, the FTA made sixteen changes to its evaluation criteria over a five-year period.[13]

Since the MTA needed New Starts funds to help pay for the Second Avenue subway, the battleground for the megaproject shifted in 2000. The most recent fight had taken place between the governor, legislative leaders, and the mayor over the MTA's five-year capital program. Transit advocacy organizations, including the Regional Plan Association (RPA) and the Straphangers Campaign, had skillfully convinced the public and elected officials to support the new subway line. Once the capital program was approved, though, the legislative leaders and the mayor had much less power than the governor over the MTA's actions and priorities.

Even though New York City residents paid billions of dollars in taxes and tolls to subsidize the transit system, the City of New York had little influence over the Second Avenue subway for four reasons. First, thanks to William

Ronan and Nelson Rockefeller, the MTA board was controlled by the governor. Second, when the state legislature approved Richard Ravitch's capital program in 1981, it instituted a series of streamlining changes that gave the MTA more autonomy and stripped city agencies of their oversight role relating to transit contracts. Third, MTA officials did not need to make any deals with the members of the city's Board of Estimate, as it did in 1968, to get city approval for the route. Fourth, the city funded only about 2 percent of the MTA's capital program; in the 1980s, the city had contributed $200 million annually, but by the early 2000s, it was contributing less than half that amount.[14]

A team of planners, attorneys, and engineers in Brooklyn and Manhattan would have to convince federal bureaucrats, not city officials, that the Second Avenue subway deserved funding. The MTA had begun the first stage of the New Starts evaluation process in 1995 when NYC Transit's Peter Cafiero kicked off his planning study. In the summer of 2001, Cafiero and his team were updating their study's results to reflect the MTA's decision to build a full-length subway from 125th Street to Lower Manhattan. Cafiero would need to prepare an environmental impact statement that evaluated air quality, noise, traffic, and numerous other resources for the entire 8.5-mile line.

The MTA was also preparing an application to the FTA seeking approval to begin preliminary engineering, the second stage in the New Starts process. NYC Transit would need to hire a team of engineers to design the Second Avenue subway and refine its cost estimates. The engineers' determinations about the subway alignment, entrance locations, construction techniques, and other details would also be used to help assess the new subway line's environmental impacts.[15]

In the summer of 2001, FTA officials in New York City and Washington, DC, gave the MTA's Jack Dean informal feedback on the proposal for a Second Avenue subway. They were impressed that the new line was expected to carry more than half a million riders on a typical weekday. This dwarfed other projects the FTA was planning on funding. For example, new light rail lines were expected to carry only eleven thousand riders per day in Dallas and thirty-seven thousand in Austin. The FTA was carefully evaluating the assumptions behind Cafiero's ridership estimates because Congress had complained that many federally funded rail projects were not meeting their expected ridership levels. The FTA's review team did recognize that the Second Avenue subway was much more likely to attract riders than projects in other cities because of the East Side's density and the city's relatively low automobile ownership rates.[16]

Only five cities in the entire country had more residents than the East Side, while more than a million people worked near the subway's proposed route. FTA officials were certainly familiar with key destinations the new line would serve, such as the New York Stock Exchange, the United Nations, and the FTA's own New York City office. Given the project's benefits and the MTA's recent successes rebuilding the subway system, FTA officials in Washington were confident that they could sell the benefits of the Second Avenue subway to members of Congress, who had final approval on the disbursement of New Starts funds. But the project's benefits alone would not determine whether the MTA would succeed in obtaining these funds. The MTA would need to submit a series of application documents over several years so that the FTA could evaluate the project's cost effectiveness.[17]

While the MTA prepared documents, the Upper East Side's representative in Congress, Carolyn Maloney, tried to pass legislation that would designate funds specifically for the Second Avenue subway. Although congressional earmarks would not require the same level of FTA scrutiny as New Starts funds, they typically did not provide more than a few million dollars, and the amount allocated by Congress would be deducted from a future New Starts grant. In the summer of 2001, when Congress appeared poised to earmark $3 million for the Second Avenue subway, Maloney proclaimed, "This is absolutely great news for thousands of straphangers riding the jam packed Lex line in stifling summer heat." Maloney's reference to $3 million as "absolutely great news" was a bit of an overstatement, though, because $3 million for the multibillion-dollar Second Avenue subway was like getting a $5 check from an uncle toward the purchase of a new car.[18]

The MTA's deputy executive director, Chris Boylan, explained why Maloney's efforts were important. "The more money we got," he said, "the more credible the project was, and the more people bought into the project. The feds will give us more money, because it's already gotten money." In July 2001, Pataki made progress on another potential source of funds for the Second Avenue subway when the Port Authority closed on a deal to lease the World Trade Center to a private developer for ninety-nine years.[19]

In July, the MTA officially ended its Lower Manhattan Access study. This study had begun three years earlier after business leaders and landlords in Lower Manhattan lobbied Pataki to provide direct commuter rail service from the suburbs. Businesses had been leaving Lower Manhattan for Midtown since the 1950s because Midtown had more space, newer office buildings, and direct commuter railroad service from the suburbs in

Westchester, Long Island, and New Jersey. As part of the Lower Manhattan Access study, the MTA's planners determined that extending commuter rail service to Lower Manhattan would not be cost effective. Instead, they recommended building a full-length Second Avenue subway with a stop underneath Metro-North Railroad's 125th Street station. This would help both New York City's northern suburbs and Lower Manhattan. In addition, the planners recommended improving connections between Lower Manhattan's numerous subway lines, an idea that would get much more attention a few months later.[20]

The MTA chair, Peter Kalikow, personally decided that the Second Avenue subway would be built with new stations all the way to Water Street in Lower Manhattan's financial district. The MTA's planners and engineers seriously considered an alternative that would have connected the Second Avenue line on the Lower East Side with an existing subway line (the J and Z trains) that went all the way downtown. Although this option would have saved hundreds of millions of dollars, Kalikow felt that the transportation, economic, and political benefits of new Lower Manhattan stations outweighed the benefits of tying into the existing line.[21]

On September 10, Cafiero met with the Upper East Side's community board to update its members on his team's progress studying alternative routes, potential stations, and the project's environmental impacts. Scheduled last on the agenda that evening, Cafiero realized that the Second Avenue subway was not an urgent topic for the board. The community had not yet understood the major disruptions that building a new subway line would entail. Instead the board's transportation committee members were spending more time talking about renaming streets and modifying parking regulations.[22]

The next morning, building a Second Avenue subway was not a priority to anyone, anywhere.

At 8:46 a.m. on September 11, an airplane traveling at over 450 miles per hour and carrying ten thousand gallons of jet fuel plowed into the World Trade Center's North Tower. Seventeen minutes later, a second airliner hit the South Tower. Lower Manhattan's Twin Towers collapsed less than ninety minutes later. More than 2,600 people died at the World Trade Center that day. The attack destroyed the Port Authority Trans-Hudson (PATH) train station at the World Trade Center, severing a vital link between New York and New Jersey. The collapse of the towers also destroyed about 1,800 feet of the tunnel used by the number 1 and number 9 subway lines, and damaged the N and the R subway lines as well.[23]

Numerous streets near the World Trade Center were destroyed, buried, or blocked for months. In the following weeks, the city instituted a virtual traffic ban in Lower Manhattan to accommodate recovery and construction equipment. Mayor Giuliani also issued an executive order banning single-occupant cars on the bridges and tunnels into Manhattan below 60th Street.[24]

The priorities of the region and the MTA were transformed. The MTA added over $500 million to its capital program to minimize its vulnerabilities to another terrorist attack. It enhanced security at its stations, bridges, and tunnels by strengthening structures, improving fire equipment, and installing electronic security and surveillance. Old ideas for improving Lower Manhattan—many of them identified in the MTA's Lower Manhattan Access study—were suddenly thrust to the forefront.[25]

US president Dwight Eisenhower would have appreciated how a study completed just weeks before a terrorist attack was now helping officials figure out how best to rebuild and revitalize Lower Manhattan. He once emphasized the importance of planning to attendees at a national defense conference, explaining that in case of an emergency, "the first thing you do is to take all the plans off the top shelf and throw them out the window and start once more.

Figure 7.1. *Lower Manhattan subway station after September 11, 2001, terrorist attack.*
Source: *Metropolitan Transportation Authority.*

But if you haven't been planning you can't start to work, intelligently at least. That is the reason it is so important to plan, to keep yourselves steeped in the character of the problem that you may one day be called upon to solve—or to help to solve."[26]

As city and state transportation officials assessed Lower Manhattan's enormous transportation needs and opportunities, one thing did not change. Lou Tomson, a top aide to Pataki, said that projects like the Second Avenue subway would keep on moving along even if the governor was not paying much attention to them. He said they were "like ball bearings in a tube. It's hard to get them into a tube, but they run forever once you do." The MTA would still build the Second Avenue Subway, with Lower Manhattan stations in the East Village, Chinatown, South Street Seaport, and the financial district. The attack only deepened Kalikow's resolve. He said, "We need more, not fewer, ways to access downtown as we begin the difficult process of rebuilding."[27]

The aftermath of September 11 highlighted how the subway had prevented the city's economy from collapsing. Despite the destruction of key transportation facilities, millions of people could still get to work every day because of the transit system's enormous capacity and flexibility. The need for another subway line along Manhattan's East Side became even clearer. Kalikow said, "We need to make people understand that mass transit functioned during this crisis, and mass-transit initiatives are imperative now." Jeff Zupan at the RPA had been trying to steer more federal transportation funds to the New York City metropolitan area for more than thirty years, and he had never seen a more favorable opinion from the rest of the country toward New York City. "It's a different world," he said.[28]

Remarkably, the attacks delayed the MTA's Second Avenue subway planning efforts by only a few weeks, and on October 11, the MTA submitted an application to the FTA so that it could begin preliminary engineering.[29]

DESIGNING A SUBWAY FOR THE TWENTY-FIRST CENTURY

Mysore Nagaraja, NYC Transit's senior vice president, would be responsible for the engineering, design, and construction of the new subway line. In 1985, the Indian-born engineer was one of the first people the MTA had ever hired specifically to manage a capital project, because the authority wanted to implement a professional project management system to effectively manage its first five-year capital program. Nagaraja learned about NYC Transit's inefficiencies on his very first project—rehabilitating the Lexington Avenue line's tracks, tunnels, pump rooms, and fan plants. Because the line had so many riders, NYC Transit would shut down service only between eleven thirty at night and five o'clock in the morning. The problem was that by the time the tracks were fully cleared and the workers were in position, they could work for only three and a half to four hours. Meanwhile, union rules required that the workers get paid for eight hours of work plus a bonus for late-night shift work.[30]

Nagaraja developed project management procedures that helped engineers manage project costs and schedules and allowed NYC Transit to avoid lingering contract disputes after construction work was completed. As he moved up the organizational ladder, some engineers protested having to work for the MTA's first high-ranking Asian American. Nagaraja was different from the other executives. He had not played stickball on the city's streets, ridden the subways to Coney Island in the summer, or attended one of the city's engineering colleges. Nagaraja was not big and gruff; he spoke with an unusual accent and talked about the benefits of collaborating, not arguing, with contractors.[31]

Nagaraja's staff managed a competitive bidding process to select the consultants who would design and engineer the Second Avenue subway. They recommended DMJM Harris/Arup, a joint venture of three firms and twenty subconsultants. Nagaraja appreciated the team's expertise and willingness to work collaboratively. Lee Sander, the former city transportation commissioner who had started the Empire State Transportation Alliance and advocated for the Second Avenue subway, was one of the joint venture's leaders. Sander had worked for more than a year putting together the team that secured the engineering contract.[32]

The project was more than just a job for many of the firms and their staffs. The opportunity to design one of the world's most notable infrastructure projects was irresistible. The consultants brought in tunneling and subway construction experts from around the world, many of whom had spent years building other megaprojects, including new subway lines in London, Puerto Rico, Singapore, and Bangkok. The consulting team included local experts like Ed Plotkin, a tunneling engineer who was excited to work on the Second Avenue subway for the second time in his career. In the early 1970s, he had walked through the basement of nearly every building along the route to determine whether it needed to be shored up during the subway's construction. He knew the location of every underground stream, and the political and logistical challenges of building a tunnel in Manhattan. He also knew whom to call at the city agencies and utility companies to get information and necessary approvals.[33]

One of the design team's leaders, Sheldon Fialkoff, also had worked on the Second Avenue subway in the early 1970s. As an MTA planner, he later convinced federal officials not to take back the funding they had provided to build the East Harlem and Chinatown tunnel segments by telling them the MTA was not abandoning the Second Avenue subway, but rather "putting it to sleep." The consultants also brought in none other than the seventy-seven-year-old Bob Olmsted, who had developed the 1968 subway expansion plan. He gave the team invaluable insight about integrating the new subway line into the existing system.[34]

Three months after the September 11 attacks, the MTA board affirmed its commitment to the Second Avenue subway by approving Nagaraja's request to award a $200 million engineering contract to design the new subway. The consulting team leased space on Exchange Place, a short walk from the World Trade Center, becoming the first major private tenant to locate in Lower Manhattan since September 11. At its peak in 2003, the office had close to three hundred people working on various elements of the new subway line. Members of Nagaraja's staff shared office space with the consulting engineers who were preparing the designs. Nagaraja wanted them to work closely together because the consultants knew more about building a new subway line, while NYC Transit's engineers had a far better understanding of how to operate and maintain one.[35]

The Second Avenue subway design team did not have to look far to see what could happen when designers failed to account for maintenance requirements. Less than eight miles away, New Jersey Transit was opening a new $700 million train station in Secaucus with a seventy-five-foot-high ceiling in its rotunda. When some light bulbs on the ceiling had to be changed for the first time, the engineers realized that the only way to reach the fixtures was to cut a hole in the roof and hoist a crane into the station. It took them two weeks and thousands of dollars to change the bulbs.[36]

Nagaraja did not want the Second Avenue subway to be a place for experimentation. He wanted practical elements that had been proven to be reliable. The new subway line would be ultramodern by New York City subway standards, but it was not going to be the first place to try something out. When someone had an idea about lighting or escalators or waterproofing, one of the first questions that was asked was whether it had worked somewhere else.[37]

New York City's subway riders were accustomed to trudging down dimly lit, steep, and crowded steps. They waited for trains on narrow platforms with low ceilings that were punctuated with support columns often spaced only fourteen feet apart. The designers of the Second Avenue subway could not and would not replicate early twentieth-century stations' approach to safety and aesthetics. Likewise, the planners and engineers could not take the 1970s designs for the Second Avenue subway off their dusty shelves because NYC Transit needed to meet much tougher building standards and the engineers could take advantage of new construction techniques.

If a fire occurred in one of the existing subway stations or tunnels, large fans were supposed to send smoke up through the metal grates in the city's sidewalks. New York City's thirty-nine thousand subway grates were sometimes referred to as "Marilyn Monroe grates" because of the iconic film scene in which Monroe stood on top of one as a passing train blew her dress up. Grates were no longer acceptable for a new subway because they allowed heavy rains to flood the subway tunnels and destroy equipment. More importantly, a match dropped down a grate or an idling truck spewing fumes could endanger people below. Working in Lower Manhattan right after 9/11, the designers were very sensitive to the potential for another terrorist attack.[38]

Instead of grates, each new station would have at least two ventilation buildings, about four to five stories tall, one to bring in fresh air and the other to exhaust the stale air. The ventilation system would include an air-cooling component designed to lower temperatures on the platforms during hot summer days. No one had to twist the engineers' arms to incorporate this feature. Their office was a five-minute walk from the Lexington Avenue line's Fulton Street subway station, where on summer days, the temperatures would sometimes exceed one hundred degrees.[39]

To accommodate passengers in wheelchairs, the new stations would have elevators and the platforms would be more than twenty-eight feet wide, four times wider than platforms at some of the older subway stations. To meet fire regulations, the stations were designed so that passengers getting off a train could clear the platform within forty-five seconds. That was a novel concept for anyone who had ever waited five minutes to get off a Penn Station railroad platform during rush hour.[40]

Because the new stations would have mezzanines to enhance passenger flow, and platforms without columns, they would not look like New York's usual dingy, claustrophobia-inducing stations. They would not sound the same either. Acoustic engineers designed the public address system so that announcements would be clearer, and both the ceilings and the track bed were designed to absorb the sounds from trains. The chief architect, Kenneth Griffin, wanted a "strong, timeless architecture" that would stand up over the decades. He was trying to avoid features that dated stations, such as the orange tile at Bowling Green. The Second Avenue stations would have white wall tiles along with stainless-steel and granite surfaces. Griffin said, "It was a decision I made early to have this light color, a sharp crisp space, and the natural concrete overhead."[41]

Mysore Nagaraja had the designers work early on with the director of the MTA's arts department. They would try to prominently feature work by artists in locations where it would be easy to maintain and where lingering passengers would not block traffic. Nagaraja also sneaked a little more money into the budget for artwork than the MTA typically allotted.[42]

Tunneling technology had come a long way in thirty years. In the 1970s, the Second Avenue subway tunnels were built using the cut-and-cover method, as well as by drilling holes through rocks and then using explosives to create larger holes. In the early 2000s, those two techniques would still be used, but a new method was now available: tunnel-boring machines that could drill through rock deep below the surface. Using a tunnel-boring machine might be more expensive than cut and cover, but it had distinct advantages. By tunneling deep below the street, construction workers were less likely to weaken the foundations of nearby buildings and disrupt water, electricity, television, phone, and internet services. Compared to cut and cover, a boring machine would be much less disturbing to the people who lived and worked on Second Avenue. That was important to the engineering consultants because they wanted to maintain community support for the project. They were well aware of how community opposition could stall or even halt a megaproject's construction.[43]

The decision to build the tunnels deeper than New York's existing subway lines added costs to other aspects of the design. Deeper stations would be more expensive to build and would require a more complex ventilation system, as well as long escalators to allow prompt and safe emergency egress. NYC Transit officials hated escalators because they were expensive to operate, inspect, and maintain. They also frequently broke down and were associated with numerous customer injuries. New York's older subway stations were just a single flight of stairs below the sidewalk. Some of the Second Avenue subway stations, though, would be almost one hundred feet, or ten stories, below the street. The 96th Street station would be only about forty-two feet deep, however, because it had to connect with the shallow subway tunnels in East Harlem that were built in the 1970s.[44]

The MTA would need to acquire private property to build and operate the new subway. While entrances at most of the existing subway stations were located on sidewalks, the new entrances would be so wide that they could not fit on the sidewalk without blocking pedestrian traffic. Because the stations were so deep, escalator shafts descending to the station mezzanine level would have to be built under numerous residential and commercial buildings. The MTA would also need to knock down some buildings so that it could build entrances, ventilation towers, emergency exits, and power substations.[45]

The MTA was fortunate that it had some properties it could use, because in 1974 the city started requiring property owners near potential Second Avenue stations to provide easements into the subway from new buildings and public plazas. As a state authority, the MTA also had the power of eminent domain, so it could acquire property from private owners as long as it paid fair market value. To avoid the need to raze small tenement buildings, the design team usually targeted portions of the ground floors in large modern apartment buildings.[46]

The team agonized and had endless discussions about how deep was too deep, how to minimize property takings, and what buildings were at risk of collapsing during construction. Designers had to prioritize one goal over another. For example, officials at NYC Transit's operations department wanted more than two tracks at certain stations, so that a disabled train could be bypassed. Engineers, however, were concerned about the risks and costs associated with building a station wide enough for a third track. Since platforms had to be wide enough to accommodate wheelchairs, a third track would require stations to extend underneath tall apartment buildings, potentially jeopardizing their foundations.[47]

The design team was torn between having one or two entrances at each station. An entrance at each end of the station would provide better access, but would cost more to build than one central entrance. The best choice, the team realized, would be to have a mix, with some stations having one entrance and others having two. This would encourage passengers to spread out along the entire ten-car train rather than cluster in the middle or the ends. The team members also had different perspectives regarding the construction schedule. Construction would be faster and cheaper if the workers could excavate materials and build the line during both day and night. But NYC Transit's community affairs office was adamant that everyone who lived along the route deserved a good night's sleep.[48]

Representatives from all of the relevant NYC Transit divisions came in for weekly meetings where they discussed, debated, and collaborated on design elements. They were curious and excited about the design process since very few of them had ever worked on the design of a new subway line. Each division gave the designers a list of requirements for the new line. The engineers tried to accommodate requests by integrating various design elements, such as combining the ventilation towers, emergency stairways, and utilities into ancillary buildings at each station.

The designers could not make everyone happy, though. For example, the Infrastructure Division said it needed workshops at the 72nd Street station with grinders, drill presses, lathes, and workbenches to maintain and repair elevators and escalators. The division also requested office space with six desks, six chairs, three coat racks, two fax machines, and telephone lines for voice, data, and faxes. Even though the workers who maintain elevators and escalators might not entertain much, the Infrastructure Division's representatives said they needed seven chairs in their office for visitors. The extraordinary challenge the designers faced was that six other divisions in NYC Transit's sprawling bureaucracy submitted their own equally detailed and extensive list of employee facilities for the same station.[49]

Sometimes the consultants needed one answer from NYC Transit but received conflicting ones. With some issues taking up to eighteen months to resolve, the engineering team set up a committee of NYC Transit executives to resolve disputes. Mysore Nagaraja found himself spending much of his time managing their expectations.[50]

In 2002, plans for the full-length subway were shaping up. The line would have sixteen stations along the East Side, with potential connections to other subway lines at five of them. The stations were in similar locations to those in the 1970s plan, except for one addition. Just as MTA chair William Ronan had added a stop at 96th Street in the 1970s because of community pressure, Peter Kalikow added a stop at 116th Street, in the heart of East Harlem.

OUTSMARTING THE FEDS

In 2001, the MTA estimated that the 8.5-mile Second Avenue subway line would cost approximately $16.8 billion, and that once construction started in 2004, it would be completed by 2020. The MTA released that information to the public. But the MTA did not reveal that completing construction by 2020 was a fantasy given the existing system's needs and the authority's high levels of debt.[51]

At least the cost estimators did not try to hide costs, as Ronan did in the late 1960s. Nagaraja's estimates included the cost of stations, subway cars, and all the components that allowed trains to move rapidly and safely. Following federal guidelines, the cost estimates included a contingency amount for unforeseen circumstances and anticipated inflation through 2020. The estimates also included over $2 billion in "soft costs" that were needed to design the subway, manage the project, acquire real estate, and purchase insurance. Even if the engineering team wanted to fudge the numbers, it would have been hard to get away with. As part of the New Starts process, FTA officials in Washington carefully reviewed the MTA's cost estimates. Congress did not want to repeat the problems of the Big Dig, a $13.6 billion highway project underway in Boston that had been initially estimated to cost $2.8 billion.[52]

In 2001 and 2002, the MTA submitted project and financial data to the FTA and waited for the New Starts team in Washington to evaluate its Second Avenue subway proposal. Until the MTA signed a final grant agreement with the FTA, the authority would have to spend a couple of million dollars every year, updating information about its financial capacity and its proposed project. Among their other tasks, planners needed to regularly update the estimates of how many people would ride the Second Avenue subway. Numerous factors, such as census data and the city's employment forecasts, affected these estimates. The computer model used to estimate how many New Yorkers would travel via various modes was sensitive to even relatively minor changes. For instance, Cafiero's team lowered its estimate for the number of riders who would use the 96th Street station when engineers realized that an average passenger would need sixty seconds to exit the station rather than forty-eight seconds.[53]

While MTA officials were honest about their ridership estimates, they were not transparent about their expected funding shortfalls; otherwise they would not have been able to obtain New Starts funding. In an internal MTA email, one MTA official wrote, "We cannot show out-year gaps because they get exponentially inflated and would show an untenable financial situation in 2023. The feds would give us an unrecommended if we showed them the model with the gaps."[54]

Although federal officials recognized the Second Avenue subway's benefits, the FTA gave the MTA some bad news in 2002 and 2003. The $16.8 billion project would not be cost effective. Moreover, the MTA was asking for nearly half of all the New Starts funds that were available for the entire country. The two most important factors that the FTA used to calculate a project's cost effectiveness were the number of expected *new* transit riders and the estimated cost. Neither factor favored the Second Avenue subway. Most of the subway riders would not be new transit riders, but rather passengers who had previously taken the Lexington Avenue subway line. Furthermore, the new subway line's construction cost was seventy times that of most of the other projects proposed for New Starts funding.[55]

After considering various ways to improve their score, the MTA's planners and executives came up with three promising ideas: change the FTA's scoring system, slash the project's costs, and ask for less money.[56]

The FTA had developed a cost-effectiveness measurement so complicated that the perception at the FTA and the MTA, and in much of the transportation consulting world, was that only one team outside the FTA really understood it. The MTA hired the leader of that team, Bill Woodford, a Virginia-based consultant who had a close working relationship with federal officials. Woodford was in the perfect position to help improve the Second Avenue subway's scoring because at the same time that he was consulting for the MTA, he was also working for the FTA's New Starts team helping them improve their ridership forecasting and project evaluation process.[57]

When Woodford talked to the FTA's Jim Ryan about the benefits of the Second Avenue subway, Ryan responded, "You don't have to give me a song and dance." Ryan explained that on a recent visit to New York City, he and his wife had tried to take the Lexington Avenue subway at Grand Central. The train was so crowded that only one of them was able to get onboard. The two of them frantically waved to each other as the train pulled away. With Woodford's help, the MTA successfully convinced FTA officials to change the cost-effectiveness measurement so that it would incorporate the benefits of alleviating crowding on existing subway lines. Instead of looking only at the number of new transit riders, the FTA agreed to also consider the benefits of reducing existing transit riders' walk times, wait times, ride times, and number of transfers.[58]

The second idea to improve the new subway's cost-effectiveness rating was to slash the project's cost by separating the subway's construction period into distinct phases. Selecting those phases was a delicate exercise because Kalikow did not want anyone to think the MTA was just building a stubway. In addition to the political considerations, Kalikow also had to consider financial, logistical, engineering, and operational factors.[59]

Nagaraja's team determined that the fastest and least expensive option would be to construct the entire subway line, simultaneously, from 125th Street in East Harlem to Hanover Square in Lower Manhattan. But this was not practical because, with so many other major construction projects underway in the region, the MTA might not be able to find enough qualified contractors, workers, and supplies. Building the entire subway at once was not financially feasible either, because the MTA would have to obtain $13 billion in a single five-year capital program in order to complete construction in nine years. The engineers recommended against beginning construction in either Lower Manhattan or East Harlem, because NYC Transit would not be able to operate train service until a track connection was made with the existing 63rd Street subway tunnel.

Kalikow did not have to be reminded of what happened to the tunnels under Second Avenue in the 1970s when William Ronan started construction simultaneously in East Harlem, the East Village, and Chinatown. Clearly, the best option was to go back to the recommendation made by the MTA's Bob Olmsted in the 1970s. That was the same "brilliant idea" that NYC Transit's planners had in the late 1980s, and the same course of action that MTA's executives had selected in the 1999 proposal that was dubbed the stubway. Based on ridership and cost estimates, Mysore Nagaraja and Peter Cafiero determined that starting at 63rd Street and working north up to 125th Street would most effectively alleviate congestion on the Lexington Avenue line and provide the biggest bang for the buck.[60]

Nagaraja's consultants prepared a construction timetable that split the entire project into four phases, each of which would cost less than $5 billion. That figure was similar to the expected cost of the Long Island Rail Road's connection to Grand Central Terminal. It was also an amount that was not expected to overwhelm future capital programs. With construction of the entire line expected to take between fourteen and sixteen years, the completion of each phase would demonstrate success to the public and help maintain support from elected officials and community groups. Building in distinct phases would also help ensure that work on a segment, once started, could be completed and made operational, without the MTA running out of money.

Kalikow agreed with Nagaraja's plan to build the Second Avenue subway in four phases, and then Governor Pataki signed off on it as well. At first MTA officials did not want to tell Speaker Silver, let alone the public, about their phasing plan. Within their offices, they coined the term "interim operating segment" to describe possible ways to phase construction. They were hoping to pin the blame for phasing on federal officials, and they got their wish in 2003 when the FTA asked them to describe how the subway would be phased and to identify the initial operating segment. The FTA did not want a repeat of the 1970s either. MTA officials were delighted because they could now tell elected officials that the FTA had told them to build the Second Avenue subway in phases.[61]

When the MTA's executive director and Nagaraja finally presented the phasing plan to Silver, he did not give them a hard time, because the MTA was accommodating his higher-priority requests. Silver, whose assembly district included the World Trade Center area, cared more about Nagaraja's plan for rebuilding Lower Manhattan's subway stations and integrating five of them into a Fulton Street Transit Center. In 2003, the plan was set for a Second Avenue subway with sixteen new stations that would be built in four distinct phases.[62]

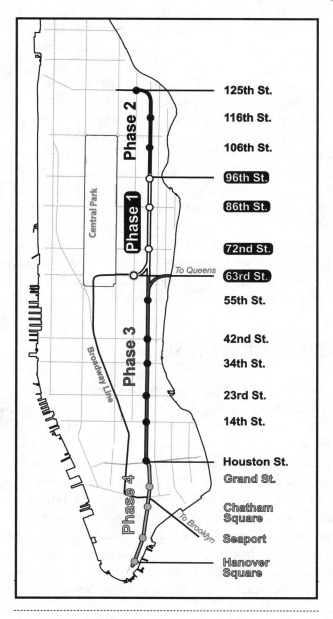

Map 7.1. Four phases of the Second Avenue subway

The first two ideas to improve the MTA's chances of obtaining New Starts funds were to revise the FTA's evaluation criteria and to phase the project. The third strategy was to ask for less money.

The MTA initially requested $8.4 billion, which was half of the total estimated cost. For advice about the New Starts process, the authority's executives turned to an old colleague, Mort Downey. Downey had left the MTA's executive suite to become deputy secretary of the US Department of Transportation, the FTA's parent organization. Although Downey was no longer at the Transportation Department, he knew how to play the New Starts game. He told Chris Boylan, the MTA's deputy executive director, "Tailor your request to the art of the possible, but push the envelope as far as you can." Downey explained that the FTA would be constrained by the total amount of funds that Congress authorized for the entire country over a six-year period, as well as the amount available in each fiscal year. After reviewing the FTA's budget and the Second Avenue subway's competition, he suggested that the MTA ask for $1.3 billion, which was one-third of the estimated cost for the first phase.[63]

The MTA's three-pronged strategy—changing the New Starts evaluation criteria, phasing the project, and asking for less money—would prove to be successful. In 2005, the FTA determined that the MTA's request for one-third of the cost of the first phase of the Second Avenue subway would be one of the most cost-effective New Starts projects in the entire country.[64]

AN EXASPERATING EXERCISE

Between 2001 and 2003, Peter Cafiero's planning team worked closely with Nagaraja's engineering team to identify all of the potential environmental impacts of the new subway line. Federal regulators did not want the public to be surprised when construction started or when the first train entered a Second Avenue subway station. The federal requirements for disclosing information had become much more onerous over time. In the 1970s, the MTA submitted dozens of pages of materials to federal transportation officials. In the 2000s, the MTA had to prepare thousands of pages of data and analyses that disclosed all potential adverse impacts. Construction would be disruptive for people living, working, and traveling along Second Avenue. The machinery would be noisy, contaminated materials uncovered, trees cut down, parks closed, businesses hurt, sidewalks narrowed, and half the width of Second Avenue closed to traffic.

Conducting the environmental analysis was costly and time consuming, but it did achieve one of its primary goals. Environmental issues were carefully considered during the design process, and the designers modified their plans when they learned about potential impacts. For example, the route south of Houston Street was modified so the subway line would be built under Forsyth Street rather than Chrystie Street. This choice was made to minimize impacts to the seven-block-long Sara D. Roosevelt Park and reduce the risk of running into long-forgotten human remains in Lower East Side burial grounds.[65]

What might seem like bureaucratic regulations run amok could be critically important. For instance, the engineers had to estimate aboveground vibration levels associated with tunnel-boring machines, even though the vibrations would be virtually imperceptible. Doctors at the New York Eye and Ear Infirmary on Second Avenue certainly appreciated the analysis, though, because they performed more than twenty thousand annual microsurgical procedures that were extremely sensitive to external vibrations.[66]

The planning and design teams were still undecided about certain construction and operational questions. In those cases, the environmental impact statement had to describe the potential impacts of each alternative under consideration. For example, to provide Second Avenue subway service, NYC Transit would need to accommodate twenty-five subway trains, each ten cars long, at a location where trains could be stored and workers could perform inspections and routine maintenance. Rather than build a new facility, the planners determined that capacity could be added at existing rail yards and maintenance shops at Coney Island, 207th Street, or the northern Bronx.[67]

The environmental analysis conducted for each of these three options was more extensive than the analysis conducted for the entire Second Avenue subway in the early 1970s. The planners analyzed whether contaminated materials would be released during construction, and whether any important public views or vistas would be harmed. They reviewed archeological documents to determine whether construction was likely to uncover any burial sites or tools used by Native Americans. They also had to gauge the effects of construction on buildings that were eligible for listing on the state and national Registers of Historic Places. And, after wading through the Coney Island Creek, environmental scientists assessed potential impacts to the plants and animals living near the Coney Island yard.[68]

Needless to say, the MTA's planners and attorneys often found the regulatory process exasperating, such as when they were asked to write both more and less. At one June 2002 meeting, FTA officials told Cafiero's team to prepare an environmental impact statement that was less than 300 pages long because federal regulations indicated that the impact statement "shall normally be less than 150 pages and for proposals of unusual scope or complexity shall normally be less than 300 pages." The MTA's environmental lawyers were taken aback by the request because federal courts required preparers to take a "hard look" at all the issues; otherwise a federal judge could bar the FTA from funding a project. In the past, judges had delayed or killed numerous transportation projects, most notably New York's Westway, because the environmental reviews were deemed to be insufficient. The MTA and FTA compromised on the length by moving much of the text to the appendices. When completed, the environmental impact statement was over 1,500 pages long, and the cost to print a copy of each document, with its color maps and long tables, was $174.[69]

The MTA planners released the environmental impact statement in March 2003 and two months later held a hearing in Lower Manhattan to highlight their findings and solicit public comments. Even though the MTA identified major inconveniences and significant disruptions, the public still supported building a Second Avenue subway. Or at least the approximately two hundred people who showed up for the public meeting did.

In an article titled "No Second Thoughts on Subway," a *Daily News* reporter wrote, "The pain will be worth the gain. That was the overwhelming consensus of transit advocates, politicians and subway riders who spoke out yesterday at the first public hearing on the long-planned Second Avenue subway." US congressman Anthony Weiner said, "This is going to be dusty. There are going to be people who are going to have their dishes shaken clear off their cabinet through part of this work. But at the end of the day I think we really can't live without the Second Avenue subway much longer."[70]

The subway's biggest supporters, though, were concerned about the MTA's proposed phasing plan. Representative Carolyn Maloney said, "It makes sense to begin building the lower portions of the subway first, to ensure that the Downtown community reaps the greatest possible benefits from the subway and to emphasize the subway's status as a component of the Lower Manhattan redevelopment project." The RPA's Jeff Zupan argued that the MTA needed to extend the subway to Brooklyn and the Bronx. He was concerned, rightly so, that the MTA would provide enough funds only for the portion from 125th Street to 63rd Street.[71]

Even though the environmental document explained that the MTA needed to purchase private property, this was not a cause of much concern at the meeting. Residents along the East Side continued supporting the Second

Avenue subway, even as helicopters conducted low-altitude aerial surveys and crews drilled over six hundred holes in the ground to determine subsurface conditions and potential soil contamination.[72]

Six months later, however, after the MTA had revealed the exact addresses where it planned on acquiring property, no one could say the Second Avenue subway had widespread community support. The Upper East Side community board sponsored a forum in September 2003 where about three hundred residents and business owners came to learn more about the project. The next day's headlines in the *New York Post* and *Daily News* declared, "E. Siders Rail against Subway Plan," and, "2nd Thoughts on 2nd Ave. Line."[73]

Attendees were angry to learn that the community board had been supporting the subway project for the past eight years but many residents were only just learning about it. Carol Ferrante, president of a co-op board on East 69th Street, said that none of her neighbors objected to the subway until they found out that an entrance was slated to be built in their building. Doron Gopstein, who lived in a twenty-one-story luxury high-rise with 695 apartments, said, "For the people who live on Second Avenue, the next five, ten, fifteen years will be a disaster." Gopstein and his neighbors would plead with the MTA, unsuccessfully, for the next ten years to move the entrance that was proposed to be built in their building.[74]

Some attendees felt the MTA did not do its homework before deciding on the station entrance locations. In response, Peter Cafiero carefully explained how the MTA had selected them. He was proud of the thorough analysis his team had conducted. Where possible, station entrances were located on corners because they would be easier to access from both Second Avenue and crosstown streets, and would discourage people from crossing in the middle of a street. Cafiero's computer models of pedestrian activity helped determine whether entrances should be located on the western or eastern side of the avenue. The planners and engineers looked for locations where they could fit both escalators and stairs, preferably in open plaza areas or where the MTA had existing easements.[75]

Instead of appeasing the crowd, Cafiero's detailed responses only heightened their concerns. Now many of the attendees thought the MTA had done so much homework that the details were a fait accompli. Although Cafiero had tried to minimize the number of people who would have to move, he might have saved the MTA time, money, and trouble if he had proposed knocking down some of the older, smaller, and more fragile tenement buildings lining Second Avenue rather than trying to take portions of buildings that contained hundreds of apartments.[76]

Nine years after NYC Transit's planners officially kicked off their alternatives analysis, the planning stage of the Second Avenue subway finally ended in April 2004 when the FTA signed off on the final environmental impact statement. A few weeks later, the MTA board authorized the MTA Capital Construction Company to seek proposals from firms to finalize the design and build the subway's first phase. The MTA indicated that it would begin construction by the end of the year, so that it could complete the first phase by 2011 and the entire line with sixteen stations by 2020.[77]

Kalikow had recently set up Capital Construction to build the MTA's megaprojects, including the Second Avenue subway, the Long Island Rail Road's connection to Grand Central, and the Fulton Street Transit Center in Lower Manhattan. Kalikow appointed Mysore Nagaraja as its first president, and Nagaraja shifted the Second Avenue subway's engineering team to the new MTA agency.

Although Kalikow proudly announced that the MTA was seeking proposals to build the new subway line, he did not intend to actually begin construction until he secured funding from Albany and Washington. Katie Lapp, the MTA's executive director, said in April 2004, "We need to make our needs known. It's up to elected officials to figure out how to provide those needs whether through dedicated taxes or other sources." One of the leaders of the DMJM Harris/Arup consulting team said the engineers were "working at 30 yard dash speed" through 2004; then everything stopped and they had to lay people off while waiting for the MTA to make a decision on whether the project would move forward with final design and construction. To keep the project team together and maintain momentum, Nagaraja extended the project's preliminary engineering stage.[78]

The Second Avenue subway was not the only megaproject seeking funding and political support. In 2004, it was fending off challengers from all across the metropolitan area.

BATTLING OVER MEGAPROJECTS

The idea of building a subway under Second Avenue had faced competition ever since it was first considered in the early 1900s. In the 1930s, Second Avenue lost out to Sixth and Eighth Avenues because those streets were closer to Manhattan's commercial center. In the 1950s and 1960s, the city expanded its highway network, not its transit system. In the 1970s, Mayor Abe Beame prioritized maintaining the thirty-five-cent fare over completing any portion of the Second Avenue subway, and in the 1990s, the state's leaders emphasized transit projects that benefited suburban commuters.

The Second Avenue subway faced new competitors in 2004. In private meetings, New York City mayor Michael Bloomberg disparaged the Second Avenue subway plan because the line would not have separate local and express stops. The mayor thought it was more important for the MTA to extend the number 7 subway line from Times Square to 11th Avenue to help transform Manhattan's far West Side from an area characterized by low-rise manufacturing and warehouse facilities into a new mixed-use neighborhood with office and residential skyscrapers. As part of Bloomberg's vision for the neighborhood, the state would expand its convention center and the New York Jets would build a football stadium that could be used for convention space and the 2012 Olympics.[79]

Bloomberg was in a hurry to start construction of the number 7 subway extension before the International Olympic Committee selected a city in 2005 to host the Olympics. Although he wanted the MTA to help pay for the subway work, he was not interested in using New Starts funding because he did not want to get tied up in the onerous federal approval process. After all, he wanted the 2012 Olympics, not the 2020 Olympics.[80]

In 2004, the state and city were still debating multibillion-dollar plans for revitalizing Lower Manhattan. Insurance proceeds and special congressional funding were expected to pay for a new PATH station and improve pedestrian circulation between subway lines at the new Fulton Street Transit Center. Although both of these projects would vastly improve passenger amenities, they would not provide any new train services.[81]

Many of Lower Manhattan's business leaders and property owners were convinced that to regain its former glory, the neighborhood needed better transit access. One of their proposals was to extend the PATH train to Newark Airport. This would give Lower Manhattan direct rail access to an airport, something that Midtown Manhattan did not have. An even higher transportation priority for them was a new "Rail Link" that would connect Lower Manhattan with Kennedy Airport and Long Island. This $6 billion project had strong support from Pataki, Bloomberg, Silver, and New York's senior US senator, Chuck Schumer. MTA officials, however, were concerned that the Rail Link would divert funds from the Second Avenue subway and the Long Island Rail Road connection to Grand Central Terminal.[82]

Another initiative on the drawing boards was a new railroad tunnel under the Hudson River connecting New Jersey with Penn Station in Midtown

Manhattan. To pay for it, New Jersey Transit had secured Port Authority funds and was on its way to obtaining the largest federal New Starts grant ever awarded. Pataki, though, was not interested in helping to pay for this project, because he had a different trans-Hudson priority: he wanted to replace the three-mile-long Tappan Zee Bridge and build a rail line on the new span.[83]

US congressman Jerrold Nadler was pushing for a New York City rail freight tunnel under the Hudson River because the closest freight train crossing was about 140 miles north of the city's harbor. This proposal had been discussed, off and on, since the nineteenth century. Nadler was convinced that a freight tunnel would help bring down the cost of goods, reduce the city's reliance on trucks, improve air quality, enhance local manufacturers' competitiveness, and resurrect Brooklyn's ports. As New York City's only member of the House Transportation Committee, he appeared to be well positioned to obtain funding for the project.[84]

Another popular project involved converting the Farley Post Office building across from Penn Station into a new home for Amtrak. Rather than navigate crowded and confusing underground passageways, Amtrak customers would be able to enter and leave the city via a grand train hall with a skylighted atrium. Megaproject ideas never seem to completely disappear, although one had fallen off the radar. Giuliani's push in the 1990s to extend a subway line to LaGuardia Airport had succumbed to community opposition in Queens.[85]

With so many valuable and important projects on the table, totaling more than $50 billion, it was not clear which ones would get built and how they would be funded. Some elected officials raised false expectations. Chuck Schumer, for instance, promoted the MTA's projects, Bloomberg's subway extension, Nadler's project, the Lower Manhattan Rail Link, Amtrak's new station, and New Jersey Transit's tunnel, as well as one more—a direct rail connection between Penn Station and Grand Central Terminal. The senator said, "I believe that, if we all work together, we can succeed in this unique moment in securing the funding needed to build all these important transportation projects."[86]

Some New Yorkers thought the private sector could save the day. A *New York Post* reporter suggested that the only way the Second Avenue subway would ever get completed would be if the real estate developer Donald Trump built it. After Pataki proposed giving the private sector the opportunity to build and operate transportation facilities, Assemblyman Richard Brodsky said, "Do we really want to have Donald Trump build the Second Avenue subway, and charge tolls for it?"[87]

The Partnership for New York City, an influential civic organization rep-resenting business leaders, saw a clear need for prioritization. Its president, Kathryn Wylde, said, "Unless we set a few priorities and relatively short-term priorities and allocate enough money to actually get them done, you'll have lots of planning and little getting done." The RPA's president, Bob Yaro, had similar thoughts. He warned, "The danger is that we end up in a traditional New York blood vendetta instead of a rational discussion. We could end up with nothing if we get bogged down in that kind of warfare."[88]

Both the Partnership and the RPA were highly respected and led by members of the business community. But they had different priorities, partly because the Partnership for New York City focused on the city while the RPA had a regional perspective. Another difference was that the Partnership talked about what the city's needs would be for the next fifty years, while the RPA had an even longer planning horizon.

Wylde thought that politics and the preferences of the transportation agencies were determining the region's priorities. She wanted the city and state to consider the economic return of the various projects under consideration, rather than focusing on the needs of the transit riders and the transportation system. In 2003, the Partnership hired consultants to evaluate and prioritize the proposed megaprojects. They had to develop their own approach to evalu-ating economic impacts because there was no standard way of measuring them. The team's analysis showed that the most valuable projects would be those that strengthened existing transportation hubs, because those were the locations most desirable for the city's employers and their employees.[89]

In the Partnership's final report, the highest-priority projects were rebuild-ing Lower Manhattan's infrastructure, extending the number 7 subway line, and moving Amtrak's station to the Farley Post Office building across from Penn Station. Wylde recalls that although extending the number 7 line would not enhance an existing hub, it was given top priority because Deputy Mayor Dan Doctoroff, the city's leading figure in redeveloping the far West Side and planning the Olympics, "put his finger on the scale." Doctoroff referred to the Second Avenue subway as "a silly little spur that doesn't generate anything other than some convenience for people who are perfectly happy to live where they lived before."[90]

The Second Avenue subway did not fare well because according to the Partnership's analysis, the project's costs exceeded its expected economic devel-opment benefits. This news was not well received by the Second Avenue sub-way's advocates. The RPA immediately prepared its own analysis that rebutted

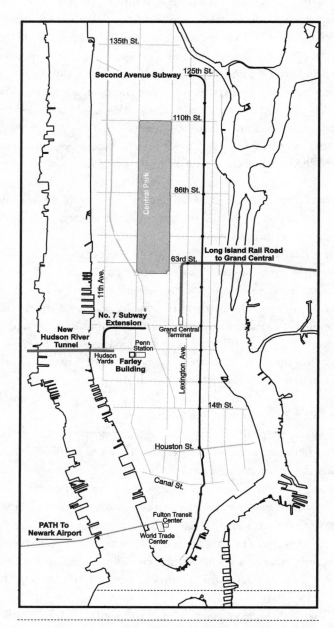

Map 7.2. Projects compared by the Partnership for New York City in 2003

the Partnership's report and demonstrated how the Second Avenue subway's benefits would, in fact, greatly exceed its costs.[91]

Bitterness would linger for years between the Partnership and the RPA over the conflicting reports and the dueling press conferences. The Second Avenue subway advocates thought the Partnership did not understand the project's benefits and deliberately tried to kill it. Those who performed the Partnership's analysis were annoyed by the criticism their report received, because no one ever came up with a better way to compare all of the different projects. In fact, the Partnership was not trying to kill the Second Avenue subway. Wylde had a different target in mind: she was trying to eliminate the Lower Manhattan Rail Link, because she was afraid it would divert resources from building the Fulton Street Transit Center.[92]

Despite attempts by the Partnership and the RPA, there was simply no definitive unbiased way to compare these types of projects. It was impossible to objectively quantify certain benefits, such as reducing crowding, cooling a station on a hot summer day, or providing service along Second Avenue if the Lexington Avenue line had to be shut down for an extended period of time. Planners did not have crystal balls that could predict all the factors that would need to be considered, including future employment, population, travel patterns, real estate values, and technological innovations. Every methodology had its flaws and relied on contested information, suspect data, shaky assumptions, and unreliable computer models.

Kalikow explained how decisions about megaprojects were actually made. He said, "I don't want you to think everybody goes to Peter Luger [Steakhouse] with cigars and doles this stuff out. Some of these decisions are the result of knock-down, drag-out battles with powerful, competing politicians at the table." With the mayor losing his battle to obtain MTA funds, Kalikow admitted, "I'm getting beaten up pretty good internally because I haven't taken my pants down over this No. 7 project."[93]

VOTE YES FOR TRANSPORTATION

By 2004, subway ridership had soared to levels not seen since the 1950s, and New York City was recovering from the 2001 terrorist attack, stronger than ever. The MTA's financial situation, however, was a different story. As the authority prepared for its next capital program, it faced huge debt levels and rapidly growing operating budget deficits. They were related. The MTA's

2000–2004 capital program had been a fiscal time bomb that had placed tremendous pressure on the operating budget.[94]

The MTA had become increasingly reliant on borrowing money against its future revenue rather than on funding from the state and city. The State of New York had contributed $1.8 billion for the MTA's first five-year capital program, but nothing for the 2000–2004 program. Meanwhile, successive mayors cut New York City's contributions to the MTA's capital programs. The public did not understand the MTA's predicament. A citywide survey indicated that most New Yorkers thought the MTA earned a profit on its subway service. In fact, subway riders paid only 44 percent of the authority's operating costs, with taxes and tolls making up the rest. In 2004, the fastest-growing portion of the MTA's budget was the interest expenses on its debt. The MTA's outstanding debt had skyrocketed from $9 billion in the early 1990s to nearly $20 billion by 2004, and its annual interest payments were over $800 million.[95]

To get out of this financial predicament, the authority would either have to scale back its next capital program or find new sources of revenue. Gene Russianoff, from the Straphangers Campaign, said, "Their credit card is maxed out." Civic groups like the RPA again called for tolls on the city's free East River bridges. Kalikow decided to raise fares. In 2003, the MTA had the largest fare increase in its history. The authority would raise fares again in 2005, 2008, 2009, and 2010, but this still would not be enough to accommodate what one bond rating agency called the MTA's "enormous and unending" needs.[96]

In July 2004, with the MTA's capital program expiring at the end of the year, Kalikow unveiled a $27.8 billion capital program for 2005–9. It included $2.3 billion for the Long Island Rail Road connection to Grand Central, $1.4 billion for Second Avenue, and $400 million for the Lower Manhattan Rail Link.[97]

Even though it was not true, MTA officials continued telling the public that the full-length Second Avenue subway with sixteen stations would be completed by 2020. According to the authority's internal documents, though, the MTA would be able to meet that deadline only if it allocated more than $5 billion for the project in its next capital program. By asking for only $1.4 billion, the MTA was quietly extending the completion date by at least five years. But adding a few years to the schedule was not the MTA's biggest concern.[98]

By 2004, the MTA had again fallen behind schedule restoring the subway's infrastructure. The subway's signals, ventilation systems, and subway stations were not expected to be in a state of good repair for at least twenty more years. Moreover, Kalikow's proposed capital program had a funding gap of more than $16 billion, even though he made a number of overly optimistic assumptions about obtaining federal funds. To fill this gap, he proposed that the state increase business, real estate, motor vehicle, and fuel taxes to generate about $850 million per year. Unless the state raised taxes, Kalikow warned, the MTA might have to sacrifice the Second Avenue subway.[99]

In December 2004, the Capital Program Review Board rejected the MTA's proposed program. Pataki wanted to cut the MTA's request by one-third, and he was not interested in raising any taxes. Kalikow was disappointed but not surprised. He said about the governor, "I know his abhorrence of taxes."[100]

During his tenure as MTA chair, Virgil Conway had cared more about the governor's political ambitions than the MTA's long-term problems. Kalikow also had a close relationship with Pataki, but in 2005 he was more concerned with his own legacy than the governor's. The longer he served as chair, the more Kalikow became a forceful advocate for improving and expanding the system. He warned that without sufficient funding, subway service would return to a level of service not seen since the early 1980s. He was prepared to drop the Second Avenue subway if he did not get enough money to maintain, restore, and upgrade the existing system. Kalikow was also prepared to resign if Albany did not approve a well-funded capital program. "I don't want to be the guy that presides over the Titanic," he told one of his aides.[101]

Kalikow spent countless hours in Albany and Washington advocating for the Second Avenue subway and the Long Island Rail Road connection to Grand Central. He lobbied legislators and threw private fundraisers for US senators who wielded influence over transportation funds. Twice he brought Senator Richard Shelby of Alabama, chair of the US Senate Appropriations Subcommittee on Transportation, to a Lexington Avenue line subway platform at rush hour so that he could understand the need for a new East Side subway line. Kalikow said, "People in Washington think I'm some kind of nut: here's a Republican asking for mass transit money. It doesn't quite fit the mold."[102]

Just as Richard Ravitch had done in the 1980s, Kalikow lobbied the business community to support new revenue sources, and the business community in turn lobbied Albany officials. He said he had to convince Pataki "that this tax is something that the business community and the people that use the system will actually see." Kalikow said that he couldn't just "bully-pulpit" the governor. "It has to be coerced—uh, I mean cajoled."[103]

Kalikow wanted to convince state legislators that the MTA's capital program would benefit New Yorkers who did not even use the authority's services. It was not an easy task considering that some members of the state legislature lived closer to Cleveland and Detroit than to New York City. Kalikow made sure they learned that the MTA was creating jobs all across the state. For instance, it purchased lighting equipment from Buffalo, ventilation systems from Auburn, fabricated metal parts from Kingston, propulsion systems from Johnson City, and sheet metal from Utica.[104]

Since the governor would not allow the MTA chair to negotiate directly with Sheldon Silver, Kalikow asked Lee Sander to serve as his intermediary and negotiate with Silver's key staff members on the MTA's behalf. Sander was a busy man. He was negotiating the MTA's next capital program, cochairing the Empire State Transportation Alliance, and directing the transportation research center at New York University. These roles all helped him in his day job as the senior vice president of the firm designing the Second Avenue subway. Thanks to Sander, the Empire State Transportation Alliance launched a media and lobbying campaign to push state lawmakers to provide more transportation funds.[105]

The MTA also had help from Jennifer Dorn, the head of the FTA, who pressured the state's leaders to provide their share of the funds for the Second Avenue subway. She did not want the FTA to award $1.3 billion in New Starts funds for the subway unless the MTA made a firm commitment to fund the rest of the project. It would have been irresponsible of her to tie up those funds when other states were vying for them. If New York did not come up with its share of the costs soon, the New Starts funds designated for Second Avenue were likely to be diverted to fast-growing cities in Arizona, Oregon, Colorado, and Texas.[106]

In March 2005, the governor and the legislative leaders agreed on a five-year MTA capital program. The program allocated only $2.5 billion for the three expansion projects: the Long Island Rail Road connection to Grand Central, the Second Avenue subway, and the Lower Manhattan Rail Link. These funding levels, however, would be contingent on the state's voters' passing a $2.9 billion transportation bond act in November.[107]

Five years earlier, the governor and Speaker had been committed to a Second Avenue subway whether or not voters supported the 2000 bond act. That was not the case with the 2005 bond act. Kalikow said that the Second Avenue subway had little chance of progressing unless voters approved the bond issue in November. He decided to hold off on the first phase's final design and initial construction, pending the voters' decision.[108]

In 2005, transportation advocates still vividly remembered how New York State's voters had turned down the bond issue five years earlier because elected officials stayed on the sidelines and voters were not convinced the bond proceeds would directly benefit them. Stephen Morgan, a leader of the New York Roadway Improvement Coalition, an Albany-based coalition that lobbied state officials on behalf of construction firms and unions, referred to that failed referendum as a "shit show." Morgan told the governor's staff in 2005 that his group would be more than happy to lead the state's efforts to pass the bond act. The governor responded, "If you guys want to run it, be my guest." The coalition went ahead and set up a not-for-profit corporation called Vote Yes for Transportation, and Morgan led its efforts.[109]

Morgan ran a full-fledged statewide political campaign, raising $2 million from a wide array of stakeholders, including contractors and consultants who would benefit from increased transportation spending. He worked closely with a Republican state senator and a Democratic assemblyman, who coordinated the legislators' advocacy efforts. He also teamed up with Lee Sander at the Empire State Transportation Alliance, who organized the transit advocates in the New York City area.[110]

The governor and the legislative leaders all supported the bond act, and they made sure the referendum question was prominently placed in the middle of the ballot. Five years earlier it had been hard to find. The governor said the act was "fiscally responsible" and would create 120,000 jobs. The state comptroller supported the referendum, as did state attorney general Eliot Spitzer, the frontrunner to replace Pataki as governor. The mayor was especially helpful. Running for a second term, Michael Bloomberg had thousands of his campaign workers hand out cards that told voters to vote for the mayor and for "Better Subways, Buses and Roads."[111]

Unlike in 2000, the governor and legislative leaders specified the exact projects that would be funded with the bond proceeds. The long list included $450 million for the Second Avenue subway, as well as funds for projects all across the state, such as dock improvements in Oswego, two hybrid-electric buses in Poughkeepsie, and security improvements at small commercial airports upstate.[112]

The coalition hired political consultants to craft compelling messages and a polling firm to figure out where the campaign should target its media buys and distribute four hundred thousand fliers. According to Morgan, they "hammered" the state's southern tier with advertising. New Yorkers living west of the Catskill Mountains near the Pennsylvania border usually voted against bond acts, but polling data indicated the popularity of funding a local highway improvement project that was tied to the referendum.[113]

The state's two most important transportation leaders also helped. Kalikow warned that the bond measure would "make or break" the Second Avenue subway because without it, New York would lose out on New Starts funding. He promoted the bond act on the MTA's website and had subway workers put up fifteen thousand posters on buses, subways, and commuter rail cars extolling the bond act's benefits to the MTA's customers.[114]

New York State's transportation commissioner, Tom Madison, was legally restricted from asking for anyone's vote, but he was allowed to talk about why voters should support borrowing for transportation improvements. He made as many as three speeches per day to civic groups, labor organizations, chambers of commerce, and construction industry advocates. He talked about the bond act at engineering award breakfasts, rubber-chicken dinners, and media interviews—"whoever would let me come do my stump speech," he said.[115]

At Morgan's suggestion, Madison traveled to the Catskills, where he persuaded the rabbis and other leaders of an ultra-Orthodox Jewish community to support the bond act. He later recalled, "I had longstanding relationships with some of them from my time in the Governor's appointments office, where the Hasids were very active in pursuing jobs for their people." Since the community nearly always voted as a bloc, Morgan estimated that Madison's trip and follow-up brought in as many as twenty thousand votes.[116]

Although some upstate newspapers and budget watchdog groups came out against the bond act, there was little organized opposition. By a margin of 55 percent to 45 percent, voters approved the 2005 bond issue. The next day, Kalikow announced that shovels would be in the ground on Second Avenue in 2006. "It doesn't get any better than this," he said.[117]

In 2005, the stars had once again aligned for the Second Avenue subway. The economy had rebounded from the terrorist attacks and the MTA had lined up sufficient funds to begin the first phase of construction. The megaproject also had widespread political and public support, while the MTA faced minimal opposition to its proposed route, phasing plan, and station locations. A week after the bond vote, the MTA board authorized $150 million for final design and construction support services for the Second Avenue subway between 63rd and 96th Streets. Several months later, the FTA approved the MTA's request to move the project into final design, the last step before it could enter into a grant agreement.[118]

As for the projects that the Second Avenue subway competed with, New York lost out to London for the 2012 Olympics, but the MTA would extend the number 7 line to the far West Side anyway. The city paid for it by issuing bonds that would be paid back with real estate tax revenues generated by new development. In Lower Manhattan, the subways and PATH would be rebuilt and improved, while the Rail Link project would die a quiet death. The Long Island Rail Road's connections with Grand Central Terminal, the project that had long been tied to the Second Avenue subway, would move forward, albeit slowly.[119]

Future governors would dream about creating a new Penn Station, building a new rail tunnel under the Hudson River, providing rail freight access across the harbor, adding train service to the Tappan Zee Bridge, and extending rail service to LaGuardia and Newark Airports. In the meantime, the MTA was getting ready to build the Second Avenue subway. Maybe not the whole thing, but at least the southern half of a stubway.

8

Building a Subway and Unleashing the Plagues

For a decade, nearly every one of Representative Carolyn Maloney's staff meetings started with the question, "What can we do to move the Second Avenue subway along?" According to Chris Boylan, the MTA's longtime director of government relations, "Maloney made noise until people squealed. . . . Maloney hounded the crap out of the FTA and the chair of the House Transportation Committee. She did what I wish every congressman would do. I would be in her office and she would get up and say to her secretary, 'Tell the chair of the committee that I'm on my way over.' Then she'd barge into his office and say something like, 'Your staff said it couldn't happen, but it has to happen.'"[1]

In New York, Boylan schmoozed visiting members of Congress and led tours for their staffs. He wore them out visiting depots, subway stations, and tunnels. "I could have taken them around in cars or buses," he said, "but I wanted them on crowded trains and long subway rides because the medium is the message." Since the Lexington Avenue line carried more people in a single day than the population of many of the states where his visitors hailed from, the crush of people "helped them understand that we really did need the money."[2]

In Washington, DC, Maloney pressured the head of the FTA to approve the Second Avenue subway's environmental impact statement, allow the MTA to begin final design, sign a grant agreement, and then start construction. The Upper East Side Democrat also teamed up with Long Island Republicans to line up support from the rest of New York's congressional delegation. The Republicans pushed for the Long Island Rail Road connection with Grand

Central Terminal, while Maloney championed Second Avenue. Together they made sure that Congress supported the FTA's funding recommendations for the New Starts program.[3]

A united effort was important because the FTA looked at how states prioritized their transit projects. Mort Downey, the US Department of Transportation deputy secretary under President Bill Clinton, said that New York improved its chances of obtaining New Starts funding for the Second Avenue subway and the Long Island Rail Road project when the state's congressional delegation, governor, and legislature, as well as the MTA board, all indicated that these were the state's highest-priority infrastructure projects. In 2007, after the FTA approved a $1.3 billion New Starts grant for the Second Avenue subway, Maloney said, "The Second Avenue subway is now inevitable."[4]

CONSTRUCTION BEGINS, AGAIN

2007 was also a year when political power in the state shifted from New York City's suburbs back to the city, as Eliot Spitzer, an Upper East Side resident, succeeded George Pataki as governor. After the gubernatorial election, Spitzer went down to Washington to talk about his priorities—including the Second Avenue subway—with New York's congressional delegation. The members of Congress praised Spitzer for his willingness to travel to Washington. Representative Eliot Engel said, "It sends a very powerful message that he wants to be partners with us."[5]

Spitzer wanted to appoint a new MTA chair; however, Peter Kalikow vowed not to step down until he was satisfied that the Second Avenue subway was underway. To place his stamp on the authority, the governor appointed Lee Sander to run the MTA on a day-to-day basis as its chief executive officer and executive director, at an annual salary of $340,000. Spitzer trusted and deferred to Sander, who had been an early adviser to his campaign.[6] Sander had been instrumental in moving Second Avenue along in three different roles: as cochair of the Empire State Transportation Alliance, director of the transportation research center at New York University, and senior executive at the engineering firm designing the Second Avenue subway. Although Sander was skeptical about the Second Avenue subway when the Regional Plan Association had first approached him about it in the late 1990s, he had become convinced that New York could not compete with London, Shanghai, and other global cities without the new subway line. In 2007, he said, "Every time I go down to 42nd Street and Lexington and I see the hordes of people, I say to myself: how can one possibly question not having a Second Avenue subway?"[7]

In March 2007, right before the MTA signed the first construction contract for the new line, Kalikow said the project "turned from doubtful to inevitable and nobody quite knows when it happened." The next month, Spitzer, Kalikow, Sander, and Sheldon Silver led a celebration in East Harlem to start the subway's construction. They held it forty feet belowground in a Second Avenue subway tunnel segment built in the 1970s. A *New York Post* reporter called the ceremony "part groundbreaking and part curse-breaking."[8]

Alluding to the recently celebrated Passover holiday, Kalikow said, "Why is this groundbreaking different than all other groundbreakings?" Then he answered his own question: "This time, we have the money and the political will." As a matter of fact, it was more a wall breaking than a groundbreaking, because the public officials used shiny new hammers to knock down a thin cement wall that had been installed in the tunnel for the ceremony. Spitzer proclaimed, "It is necessary that we build the subway so that it not only goes down to Lower Manhattan and 125th Street, but also further north and further south." He noted that the ceremony for building a Second Avenue subway was "déjà vu all over again, all over again, all over again."[9]

Peter Cafiero, who had been promoted to NYC Transit's director of operations planning, helped the eighty-two-year-old former MTA planning director Bob Olmsted through a rectangle-shaped manhole in the sidewalk and down the steep ladder into the tunnel. Olmsted was still providing critical advice to planners, engineers, construction officials, and even Mysore Nagaraja, president of MTA Capital Construction. Olmsted had told his cardiologist, "You have to keep me alive until the Second Avenue subway opens."[10]

Cafiero later said, "There was no such thing as an original transportation idea in New York because invariably Olmsted had thought of it thirty years before." Thirty years was actually an understatement. Olmsted had published an article about the future of New York's transportation system sixty-five years before the 2007 groundbreaking. At the time of the ceremony, he was working on another one, titled "Rail Transit in New York: The Next 25 Years."[11]

While politicians patted themselves on the backs about the Second Avenue subway, Gene Russianoff worried about the MTA's future. The Straphangers Campaign leader said he would not be surprised if financing for mass transit "turns to guacamole." A newspaper columnist subsequently opined that "the city may yet be left with a runt of a line consisting of only a few stations—a stubway, as some have called it."[12]

In 2008, Sander unveiled the MTA's most ambitious expansion plan since William Ronan introduced his *Program for Action* forty years earlier. Drawing on work prepared by the Regional Plan Association (and of course Bob Olmsted), Sander outlined a building program over the next twenty-five to forty years that would take advantage of underutilized freight and commuter rail rights of way. He proposed new rail lines all across the region, including an extension of the Second Avenue subway to Brooklyn and Queens.[13]

Several months later, New York's financial institutions were hit hard by a slowdown in the nation's real estate market and defaults on home mortgages. As the economy soured, the MTA's revenues from taxes on mortgages, real estate transactions, and corporate profits plummeted. The MTA also lost the opportunity to obtain $4.5 billion for its next capital program after the state assembly rejected Mayor Bloomberg's proposal to charge drivers a fee to enter Manhattan below 86th Street.[14]

Sander scaled back not only his vision, but also the MTA's ongoing capital program by cutting funds for station renovations, signal modernization, and upgrades to pumping and ventilation equipment. The MTA continued falling behind its promise of bringing the subway system up to a state of good repair. For example, in 1992, the MTA expected that upgrades to the giant fan plants that remove smoke from subway tunnels would be completed by 2007, and signal system upgrades by 2012. By the time of the Second Avenue subway's groundbreaking, the MTA had already extended the completion date for the signal work by fifteen years and the fan plants by twenty-one years.[15]

Sander's boss was preoccupied with his own troubles. Spitzer resigned in March 2008 after he was caught on a federal wiretap arranging to meet with a prostitute at a Washington hotel. His visits to the US capital had apparently included other agenda items besides the Second Avenue subway. But neither the weak economy nor the elevation of Lieutenant Governor David Paterson (a longtime Harlem resident) to governor slowed down MTA Capital Construction's work on the first phase of the Second Avenue subway.

Mysore Nagaraja was responsible for more than building a Second Avenue subway between 96th and 63rd Streets. He was also leading the efforts to extend the number 7 train to the far West Side, rebuild subway stations in Lower Manhattan, and connect the Long Island Rail Road with Grand Central. But his MTA subsidiary needed only 130 full-time employees, because nearly all of its work was performed by consultants and contractors. This allowed Nagaraja to hire people with highly specialized skills without burdening the MTA with a large staff after the project was complete. Consulting services did not come cheap, though. The engineering firms DMJM Harris and Arup would earn more than $420 million for their work designing the new subway line, helping the MTA select contractors, inspecting materials, and then modifying designs when contractors came across unexpected site conditions.[16]

Nagaraja decided to divide the construction work for the Second Avenue subway into six separate contracts as a way to entice more firms to submit proposals. But the contracts were still too large. When MTA Capital Construction started soliciting bids, the contractors had trouble obtaining the performance and payments bonds they were required to secure. These bonds (similar to insurance policies) would guarantee that if the contractor went bankrupt, the work would still be completed and all of the subcontractors, workers, and suppliers would still be paid. To reduce the size of the contracts, Nagaraja decided to split the construction work into ten, rather than six, contracts. Although this did help increase the number of bidders, it also increased the complexity of managing and coordinating the construction of the Second Avenue subway.[17]

To coordinate the work of the design firm and ten separate construction contracts, MTA Capital Construction hired yet another firm, Parsons Brinckerhoff, as its construction manager. This firm, which had built New York's very first subway more than one hundred years earlier, assigned approximately 120 people to work on the project. The MTA also spent millions of dollars making sure the contractors and their dozens of subcontractors complied with all federal and state requirements, including those relating to civil rights, the environment, and labor. No one ever calculated how long it would have taken and how much it would have cost to build the new subway line if the MTA officials did not have to worry about all of the requirements imposed on them. Instead those requirements were just a given—the cost of building a subway line in New York.[18]

The first construction contract was awarded to a consortium of three construction companies, with Alaeden Jlelaty leading the project. His team was hired to build a trench between 92nd and 95th Streets, the size of an eighty-story apartment building lying on its side: about eight hundred feet long, sixty-two feet wide, and sixty-five feet deep. The trench was designed to serve two purposes. First, it would be used to launch a tunnel-boring machine that would excavate belowground to the existing east–west 63rd Street subway line. Then the trench would be transformed into the 96th Street subway station.[19]

After construction workers dug up Second Avenue's asphalt surface and the concrete below it, they had to relocate utility lines and support them underneath a temporary roadway. The city-owned water and sewer pipes, as well as equipment owned by private utilities, were not under just Second Avenue; they were also under every single east–west cross street. Ever since an 1888 blizzard had knocked out overhead wires and endangered pedestrians, the city had required utility companies to install their electric, phone, and telegraph cables under the streets. Over time, more utilities were installed to serve a growing population and provide new types of services, such as cable TV and internet.

In the 1970s, the number of utilities belowground was one of the MTA's biggest challenges during construction. After construction began in 2007, another generation was surprised by the complexity of building a subway within the world's largest underground utility system. According to Ed Plotkin, a tunneling engineer, although the Second Avenue subway's designers and contractors had maps of the underground utilities, "drawings mean nothing." The utility companies did not keep perfect records because it was costly; plus they did not want to reveal too much information to competitors or potential terrorists. Don Phillips, another tunneling engineer, said that opening up a street was like "looking at rubber bands in a tin can."[20]

Nagaraja's successor as MTA Capital Construction president, Michael Horodniceanu, said that relocating the lines while trying to minimize outages to utility services was like "trying to ride a bike and change the tire at the same time." Maintaining service was especially challenging for buildings, such as nursing homes, that required uninterrupted electrical service. Con Edison's electric, gas, and steam services were the most complicated and expensive to accommodate. The firm, which traced its history back to the 1820s, had cables, pipes, transformers, regulators, conduits, and other equipment belowground. On Second Avenue, not only did the MTA pay the costs of moving and upgrading Con Edison's equipment, but it even had to pay for Con Edison's workers to monitor the MTA's contractors, just in case construction workers impacted Con Edison's services.[21]

Construction workers uncovered other items besides utilities. When the engineers were conducting test borings to determine the properties and the depth of soil and bedrock all along the route, their drill hit something that was neither rock nor soil. Nor did it appear to be any type of hazardous material they were familiar with. On closer inspection, they realized that sixty-five feet below the 96th Street station area, their drill had hit a brass button from a Civil War jacket that had apparently flowed along an underground stream before resting deep below Second Avenue.[22]

Since the neighborhood near the 86th and 96th Street stations had once been home to many German immigrants and breweries, the construction team was not surprised when beer bottles, dating back more than a hundred years, were found during excavation. But none of the engineers or construction workers expected to come across a 15-foot-high, 212-foot-long concrete wall below the street. It was a remnant of the Jacob Ruppert Brewing Company, which had expanded its underground cellar to store barrels of beer in a cool spot. New Yorkers might have forgotten about the brewery, but many of them remembered that the brewery owner had lured Babe Ruth to play for his baseball team and then built them a massive ballpark called Yankee Stadium.[23]

Construction workers building the eight-hundred-foot-long trench excavated soil and then drilled small holes into the bedrock. Then they filled the holes with explosives and carefully detonated them. When the trench was completed in 2010, Michael Horodniceanu decided that Jlelaty's team was ready to start using the tunnel-boring machine. The 485-ton machine had dozens of teeth that sliced through bedrock and ejected rock chips. Named "Adi" after Horodniceanu's two-year-old granddaughter, the machine was over a football field long and included a locomotive and eighteen double-deck rail cars to transport the rock fragments back to 92nd Street. The contractor was not pleased that the union required the firm to have twenty-five workers operating the machine even though only nine were needed to operate a similar machine in Spain.[24]

As soon as the boring machine began drilling south, Horodniceanu wished that his predecessor had conducted more test borings to determine Second Avenue's subsurface conditions. Just south of 92nd Street, the tunnelers came across soil and crumbly rock, not something the boring machine was designed to dig through. If they kept on going, they could have caused catastrophic damage if underground water flowed into the tunnels and buildings collapsed.[25]

Horodniceanu's motto was, "You have a plan and it changes on Day One." After numerous meetings, Horodniceanu's team decided to drill a series of eighty-foot-deep holes where workers inserted steel pipes and pumped in a liquid chilled to thirteen degrees below zero. Several months later, the earth was frozen solid enough so that the tunnel-boring machine could work its way south. The boring machine cut through about sixty feet of solid rock every day until it reached the existing 63rd Street line in 2011. Then the machine was disassembled, pulled back by locomotive to 92nd Street, and used to dig a second tube that would one day accommodate northbound trains.[26]

Of the three new stations, only the 96th Street station was built using the cut-and-cover construction method. It had to be relatively shallow so that it would connect with the East Harlem tunnels built during the 1970s. At the

72nd and 86th Street stations, the workers built construction shafts reaching about a hundred feet below the surface that were used to bring workers and equipment down, and the rock and soil up. Then they built an underground cavern that stretched approximately one-quarter of a mile, with entrances at either end. One NYC Transit official said, "It was like building a four-story building, a hundred feet belowground."[27]

More than a million cubic yards of rock and soil, known as "muck," had to be excavated and removed to build the tunnels and stations. That was enough to fill more than half the Empire State Building. The muck was brought up from belowground into "muck houses" about two hundred feet long, two traffic lanes wide, and four stories high. The tunneling contractor had suggested that the MTA use these muck houses to minimize dust and noise, and the idea was quickly embraced by Nagaraja. At the northernmost muck house, as many as 140 trucks a day picked up the crushed rock and hauled it to New Jersey, where it was used for walls, building foundations, and even a new golf course in the Bronx. At the Trump Golf Links at Ferry Point, golfers would play on fairways and bunkers that were built on top of Second Avenue bedrock.[28]

Figure 8.1. *Utility work under Second Avenue in April 2015. Source: Metropolitan Transportation Authority.*

Figure 8.2. *Tunnel-boring machine at 92nd Street in 2010, after the two starter tunnels were blasted out of the bedrock. Source: Ben Heckscher/The Launch Box*

Figure 8.3. *Excavating rock for the 72nd Street station in 2012. Source: Metropolitan Transportation Authority.*

Figure 8.4. *Muck house at 72nd Street in November 2011. The muck house sat atop an access shaft approximately ninety feet deep. After explosives were set off, dust and smoke were exhausted out of the vents. Source: Ben Heckscher/The Launch Box*

Figure 8.5. *Narrowed sidewalk between 93rd and 94th Streets in 2008. Source: Ben Heckscher/ The Launch Box*

UNLEASHING THE SECOND AVENUE PLAGUES

Before construction work began in 2007, the New York City Department of Transportation's traffic engineers told the MTA that it needed to keep at least three of Second Avenue's six traffic lanes open at all times so that vehicles did not overwhelm the already highly congested parallel highways and avenues. City officials knew the MTA would save money by shutting down the avenue's traffic, but they did not want New Yorkers to bear the cost of late deliveries and longer travel times. To maintain three lanes, the construction team severely restricted curbside parking, pickups, and deliveries. Sidewalks that had been more than twenty feet wide were narrowed to as little as seven feet. Horodniceanu later admitted that his team did a better job accommodating vehicles than pedestrians.[29]

Despite the MTA's extensive efforts to minimize impacts, the businesses and residents along Second Avenue had little patience for the construction. Alaeden Jlelaty said that while previous generations were able to live without functioning streets and utilities, "now, if people lose heat or cable TV for an hour, they are up in arms." Building the Second Avenue tunnel while trying to minimize every possible disturbance, he explained, was as ridiculous as painting a small home office with the owner trying to work in it. He described the absurdity of the painter shifting everything in the room from one side to the other so that the owner could continue working while painting was underway. Furniture and office supplies would have to be moved, along with electrical wires, internet connections, and phone cables. Then the painter would have to set up a plastic screen and ventilation system to protect the furniture and the owner. After the paint was dry, everything would have to be moved again, to paint the other side of the room. "You're jumping through hoops because you don't want to inconvenience anyone," Jlelaty exclaimed. "You're doubling the cost and taking twice as long to paint the room!"[30]

On Second Avenue, he recalled, "we moved the traffic from right to left and left to right." Starting on one side of the street, his team removed trees, light fixtures, and fire hydrants. From one side to the other, the construction workers moved utilities, restored the street, built underground walls, and moved traffic. Because he could cut off only half of the avenue at any one time, he said, "we had to move men and equipment eight times." The MTA paid for traffic enforcement agents to maintain traffic along Second Avenue during construction. One senior Department of Transportation official said, "It wasn't pretty, but it worked." Driving down Second Avenue was like going through a ski slalom, shifting between three lanes located on the left, right, and center.[31]

Jlelaty estimated that the MTA could have saved hundreds of millions of dollars if it did not have to continuously keep traffic flowing. He listed a whole cadre of people who could have been cut, including inspectors, safety officers, shop stewards, foremen, planners, and schedulers. But although Jlelaty talked tough, he had his soft spots. A woman in a wheelchair pleaded with him to allow her daughter to park in front of her assisted-living facility so that she could be picked up every Thursday at ten o'clock in the morning. "It was the most important thing in her life," he said, so "we allowed it."[32]

At the 2007 Second Avenue subway groundbreaking, Kalikow had alluded to a Passover Seder when he asked, "Why is this groundbreaking different than all other groundbreakings?" In keeping with the theme of the Jewish holiday that celebrates the Israelites' escape from Egypt, Horodniceanu unleashed what Upper East Siders perceived as a series of plagues.

Residents lived with loud noises outside their windows, especially when steel pipes were hammered into solid rock and cranes moved materials. One observer said that the underground explosions, accompanied by "shrill warning horns reminiscent of World War II air-raid sirens," sounded like buildings getting demolished. The noise was more than just an annoyance for parents trying to put their children to sleep and for those who worked at night and tried to sleep during the day. The construction work also created vibrations that cracked building foundations and detached facades from buildings. A liquor store owner worried that the blasting would shatter his front window and knock wine bottles off their shelves. One resident said that the first time she heard the underground explosions, "I fell out of bed. It scared me to death. I thought the ceiling was falling in on me."[33]

Residents also complained about dust; one said it was worse than "bad military situations" he had been in. A man who lived on the eighth floor of a building on 70th Street said, "Smoke just comes straight into our apartment. It's so thick you're gagging." MTA officials suggested that residents keep windows closed, use filters in their air conditioners, and avoid going outside when the construction workers were blasting rocks. The muck houses did help contain the dirt and noise, but Upper East Siders whose apartments faced them looked at a wall of white for several years.[34]

Despite the MTA's extensive precautions, water, electricity, cable, and telephone service were periodically halted. Construction workers installing equipment accidentally flooded the basement of the Memorial Sloan Kettering Cancer Center. Other workers inadvertently turned off a gas line that led to more than 1,200 apartments; these residents were not able to use their ovens and stoves for nine days.[35]

Navigating the streets could be disorienting. After Manhattan's borough president, Scott Stringer, left his apartment at 83rd Street and Second Avenue one morning, he remarked, "I did not know which way to walk or how to navigate the streets. Do you go left, under the crane, or do you go around the corner, under the cement truck?" He referred to the neighborhood as an "outdoor storage bin." Along Second Avenue, trash started piling up because apartment buildings lost storage space and sanitation workers were not sure where to pick up bags of garbage. The exterminators appreciated an uptick in business, though, when they were called in to get rid of swarming flies as well as rats, some of them the size of small cats.[36]

Like the rest of Manhattan, Second Avenue is pedestrian friendly; most people walk, not drive, to their local shops, grocery stores, and restaurants. The ongoing subway construction hurt Second Avenue retailers because people wanted to avoid the narrow sidewalks and the guardrails, chain-link fences, concrete barricades, muck houses, scaffolding, and construction equipment. Storefront signs were hard to see because the MTA removed canopies and large awnings. Retailers were also hurt by the traffic conditions. Parking a car near Second Avenue stores had never been easy, but with curbside parking prohibited, drivers could no longer run into their favorite shops and grab something quickly. Not surprisingly, two years after construction began, more than 90 percent of fifty-nine businesses polled near the construction said their sales were down, and nearly half had to lay off workers. One café manager called Second Avenue a "war zone," saying that it was "just awful to look at."[37]

Business owners along Second Avenue had not expected construction to be so intrusive. Hardest hit were those entrepreneurs, like Eddie Crowe and Young Yoo, who had signed long-term leases and poured their life savings into new businesses right before construction began. Both of their businesses, the Crowe's Nest Bar and the Buddha BBeeQ restaurant, closed well before construction was completed. Joe Pecora, the owner of an Italian restaurant, had spent thousands of dollars building an enclosed sidewalk area for his restaurant. The city took away his sidewalk permit when construction started. He lost power several times while contractors were working on utility lines, and in one unforgettable incident, his employees and customers fled the restaurant after an electrical panel exploded in the basement.[38]

Pecora and several other business owners set up a Second Avenue Business Association and lobbied the MTA for financial assistance, but the MTA's executive director, Lee Sander, said the agency could not afford to compensate them. Although the state legislature subsequently passed a bill that would have provided grants to businesses, Governor Paterson vetoed it. He was concerned about the statewide fiscal implications of reimbursing businesses whenever they were impacted by a public works project.[39]

The woes of 350 stores affected by construction sparked publicity and empathy because the business owners put a familiar face on the construction impacts. When the media covered the Second Avenue subway, Upper East Siders recognized and understood what was happening to their favorite pizzerias, grocery stores, and delis. But the subway was not the only cause of the retailers' problems. Barry Schneider, cochair of Community Board 8's Second Avenue Subway Task Force, said, "It's a perfect storm. The subway construction collided with the economic downturn, and the victims are the businesses on Second Avenue."[40]

Representative Carolyn Maloney said that the best way to solve the community's problems was to finish the project promptly. Ed Plotkin, the tunneling engineer, had a similar thought. When people complained to him about construction impacts, he would ask, "Would you rather have the dentist pull your tooth slowly or fast?"[41]

The Upper East Side has long been one of the country's most affluent neighborhoods. In 2010, the average price for a two-bedroom co-op apartment was $1.5 million. The average cost of a townhouse, one of New York's ultimate status symbols, was over $9 million, which could have paid for thirty-three average American homes at the time. Many of the neighborhood's residents knew how to advocate for themselves and expected government officials to respond promptly to their complaints. After Andrew Cuomo became governor in 2011, his sister Madeline frequently called and emailed government officials to complain about conditions on Second Avenue.[42]

The sense of entitlement became more pronounced as the MTA started working closer to 63rd Street. One official remarked that further south, the MTA's construction team encountered people with more money, power, and influence. These residents, she said, did not ride the subways and did not want a subway entrance near their apartments; they had a "let-them-eat-cake attitude." Store owners who shared their woes of financial hardship did not always engender compassion from the construction team. When Cantaloup Kids, at 72nd Street and Second Avenue, put up a sign proclaiming that the "Second Avenue Subway Is Putting Us Out of Business," a NYC Transit official said to herself, "Maybe it's because you're selling kids' shoes for three hundred dollars."[43]

Compared to subway construction in the twentieth century, the MTA was taking extraordinary steps to mitigate noise, dust, safety hazards, and other construction impacts. But it was not nearly enough to satisfy residents and community leaders. One construction official thought the type of community opposition the agency encountered "wouldn't have happened anywhere else." Guido Schattanek, the team's air-quality specialist, said that Upper East Siders had time to fight, money to hire professionals, and access to the press. "We had to react," he said.[44]

In addition to the area's wealth and influence, the Upper East Side was different from the rest of the country in another important way. Only six census tracts outside New York City were as densely populated as the Upper East Side. Horodniceanu liked to joke that three of them were in places where people actually appreciated tunnels getting built under their homes: San Quentin State Prison, Maryland Penitentiary, and Trenton State Prison.[45]

New York City's newspapers and TV stations regularly reported on the plight of Second Avenue's businesses and residents. The stories struck a chord with many New Yorkers because construction was taking place in a well-known neighborhood and was caused by an unpopular transportation agency. As the transportation reporter for the *New York Post* in 2009 and 2010, Tom Namako covered every transportation mode from gondolas to rickshaws. During those two years, he wrote and edited twenty articles about the Second Avenue subway construction, with headlines such as "Co-op Owners Vent Rage at MTA" and "2nd Ave. Tenants Rip Train Wreck." Business owners and residents reached out to him and he cultivated an ongoing relationship with them. According to Namako, the *Post* did not have any sacred cows when it came to covering city hall and the transportation agencies. "If people are getting screwed," he said, "the *Post* will gleefully punch."[46]

Namako heard two very different perspectives about community impacts. The MTA seemed to think it was inevitable for some businesses to suffer while it undertook a massive construction project that would have widespread benefits. After all, as New York's master builder, Robert Moses, had often remarked, "You can't make an omelet without breaking eggs." Meanwhile, Namako realized that Upper East Siders had little trust in the MTA, especially because they considered the Second Avenue subway to have been a decades-long boondoggle. He talked with many residents who were skeptical that the new stations would ever open, and who questioned whether it was worth the inconvenience.[47]

LISTENING TO THE COMMUNITY'S COMPLAINTS

Manhattan's Community Board 8, which covers the Upper East Side between 59th and 96th Streets, served as a conduit between the community and the MTA. Although the board has a purely advisory role in city government, its members have the ears of elected officials as well as city agencies.

Barry Schneider, who cochaired the board's transportation committee and later its Second Avenue Subway Task Force, had been a strong advocate for the new subway line ever since NYC Transit's Peter Cafiero started talking to the board about it in the 1990s. When construction started, Schneider and the rest of the board were bombarded with complaints from residents. Schneider was not a transportation expert; he had owned his own advertising agency before retiring in the 1990s. But he did know how to access resources and effect change. His task force cochair said, "For Barry, it's like a full-time job. He has energy, time, and sophistication."[48]

MTA officials and their contractors gave periodic presentations to the community board; however, they used a great deal of technical jargon and much of what they presented was not relevant to the audience. One official recalled that contractors discussed the scope of work in their contracts, but did not adequately answer more pertinent questions, such as, "What was going on inside people's buildings, and when can I tell my kids they won't wake up from blastings?" She said, "The MTA stonewalled, and sent people who were ill equipped or unequipped to answer questions." Likewise, according to Schneider, the MTA was defensive and not forthcoming with information. "There wasn't a dialogue" when construction began, he said.[49]

In March 2010, Schneider set up a public meeting for Upper East Siders to discuss the project with the MTA's representatives. The attendees had a long list of concerns, including the siting of ancillary facilities, loosened facades, noise, dirt, displacement of residents, loud blasts, cracked walls and ceilings, narrow and uneven sidewalks, rats, blocked building entrances, trash not getting picked up, unsightly ripped fencing, and difficulties obtaining deliveries and parking vehicles. Residents were zigzagging around the construction area on poorly lit, narrow sidewalks. They no longer felt safe crossing the streets in their own neighborhood.[50]

Schneider's meeting was lively and well attended, but the guests of honor were no-shows. The MTA did not want to participate because of pending litigation related to a proposed East 69th Street ancillary facility. Schneider was furious, and the community board subsequently passed a resolution by a vote of thirty-six to two, declaring that it found "the MTA's failure to attend unacceptable, disrespectful and an insult to the community board and the concerned members of the public who attended."[51]

The MTA, a sprawling state authority with over fifty thousand employees, had split up responsibility for the Second Avenue subway in a way that was not conducive to community relations. MTA Capital Construction was in charge of design and construction, while NYC Transit managed the community affairs aspects of the project. NYC Transit had more than four hundred other capital projects underway, and Lois Tendler, its vice president for government and community relations, did not have enough resources to meet the very high expectations of the Upper East Side community. Mild mannered and reserved, Mysore Nagaraja had tried in his cooperative manner to obtain additional resources from Tendler, but she could assign only one person to work on community issues for the entire East Side of Manhattan, an area that covered five community boards with a population of over six hundred thousand people.[52]

The Second Avenue subway was fundamentally different, though, from every other subway project, because of its scale, the neighborhood's density, and the fact that no one needed to go belowground or aboveground to be impacted by it. The construction was affecting not only existing transit riders, but an entire neighborhood. Jay Walder, who served as MTA chair between 2009 and 2011, admitted that the "scale and size of what we're doing is beyond anything that we've ever attempted before." He said, "It's not just a little more complex; it's a totally different league."[53]

Tendler's staff who were assigned to the project tried responding to issues and placating the community. For example, they told the contractors that blasting during holiday dinners was unacceptable and that the construction crews needed to accommodate cars at funeral homes. Despite accusations from community members, one of the staff members said, "we weren't heartless and cold."[54]

Tendler explained, "NYC Transit had way too much to do with not enough resources, human or financial. I wanted to be equitable across the city and be more sensitive to lower-income communities that were not getting as much attention." She referred to the Upper East Siders as "whiners" and thought the retailers were exaggerating the impacts on construction. "People don't go out of their way to do their dry cleaning," she said. She had a point. Although store-front vacancies on Second Avenue did rise after construction began, the recession also caused a spike in vacancies on First and Third Avenues.[55]

As president of MTA Capital Construction, Horodniceanu was frustrated that he could not control his own community affairs efforts, and he battled NYC Transit to secure more resources. Tendler thought Horodniceanu should focus on getting his contractors to meet their obligations regarding cleanliness and working hours, because that would improve community relations and help the MTA's credibility. "You need to do the meat and potatoes before the gravy," she said.[56]

Horodniceanu was known for his large ego and a tendency for self-promotion. Unlike most of the other senior MTA officials, he was media savvy and made a concerted effort to engage with the press. New Yorkers were accustomed to hearing about the Yankee third baseman Alex Rodriguez, nicknamed "A-Rod." Among themselves, the reporters who covered the MTA referred to the Capital Construction president as "H-Rod." Horodniceanu's interest in promoting himself would come in handy, though, because it would help MTA Capital Construction dampen community opposition, generate enthusiasm for the project, and pressure the contractors to be more sensitive to the new subway line's neighbors.[57]

After the MTA failed to show up to the March 2010 community board meeting, Schneider called Horodniceanu, someone he had never met before. As a community board leader, when Schneider encountered a problem, he always went right to the top. When Schneider told me this story, I said with surprise, "You just called the president of the MTA Capital Construction Company to complain?"

"No, no, no," he responded. "I never like to complain." Instead Schneider asked Horodniceanu whether they could get together and talk about the Second Avenue subway. Horodniceanu immediately agreed, and over lunch, Schneider gave Horodniceanu three suggestions: host a town hall meeting, come out from behind the curtain, and get help from Sam Schwartz, the owner of Sam Schwartz Engineering.[58]

Schneider did not have to twist Horodniceanu's arm about hosting a meeting, taking center stage, or hiring Schwartz's firm. Horodniceanu enjoyed the spotlight and did not want community opposition to slow down or stop his project. He was also longtime friends with Schwartz. Schneider's phone call and lunch had a lasting effect; Horodniceanu liked Schneider and realized they could help each other. The community board could become an effective advocate for the project and help minimize the hostility the MTA was facing from residents and businesses. Over time, the two men developed a strong and trusting relationship, and Horodniceanu provided Schneider invaluable access and information.[59]

Schneider was not the only one offering suggestions to Horodniceanu. City council members, state legislators, and members of Congress all heard about the ongoing problems on Second Avenue. Facing intense pressure, Jay Walder gave Horodniceanu marching orders to complete the project on time and on budget, and to control and minimize community impacts.[60]

Horodniceanu wore Tendler down in their bureaucratic tussle, and she agreed to cede control of the project's community relations role to MTA Capital Construction. Horodniceanu then brought in his old friend Sam Schwartz for help. In 2011, Schwartz's team prepared a list of potential strategies, including what they considered some "pie-in-the-sky ideas" that MTA Capital Construction could implement to foster better community relations. The strategies built on pedestrian safety and communications initiatives the firm had implemented for the Port Authority in Lower Manhattan after the September 11 attacks. Schwartz's team also incorporated ideas developed by a group of students at Hunter College's Master of Urban Planning program.[61]

Much to the surprise of Schwartz's team, Horodniceanu agreed to undertake all of the team's recommendations. "In order to get the credibility and the trust of the residents," he said, "I needed to put my face on the project. What I mean by that is, I needed them to trust me in what I do and I needed them to hear that the buck stopped with me." Horodniceanu and Schwartz implemented what was by far the most ambitious community outreach effort the MTA had ever conducted. At its peak, the Second Avenue Subway outreach team, including both MTA Capital Construction staff and its consultants, included seven full-time people. They were able to accomplish much more than just one person working on it part time could have.[62]

Schwartz's team introduced three significant improvements. In retrospect, it is surprising that the MTA did not implement them earlier. First, community liaisons were assigned to each of the stations. They regularly walked the construction areas and listened to the concerns of residents and business owners. As active participants in the construction team's regular meetings, the liaisons raised quality-of-life issues and then followed up to make sure they were resolved.[63]

Second, Horodniceanu set up community meetings and public workshops where the public could meet with representatives from the contractors, the MTA, and various city agencies, including the Transportation, Police, Sanitation, and Health Departments. At the first workshop, almost two hundred people sat around tables with facilitators to discuss issues and develop practical solutions. After the workshop, the MTA added more dust control measures, changed the blasting methods, and established new ways to keep the community informed.[64]

Third, for $176,000 per year, the MTA rented a storefront where it set up an information center. Horodniceanu realized that this would change how people thought and talked about the new subway. While getting their questions answered, visitors could learn more about the construction, subway route, and station entrances. The center, with its displays, meeting rooms, and interactive exhibits, provided a space for children and adults to get excited about their neighborhood's long-promised subway service.[65]

Lois Tendler had wanted Horodniceanu to make sure his contractors were complying with their commitments rather than spending millions of dollars on more community outreach efforts. But the two strategies complemented each other. The station liaisons learned about problems, monitored them, and then made sure that workers cleaned up their trash, maintained pedestrian and vehicle access, stored their equipment appropriately, and did not work late in the evening.[66]

Horodniceanu's efforts helped Upper East Siders understand the project's enormous scale and the MTA's extensive efforts to minimize construction
impacts. Likewise, construction officials became much more sensitive to the
community when they heard directly from residents and business owners at
workshops. Barry Schneider was delighted that the MTA had started engaging
in a dialogue and becoming "much more transparent."[67]

When construction first began, Ben Heckscher, an amateur photographer
who set up a highly informative blog about the ongoing construction, rarely
got more than one-sentence answers when he asked the MTA questions. "The
MTA was like the East German government," he said. "It was almost chilling."
He noticed that workers who posted construction-related photos and videos
on their social media pages were forced to take them down because the MTA
wanted a tight grip on information, or a lack of information. MTA officials,
Heckscher realized, were not going beyond meeting the federal requirements
for public outreach, and he watched as the "public's frustration built and built
until it blew up." But after Horodniceanu brought in Sam Schwartz's team, he
said, "community outreach went from an F to an A-minus or a B-plus."[68]

Horodniceanu explained, "People do not like surprises unless it comes out
of a cake—and maybe is naked. You have to work with these people so they
become your allies. When people complain, you can't say, 'Go the fuck away.'
You have to listen to what they say, and say, 'O.K., help me to help you.' We
want to get out of here as soon as possible. We have to build. If you've got good
ideas, I'll listen to you. Tell me what I can do."[69]

A community outreach initiative introduced in December 2011 softened
even the project's most bitter critics. Horodniceanu started leading monthly
underground tours for people living and working near the construction. "It was
the best investment I could make," he later said. Over the next few years, more
than two thousand Upper East Siders were awed by the size and scale of the
work as they toured the station caverns and tunnels. On the eighty tours he led,
someone would invariably ask, as they walked more than seventy feet below the
surface, "What was here before?" Horodniceanu would respond, to quizzical
looks, "Solid rock."[70]

Michael Porto, a community outreach leader, said the tours helped those
who had been complaining about the muck houses finally understand how the
MTA used them to contain dust and noise. "We got people invested" in the
project, he recalled. One underground visitor said, "When you see the scope of
the excavation, you understand a little bit better why there is so much surface
disruption." But, she added, "it didn't really make me any happier."[71]

One of the construction team members said, "The tours were brilliant because they changed the tone of the community and people became supportive of the project." According to another member of the team, "Michael pats himself too much on the back, but that's something he accomplished that went a long way." MTA Capital Construction had no greater critic than Richard Bass, an urban planner who was hired by twenty-six different buildings along Second Avenue to provide them with technical and political assistance during construction. "When the tours started," he said, "a lot of opposition drifted away."[72]

The tours also helped the MTA's relationship with the media. The *New York Post*'s Tom Namako remembered how going underground gave him a better understanding of the ongoing construction and a frame of reference to appreciate the project's scale. With reporters becoming more sensitive to the MTA's needs, the MTA received more positive coverage, which in turn diminished community opposition. "Everyone loved those tours," Schneider said. After his fellow community board members praised the MTA's newsletters, construction tours, and workshops, a March 2012 *Post* article asked, "What's next? Peace in the Middle East?"[73]

Lois Tendler thought that in a world of unlimited resources, all of Horodniceanu and Schwartz's initiatives would be wonderful. But, she said, "we did things on Second Avenue that were close to being extortion because we didn't have the balls to say, 'Go fuck yourselves.' We do that all the time on the Upper East Side. We made decisions that were costly, just to stay out of the press."[74]

The MTA was not the only one taking heat for construction-related problems. Michael Bloomberg's neighbors pleaded with him for help. The billionaire mayor lived on 79th Street, just four blocks west of Second Avenue, and he hosted functions at Gracie Mansion, the mayor's official residence, on 88th Street, three blocks east of Second Avenue. Bloomberg warned in 2009 that construction was "literally destroying every business on Second Avenue.... It is an economic disaster for the people who have stores and restaurants on Second Avenue and we have to find something to do for them."[75]

Bloomberg assigned his deputy mayor, Steven Goldsmith, to coordinate the city's efforts. Nancy Ploeger, president of the Manhattan Chamber of Commerce, subsequently said that when she called Goldsmith about a problem on Second Avenue, "the city was there in a heartbeat." Thanks to Goldsmith and Sam Schwartz's team, the MTA's construction officials began meeting regularly with city agencies, business owners, building representatives, the Chamber of Commerce, and elected officials to address problems. As a result, public officials made numerous changes. For example, the Sanitation Department improved its trash pickup and stopped issuing summonses to businesses for garbage left by the subway's construction workers. Traffic enforcement agents stopped giving tickets to delivery trucks that had to double park because of construction. And the MTA hired more crossing guards, added lighting, improved sidewalks, and cracked down on contractor cleanliness to help control the rats and flies.[76]

Sometimes Upper East Siders took compliance into their own hands. At a June 2011 community board meeting, an MTA Capital Construction official said that blasting to build the 72nd Street station would occur only occasionally after seven o'clock in the evening. That was an invitation for Steve Broer, an East 70th Street resident, to take out his stopwatch and calendar. Over the next two months, Broer counted twenty-eight blasts after seven o'clock, including nineteen after nine o'clock. Broer's elected representatives then pressured MTA officials to keep their word, and two months later, the MTA capitulated and agreed to ban all blasting after seven.[77]

Greater responsiveness, however, did not stop the complaints about the debris and clouds of smoke. One local doctor talked about "the Second Avenue cough," and many Upper East Siders worried that exposure to the blasts would lead to serious long-term respiratory effects, like those experienced by the World Trade Center's first responders after 9/11. After hashing out options with local politicians and community leaders, Horodniceanu agreed in November 2011 to halt blasting for more than two weeks while MTA Capital Construction implemented new measures to minimize blast levels, contain the debris and noise, and revamp the exhaust systems. Despite reservations from his team, Horodniceanu also decided to hire consultants to undertake a comprehensive air monitoring study—though one MTA official remarked, "That's the last thing you want to do because you don't know what you will find." Discovering a hazardous condition would have had costly results in terms of both time and money. Horodniceanu was confident, though, that the explosives were safe. "If something is wrong," he said, "we'll correct it."[78]

Measuring air quality required some creativity. After obtaining air monitoring devices, the consultants, led by Guido Schattanek, had to find appropriate locations to install them—not where someone might tamper with them, not in the mouth of an exhaust, not where people might smoke, not too high off the ground, not too low off the ground, and somewhere with access to electric power. In consultation with the US Environmental Protection Agency, Schattanek determined which pollutants to measure and the thresholds considered harmful to human health. These choices were not clear cut, because some people were breathing the air forty stories above the street, while others, like street vendors, construction workers, and security guards, were on the street for hours a day. Schattanek tried to capture the pollution from numerous construction sources, including excavation, blasting, spoils removal, and demolition, as well as the exhaust from the diesel engines that powered construction equipment and trucks.[79]

During a four-week period in the fall of 2011, the air monitoring equipment collected over three million minute-by-minute pollutant measurements. Some of the particles were large and dark enough to be seen with the naked eye, while others were so small they could be seen only with an electron microscope. While most of the air quality results were as expected, Horodniceanu lost his temper when he learned that the equipment showed what the construction team considered "enormously high levels" of sulfur dioxide, a colorless gas that can cause coughing, shortness of breath, and even death. For weeks, the construction team could not figure out where the sulfur dioxide was coming from. Although the levels rose before the blasting events, the toxic gas could not be correlated with these blasting operations.[80]

Horodniceanu decided not to tell the public until his team could pinpoint the cause. After extensive testing, the consultants determined that a chemical in the blast emission was causing a false reading and the public was never in any danger. The air quality team then prepared a report indicating that certain pollutants did exceed certain health standards, but they were caused by passing trucks and old boilers in buildings, not the subway construction. Horodniceanu did not want to take any chances with how people might perceive the consultants' findings, so he made numerous revisions to the final report and even set up a mock presentation with more than twenty members of his construction team so that Schattanek could practice answering questions from the public.[81]

In January 2012, Horodniceanu released the air quality report and held a public meeting with nearly three hundred people attending. Although MTA Capital Construction already had an extensive air quality program in place, Horodniceanu agreed to undertake even more rigorous and expensive procedures, including installing new rooftop vents on the muck houses, sealing door leaks to contain the smoke in the muck houses, and increasing the time interval between each blast. After residents listened to Schattanek and the other scientists go through their well-rehearsed presentation, Upper East Siders stopped talking about the Second Avenue subway cough.[82]

Accommodating the community's concerns, however, did not come cheap. Restricting the hours of blasting added $7.3 million to the cost of building the 72nd Street and 86th Street stations. The new emissions monitoring program added $1.1 million, and acoustic panels added another $377,000.[83]

On August 21, 2012, the MTA again had to halt blasting at the 72nd Street station after an explosion rocked the neighborhood. The incident revealed the potential dangers of explosives to residents and workers. Forty feet below the street, workers had mistakenly placed explosives at the wrong angle and did not properly anchor down an 1,800-pound steel deck covering the hole where they placed the explosives. The explosion knocked away the steel deck and sent a shower of boulders, dirt, and debris eighty feet into the air. Although no one was hurt, buildings shook, construction equipment was ruined, and windows were shattered.[84]

While Upper East Side residents were nervous about the blasting, the men and women building the tunnels and caverns were the ones who were really at risk. The hundreds of workers operating the boring machines, drilling into

Figure 8.6. *Blast at the 72nd Street station on August 21, 2012. Source: John Wilson.*

rock, and setting off explosives in tight quarters were members of the Laborers' Local Union No. 147, affectionately known as the sandhogs. Julie Freitas, a geologist on the construction team, said that these workers "understood the geology and made things more efficient because they knew what they were doing." Even though the sandhogs wore respirators and air quality monitors, they were the ones who most had to worry about developing emphysema and silicosis, two lung diseases associated with breathing the chemical fumes and inhaling the dust.[85]

WATCHING THE CLOCK AND THE BUDGET

The MTA's ongoing coordination with residents, businesses, and city officials helped prevent serious protests and significant disruptions to the construction schedule. An even more important type of coordination was occurring behind the scenes. MTA Capital Construction was building the subway, but it had to make sure NYC Transit was satisfied with the results.

Carmen Bianco started overseeing NYC Transit's Subways Department in 2010 and later served as NYC Transit's president between 2013 and 2015. He was not as concerned as Horodniceanu about adhering to the Second Avenue subway's schedule and budget. He worried more about the subway system's aging ventilation fans that were needed in case of a fire, the tracks that needed to be upgraded, and the eighty-year-old signal systems that could not accommodate the growing number of riders. Most of all, he lost sleep worrying about a potential terrorist attack.[86]

Regarding the Second Avenue subway, Bianco said, "I had to make sure that when [Horodniceanu] handed me the keys, it's a subway system that I can run. I don't want a system that I can't operate and I don't want be in a position where I can't maintain it. The Capital Construction Company's mission is to design and construct the subway, but they are walking away and don't have to look back. I inherit it for the next hundred years." Wynton Habersham, a senior NYC Transit official, thought of himself as MTA Capital Construction's client. "You need to build my house according to my specs," he said.[87]

Bianco set up a team to make sure that every piece of equipment, from light bulbs to ventilation systems, would be easily accessible and could be properly maintained. While Horodniceanu wanted to install cutting-edge technologies, NYC Transit's engineers were more comfortable with equipment they thought had a better performance record. Bianco also wanted to make sure that MTA Capital Construction minimized its interference with NYC Transit's services and customers at the 63rd Street line's Lexington Avenue station, which had to be modified and expanded to accommodate Second Avenue subway service. Usually Capital Construction's engineers modified their plans in accordance with NYC Transit's requests; when they did not, Bianco had the MTA chair tell Horodniceanu to accommodate the transit operator's concerns.[88]

Horodniceanu's team was forced to make thousands of design changes as work progressed. The MTA had to juggle demands from NYC Transit as well as the Fire Department, building owners, and the utility companies. Con Edison's engineers literally held all the power, because if the MTA did not accede to their demands, the subway could not connect with Con Edison's electrical grid.

Many standards had changed since the design team had started working in 2002. For example, climate change issues rose to prominence after Hurricane Sandy hit New York's harbor in 2012. The MTA chair, Joe Lhota, called the hurricane the most devastating disaster to impact the subway system in its 108-year history. The stairways, grates, and elevators all became massive waterfalls into subway stations. Seven subway tunnels under the East River flooded with salt water, some all the way to the ceiling. After the hurricane, Second Avenue subway designers went back to the drawing board, redesigning the stations so that equipment rooms, electrical components, and signals would stay dry in the event of another major storm. If the new tunnel were to have a leak—whether from an underground stream, an overflowing sewer, or a storm surge—pumps and a drainage system would remove all the water.[89]

Some design changes required years of debate and numerous meetings to resolve. For example, the 72nd Street station was expected to have a third track that would be used to store subway cars and allow trains in service to divert around stalled trains. But MTA Capital Construction engineers were not comfortable constructing a station wide enough for two platforms and three tracks, because it would require excavating below tall apartment buildings on both sides of Second Avenue. After the NYC Transit president agreed to eliminate the third track, the subway construction team saved about $200 million and had one fewer thing to worry about.[90]

The project's budget and schedule were fluid documents. In the late 1990s, the MTA had estimated it would cost $3.6 billion (in 1997 dollars) to build the Second Avenue subway between 63rd and 125th Streets. By 2004, the cost estimate had risen to $3.8 billion, and that was only for the portion between 63rd and 96th Streets. Over the next five years, the figure rose another 17 percent to $4.35 billion. To keep costs from rising even further, MTA officials used the same trick that William Ronan, the MTA's first chair, had used forty years earlier. They cut $213 million from the Second Avenue subway's budget by shifting the cost of additional subway cars to NYC Transit's capital program.[91]

The scheduled completion date also slipped. In 2004, all four phases of the full-length Second Avenue subway were supposed to be complete by 2020. Not long after that, the MTA stopped talking about a completion date for the entire project. In 2004, the first phase was supposed to open by 2012, a target that Mysore Nagaraja subsequently extended three times, finally settling on June 2015. When he retired as MTA Capital Construction president, Nagaraja did not think construction would actually be completed by June 2015, but he did not change the completion date again because he wanted his team to have an ambitious goal and he thought it was still theoretically possible to make up for lost time.[92]

After Horodniceanu replaced Nagaraja in 2008, his first job was to look at the budgets and the schedule for the agency's projects. He determined that the Second Avenue subway schedule was totally unrealistic; in fact, he referred to it as a "lie." Horodniceanu added an additional eighteen months to the scheduled completion date, postponing it until December 2016. He also increased the cost estimate by $100 million, to $4.45 billion. "We will deliver," he told the MTA's board members. "You can hold me accountable."[93]

By early 2015, even though MTA Capital Construction officials were skeptical that they could actually finish construction by the end of 2016, they continued to tell the public that that was when the subway would open. For MTA executives, a delay of a few months in completing the first phase was relatively unimportant. After all, construction on the Long Island Rail Road connection with Grand Central had fallen about ten years behind schedule. They reasoned that if the first subway had opened in January 1905 rather than October 1904, would it really have mattered very much?[94]

But in late 2015, the governor of New York, Andrew Cuomo, did not share the MTA's seemingly lackadaisical approach to its deadline. To him, a delay of a few months, a few weeks, or even just one single day after January 1, 2017, was simply unacceptable.

Figure 8.7. *Getting ready to line the 72nd Street station cavern with concrete in 2013. Source: Metropolitan Transportation Authority.*

Figure 8.8. *Completion of 86th Street cavern in 2014. Source: Metropolitan Transportation Authority.*

Figure 8.9. *Structural steel work for new entrance in an apartment building at the corner of Third Avenue and 63rd Street. Source: Metropolitan Transportation Authority.*

Figure 8.10. *On a 2014 tour, Michael Horodniceanu (at right) looks on after a city planner told his girlfriend, "Just like New Yorkers, I've been waiting a long time for the Second Avenue subway. I have also been waiting a long time to ask you this question, which is: Will you marry me?" To the delight of everyone on the tour, she responded, "Oh my God, one hundred percent!" Source: Metropolitan Transportation Authority.*

Andrew Cuomo's Finish Line

First elected in 2010, Andrew Cuomo had a reputation as governor for meticulous control of information and an intense management style, unlike anything New York had ever seen. Like his father, the three-term governor Mario Cuomo, Andrew was a tireless, secretive micromanager. Andrew had an even tighter grip over the state's apparatus, however, because twenty-first-century technology allowed him to monitor the news, obtain information, and communicate with the state's agencies far faster than his father ever could have imagined.[1]

Cuomo's first foray into a large transportation infrastructure project was his 2011 decision to replace the New York State Thruway Authority's aging Tappan Zee Bridge with one of the world's widest, longest, and most expensive bridges. Cuomo's three predecessors had been unable to finalize plans for a new Hudson River crossing because the project included building an unaffordable thirty-mile-long rail line. Cuomo eliminated the rail component, broke a decade-long stalemate, and then showered the Tappan Zee with his attention and the state's resources. In return, he received accolades across the state and nation. The governor told audiences that after decades of people talking about replacing the bridge, he was the only governor who had the political strength to get it done. He liked to say that the state could still accomplish big things, that no challenge was too great and no project too grand.[2]

Convinced that bureaucrats did not have his drive to deliver on the new bridge, Cuomo took away powers from the Thruway Authority and beefed up the size and responsibilities of the governor's office to expedite the bridge's replacement. In early 2014, Cuomo took on a second multibillion-dollar infrastructure initiative: rebuilding LaGuardia Airport in Queens. By the time Cuomo kicked off his 2014 reelection bid, he had started to develop a national reputation as the infrastructure governor.[3]

Cuomo had a keen understanding of New York's history and he knew the pitfalls of being associated with the MTA's problems. Lois Tendler, NYC Transit's longtime government affairs executive, said that taking responsibility for the MTA "is a losing proposition," because the MTA generates more bad news than good: everything from fare increases and toll increases to service delays and construction impacts. Those seen in charge of running the subways and buses rarely receive acclaim. Jim Brennan, a state assemblyman who led the committee overseeing MTA issues, said that in his first term Cuomo "badly mistreated" the authority. He "wouldn't address its problems," and he "pretended he didn't have anything to do with the MTA."[4]

One longtime MTA executive was confused and frustrated by Cuomo's attitude. Not only had Cuomo publicly disassociated himself from the MTA, but he was not interested in working with MTA officials in private either. Under previous governors, MTA officials promptly answered questions from the governor's office and managed the governor's expectations about transportation services and projects. MTA leaders were accustomed to holding press conferences where governors could take credit for the authority's new initiatives. Cuomo's staff, however, was not at all interested in working with the MTA. According to the MTA executive, the attitude of Cuomo's staff toward the MTA was, "Your job is to stay out of sight and mind. Don't talk to us; we'll tell you what to do." About Cuomo, he said, "You can't work too long for him. You need a relationship where there's some give and take—some ability to figure out strategy and change course and direction. And to like the people you work with. It wasn't possible with Cuomo."[5]

The Thruway Authority had a different kind of turmoil. The effort to replace the Tappan Zee Bridge was so intense, the governor demanded so much, and he worked the senior staff so hard, that he went through six different Thruway Authority executive directors in a six-year period. Another senior state transportation official noted that except for the Tappan Zee Bridge and LaGuardia Airport, Cuomo did not get involved with infrastructure during his first term. "No legacy shit," he said, "nothing someone else started." One state assemblyman said that for Cuomo, "If he didn't come up with the idea while taking a shower, it's not a good idea."[6]

When Cuomo's father first took office, he ignored Richard Ravitch, the MTA chair at the time, and Ravitch resigned as a result. A similar situation occurred with Andrew Cuomo and the MTA chair he inherited, Jay Walder. One of Walder's conditions before accepting the chairmanship was that he would deal directly with Governor David Paterson or Paterson's top aide. When Cuomo took office, he wanted Walder to deal with someone an MTA executive referred to as a "pretty low-level functionary."[7]

Getting Cuomo's attention had its drawbacks for Walder. As a tropical storm was approaching New York City in 2011, Cuomo wanted to be seen as the person in charge of the government's response. Moments before Mayor Michael Bloomberg held a press conference, Walder got into a loud and angry phone argument with a governor's aide who tried to stop him from appearing with the mayor. According to an MTA executive, the governor was "insanely out-of-his-mind pissed" that Walder would share the stage with the mayor.[8]

Cuomo made a number of budget decisions to the detriment of the MTA. In his first four years in office, he diverted $456 million that had been dedicated to the MTA's operating budget. When the state received nearly $9.9 billion from seven financial institutions as a settlement for violating laws, he allocated $2 billion to help the Thruway Authority pay for the new Tappan Zee Bridge and prevent a toll hike. The Thruway Authority received the equivalent of more than $14,000 for each driver crossing the bridge on a typical day, while NYC Transit was allocated less than $10 for each of its daily passengers.[9]

Assemblyman Brennan placed Cuomo's neglect into context, explaining that for the MTA, the 2008 recession had been a financial catastrophe, Hurricane Sandy had been a physical catastrophe, and Governor Cuomo was a political catastrophe.[10]

ADDING A PET PROJECT

In 2013, Cuomo interviewed Tom Prendergast for the position of MTA chair and chief executive officer. Cuomo wanted to make sure Prendergast had the stamina and the passion to lead the MTA. He asked, "Do you want it? Do you really want it? Do you really really want it?" The governor warned Prendergast that he would be subject to harsh criticism from the public. Prendergast responded, "Yes, I do really want it."[11]

No chair in the MTA's history knew more about the subways than Prendergast. He was not an academic, a financial wizard, a political party leader, a real estate developer, or a politician. Prendergast had worked at Chicago's transit authority in the 1970s before becoming NYC Transit's assistant director of system safety in 1982. He was promoted to lead the Safety Department and then served as chief electrical officer, senior vice president for subways, and later president of NYC Transit.[12] At his job interview, when Cuomo emphasized the political role associated with the MTA chair's position, Prendergast admitted that he might not have the necessary experience and acumen for the political arena. Cuomo told him not to worry: "I can help you with the politics," he said. As it turned out, Prendergast would find the politics even more challenging than he expected. Referring to a 1991 subway derailment that killed five passengers, he said, "You don't like dealing with stuff like that, but you deal with it." Prendergast found that such incidents "pale in contrast to the difficulties of dealing with political issues."[13]

Under Prendergast's leadership, the MTA conducted an extensive analysis of its assets and needs for the next twenty years. The results were used to develop a five-year, $32 billion capital program that the MTA board released in September 2014. Although most of the funds were directed toward state-of-good-repair and normal replacement projects, it also included $1.5 billion to start the second phase of the Second Avenue subway. Prendergast assumed that the Federal Transit Administration (FTA) would fund about one-third of the cost to build the line between 96th Street and 125th Street.[14]

Prendergast thought he had Cuomo's support for the MTA's capital program; however, he had talked about it only with Cuomo's aides, not the governor himself. Just a few days after the MTA board approved it, the governor called the program "bloated" and rejected it. Disappointed and frustrated, Prendergast regretted that he had not done a better job selling the program to the governor. He sincerely thought that every element of the program was necessary. Prendergast had not played any bureaucratic games with his request, such as asking for more money than he needed in the expectation that others would trim it. Gene Russianoff, leader of the Straphangers Campaign, lamented that Cuomo had shown a "shocking indifference" to the MTA's issues.[15]

Over the next year, the debate about the capital program played out differently than previous ones had, because of political turmoil and the loss of the Second Avenue subway's most important champion. Sheldon Silver resigned from the state assembly after the FBI arrested him on bribery charges. Three months later, the FBI arrested the leader of the state senate on corruption charges. Behind-the-scenes negotiations with legislative leaders were then overshadowed by a feud over the capital program between Cuomo and New York City mayor Bill de Blasio.

Governors and mayors had long clashed over transit funding, but in 2015 the state's two leading Democrats were barely speaking to each other. The relationship came to a head in June when the governor ridiculed the mayor to *Daily News* and *New York Post* reporters. A few days later, de Blasio retorted, "I started a year and a half ago with a hope of a very strong partnership. I have been disappointed at every turn." Unleashing his frustrations about the governor, de Blasio said, "What I found was he engaged in his own sense of strategies, his own political machinations, and what we've often seen is if someone disagrees with him openly, some kind of revenge or vendetta follows." When the state's top education commissioner heard about the mayor's response, she said, "Oy. If I was unburdening, I'd generally do it to my mother, not to a reporter."[16]

The MTA's capital program got caught up in the drama as Cuomo told the city that it would need to pay for a greater share of NYC Transit's capital improvements. The city's direct contribution to the MTA's first five-year capital program in the 1980s averaged $136 million a year. If the city kept increasing that amount to adjust for inflation, the city would have contributed $363 million in 2014; instead it gave only $100 million. As the governor and mayor sniped at each other, former MTA chair Richard Ravitch called the MTA's funding "a mess" and suggested that part of the solution would be to "elect better politicians." In the fall, the mayor acquiesced to the governor's demands and promised to dramatically increase the city's contribution to the capital program.[17]

Cuomo and de Blasio also agreed to cut $3 billion from the capital program and reduce funding for the second phase of the Second Avenue subway from $1.5 billion to $500 million. In October 2015, the MTA board approved a revised capital program. The Second Avenue subway advocates, however, still had some political clout. At a rally on 96th Street, a coalition—including city council members, state legislators, contractors, the Regional Plan Association president, the city comptroller, the Manhattan borough president, environmentalists, and labor unions—urged the MTA to restore the $1 billion that was cut from the project's second phase. They were afraid the MTA would abandon future phases after it opened the stations at 72nd Street, 86th Street, and 96th Street. Extending the subway to East Harlem had become an issue not only of transportation but of environmental justice, with the funding cut seen as a slap in the face to East Harlem's predominantly Hispanic community.[18]

State legislators all across the city understood the need to relieve crowding on the Lexington Avenue line, according to Assemblyman Brennan. He said, "The concept of abandoning the Second Avenue subway, especially for the Manhattan delegation, was not even discussable, not even conceivable." Even though the mayor had agreed with the governor in private to cut funding for the second phase, de Blasio joined all of Manhattan's elected officials in criticizing the MTA.[19]

Behind the scenes, Silver's successor as assembly Speaker, Carl Heastie, told the governor that he could not get enough votes to pass the state budget unless the MTA restored funding for the second phase. Prendergast appeased the state legislators with a meaningless promise. He told a delegation of elected officials that the MTA would speed up the timetable for the second phase and seek additional funds. The capital program that was finally approved by the governor and legislative leaders in 2016 included a total of $1 billion for the second phase, with an assumption that the FTA would provide $500 million in New Starts funds.[20]

In the summer and fall of 2015, as the governor and mayor clashed over the MTA's capital program, Cuomo started to become engaged with the MTA's issues, and his involvement intensified over time. Although he had been hesitant about being associated with the MTA's affairs, its $6 billion annual capital program offered an irresistible opportunity for the infrastructure governor. Cuomo wanted the MTA to focus on short-term initiatives that would have widespread appeal. To reinforce his influence, the MTA was told to hire people whose first loyalty was to the governor. One MTA executive said the governor went from staying away from the MTA to getting overly involved in its details. He rhetorically asked, "Why is Cuomo designing the look of MTA's buses?" Another senior official grumbled that the governor wanted the color of tiles in a renovated station to be the same blue as the one on the state's flag, even though NYC Transit officials thought it was much too dark for an underground station.[21]

A self-described "control freak's control freak," the governor began to treat the MTA like other state agencies, even though the MTA had its own independent board of directors. In 2015, he appointed one of his most loyal aides, Larry Schwartz, to serve on the MTA board. In Albany, Schwartz was known as the governor's "political enforcer" and "all-purpose hatchet man." Fred Dicker, a New York Post reporter, said that Cuomo admired Schwartz's work ethic and unrelenting viciousness. You could send out Larry Schwartz as your attack dog, he said, "and no one will out-attack you."[22]

Until Schwartz was appointed to the board, MTA executives were not accustomed to screaming, cursing, and threatening phone calls from one of their own board members. One senior MTA official referred to Cuomo as a thug and Schwartz as "the thug's thug." When another MTA official reminded

Schwartz that its board members were independent and had a fiduciary responsibility to act in the best interests of the MTA and its mission, Schwartz responded, "You work for the governor, fuck the fiduciary."[23]

Larry Schwartz shared his boss's focus, boundless energy, and disdain for many government bureaucrats. Sometimes he called state officials every day to remind them of a deadline; he was convinced that little would get done otherwise. He challenged people's competence by saying things like, "You said you could do it, but you can't." When necessary, Schwartz would work ninety hours a week, sometimes until two or three o'clock in the morning. He complained about an official who had the audacity to go for a one-and-a-half-hour bicycle ride on a Saturday without his phone.[24]

In 2015, the governor appointed Rick Cotton as his special counsel for infrastructure projects. A low-key problem solver, Cotton would set high expectations with strict deadlines. He was the perfect counterpart for Schwartz. Cotton would figure out what needed to happen and how to get it done, then Schwartz would make sure the plan was executed. But the two men bumped up against the MTA's huge bureaucracy, whose goals did not match their own.[25]

Prendergast thought about the MTA's long-term needs, asked questions about the life-cycle costs of investments, and wanted to upgrade decrepit maintenance facilities that were never seen by the MTA's customers. In contrast, Cuomo and his staff focused on projects where they could make a difference in a matter of months so the governor could burnish his image in the media. One NYC Transit senior official recalled that before Cuomo started paying attention to the MTA, she spent most of her time working on capital programs and financial plans. Between 2015 and 2017, however, nearly all of her work consisted of preparing information that would be incorporated into the governor's next set of press releases.[26]

Cuomo had a long list of priority projects, including bringing Wi-Fi coverage, cell phone service, and countdown clocks to every subway station. He wanted subway riders to be able to swipe through the turnstiles using bank cards and smartphones, and he wanted USB chargers in stations, trains, and buses. He wanted the MTA to accelerate the purchase of new subway cars featuring accordion-like connectors, and he wanted his own aides to select the stations that would be renovated. He also wanted toll barriers to be removed from the MTA's bridges and tunnels. For the most part, he got what he wanted.[27]

The governor cared about aesthetics and was a stickler for details. He urged the MTA to install LED lights on its river crossings at a cost of more than $200 million, so the bridges could offer extravagant multicolored light shows choreographed to music. The completion of a new concourse at Penn Station for Long Island Rail Road customers was delayed six months because he wanted more digital information screens and ceiling-mounted LED displays.[28]

Cuomo's staff was critical of the MTA's culture because the authority was slow to implement new technologies and customer-friendly initiatives. Few outsiders understood that this culture was a product of Richard Ravitch's tenure as chair, when the MTA first began to focus on bringing the system up to a state of good repair and replacing every asset once it reached the end of its useful life. Many of the MTA's senior managers, like Prendergast, remembered the condition of the subways in the 1980s and how Ravitch had rescued New York's transit system. They worried about the implications of prioritizing the governor's short-term projects over the system's long-term needs.

Although the subway cars and tracks were in a state of good repair, nearly every other asset was still years away from achieving that goal. Something relatively straightforward, such as converting incandescent fixtures to fluorescent ones, was going to take twenty years longer than had been expected several years earlier. In 2014, the Citizens Budget Commission warned that subway service was likely to have more disruptions and safety issues because NYC Transit was making little progress modernizing its infrastructure.[29]

In late 2015, Cuomo identified one more project that he wanted to place ahead of the MTA's other priorities. The governor's ears pricked up when he heard that the first three stations of the Second Avenue subway were scheduled to open on January 1, 2017. New Year's Day held a special significance for him because on the first day of 2015 he was sworn in for his second term as governor. A few hours later, his father died at his Upper East Side home.[30]

The first phase of the new subway line, Cuomo learned, was expected to carry about two hundred thousand daily riders, which was substantially more than the number of Tappan Zee Bridge or LaGuardia Airport users. Cuomo often talked about how government officials were unable to replace the Tappan Zee Bridge until he came along. The saga of the Second Avenue subway was even bigger and better, because New Yorkers had been talking about it for nearly a century. Moreover, the three new subway stations would be within walking distance of the very heart of the world's media capital, and the Upper East Side was home to the nation's elite, many of whom used the subway on a regular basis.

If Andrew Cuomo could open the subway line on time, he would not be just another politician eyeing national office. He would have another multibillion-dollar physical symbol of his ability to overcome enormous obstacles. No other elected official in the country would be able to point to such mega-accomplishments. The governor's first two pet projects were the Tappan Zee Bridge (which he would later rename after his father) and LaGuardia Airport. In late 2015, Cuomo selected his third.

Michael Horodniceanu was surprised by the governor's newfound interest in the Second Avenue subway. The MTA Capital Construction president said, "He never really came to our projects. It took him five years for him to figure out we existed." Cuomo had not been interested in the extension of the number 7 line because it was so closely associated with Mayor Bloomberg. He paid little attention to the Long Island Rail Road's connection with Grand Central Terminal because it would not open for at least seven more years. Likewise, he did not mind gutting funding for the Second Avenue subway's second phase because it was unlikely that he would still be governor by the time the subway reached 125th Street. In fact, the second phase was a distraction. It would take attention away from the first phase and remind people that the first three stations were just a modest beginning to the long-promised Second Avenue subway.[31]

Rick Cotton, the governor's infrastructure czar, realized the MTA would not be able to open the first phase by the end of 2016 without the governor's intervention. He thought the MTA's definition of a deadline was, "It's time to set another deadline." After a career in the private sector, he recognized that "the words 'speed' and 'government' did not usually go together." Cotton had some ideas to expedite the project, including providing contractors with more incentives to complete it on time, and giving Horodniceanu more autonomy so that decisions could be made faster. Most importantly, Cotton wanted to eliminate unnecessary regulations and layers of approvals that had been put in place because something had gone wrong in the past. NYC Transit officials, he believed, had a greater allegiance to processes than to deadlines.[32]

Now under pressure from the governor's office, at an "all-hands meeting" that also doubled as a Christmas celebration in 2015, Horodniceanu reminded his team about the January 1, 2017, deadline and proclaimed, "We're getting this done."[33]

QUASI-INDEPENDENCE

Prendergast was immensely proud of his role in rebuilding New York's subway system. In 1982, when he first started working at NYC Transit, travel writers warned tourists about the dismal and hazardous conditions of the New York subways. "Things were pretty bad," Prendergast recalled. "We had derailments every twenty-seven days; we had car fires all over the place; we had graffiti on every inch of the system." In 2015, the travel guide Frommer's referred to the New York City subway as "the single most efficient, rapid, easy, and affordable way to get just about anywhere you'd want to go in Manhattan, with the exception of some of the far eastern sections of the Upper East Side (and that will change once the Second Avenue subway is completed)."[34]

He had been at the MTA long enough to know that the governor and his staff were controlling the MTA more than any previous governors had. The MTA and Cuomo had "a singular message," he said. Prendergast had no choice because the governor was keeping a close eye on him. For instance, Prendergast liked to tell audiences that the MTA's facilities and equipment were worth a trillion dollars. If each of those assets had a thirty-year life span, then the MTA would need to invest about $30 billion a year upgrading them. Prendergast said the authority was falling behind because it had allocated $30 billion for a five-year, not a one-year, capital program. When Cuomo heard about Prendergast's trillion-dollar reference, he had his aides tell the MTA chair to stop using it.[35]

Prendergast always tried to anticipate the needs of his demanding boss. Whenever an accident involving the MTA's services occurred, Prendergast made sure to arrive at the scene of the incident before the governor did. He would mentally prepare answers for all of the tough questions that Cuomo would invariably ask when he arrived with his entourage.[36]

The governor's office would not let Prendergast negotiate directly with legislative leaders, as Ravitch and some other MTA chairs had. When Cuomo and the legislature were identifying the best use of the $9.9 billion windfall from the state's settlement with financial institutions, Prendergast was not allowed to lobby for the MTA's needs. Instead he had to wait for the crumbs to appear.[37]

Prendergast liked many of Cuomo's initiatives; after all, he wanted to improve customer amenities as much as anyone else. But he was not comfortable taking resources from other projects to pay for them. The other members of the MTA's board of directors went along with the governor's priorities in 2015 and 2016, in part because the board members relied on the chair and the MTA staff for information and advice. Every month, the members were given books containing hundreds of pages of tables and text about the MTA's expenses, revenues, and performance, along with background information for decisions they needed to make about setting fares, raising tolls, approving contracts, modifying services, settling lawsuits, hiring consultants, and acquiring real estate. As volunteers, they had limited time to absorb the complex issues associated with the vast agency. The MTA's operating and capital expenses were over $20 billion a year, and the authority along with its subsidiaries employed sixty-eight thousand people. On a typical day, the MTA carried 8.7 million people on its trains and buses, twice as many riders as the combined total in Chicago, Los Angeles, Boston, and Washington, DC.[38]

Many of the board members first learned about new MTA appointees and programs from the news media. Although the board had to approve the capital program, its members had limited influence in developing it; they could only approve or reject it as a body of work. In 2015 and 2016, they were not given straight answers about how the governor's initiatives would be funded. According to one board member, Veronica Vanterpool, the governor had "neutered the board." Prendergast was sympathetic to her. "It was a product of the governor," he said.[39]

Watching from the sidelines, many current and former MTA officials were disturbed. Richard Ravitch was outraged by the board's impotence. The former MTA chair thought Cuomo was violating state law by appointing his own people to MTA staff positions and usurping the authority's powers. One MTA executive recalled a time when MTA leaders did not always return phone calls from the governor's office. Shaking his head, he said, "Compare that with today, when it's stoop over and how far."[40]

When asked whether Tom Prendergast could have rebuffed the governor's requests, a former governor's senior aide said, "Cuomo knew how to use his powers. He got his way with legislators and he would have walked all over Tom." The aide noted that Cuomo was vengeful and quick to criticize other officials both on and off the record. "No one wants to incur his wrath," he said. The governor, he explained, could have made Prendergast's life miserable by cutting state funding, disrupting bond deals, putting pressure on other board members, and appointing people to the board who would give him trouble.[41]

Prendergast said the governor "never asked me to do anything illicit, illegal, or immoral." And the MTA chair stood up to the governor's aides when they suggested something that he thought would directly jeopardize the safety of his customers. As the former safety director for the subways, he could still remember the dates and details of subway derailments and other serious accidents that occurred under his watch. The Second Avenue subway stations might not be perfect when they opened, and some corners might have to be cut, but Prendergast was not going to begin operating trains unless he was confident that the service would be safe.[42]

A VERY LONG TO-DO LIST

In late 2015, when the governor decided to prioritize the Second Avenue subway, completing it by the end of 2016 was more of an aspirational goal than a realistic one. Michael Horodniceanu could not just pressure one firm to expedite work, because MTA Capital Construction had hired one consultant to design the subway and ten different contractors to build it.

In the tunnels, Horodniceanu's contractors were still finishing the installation of tracks, power supplies, and ventilation fans. In the stations, they were installing ceiling panels, walls, and floor tiles, along with ductwork for the ventilation and conduits for the electricity. Not all of the escalators had been delivered yet, let alone installed. On the street, contractors were still replacing utilities and building the ancillary facilities that would incorporate the ventilation equipment and emergency stairways.[43]

The schedule Horodniceanu had developed four years earlier assumed that by the end of 2015, most of this work would have already been completed and successfully tested. Now his schedulers had an enormously complicated task ahead: figuring out when each contractor would work, how much time they would need, and how they could all share work spaces. One contractor's problem could cascade into extensive delays.[44] Determining who was to blame for falling behind schedule was not easy. For example, any and all of the following parties might be responsible for the delays associated with installing the water mist system, which would be used to extinguish fires in an emergency situation:

+ MTA Capital Construction and its designers, for specifying an overly complicated system
+ Contractors who took longer than expected building the station cavern and laying the tracks
+ The manufacturers and suppliers who were providing the pipes, connectors, valves, pump controllers, nozzles, alarm devices, and pressure gauges
+ FTA officials who determined, after a lengthy review, that each of these components had to be manufactured in the United States
+ Workers who were installing all of these components in the stations
+ The NYC Fire Department and NYC Transit, which had extensive testing procedures to make sure everything was safe, effective, and easy to maintain[45]

In the beginning of 2016, with the governor breathing down their necks, the leaders of the Second Avenue subway construction team did not have the luxury of assigning blame. They needed to work together, or they would never meet the January 1, 2017, deadline. One of their biggest challenges was finding time to perform all the tests that had been planned. Testing first started when Horodniceanu sent engineers to factories all across the country to inspect various components such as signal equipment, transformers, escalators, and elevators. These trips identified problems that could be addressed early on, and would later help rule out the causes of problems that occurred in New York. Equipment and machinery were tested when they were delivered, after installation, and yet again after they were hooked up to other equipment. For example, electronic signs needed to display the letters and numbers clearly and with the proper illumination. After the signs were connected to NYC Transit's Rail Control Center, they needed to correctly display the proper information about train services, and the messages had to be consistent with those heard over the public-address sound system. These extensive testing procedures ensured that MTA Capital Construction's contractors turned over stations and equipment that would meet NYC Transit's stringent specifications and performance standards.[46]

To expedite testing for the New Year's deadline, NYC Transit would have to take personnel who had been assigned to work on other projects and other lines. That would be problematic since the MTA's inspector general had recently found that the subway's Maintenance Department needed to be conducting more, not fewer, regular inspections and tests of its tracks, equipment, and structures. NYC Transit did have not enough staff to expedite Second Avenue subway testing and conduct all of its routine tests, let alone meet the promises it had made in response to the inspector general.[47]

In January 2016, a very anxious Salvatore DeMatteo was raising concerns. His firm had a contract to install tracks, signals, and communications systems. The communications component was an example of the project's extraordinary complexity. DeMatteo was installing nineteen different communication systems, including those relating to intercoms, intrusion detections, closed-circuit television, service announcements, telephones, emergency booths, police and fire radios, emergency broadcasts, and fire-alarm/pull stations.[48]

DeMatteo began installation where he could, but he had to wait until many other contractors completed their assignments. His workers needed to connect equipment to permanent power supplies that were not yet available, and to install cables through conduits that had yet to be put in place. His team could not hang antennas until ceiling panels were installed or connect heat detectors to elevators that had not been lowered into stations. Because DeMatteo's work came after most of the other station work was completed, he said, "Everything falls on us. We need to test and put everything into service. We become the whipping boy." He made sure that MTA Capital Construction and the other contractors knew about his problems. He yelled and screamed; otherwise, he said, "things accumulate and come on us." He explained, "If I don't tell people in advance, we get blamed."[49]

The trickiest part of the communications system was the fire-protection component. In each station, DeMatteo had to install hundreds of smoke and heat detectors, each with their own internet address, that would trigger a complicated sequence of actions depending on the location and seriousness of the incident. Detectors would alert NYC Transit's Rail Control Center and the city's Fire Department with a fire's exact location. Elevators would go to a preprogrammed stop, while the escalators would either stop, reverse direction, or continue moving along, depending on the situation. Electronic signs and the public-address system would direct riders to the appropriate exits, while customers with difficulty evacuating would be accommodated in safe areas where they could communicate with emergency personnel.[50]

The safety systems were designed to meet the highest standards. The MTA had little choice. Since the September 11 attacks, terrorists had targeted train stations in Moscow, Madrid, London, India, and Sri Lanka.

Opening up the Second Avenue subway on time was certainly a popular idea. The Upper East Side's businesses and residents, including the governor's own sister, were tired of the construction. Elected officials were anxious to cut the ribbon, and subway riders were looking forward to new services and the easing of crowding on the Lexington Avenue line. The contractors also wanted to move on to other projects.

While the MTA had been poised to postpone the opening date of the subway before the governor intervened, Horodniceanu and Prendergast had their own personal incentives for finishing the project on time. Horodniceanu hoped to meet the deadline he had set in 2009 when he declared, "You can hold me accountable." Prendergast had been ready to retire in March 2016, but continued working only because the governor asked him to stay until the Second Avenue subway opened.[51]

When making decisions about the Second Avenue subway, MTA officials always had to balance various factors, including budget, schedule, and quality. Cuomo changed the MTA's priorities to emphasize speed. As a result, some factors were deemphasized, such as NYC Transit's concerns about maintainability, budget officials' worries about cost overruns, and engineers' expectations that they would thoroughly test every single component. The governor's insistence on meeting the New Year's deadline would consume the MTA as it turned its attention from other projects, other escalators, and other signal systems.

In February 2016, with the schedule more important than the budget, the MTA board awarded an additional $66 million to accelerate the subway's construction. The board members understood from the governor's public statements that this was important to him. Only one board member, Andrew Albert, spoke up at the meeting. He said, "This is really good news."[52]

The governor did not just want the subway opened by New Year's Day; he also wanted the streets rebuilt, with the equipment, trash, trucks, and muck houses all removed. So, the following month, the board awarded additional funds to complete the surface restoration of Second Avenue as quickly as possible. This construction work would involve laying down all the utilities in their permanent locations, installing a concrete roadway base and asphalt above it, putting in steel curbing, rebuilding sidewalks, and installing light poles and traffic signals. The contract would include an incentive if the contractors completed their work early and a penalty for late completion.[53]

With the board's approval, funds were taken out of the project's contingency budget and were used to pay for extending work shifts, additional shifts, and weekend work. At its peak, over five hundred union electricians were working simultaneously on the Second Avenue subway. Their regular salary was $54 per hour, plus $52 per hour in benefits, although when they worked overtime, they could earn $106 per hour, with an additional $70 per hour in benefits. One contractor said that at the end of 2016, many of his workers earned the equivalent of three weeks' salary in just one week.[54]

Money could only do so much, however. Cuomo and Prendergast had to move the Second Avenue subway to the top of everyone's to-do lists. Alaeden Jlelaty, the senior project manager who oversaw tunneling construction, said, "Life is about getting approvals." The governor got people to pay attention, turn up at meetings, and provide prompt feedback. Vacations were canceled, and when people responsible for sign-offs were unavailable, they identified someone else in their departments who would take their place. When MTA Capital Construction needed a part or service, Jlelaty said, they did not conduct their usual evaluation, solicit three prices, and then negotiate the best price. The governor, he explained, "pushed people out of their comas." Likewise, Pablo LeMus, a construction project manager, said the governor's deadline "got people's attention to the bullshit that was going on." The MTA, he recalled, "cut out the bullshit" and finally made decisions about various issues that had been lingering for months, such as the location of artwork, the type of ceiling paint that would be used, and the design of the token booths.[55]

Before Cuomo's team started riding roughshod over the project, MTA Capital Construction was beholden to its sister agency, NYC Transit. The transit divisions responsible for maintaining signals, tracks, and stations had forced Horodniceanu to revise his designs even as construction was underway. Since construction had been taking so long, the engineers wanted to update elements of the original designs. By the beginning of 2016, though, NYC Transit was allowed to make only those design changes that were either safety related or required by a building code.[56]

MTA Capital Construction's construction management firm, Parsons Brinckerhoff, brought in Larry Reuter to help coordinate construction work with NYC Transit. Before retiring in 2007, Reuter had been NYC Transit's longest-serving president. In 2016, he facilitated meetings, encouraged people to make prompt decisions, and helped secure NYC Transit staff to work on the Second Avenue subway. Reuter warned Prendergast, "We're going to drain your resources."[57]

The number 7 line extension, which opened in 2015, had been delayed because NYC Transit officials needed extra time to finish testing all the components. Delaying the Second Avenue subway in order to test every component was not acceptable. To expedite its work, NYC Transit would have to dedicate more resources, open up a testing office on Second Avenue, and scale back some of its requirements. According to the original schedule, DeMatteo would have nearly a year to conduct his testing. He was given less than three months.[58]

Since permanent electrical power was not yet available, Horodniceanu decided to use temporary power sources to test signals, lighting, pumps, elevators, and other components. This was somewhat risky because the components might not perform the same way with temporary power, and the temporary power could damage electrical components. Horodniceanu's decision was also costly, because the MTA and its contractors would have to conduct the tests all over again with full power. But testing with temporary power did reveal some issues the contractors were able to address earlier than they otherwise would have. Testing with permanent power had to be conducted more than once because all of the new stations had two separate electrical feeds from

Con Edison, in case of a power outage. So the construction team had to test the electronic devices with each feed and then ensure that all the equipment worked correctly after switching from one to another.[59]

The escalator testing was especially challenging. The new subway escalators were among the sturdiest found anywhere in the world. Compared to escalators in department stores and hotels, the subway escalators were designed more like stainless-steel tanks that could operate under extreme weather conditions, twenty-four hours a day, seven days a week, carrying a constant flow of customers with food, drinks, bags, strollers, and luggage. Some MTA contractors even ignored the rules and used the new escalators to move their construction equipment.

Kone, an escalator company based in Illinois, compressed about three months of work into six weeks by flying installers, electrical experts, and workers from its factory to expedite the installation, adjust the equipment, and order necessary parts. The escalators had to be sufficiently sturdy, yet pass a battery of sensitivity tests to ensure that they would automatically stop when a child caught a hand or shoelace on a moving escalator. They could not be too sensitive, though, or the automatic shutdown feature would stop the escalators every time passengers spilled their drinks or dropped their MetroCards.[60]

THE HANDS-ON GOVERNOR

In the summer of 2016, Andrew Cuomo, for all intents and purposes, took over Horodniceanu's role as the executive in charge of the Second Avenue subway. The governor started leading regular meetings of a construction management committee whose attendees included his trusted advisers (Rick Cotton and Larry Schwartz), MTA senior officials (Prendergast and Horodniceanu), and executives and supervisors from the construction firms. In the governor's conference room thirty-nine floors above Third Avenue, Cuomo told the committee that everyone had said he could not build a new Tappan Zee Bridge, but he got it done anyway. On Second Avenue, he declared, "We'll move heaven and earth" and "defy all expectations."[61]

At each meeting, the governor went through the outstanding issues and asked where and how he could help. He grilled the MTA officials and the contractors. Attendees came out of the meeting shaken up because he would not take no for an answer. Instead he wanted to know how they would get to yes.[62]

Many MTA officials and contractors who dealt directly with Cuomo described him as a bully. One construction manager said, "He squeezed people. He whipped people and scared them about their jobs and companies." The governor, he recalled, "had everyone running like when you're at a beach and someone comes up from behind you and yells 'shark.'" Another construction manager said that Cuomo was a bully, and one who was "effective as hell." According to a construction executive, "He went right for the jugular. It was my way or the highway. He's a bully; he does it well, an eloquent bully. He lets you know this is the way it's going to be. If you're not tough enough, find another place to work." DeMatteo said that the governor made everyone aware that "you needed to be on his team or he would get someone else."[63]

Tom Prendergast would not describe Cuomo as a bully, although he did say the governor was direct, held people accountable, and was "not happy with horseshit excuses." Prendergast said with a smile that Cuomo was not the proverbial eight-hundred-pound gorilla in a room. "That would be the vanilla version of the governor." Cuomo was more like an "eight-thousand-pound gorilla. If he is sitting on your side of the table, you love it." Prendergast felt intense pressure and developed migraine headaches, but recognized that if he wanted the responsibility and authority of leading the MTA, he needed to take the heat.[64]

Prendergast credited the governor with creating an "esprit de corps," and most of the contractors I talked with used similar terms. DeMatteo was impressed by Cuomo's leadership, tenacity, and focus: "He put us all in one boat and said, 'Let's get past the me versus you.' He made it clear, if there's a hole in the boat, we're all going to sink." Contractors, DeMatteo said, will often point fingers at each other and claim they were not the ones responsible for a problem. Until Cuomo brought them together, the construction executives were not accustomed to meeting with each other or working closely together. The governor forced them to help each other out. One contractor said, "When the governor of the state of New York gets involved, you feel more important about it and more focused on it."[65]

When a company responsible for installing conduits fell behind schedule, another firm stepped in and installed them, even though the firm doing the work was not sure whether it would be fully reimbursed. A senior construction manager said, "We put financial and commercial issues aside" because of peer pressure. "People," she added, "wanted to keep their reputations." Likewise, while Con Edison's Alphonse Calvanico was coordinating work with nine different departments at his company, he kept his supervisors in the loop because they were "feeling the political heat." He said, "We made sure that we weren't going to be the cause of a delay."[66]

One of Cuomo's most effective tactics was threatening suppliers and subcontractors. The governor called and sent out letters telling them that if they did not meet the MTA's deadlines, he would make them ineligible to work on the state's future projects. He even warned them that the impact would be so significant to their business that the publicly traded construction companies might have to notify the Securities and Exchange Commission. His threats were mostly a bluff, but the companies decided it was less expensive to spend money on overtime than on litigation. According to Horodniceanu, "When the governor calls, people listen." Often the governor did not even need to make a call, because word spread quickly throughout the construction world that Cuomo meant business.[67]

Bob DeThomasis's firm was responsible for the stations' interior finishes, such as canopies, glass enclosures, escalator paneling, and ornamental steel iron. Like DeMatteo, he was at the mercy of nearly every other contractor, because he had to wait for them to complete their work. DeThomasis was genuinely worried that "if we don't get it done, we would close up shop—and never get another public works project." With Cuomo making frequent visits to inspect the subway's progress, DeThomasis said, "we were always under the gun." He found the governor intimidating and the scrutiny intense. "The governor made it clear that we will be done. There were no negotiations. You had to do whatever you needed to do."[68]

The glass canopy for a 72nd Street station entrance could not be ordered until another contractor completed its work and let DeThomasis's crew take final measurements. The supplier said that once the order was placed, it would take six weeks to manufacture and deliver the canopy to New York. Cuomo offered to call the glass company himself to expedite the work, but that would not be necessary: DeThomasis flew to Minneapolis and warned his supplier, "The next call you get will be from the governor's office and you will no longer be on the preferred contractor's list for the MTA. . . . The governor is pissed off at us, and you won't get anything more from him or us." The threat worked. DeThomasis's firm gave the glass company additional money and the canopy was shipped and installed in two weeks rather than six.[69]

The governor "did the right thing," DeThomasis maintained. "He made a goal for everybody to achieve. . . . In the construction business, the only language that people we deal with understand is, who has the biggest stick, mouth, and checkbook—that's what gets it done. When someone tries to expedite a construction job, usually people will just look at them and laugh."[70]

When Cuomo visited Second Avenue in the fall of 2016, he asked workers, inspectors, and engineers about the problems they were encountering, how he could help, and whom he could call. According to one member of the construction team, he set a tone: "We will get this done." DeThomasis recalled that "when he started to show up, it made the men more confident and comfortable." The governor said to the workers, "If you're having a problem with your boss, you tell me. Tell us what you need from us—whatever you can think of."[71]

DeThomasis appreciated Cuomo's attentiveness because the governor was talking not just to the construction executives, but also to the workers who had the best understanding of the problems underground. "If workers feel comfortable," DeThomasis explained, "they will work harder. If you set goals, they will be receptive." He said that Cuomo's approach was much more effective than the MTA's typical pace of "we will get it done, sometime." Even though the union workers were earning lucrative salaries by working overtime, by all accounts they were not slowing down the project to pad their pockets. DeThomasis recognized that "they wanted to get it done. They didn't want to hold it up." Clearly, no one wanted to be blamed for a delay.[72]

Although Andrew Cuomo can be charming, it is not his natural and typical demeanor. At the Second Avenue subway meetings, he would ask how many people the contractors would have working at the stations. Then, on his way home, Cuomo said, "I would stop at one of the stations. I'd go down and count how many people were down there." He shouted when he saw something he did not like. One day, Cuomo was so angry when he did not see anyone working on a faulty escalator that he walked around yelling, "Who is working on the escalator?" until someone finally appeared. On another occasion, he was so frustrated that he reportedly "threw a fit" and stormed off.[73]

Michael Horodniceanu had been the face of the Second Avenue subway when the streets were getting ripped up, Upper East Siders were coughing, and explosions were scaring residents. With the opening only weeks away, Cuomo was in the spotlight, basking in the MTA's accomplishments. Cuomo lambasted the MTA's lackadaisical approach to the project before he got involved, saying that "there had been no sense of urgency" and that the MTA bureaucracy had developed its own culture in which it set a deadline but nobody was responsible and accountable for it. Belittling Horodniceanu's painstaking efforts, he said, "Now, I'm sure the people who picked the deadline in 2009, basically threw a dart at a calendar and it landed on January 2017. And I'm sure the people who set the date in 2009 said, 'Well let's pick a date where none of us are going to be here so we can't be held accountable.' And they came up with 2017."[74]

In 1968, Nelson Rockefeller had unveiled his ambitious transportation plan as a way to burnish his credentials on the national stage. In a similar way, Cuomo took advantage of his accomplishments with the Tappan Zee Bridge, LaGuardia Airport, and the Second Avenue subway. In December 2016 he boasted, "We haven't built big projects, ambitious projects in a long time. Not just this state—this nation. Last time we built a new airport was Denver, like twenty years ago. Last time we built a new bridge was the Verrazano, like 1960. Our appetite for big projects waned."[75]

Cuomo took full advantage of the impending subway opening with multiple media events. He gave tours of the stations, unveiled the stations at open houses, and introduced the stations' artwork at the Museum of Modern Art. National TV crews and newspaper reporters followed him around as he inspected the ongoing progress. He proudly pointed out, as if he had designed it himself, the stations' sense of openness and their spectacular art. He exclaimed, "That claustrophobia that descended upon you when you walked into a subway station is gone."[76]

The governor's press office skillfully shaped the coverage of the subway megaproject. Reporters did not refer to the new line as a short extension of an existing subway line. The media did not discuss the lack of a financial plan for the second, third, and fourth phases. Instead, most reporters said that thanks to Andrew Cuomo, the long-awaited Second Avenue subway would finally open. Cuomo was given credit for helping to secure more than $1 billion in federal funds, even though he had not been the governor when the FTA awarded its grant. Instead of sharing the credit with his predecessors, Cuomo tended to exaggerate his own role. For instance, he claimed that even though public authorities were supposed to be efficient, effective, and faithful to deadlines, he reversed the equation by getting the subway opened on time.[77]

The governor took obvious delight in answering reporters' questions. While riding on a train through the new stations, an NBC *Today Show* correspondent asked Cuomo, "What can other cities learn from what you guys have managed to pull off here?" CBS's morning show asked him whether his accomplishment was a model for how governments could complete big projects efficiently. When questioned about whether he was running for president, Cuomo would invariably chuckle. In words that would come back to haunt him the following year, the governor explained that he controlled the MTA because he appointed the majority of its board members. "I'm going to step up and take responsibility," he said on December 15. "If it doesn't open on January first, it's me. It's me. I will have failed."[78]

When Cuomo was sufficiently confident about meeting the project deadline, invitations were sent out to over five hundred people for an exclusive New Year's Eve party in the 72nd Street station. The station was filled with purple, pink, and orange lights, and the newsstand was converted into a beer bar. On December 30, the governor checked out the new station one last time and told the workers he wanted the walls cleaned and the floors scrubbed for the next evening's gala.[79]

On New Year's Eve, the MTA gave Cuomo and his guests rides back and forth between the new stations. The sounds of the trains did not drown out the five-piece band, thanks to the rubber pads on the tracks and the sound-absorbing panels on the ceiling and walls. Cuomo told his guests that the new subway was a vindication of his vision. "We needed to show people that government works and we can still do big things and great things and we can still get them done," he said. "This isn't your grandfather's subway," he told the partygoers.[80]

The stations received rave reviews. The news columnist Ralph Gardner Jr. called the Second Avenue subway "amazing." He told radio listeners, "Unlike the typical station where the ceilings are so low you can almost bump your head on the mechanicals, or get dripped on by strange fluids, the new stations are spacious, brightly lighted and filled with art."[81]

On New Year's Day, Cuomo came back to 96th Street to welcome the public for the Second Avenue subway's first day of service. From the front car, he announced over the public address system, "Rest assured, I am not driving the train." Thousands of smiling people walked around the stations and admired the artwork as though they were visiting a museum. Barry Schneider, the community board leader, remembering how he had lived through the filth, the dirt, the muck, and the dislocation, said, "Here we are today in a world-class, otherworldly train station. It should have a special name. It's better than a train station."[82]

One of the biggest surprises to many people were the massive art installations commissioned by the MTA. When Cuomo unveiled the artworks, he called them "the largest permanent public art installation in New York State history." At 63rd Street, an artist used old photos of the Second and Third Avenue elevated trains to create compositions of riders and pedestrians. At the 72nd Street station, glass mosaics and laminated glass displayed more than three dozen characters, including a restaurateur holding a bag with a fish tail sticking out, and a police officer with a dripping popsicle stick. At 86th Street, mosaic-tiled portraits nearly nine feet high reflected the diversity of the subway's riders, while the 96th Street station featured over four thousand porcelain wall tiles.[83]

As MTA officials and construction workers walked through the new stations on New Year's Day, their favorite part was watching people's faces. Strangers walked up to them and said thank you. As a team they had accomplished what many of them had thought was impossible, achieving in the last two months what was expected to take nearly a year. One senior construction manager fled Second Avenue as soon as she could, taking a long-planned family vacation, something she had not done in three years. She said that building the Second Avenue subway had been her company's most challenging project, and added, "I hope that we don't do the second phase."[84]

Peter Cafiero, the head of NYC Transit's Operations Planning division, was thrilled when he overheard a woman say, "This is so wonderful—I wish all stations could be like this." He was also delighted to have paid tribute to his mentor, Bob Olmsted, who had died seven years earlier. Cafiero invited Olmsted's son, Alan, to join him at the 96th Street station to ride in the front car with the governor. Bob Olmsted had first sketched out a Second Avenue subway in the 1940s, and he developed the MTA's expansion plan in the 1960s. He had helped MTA officials, consultants, contractors, and transportation advocates as they were planning, lobbying for, designing, and constructing the Second Avenue subway in the 1990s and 2000s. Cafiero told Alan, "I always marveled that, no matter what wild and crazy ideas I or our team came up with, your dad would whip out a hand-drawn but incredibly neat scale plan and profile of that very idea that he had sketched out 20 years before."[85]

On January 1, Second Avenue was filled with many happy people who did not need to venture belowground. The MTA had restored the streetscape so that it looked better than ever, with new trees, benches, trash cans, and lighting. Crossing distances were reduced for pedestrians and a lane was taken away from motor vehicles and dedicated to bicyclists.[86]

Business owners breathed a sigh of relief. A wine shop owner exclaimed that the new station attracted people "like it was the premiere for a movie." One restaurant owner declared, "The noise, the jack-hammering, smoke, and being blocked and obstructed behind construction equipment won't be missed." Another restaurant owner said, "We've been here for nine months and when the barricades came down, customers were surprised to see us here, with some even asking if we were new to the area."[87]

Governor Cuomo had pressed the right buttons to open up the Second Avenue subway on the first day of the new year. But New Yorkers did not realize what happens when a public agency pours too much of its attention and resources into expediting one megaproject.

Figure 9.1. *96th Street station platform in December 2016. Source: Metropolitan Transportation Authority.*

Figure 9.2. *View of the 96th Street station platform from the mezzanine in December 2016. Source: Metropolitan Transportation Authority.*

Figure 9.3. Glass mosaic and laminated glass by Vik Muniz, at the 72nd Street station. Source: Metropolitan Transportation Authority.

Figure 9.4. Governor Andrew Cuomo (left) and Tom Prendergast (right) rode the first train on January 1, 2017. Michael Horodniceanu, looking forlorn, is wearing glasses and a scarf in the background. Source: Metropolitan Transportation Authority.

CONCLUSION

Delays Ahead

In early 2017, the Second Avenue subway was no longer a joke or a metaphor for the city's failures. Those who lived and worked near Second Avenue were relieved that the barricades were down, the sidewalks clear, and the muck houses removed. Property owners were thrilled as the number of vacant storefronts plummeted and rents for commercial space and apartments soared.[1]

After leading the Second Avenue subway's planning efforts for the previous twenty-five years, NYC Transit's Peter Cafiero was delighted that more than 150,000 passengers were using the new subway service every day and that ridership at the Upper East Side's Lexington Avenue stations decreased by nearly 30 percent. Subway riders could travel between the Upper East Side, Times Square, Herald Square, and Coney Island without having to transfer trains. They had shorter walks, faster rides, and more comfortable trips.[2]

Spending $4.6 billion to build a 1.5-mile subway line was not necessarily a cause for celebration, though. Per mile, the subway cost more than four times as much as new subway lines in Amsterdam, Barcelona, Berlin, Copenhagen, Paris, and Tokyo. The *Wall Street Journal* referred to the Second Avenue subway as "by far the most expensive train track in the history of the world." MTA officials would have another reason to temper their pride, because the repercussions of meeting the governor's deadline were about to impact just about every single subway rider.[3]

TRIGGERING A STATE OF EMERGENCY

A month after the subway opened in 2017, MTA Capital Construction was tracking a mind-boggling 17,260 discrepancies between items the contractor was required to address and the actual work completed. Some of these "punch list" items were relatively minor, such as toilet paper rolls hanging by strings and identification tags missing from cables. Others were not so minor, such as active leaks in seventy-five different locations, and malfunctioning fire-alarm and fire-suppression systems.[4]

Federal officials overseeing the MTA's efforts found that such a large number of discrepancies indicated a breakdown in the contractors' quality assurance programs and the subcontractors' quality control programs. In a rush to meet the New Year's deadline, the MTA did not have enough time to follow all of its standard procedures and testing protocols. MTA officials circumvented their own process for certifying the safety of the Second Avenue subway before passenger service began. Quality, federal officials concluded, was clearly compromised to accelerate the schedule.[5]

Haste made waste. After the line opened, fixing problems became more expensive and time consuming because trains were running all day and all night. Transit officials also found it difficult to assign responsibility to contractors. One transit official explained that it was like a homeowner "buying a house without doing a full inspection and then noticing a problem three months later. . . . You're going to have trouble getting the former owner to fix those defects. They'll just blame you for causing the problem."[6]

After the new stations opened, NYC Transit was still testing the water mist systems, escalators, elevators, communication systems, signals, and tracks. Since the fire and intrusion alarms did not work properly, NYC Transit had to train and hire temporary workers to act as human fire alarms, around the clock. The MTA spent more than half a million dollars every month in 2017 for three safety officers at each of the Second Avenue stations, while two stood guard at 63rd Street. The new stations, which had wide corridors and emergency ventilation, were arguably much safer than many of the older subway stations. New stations, however, had to comply with modern fire safety standards, while the older stations were exempt.[7]

Numerous incidents occurred on Second Avenue that would have been prevented if the MTA had not been in such a rush to begin subway service. Less than three weeks after the 96th Street station opened, fire sprinklers spewed out water that flooded the escalator equipment; the escalators were then taken out of service for the next sixty-three days. Similarly, the station entrance at 83rd Street was closed after a defective sensor triggered the sprinklers and damaged three escalators. In other instances, firefighters rescued passengers stuck in elevators that repeatedly blew circuits, and rain caused an entrance to be shut down because a canopy installed days before the opening was not sealed properly.[8]

While the MTA's contractors worked on Second Avenue subway glitches, NYC Transit faced a more serious issue. Shifting the MTA's priorities and accelerating construction of the Second Avenue subway led to a system-wide subway crisis in 2017. Governor Cuomo was not the first elected official to put his own short-term priorities ahead of the subway's long-term needs. It had been a recurring pattern, not the exception, for more than a century.

Because successive mayors opposed raising subway fares to meet rising expenses, the private railroads cut back on basic subway maintenance in the 1910s, 1920s, and 1930s. After taking over the transit system in 1940, city leaders prioritized low fares and generous union contracts over infrastructure investments. In the late 1940s and early 1950s, the city lied about its ability to expand the subways so that it could borrow more money for other uses. In the 1960s, the governor pursued expansion projects that led to the deterioration of subway services in the 1970s. In the late 1990s and the 2000s, the state's elected officials forced the MTA to take on too much debt, and then the MTA had to cut expenses when the city was hit by a recession and a hurricane.

In 2016, the MTA diverted its attention and resources to accommodate Cuomo's priorities. One MTA official said that "the governor through brute force" opened the Second Avenue subway by New Year's Day, but "we paid dearly." He added, "Protecting the integrity and safety of the system needs a minimum investment. You fuck with that at your own risk." A NYC Transit executive noted, "There is only so much bandwidth an organization has. Eventually the base system falls apart."[9]

After he retired as MTA chair, Tom Prendergast was candid about the challenges he had faced trying to meet the governor's deadline. "We took our eyes off the ball," he acknowledged. "We stressed the organization and the people—and problems occurred. It had unintended consequences." Prendergast used an analogy of a family car trip. "You know the car really well," he said. "You watch the dashboard metrics like water temperature and coolant. But when the kids start complaining and your spouse distracts you, you take your eyes off the dashboard. Then the needle is in the red and you have a bigger problem." He explained, "The MTA is like an iceberg. Only 10 percent is visible above the water line. What sinks the boat is below the water line."[10]

Starting in 2015, NYC Transit allocated additional resources for the Second Avenue subway project because it was falling behind schedule. Since hiring and training new employees or bringing in qualified consultants would have taken about six months, NYC Transit executives reassigned existing staff to work on Second Avenue. They selected experienced personnel who had the necessary skills, understood NYC Transit's culture, and knew the relationship between the various divisions within the Department of Subways. Wynton Habersham, who headed the department, acknowledged that "we had to pull the best and the brightest from the existing system," and that reassigning people who normally inspected, tested, and troubleshooted equipment created problems throughout the rest of the subway system.[11]

NYC Transit routinely inspects and tests subway components to ensure their reliability and structural integrity. In 2016, some of those routine tests were put off in order to focus on Second Avenue issues. "We lost sight of more important things and paid for that in 2017," Habersham admitted, adding that the "quality of maintenance and testing waned considerably in 2016," which delayed other projects. Even when inspections were conducted, the quality of work suffered because many replacement workers did not understand the idiosyncrasies of the equipment they inspected. Habersham compared this to "taking your car to Jiffy Lube rather than your regular mechanic, who knows your car better than you in some ways."[12]

According to Samuel Wong, a NYC Transit data scientist, analysts who typically looked at the root causes of subway problems were pulled off to work on the Second Avenue subway. These analysts were like doctors who diagnose a patient's symptoms and recommend a treatment plan. When they were reassigned to Second Avenue, the symptoms on the existing subway system did not go away; they were just ignored. The Second Avenue subway, Wong explained, "literally affected hundreds of projects." In the operations and maintenance divisions, engineers who usually developed solutions to subway problems were told to focus on Second Avenue issues. Consequently, they did not order materials, schedule crews, or coordinate work for other projects. With fewer people developing treatment plans and planning projects, the symptoms worsened. "If you're not inspecting, not seeing, and not fixing," Wong said, "it's going to create problems."[13]

Among the hardest-hit divisions was the Subway Department's electronics maintenance division, which was responsible for the subway's electronics and communication systems. In 2016, nearly 20 percent of the division's two-hundred-member staff were dedicated full time to the Second Avenue subway. They were also devoting numerous resources to Cuomo's other priorities, such as countdown clocks and wireless connectivity projects. Even before Cuomo shook up the MTA's plans, this division had been unable to comply with its own schedule for maintaining and monitoring equipment.[14]

After New York diverted resources to focus on system expansion projects in the 1970s, trains broke down four times as often. A similar situation occurred after the opening of the Second Avenue subway. In early 2017, subways were delayed more than seventy thousand times a month, up from twenty-eight thousand a month five years earlier. Only 65 percent of weekday trains reached their destinations on time, the lowest rate since the transit crisis of the 1970s. On the list of the twenty most heavily used rapid-transit systems in the world, New York's on-time performance ranked at the very bottom. A 2017 Quinnipiac University poll found that less than one-quarter of New York City voters rated subway service excellent or good.[15]

The Second Avenue subway helped alleviate some overcrowding on the Lexington Avenue line, but the line's problems were far from solved. In the first three months of 2017, the local trains on the Lexington Avenue line ran on schedule less than one-third of the time. In comparison, the on-time performance of some subway systems in Asia was 99 percent.[16]

The media's praise for the MTA earlier in the year had been fleeting. In the spring of 2017, newspapers, television, radio, and websites reported on problems across the subway system. Derailments and delays took center stage to an extent not seen since the early 1980s. The Daily News referred to the subways as "on the brink," "sick-as-a-dog," and "beleaguered," while the New York Post declared, "Subway delays have hit a crisis point." The New York Times observed that "each new revelation about the degradation of New York's subways seems more shocking than the last."[17] Social media amplified the MTA's woes. Passengers took photos and videos of track fires, crowded stations, and the passengers trapped between them. The images were instantly shared because, thanks to Cuomo, all of the subway stations had Wi-Fi and cell phone service by 2017.[18]

Although the deterioration of service accelerated in 2016, it had started years before. The MTA pared expenses during the 2008 recession by cutting back on maintenance, training, and inspection. To cope with plummeting tax revenue, the MTA reduced the maintenance of subway cars, postponed track-maintenance overhauls, and inspected equipment less frequently. In 2017, the new MTA chair, Joe Lhota, acknowledged that "the maintenance intervals were stretched, and they were stretched too far." The MTA diverted even more resources from planned work after Hurricane Sandy battered the city in 2012. As a result, NYC Transit continued to fall behind in bringing the subway system into a state of good repair. Between 2011 and 2017, subways broke down more frequently every single year, the longest decline since 1982.[19]

As the subway troubles intensified in May 2017, Cuomo first tried to claim that he had little control over the MTA by pointing to other elected officials, including the mayor, who had representatives on the MTA's board. Reporters would not let the governor shirk his responsibility, though, since they had recently covered him taking credit for the subways at numerous Second Avenue subway events. In May 2017, headlines in the *Daily News* and *New York Post* proclaimed, "Straphangers to Cuomo: Fix This," "Get on Track, Gov," and "Rail Mess Is on Gov." The website Gothamist published an article titled, "Cuomo Denies Controlling the MTA despite Controlling the MTA." New York City's exasperated mayor, Bill de Blasio, said about the governor, "He should just own up to it and take this responsibility seriously." Many New Yorkers echoed the newspapers and the mayor in their social media posts by including the hashtag #CuomosMTA.[20]

In June, after a train derailment injured dozens of passengers in Harlem and caused system-wide delays, Cuomo signed an executive order declaring a state of emergency in the MTA region so that subway repairs could be expedited. The usually thick-skinned governor complained that riders "tweet nasty things about me all day." No governor could solve all the transit problems in a couple of months, a couple of years, or even a couple of decades.[21]

Making matters worse, the public and even the MTA's board members did not understand the causes of the transit failures because MTA officials hid information and manipulated data to serve the governor's purposes. Likewise, the board and the public were not told that six months after the Second Avenue subway opened, MTA Capital Construction still had over six thousand items remaining on its punch list. They were kept in the dark about the costs associated with accelerating the subway schedule because that information would have diminished one of the governor's signature achievements.[22]

THE MOST EXPENSIVE SUBWAY IN THE WORLD

Since the 1960s, the Regional Plan Association, the influential civic organization, has made the Second Avenue subway a centerpiece of its proposals to improve transportation in the metropolitan area. In 1999, the association's cost estimate of $1 billion per mile helped spur public support for building an 8.5-mile line from 125th Street to Lower Manhattan. After the first phase opened at a cost of $3 billion per mile, Richard Barone, the association's vice president, said, "There's no disputing that on a per-mile basis Second Avenue is the most expensive subway extension in the world. That's just the honest-to-God truth."[23]

Even after taking inflation into account, the cost per station to build the Second Avenue subway was twenty-five times higher than the subway's construction cost in 1904 when workers used pickaxes, not tunnel-boring machines. Despite the new subway line's astronomical costs, it would not even be able to offer express and local service, like New York's older subway lines, because Second Avenue had only two tracks, not four.[24]

The cost of the first phase was astronomical because of (1) inefficient phasing and high real estate costs, (2) powerful unions earning high wages and dictating costly work rules, and (3) regulations and environmental sensitivities. Neither the MTA nor New York's elected officials like to discuss many of these factors, since they relate to issues and problems that politicians are loath to confront.

Factor 1: Phasing and Real Estate

The cost per mile would have been significantly lower if workers had built the subway line from East Harlem to Lower Manhattan without stopping. Instead, the MTA's contractors acquired a tunnel-boring machine and shipped it to New York, where they built a trench, launched the machine, and operated it between 92nd and 63rd Streets before dismantling and removing it. For the next three phases, the MTA must again select new teams that will need to mobilize personnel and equipment. By ending the first phase before beginning the second phase, the MTA also lost talented workers and engineers who had learned valuable lessons (not captured in construction drawings) about digging up streets, supporting old tenement buildings, and building a subway. No one wanted to repeat the lesson of the 1970s, when construction started and then stopped on tunnels in East Harlem, the East Village, and Chinatown, but building one short segment and then restarting construction years later is a terribly inefficient way to build a subway line.

The population density and high real estate values on the Upper East Side added to the subway's construction costs. The neighborhood did not have any vacant parcels or parking lots where workers could build entrances, construction shafts, ancillary facilities, and emergency exits. As a result, the MTA spent more than $215 million on real estate–related expenses for the subway's first phase. These expenses included acquiring easements through the basements of apartment buildings and then relocating equipment that was in the way. For instance, the MTA gave the owners of an East 87th Street building $19 million to move their mechanical, electrical, plumbing, and fire-protection equipment. The cost included nearly $500,000 just to remove and dispose of asbestos.[25]

During construction, several buildings had to be temporarily evacuated between 92nd and 97th Streets when the MTA's contractors found they were leaning and their facades cracking. Although the problems existed before the MTA started construction, the MTA paid nearly $1 million to stabilize the buildings. The other choice was to wait for a court to force landlords to bring their buildings up to code, but that would have been more costly because it would have delayed the construction work. Tenants who were temporarily evacuated from their apartments were certainly treated well: the MTA paid for their rent and utilities, plus $9,000 per month (for those who lived in two-bedroom apartments) to find another place to stay. The tenants were given the option of staying free at a nearby hotel with a stipend of $40 per person, per day, for meals.[26]

New York construction costs were higher because of other factors. Delivering materials and removing spoils was expensive because Manhattan has no train lines to carry freight, and barges were ruled out for environmental and logistical reasons. The city's notorious traffic conditions added to delivery costs, and contractors had to use smaller-than-ideal trucks because of height and weight restrictions on the city's highways.[27]

In retrospect, MTA officials wished they had offset their costs by having property owners in the neighborhood pay for a portion of the project. Although property values along Second Avenue soared thanks to the new subway, the MTA did not recoup any of this increase. In fact, the MTA gave money to property owners to shore up old buildings that were slated to be torn down for new developments.

Factor 2: Powerful Unions

One Second Avenue subway executive told me, "Costs in New York are astronomical. You can't admit it, but a lot has to do with the unions." Even though MTA Capital Construction solicited bids from contractors and then selected the lowest qualified bidders, the public did not benefit from the efficiencies of a competitive marketplace. Few firms competed for the MTA's contracts, and the state required that union members perform all the construction work—all 15.3 million hours of it.[28]

New York City's construction unions operate under an anachronistic and highly inefficient system. The MTA does not determine wages and benefits for the workers who renovate and build its subways. Neither do the contractors who hire the workers. Instead, the contractors' trade associations and the unions' representatives negotiate wages, benefits, and work rules that apply to all construction projects in the city. The subway's construction workers earned 50 percent more than those in Amsterdam, Houston, Munich, and London, and more than twice as much as those in Seoul, Hong Kong, and Tokyo. New York's tunnel workers in 2015 earned $57 per hour, plus $48 in benefits—and double time after an eight-hour day. With benefits, electricians earned $104 per hour and plumbers made $94 per hour in 2015.[29]

The MTA's contractors paid for items that were not typically part of construction costs in other countries, such as health care, retirement benefits, and apprenticeship programs. Since many of New York's union members do not work an entire year, salaries were expected to cover long periods of unemployment. A small portion of the labor costs even flowed into the unions' political action committees, which the unions use to help their favorite politicians.

The construction unions made sure that workers were extensively trained and highly skilled, and that they performed their work in an extraordinarily safe manner. MTA Capital Construction president Michael Horodniceanu thought union workers could also be productive, as long as he could keep them busy all day long. He knew that was impossible, though, because union work rules mandated that contractors hire far more workers than were needed.[30]

Before working at the MTA, Horodniceanu owned an engineering firm, where he managed the construction of a soccer stadium in Queens. Horodniceanu complained to me that he had to hire a master mechanic for every five pieces of large equipment that were used to build the stadium. "You needed to have a guy who was supposed to fix something," he said, "but instead he just called someone else to fix it. They had a fat guy sitting in a chair smoking a cigar like in *The Sopranos*. When a sixth piece of equipment came in, you needed another master mechanic. That was the rule." The unions also required master mechanics for the Second Avenue subway construction, although Horodniceanu was not aware of this when I interviewed him. He explained, "I was interested more in the soccer stadium, because I personally paid for it."[31]

Master mechanics were just one example of unnecessary workers. The union agreements between the trade unions and the contractors association spelled out how many workers were needed to perform various tasks, from driving piles to bending metal. Referring to the unions, a cost estimator who has worked in twenty-seven different states said, "It's amazing how much they dictate everything that happens on a job in New York." The tunnel-boring machine was staffed with more than twice as many workers as in most other cities. An electrical contractor had to pay a shop steward to check whether union workers were certified and whether truck drivers delivering materials were union members. One Second Avenue subway contractor complained, "Sometimes you need two guys if you want to turn a screw."[32]

The union contracts had clauses that bordered on extortion, such as the requirement that contractors pay the tunnel workers' unions $450,000 to use a large tunnel-boring machine because it was ostensibly taking jobs away from workers. Contractors had to hire elevator operators who did little more than push buttons, and crane oilers who were paid to oil machinery that needed little oiling. Contractors even needed to hire union members to monitor break rooms and changing rooms, despite the fact that the workers were no longer in middle school.[33]

The MTA's construction team needed to respect the rules of individual unions as well as the rules that dictated which unions could do a certain type of construction work. For example, only members of the laborers' union could dig trenches, while only members of the tunnel workers' union could change the cutters and bits on the tunnel-boring machines. The carpenters' union set traffic barriers, while the operating engineers' union installed temporary power and lighting, and the timbermen's union maintained wooden support systems for temporary roadways. All of the trade unions—including the ones representing carpenters, sheet metal workers, tunnel workers, operating engineers, electricians, concrete workers, and plumbers—jealously guarded their roles, and would not let workers from other unions encroach on their work. As a result, workers in one trade often had to stand by while workers in another trade completed their work.[34]

Before soliciting bids, the MTA missed an opportunity to lower construction costs by not developing a "project labor agreement" with the unions. Such an agreement might have eliminated the most egregious work-rule practices and reduced some of the costs associated with union jurisdictions, work hours, and the number of people required to perform each task. In retrospect, MTA Construction's first president, Mysore Nagaraja, conceded that it would have helped reduce costs, but no one on his team had thought about it.[35]

Looking ahead, the relationship between subway expansion and construction unions appears to be paradoxical. Unions are politically powerful in New York because their members make phone calls, campaign door to door, attend rallies, and help turn out the vote for the unions' favorite candidates. Unions are especially influential in legislative districts that are heavily Democratic because candidates usually need only a few thousand votes to win the primary and then are virtually assured of winning the general election. Both public- and private-sector unions can also be instrumental in generating support in Albany for the MTA's multibillion-dollar capital programs. Because union labor is so expensive, however, it may not be possible in the foreseeable future to obtain enough money to complete the Second Avenue subway. Building the subway without union labor may not be a viable option either, because without union support, the MTA would not be able to generate sufficient funding.

Factor 3: Regulations and Sensitivities

The third reason why the Second Avenue subway was so costly relates to regulations and standards that have built up over time, and the ever-increasing desire to minimize disturbances associated with construction.

To meet rigorous fire-safety and disability-access regulations, the stations needed costly ventilation systems, wide platforms, spacious entrances, and numerous elevators. Other features that once might have been considered extravagant, New Yorkers now considered mandatory. Stations have mezzanines that reduce passenger crowding on platforms, and they are connected via escalators to both the platform and the street. In the summer, a climate-control system lowers the temperature in the stations. The stations were also designed to minimize noise and vibrations. In fact, they are so quiet and spacious, and boast such spectacular artwork, that they hosted a delightful New Year's Eve party for a governor. All of these features of the Second Avenue subway stations are certainly desirable, but they do drive up the cost of building new subway lines.

Since construction affected one of the nation's busiest neighborhoods, contractors had to take extensive and expensive precautions to minimize construction hours, noise, dust, and traffic impacts. Not only did the MTA have to avoid utility outages, but the authority also had to pay the cost of moving old electric, phone, television, and internet lines, as well as installing new ones. A city transportation official said about the utility companies, "Obviously they're going to milk this." He could have said the same thing about the city, since the MTA paid for new municipal water and sewer lines, as well as street lighting, curbs, and trees. The MTA even paid to improve several streets it did not rip up, just so Second Avenue would have a consistent look.[36]

The MTA was saddled with numerous regulations and programs that may have provided social benefits, but adhering to them was costly and time consuming. For example, the federal government's "Buy America" provision required the MTA to use steel, iron, and manufactured goods produced in the United States, although the FTA did grant some exceptions, such as for product subcomponents. When the acoustical engineers specified a particular pad for the train tracks that was designed to minimize noise and vibration, they assumed the pad would be exempt from the Buy America rules because it was a subcomponent. A year after the MTA's contractor purchased the pads from a Swiss company, however, the FTA said the pads were actually a component and not a subcomponent.[37] MTA officials scrambled to find a US company willing and able to manufacture the pads, which had billions of tiny bubbles. They worked with the FTA, the US Department of Commerce, and the National Institute for Standards and Technology to find a manufacturer. After failing to find one, the MTA sought a waiver to exempt the pads from the Buy America clause. Two years after the MTA's contractor initially purchased the pads, and after numerous reports, legal analyses, and memos, the FTA granted the waiver and allowed the MTA to install them.[38]

Another set of requirements related to affirmative action. Following the state's lead, the MTA established a goal that at least 20 percent of work performed on construction contracts should go to contractors owned by minorities and women. The FTA had its own set of rules to help "disadvantaged business enterprises." To meet the state's goal and comply with federal regulations, contractors had to split up their work into small-enough components so they could find enough qualified minority- and women-owned subcontractors. After E. E. Cruz & Company signed a contract to build the 96th Street station, the construction company awarded work to thirty-eight different firms owned by women and minorities. Entering into dozens of contracts, and then monitoring and coordinating them, added to the complexity, cost, and risks of construction. E. E. Cruz supervisors had to make sure there was no overlap in the work assigned to all of its subcontractors, and equally important, they had to make sure there were no gaps in the work assigned.[39]

There was another reason why contractors complained about having so many small firms: they were usually less experienced, so they needed more attention and oversight. Some problems occurred during construction that could be traced back to the multitude of subcontractors. For instance, one firm installed conduits that were too small for the firm that was hired to pull cables through those conduits. When such problems occurred, assigning responsibility and holding firms accountable was difficult and contested.[40]

The contractors had to take state and federal regulations seriously because so many government agencies were looking over their shoulders. For instance, to make sure that women and minorities were actually controlling the thirty-eight subcontractors, E. E. Cruz hired a compliance officer who conducted site visits and reviewed documentation. The MTA hired its own compliance firm to monitor E. E. Cruz and the other contractors. In turn, the MTA's program to assist disadvantaged minority- and women-owned businesses was monitored by state and federal regulatory agencies, state legislators, and even the Manhattan district attorney.

Given the difficulties of working with New York's regulations, its unions, and the MTA's bureaucracy, not as many firms bid on the large transit projects in New York compared to other cities, an important factor behind the Second Avenue subway's high construction costs. News reports have insinuated that the MTA's bidding process is "rigged" to favor certain contractors who have close ties with MTA officials. This is a costly perception because fewer firms prepare bids for projects when they think the deck is stacked against them.[41]

According to Mysore Nagaraja, "When contractors bid, they look at the agency's track record for paying for all their expenses and timeliness in paying them—how much crap they give them and whether an agency is considered fair." He said the MTA's current system of working with contractors leads to extensive conflict because it is "based on the idea that contractors are liars." This tension between the MTA and its contractors was exacerbated at the end of the first phase because the MTA made thousands of design changes after construction contracts had already been awarded. Accelerating the work to meet the governor's deadline did not help the relationship going forward, since contractors had trouble getting reimbursed for the additional costs they incurred to open the stations by New Year's Day.[42]

THE $20 BILLION QUESTION

Despite spending $4.6 billion, the New York metropolitan area still has not realized the full benefits of the long-promised Second Avenue subway because it remains a short spur on the Upper East Side. The first phase alleviated some crowding on the Lexington Avenue line, but conditions are expected to worsen because the city is encouraging even more residential and commercial development on the East Side. In addition, when the Long Island Rail Road completes its connection to the East Side, more than eighty thousand people are expected to take the railroad to Grand Central Terminal every weekday morning, and thousands of them will walk directly to the adjacent subway station on the Lexington Avenue line. A Second Avenue subway along the full length of Manhattan would not only alleviate crowding; it would also improve service reliability and reduce travel times for hundreds of thousands of passengers.

After the first phase of the Second Avenue subway opened in 2017, MTA Capital Construction started spending millions of dollars preparing for the construction of the second phase. Engineers analyzed potential environmental impacts and conducted preliminary engineering efforts. They also evaluated subsurface conditions by surveying building utilities and digging test pits along the proposed route. The second phase is planned to run north of 96th Street on Second Avenue and curve west to 125th Street and Lexington Avenue. The line will include three new stations in East Harlem, and passengers will be able to transfer at 125th Street to the Lexington Avenue's 4, 5, and 6 trains, as well as Metro-North Railroad's station.[43]

In some ways, the second phase will be easier to build than the first one because two East Harlem tunnels were already constructed in the 1970s: between 99th and 105th Streets, and between 110th and 120th Streets. Construction will also be less disruptive to the community because of demographic and land use differences. Second Avenue on the Upper East Side is characterized by twenty-five-to-thirty-story luxury apartment buildings with ground-floor retail. In East Harlem, the avenue has fewer retail uses, and its numerous public-housing buildings are set further back from the street than the Upper East Side's buildings.

In other ways, the second phase will be harder to build because the line will go under numerous apartment buildings as it curves west from Second Avenue to Lexington Avenue. Building the 125th Street station that will connect with the Lexington Avenue line will be so complicated that it could cost nearly $1 billion. Alaeden Jlelaty, who managed tunneling work for the first phase, warned that because building a subway in New York has become so expensive and complex, requiring so much energy and coordination, it has become nearly impossible to do.[44]

Design and construction costs have increased every generation as the number of requirements and regulations has multiplied. Governor Cuomo's

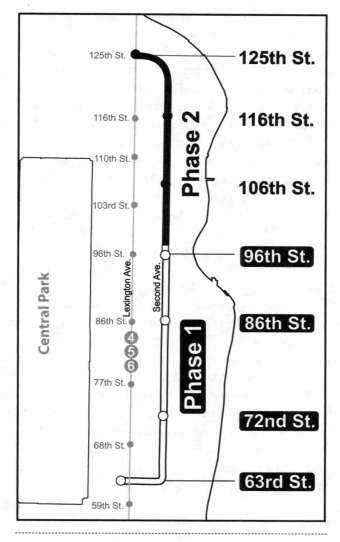

Map C.1. First and second phases of the Second Avenue subway

infrastructure czar, Rick Cotton, complained about the maze of governmental agencies and regulatory oversight involved in building the first phase. "Every time something has gone wrong in an agency's past," he said, "it has added another layer of approval. It has added another regulatory experience." He added, "Once a requirement, approval, and a process is put in, it never goes away."[45]

The first phase has become the standard for future phases. Stations in future phases will be just as spacious, quiet, and impressive. They will also be cooled in the summer and at least equally resistant to fires, floods, and terrorists. To minimize community impacts, the MTA will have to take the same expensive steps of maintaining traffic, erecting muck houses, and limiting construction hours. The level of community outreach for the second phase is indicative of how construction costs keep getting more expensive: For the first phase, the MTA opened an information center and hired community outreach staff only after construction was well underway. In preparation for a second phase, however, the MTA opened a center on 125th Street in 2017 as part of an outreach program costing more than $1.5 million per year. When the center opened, visitors were told that the beginning of construction of the second phase was imminent.[46]

Completing the second, third, and fourth phases will likely cost more than $20 billion, and then billions more will be needed if the line is ever extended to the Bronx, Brooklyn, and Queens. Obtaining sufficient funds to build the next three phases will be no easy feat since they are less cost effective than the first phase. For example, the East Harlem portion will cost more to build than the Upper East Side portion, yet will carry only half as many passengers.

Instead of funding the completion of the Second Avenue subway, billions of dollars may very well be used for other transportation megaprojects in the New York metropolitan area, such as constructing a sorely needed new Hudson River railroad tunnel for New Jersey Transit and Amtrak, replacing the world's busiest bus terminal at 42nd Street, and improving rail connections to the region's airports. The MTA still needs to finish the Long Island Rail Road connection to Grand Central Terminal, a project that started along with the Second Avenue subway in the 1960s. Nagaraja, who as president of MTA Capital Construction was once responsible for its construction, referred to this project as "one of the biggest disasters in transit history."[47]

So, what should be New York's highest-priority project? Unfortunately, no objective measure or crystal ball exists to answer that question. Peter Hall's 1982 book, *Great Planning Disasters*, reveals the difficulty of trying to assess and compare megaprojects. The author, a world-renowned urban planner, singled out the Sydney Opera House and San Francisco's BART rail system as planning disasters. The opera house had faced massive cost overruns and its design made it unable to function as a major opera house, while the BART system was attracting far fewer riders than expected. Hall had no idea that these two projects would prove to be wildly successful. The opera house is now Australia's top tourist destination and the country's most iconic structure, while BART has become essential to the economic health of the San Francisco Bay Area and the backbone of its transit system. Hall's effort to determine the success of these two projects *after* they were built was relatively straightforward compared to a task that requires even more guesswork—assessing projects *before* they are built, when estimates of both costs and benefits are subject to wide debate and manipulation.[48]

One thing is crystal clear when considering the Second Avenue subway and other transportation megaprojects: New York's most important priority should be repairing and upgrading its existing transit network. Allowing the system to deteriorate will lead to more frequent service disruptions and accidents, as well as higher costs over the long run. Every subway rider wants to see new routes and stations. More important, though, is improving the infrastructure that the public does not see, such as the signals that keep trains from crashing, the pumps that protect equipment from getting flooded, and the ventilation systems that prevent smoke from asphyxiating riders.

Since 1982, the MTA has spent more than $120 billion on its capital projects, yet the subway system is still not in a state of good repair. The subway's infrastructure has yet to make up for one hundred years of wear, tear, and neglect. One-third of the subway cars are more than thirty years old; some of them have been in service before most subway riders were even born. Moreover, much of the equipment that was upgraded in the 1980s and 1990s is already beyond its useful life and has to be replaced again.[49]

The signals alongside the tracks that help keep trains a safe distance from each other are one of the most important components of the subway system. The signals' red, yellow, and green lights tell the subway train operators when they should go, slow down, and stop. Much of the signal system was installed in the 1930s, and transit employees now have to fabricate their own replacement parts for obsolete equipment. While subway riders have to rely on this century-old technology, New York's automobile drivers take advantage of traffic signals that are part of a sophisticated information network. Above the streets, the city's Department of Transportation monitors data from sensors and video cameras to identify congestion choke points, and then remotely adjusts computerized traffic signals to optimize the flow of vehicles. Drivers obtain accurate, real-time traffic condition information via electronic signs, computers, and smartphones.[50]

For numerous reasons, the old subway signals should be replaced with computerized signal systems that track the exact location of trains. New systems would be more reliable, an important concern since signal problems are a major cause of delays. New signals would also add subway capacity by allowing trains to operate closer to each other, with more frequent service. At the same time, they would enhance safety because the new signals would prevent trains from operating too closely to each other. Furthermore, new signal systems would collect real-time data that would help NYC Transit respond to incidents faster and provide customers with more accurate and up-to-date information about services and delays.

New signals had been a top priority for Tom Prendergast, the former NYC Transit president and MTA chair, ever since a train traveling over forty miles per hour in a ten-mile-per-hour zone killed five people in 1991. After retiring, Prendergast regretted not making the signals an even higher priority. In 1997, the MTA had expected that new signals would be installed throughout the subway system by 2017. At its current pace, though, upgrading the signals system will probably cost about the same amount as finishing the Second Avenue subway and will not be completed until after 2065. The signal work is expensive and disruptive because transit workers need to install new equipment every five hundred feet on the tracks and purchase new equipment for every train.[51]

In addition to replacing the old signals, NYC Transit also needs to repair and prevent water damage. Over time, water from storms and underground streams has corroded steel and damaged equipment. Water also flows into the subways from breaks in the city's water pipes, whose average age is nearly seventy years old. On a typical day, when it is *not* raining, NYC Transit pumps a remarkable thirteen million gallons of water out of the subway system. During construction of the Second Avenue subway's first phase, engineers took extensive precautions to make sure underground streams did not cause tunnels to cave in or buildings to collapse. The tunnels and stations were also carefully waterproofed to protect structures and equipment for the rest of the twenty-first century. While the new tunnels and stations were designed to withstand more frequent and severe storms, the city's hundred-year-old tunnels and stations were not.[52]

Few cities in the United States are as vulnerable to rising sea levels as New York, and the city's underground subway tunnels are among its most vulnerable public facilities. Although the MTA has made some progress, it still needs billions of dollars more to protect its flood-prone equipment from storm surges.

Many of its maintenance and storage facilities are located in areas susceptible to flooding, and all across the subway system, new pumping equipment needs to be installed, electronic equipment elevated, and thousands of ventilation grates replaced. Neglecting to protect the subways can be much more expensive and disruptive than prevention. For instance, in the early 2000s, the MTA spent more than $500 million rebuilding the South Ferry subway station in Lower Manhattan. In 2012, only three years after the station opened, Hurricane Sandy dumped 14.5 million gallons of water and sewage into the station. After another $369 million was spent on repairs, the station reopened in 2017.[53]

Subway stations have been getting warmer from the heat released by the air conditioning units on subway cars and all of the equipment associated with countdown clocks, cameras, alarms, communications systems, and MetroCard readers. With climate change exacerbating this trend, NYC Transit will need to invest billions of dollars in upgrading the subways, because the heat can disrupt service, deteriorate equipment, cause train tracks to buckle, and, of course, make travel unpleasant for subway riders.[54]

While NYC Transit executives dream about new signals and other necessary infrastructure improvements, they have nightmares about the consequences of a terrorist attack. Their concern is well founded, because New York's subway stations were designed with narrow stairways, few exits, and poor ventilation. While airports have officers checking identification and metal detectors inspecting belongings, most subway stations do not even have cameras. Anyone can carry a backpack or wheel a suitcase into the subway.

In case of a fire, not all the subway tunnels have ventilation equipment to remove smoke. Of those that do, more than one-third are more than fifty years old and have never been rehabilitated. After the failure of ventilation equipment contributed to the deaths of two people in a 1990 subway tunnel fire, NYC Transit identified its one hundred most vulnerable underground tunnel segments. Nearly three decades later, only twenty-one of them had met modern fire-safety standards. But fires are not the only reason why the subways need an adequate ventilation system. In 1995, members of a religious cult killed thirteen passengers and injured thousands of others by releasing sarin gas into Tokyo's subways.[55]

Because MTA officials, understandably, do not want to draw attention to the subway system's vulnerabilities to fire and terrorism, they have trouble obtaining sufficient resources to address these problems. The resources needed are enormous. Improving pedestrian circulation and emergency egress in just one busy station can cost hundreds of millions of dollars.

TURNING POINTS

The Second Avenue subway saga reveals an important lesson about the need for creative transportation officials, active civic leaders, and farsighted elected officials who can ensure that sufficient investments are made to both upgrade the existing infrastructure and embark on projects needed to support New York's future prosperity. Turning points in the subway's history have been marked by transportation leaders who developed comprehensive plans and then built support to pursue them. In 1968, William Ronan and Bob Olmsted created a plan to integrate and expand the region's subways and railroads. In 1981, Richard Ravitch developed the MTA's first multiyear capital program, and in the early 1990s, Robert Kiley convinced elected officials that strategic investments would dramatically improve transportation services.

Civic organizations, business leaders, subway rider groups, and unions have played key roles in generating support from elected officials, the media, and the public. The first phase of the Second Avenue subway would not have been opened by 2017 if the Regional Plan Association and Lee Sander had not created a coalition twenty years earlier around a plan to reduce crowding, provide new services, and promote economic growth. Likewise, the MTA has obtained more resources because those who have a financial interest in subway improvements (including construction firms, trade unions, and property owners) have lobbied elected officials, donated money to political campaigns, and funded advocacy efforts.

In addition to the transportation and civic leaders, subway expansion projects have always needed champions—elected officials who can secure resources, battle away competitors, and overcome opposition to advance their pet projects. For example, Mayor John Hylan and Mayor Fiorello La Guardia led efforts to build the IND lines and unify the transit system. Governor Nelson Rockefeller forged a regional coalition, created the MTA, and secured the approval of a transportation bond issue. Assembly Speaker Sheldon Silver held up the entire state budget until the MTA agreed to build a full-length Second Avenue subway.

Most recently, Governor Andrew Cuomo became an unexpected champion for improving the subway system. Although he tried to deflect responsibility for the problems that occurred after accelerating the Second Avenue subway schedule, he eventually declared a state of emergency and resurrected a proposal for a congestion pricing program that would charge vehicles a fee to enter Manhattan's central business district. The governor decided that obtaining a new revenue source for the transit system would be one of his top priorities in 2019, and he put legislative leaders on the defensive by claiming that "the real choice is between congestion pricing or a thirty percent MTA toll and fare increase. Those are the only real options." He overcame resistance from the mayor and key legislators by agreeing to allow exemptions for certain drivers and by incorporating congestion pricing legislation into the center of negotiations over the state's budget.[56]

Another lesson from the history of New York's subways, and the Second Avenue subway in particular, points to a less auspicious outcome than a subway renaissance. If the public, media, and elected officials are ignorant about the subway's needs and limited resources, then New Yorkers will continue to deal with unappealing stations, unreliable service, and overcrowded trains. They will grumble about high fares, no matter how much they pay, while not enough resources will be available to adequately maintain the system. Ignorance will leave a void that may get filled by uninformed and/or self-serving individuals who foster false expectations about maintaining and expanding the transit system. That has happened throughout the history of New York's subways.

Because it is not in their interest to do so, many officials have not been straightforward about the challenges involved in raising enough money to modernize the subway, protect it from potential threats, and build new lines. Upgrading the existing system is not necessarily popular, because it is costly and disruptive to passengers. Subway expansion projects require raising taxes, fares, or other fees. Many voters want to hear about solutions, not problems, and politicians cater to them. Mayor John Hylan, Mayor William O'Dwyer, Governor Nelson Rockefeller, and others promised that the city and state could have a financially self-sustaining transit system and expand it at the same time. The media were complicit in creating these false expectations. If the two mayors were more honest, the city might still have an elevated line on Third Avenue. If Rockefeller had been more forthright, New York would not have started and then abandoned construction of four Second Avenue subway tunnel segments.

Politicians in office today, and those who will be running for office tomorrow, have a strong incentive to support completing the Second Avenue subway, because it is popular among residents, businesses, and property owners. But they have less of an incentive to actually build it, because each phase takes about ten years to complete. Life will be unpleasant during construction, and by the time the ribbon is ready to be cut, some other governor or mayor is likely to get the glory. The hero on January 1, 2017, was Andrew Cuomo, not those who secured funding and started construction of the first phase. One of the cynical lessons learned from the past century is that New York's politicians benefit when they tell people that they are studying, planning, designing, and preparing for the Second Avenue subway. They do not have to actually start building it to reap rewards.

In the foreseeable future, New Yorkers are likely to find themselves in familiar territory—waiting for the completion of a new subway line that is too popular to be canceled and too expensive to build. That was the situation when the Second Avenue subway was delayed for several years in 1932. Likewise, in 1944, Fiorello La Guardia told city council members that "the preparation of engineering plans for the construction of the Second Avenue subway has not been interrupted." In a similar manner, the subway was postponed for further study in 1953. When construction was halted in 1975, Mayor Abe Beame declared, "We cannot abandon the Second Avenue subway; we must, however, defer it." The following year, when asked whether the line would ever be completed, the MTA chair, David Yunich, responded, "Well, 'ever' is a long time."[57]

In 2004, New Yorkers were told that an 8.5-mile Second Avenue subway with sixteen stations would be completed by 2020. Its completion—along with a subway system in a state of good repair—remains decades away.

Figure C.1. *Pumping out water from a subway tunnel after Hurricane Sandy in 2012. Source: Metropolitan Transportation Authority.*

Figure C.2. *Chambers Street station: one of New York's most dilapidated subway stations in 2018. Source: Philip Mark Plotch.*

Figure C.3. *The abandoned Second Avenue subway tunnel in Chinatown, as of 2015. Source: Stuart McAlpine, Creative Commons.*

ACKNOWLEDGMENTS

I have many people to thank, starting with two wonderful individuals—the transit historian Peter Derrick and the political scientist Patrizia Nobbe, who collected the initial materials for this book and then gave me their encouragement, insight, time, and carloads of papers. Numerous reference librarians, archivists, and officials went out of their way to help, including my favorite librarian (Daisy DeCoster at Saint Peter's University) and the staffs at City College of New York, the La Guardia and Wagner Archives, the Maurice M. Pine Library, the Metropolitan Transportation Authority (MTA), the New York City Municipal Archives, New York City Transit, the New York Public Library, the New York State Archives, the Permanent Citizens Advisory Committee to the MTA, the Regional Plan Association, the Richard Nixon Presidential Library and Museum, the Rittenberg Law Library at St. John's University, the Rockefeller Archive Center, the Transit Museum, and Yale University.

Thanks to Michael McGandy at Cornell University Press, for raising the bar, and to his team (Bethany Wasik, Eric Levy, Karen Hwa, and Meagan Dermody) for their remarkable attention to details. Calvin Brown, a proud graduate of Hunter College's Master of Urban Planning program, did an extraordinary job creating the maps for this book.

More than one hundred people generously shared their insights and stories about the planning, design, construction, financing, politics, reporting, and community engagement associated with New York transportation projects. Thanks to Aaron Gordon, Alan Olmsted, Albert Appleton, Alphonse

Calvanico, Andis Woodlief, Andrew Bata, Anthony Semancik, Audrey Heffernan, Barry Schneider, Ben Heckscher, Bill Wheeler, Bill Woodford, Bob DeThomasis, Bob Yaro, Boris Pushkarev, Brian Rosenthal, C. Virginia Fields, Carl Weisbrod, Carlisle Towery, Carmen Bianco, Carolyn Maloney, Chris Boylan, Chuck Kirchner, Clarice Blackman, Craig Lader, Dan Jacobs, Dan Quart, Dana Rubinstein, Daniel O'Connor, Don Phillips, Ed Plotkin, Elaine Eisenberg, Emil Frankel, Floyd Lapp, Fred Dicker, Gene Russianoff, George Haikalis, George Pataki, Glenn Lunden, Guido Schattanek, Herbert Levinson, Jack Dean, James Brennan, Jay Kriegel, Jeff Zupan, Jodi Shapiro, Joe Clift, Joe Raskin, John Reinhardt, Jon Melnick, Judy McClain, Larry Fleischer, Larry Penner, Larry Reuter, Laura MacNeil, Lee Sander, Lois Tendler, Lou Sepersky, Lou Tomson, Marc Albrecht, Mark Nachbar, Maryanne Gridley, Matt McElroy, Michael Horodniceanu, Michael Porto, Minna Elias, Mort Downey, Mysore Nagaraja, Nancy Danzig, Nancy Ploeger, Naomi Doerner, Nicole Gelinas, Norm Silverman, Pablo LeMus, Peter Cafiero, Peter Goldmark, Richard Barone, Richard Ravitch, Robert Newhouser, Ronay Menschel, Ross Kapilian, Ryan Kaufman, Sal DeMatteo, Samuel Wong, Sandy Hornick, Sarah Rios, Stephen Morgan, Stephen Polan, Steve Strauss, Steve Weber, Subutay Musluoglu, Todd DiScala, Tom Harknett, Tom Jablonski, Tom Madison, Tom Namako, Tom Prendergast, Veronica Vanterpool, Virgil Conway, and Yossi Berechman. Also, thanks to Pilar Wyman for preparing the extensive index, and to my friends Bill Armbruster, Craig Avedisian, Adam Feinberg, and Carla Van de Walle for their careful attention to detail and all of their helpful suggestions as they read draft versions of this book.

I truly enjoyed every single interview I conducted. Learning about people's lives is certainly more fun than writing all of the endnotes at the end of a book. The endnotes, however, do provide valuable information, including the locations and dates of each interview. Note that those candid interviewees who wished to remain anonymous are referred to by their roles, such as "former MTA executive" or "New York state assemblyman," and that some references citing these interviews omit locations and dates in order to protect the subjects' identities.

1878: Third Avenue elevated line opens between Harlem and Lower Manhattan. Service is later extended to the Bronx.

1880: The 7.5-mile Second Avenue elevated line opens, eighteen months after construction began.

1903: New York State considers the first proposal to build a Second Avenue subway.

1904: Private railroad company builds New York's first subway.

1920: State proposes a second East Side subway line.

1922: New York City mayor John Hylan proposes a new East Side subway as part of a subway system owned and operated by the city.

1929: City announces that the centerpiece of the next subway expansion program will be a Second Avenue subway between the Bronx and Lower Manhattan.

1940: City takes control of subways from private railroad companies.

1942: City begins demolishing Second Avenue elevated line.

1947: Mayor William O'Dwyer proposes raising transit fare and building a Second Avenue subway.

1951: Voters approve $500 million bond issue to build Second Avenue subway.

1953: State takes control of subways away from the city and sets up NYC Transit Authority.

1955: City begins demolishing Third Avenue elevated line.

1965: City Planning Commission proposes a new East Side subway.

1967: State voters approve bond issue for transportation improvements, including Second Avenue subway.

1968: Newly established Metropolitan Transportation Authority (MTA) proposes Second Avenue subway.

1972: Construction of the Second Avenue subway begins in East Harlem.

1973: Construction begins in Chinatown and the East Village.

1975: Construction terminated.

1980: Subways break down four times more frequently than in 1968, and one-third of all subway cars pulling into stations have broken doors.

1981: State approves MTA's first five-year capital program.

1995: MTA begins study of transportation needs on Manhattan's East Side.

1999: MTA proposes Second Avenue subway between 125th Street and 63rd Street, which the media deride as a "stubway."

2000: Governor George Pataki and legislative leaders agree to build 8.5-mile Second Avenue subway that would run the full length of Manhattan.

2001: MTA estimates new subway will cost $16.8 billion; work is expected to start in 2004 and finish by 2020.

2003: MTA splits construction into four phases, the first of which will run from 96th to 63rd Streets, with new stations at 96th, 86th, and 72nd Streets.

2004:   MTA estimates that the cost to build the first phase will be $3.8 billion, and that it will be completed in December 2012.

2005:   State voters approve transportation bond with funding for Second Avenue.

2007:   MTA begins construction after Federal Transit Administration awards $1.3 billion for subway.

2009:   Budget for first phase increases to $4.5 billion and completion date deferred to December 2016.

2011:   MTA transforms community relations program to address complaints about construction.

2015:   Governor Andrew Cuomo demands that MTA meet its scheduled deadline for the first phase.

2017:   Second Avenue subway's first phase opens to public on January 1.

2017:   Cuomo declares a state of emergency to address transit problems on June 29.

2019:   State approves congestion pricing program to fund transit improvements.

Introduction

1   Nicholas B. Penny, "The Commercial Garden Necropolis of the Early Nineteenth Century and Its Critics," *Garden History* 2, no. 3 (1974): 61–76; Blair Kamin, "Frank Lloyd Wright's Mile-High Skyscraper Never Built, but Never Forgotten," *Chicago Tribune*, May 28, 2017.

2   Emma G. Fitzsimmons, Ford Fessenden, and K. K. Rebecca Lai, "Every New York City Subway Line Is Getting Worse; Here's Why," *New York Times*, June 28, 2017.

3   MTA, "Governor Cuomo and Chairman Prendergast Celebrate On-Time Opening of Second Avenue Subway with Inaugural New Year's Eve Ride," press release, December 31, 2016.

4   Jen Kirby, "What Is Wrong with the MTA—and Can It Be Fixed?," *New York*, June 29, 2017, http://nymag.com/intelligencer/2017/06/what-is-wrong-with-the-mta-and-how-could-it-get-fixed.html; Stephen Jacob Smith, "Dan Doctoroff and John Zuccotti Don't Think the East Side Needs Another Subway," *New York Observer*, July 31, 2013; Urban Engineers of New York (prepared for the Federal Transit Administration), *PMOC Monthly Report: Second Avenue Subway Phase 1 Project*, report period for December 2017.

5   Partnership for NYC Quality, "Quality of Life," accessed January 14, 2017, https://pfnyc.org/quality-of-life; Dana Rubinstein, "Where the Transit-Build Costs Are Unbelievable," *Politico*, March 31, 2015, https://www.politico.com/states/new-york/city-hall/story/2015/03/where-the-transit-build-costs-are-unbelievable-000000.

6   MTA, *MTA 2017 Adopted Budget: February Financial Plan 2019–2022*, February 2019, II-8; Federal Transit Administration, *Transit Profiles: 2017 Report Year Summary*, September 2018.

7   One hundred thousand daily riders are expected in the second phase, per MTA, "Capital Program Oversight Committee Meeting: March 2017."

1. From a Compact City into a Metropolis

1   Robert C. Reed, *The New York Elevated* (South Brunswick, NJ: A. S. Barnes, 1978), 106, 107, 119–22.

2   Construction began on February 24, 1879, and train service started between South Ferry and 127th Street on August 16, 1880. Public Service Commission, *Report of the Public Service Commission for the First District of the State of New York for the Year Ending December 31, 1913*, vol. 5, *Documentary History of Railroad Companies* (Albany, NY: J. B. Lyon, 1913), 666.

3   Clifton Hood, *722 Miles: The Building of the Subways and How They Transformed New York* (Baltimore: John Hopkins University Press, 2004), 98; Reed, *New York Elevated*, 123; Peter Derrick, "Catalyst for Development: Rapid Transit in New York," *New York Affairs* 9, no. 4 (Fall 1986): 29–76; Mayor's Committee on City Planning, *City Wide Studies: Part II; The Planning of Public Services for the City of New York*, 1940.

4   "New-York's Imperial Destiny," *New York Times*, February 5, 1888.

5   Peter Derrick, *Tunneling to the Future: The Story of the Great Subway Expansion That Saved New York* (New York: New York University Press, 2001), 33.

6   "Birth of a Subway Crush," *New York Tribune*, October 28, 1904.

7   Vollmer Associates, SYSTRA Consulting, and Allee King Rosen & Fleming (prepared for MTA New York City Transit), *Manhattan East Side Transit Alternatives (MESA)/Second Avenue Subway Summary Report*, October 2001, 3–4. A Second Avenue subway was considered in 1903; "Metropolitan Would Build Subways," *New York Times*, December 18, 1903. A First Avenue subway was considered in 1905; "East Side Subway Plan Gains Favor," *New York Times*, January 27, 1905.

8   Day & Zimmermann and Coverdale & Colpitts, *Joint Report of Engineers on the Organization, Methods and Procedures of the Board of Transportation and Its Various Departments, Its Facilities and Its Operations to the Board of Transportation of the City of New York, N.Y.*, November 5, 1951; Roger P. Roess and Gene Sansone, *The Wheels That Drove New York: A History of the New York City Transit System* (New York: Springer, 2013), 161–62, 199.

9   Roess and Sansone, *Wheels That Drove New York*, 281.

10   Hood, *722 Miles*, 185–93 (Hylan worked for an elevated line that was later taken over by the BRT); Ben Procter, *William Randolph Hearst: The Early Years, 1863–1910* (New York: Oxford University Press, 1998), 261; New York Transit Museum with Vivian Heller, *The City Beneath Us: Building the New York Subways* (New York: W. W. Norton, 2004), 41–42.

11   Hood, *722 Miles*, 189; Gerhard M. Dahl, letter to Hylan, August 4, 1924, in Gerhard M. Dahl, *Transit Truths* (New York: Era, 1924), 54, http://quod.lib.umich.edu/m/moa/afu3837.0001.001/60; John F. Hylan, "Traction and Finance," *Forum* 65 (1921): 257–66; Elmer D. Graper, "The New York City Election," *American Political Science Review* 16, no. 1 (February 1922): 79–83.

12   LeRoy T. Harkness, "Transit Tendencies in New York City," *Electric Railway Journal* 58, no. 11 (September 10, 1921): 403–8. Rapid transit ridership was 1,097,150,230 passengers per year in 1918–19 and 1,744,130,401 in 1925–26; numbers obtained from Robert Hickey (NYC Transit's Operations Planning Department), June 27,

2017. The Harkness quotation is from LeRoy T. Harkness, "A Review of New York's Transit Situation," *Electric Railway Journal* 62, no. 14 (October 6, 1923): 554.

13   Henry Collins Brown, *Valentine's City of New York: Guide Book* (New York: Chauncey Holt, 1920), 14.

14   Brown, *Valentine's City*, 128, 157, 168, 365.

15   Office of Transit Construction Commissioner, *A Report by the Chief Engineer Submitting for Consideration a Comprehensive Rapid Transit Plan Covering All Boroughs of the City of New York*, August 1920; "Transit a Social Problem," *New York Times*, June 1, 1922. Jurisdiction for planning new routes was held by the Board of Rapid Transit Railroad Commissioners until 1907, the Public Service Commission of the First District from 1907 to 1919, the Office of Transit Construction Commissioner from 1919 to 1921, and the New York State Transit Commission from 1921 to 1924. Board of Transportation of the City of New York, *Report Including Analysis of Operations of the New York City Transit System for Five Years Ended June 30, 1945*, 1945.

16   Office of Transit Construction Commissioner, *Report by the Chief Engineer*, 16.

17   "Hylan Announces His $600,000,000 Plan for Transit," *New York Times*, August 28, 1922; "Hylan Subway Plan Calls for 35 Lines: Cost $600,000,000," *New York Herald*, August 28, 1922; "Hylan Plans 4-Track Subway on First Avenue below Bronx," *New York Tribune*, August 28, 1922 (the plan included a First Avenue line); Hood, *722 Miles*, 196; John Hylan, "Mayor Hylan's Plan for Real Rapid Transit in New York City: Submitted to the Board of Estimate and Apportionment," September 6, 1922.

18   "Hylan Names Smith Only Once at Rally," *New York Times*, November 2, 1922; Board of Transportation of the City of New York, *Report Including Analysis*, 5; "Hylan Subway Plan Links Four Boroughs at $450,000,000 Cost," *New York Times*, December 10, 1924; "New Subway Routes in Hylan Program to Cost $186,046,000," *New York Times*, March 21, 1925; "City Soon to Launch $600,000,000 Subway for the East Side," *New York Times*, April 5, 1929.

19   "Hylan Hits Harkness as a Law Partner of an I.R.T. Director," *New York Times*, March 15, 1925.

20   Mason B. Williams, *City of Ambition: FDR, La Guardia, and the Making of Modern New York* (New York: W. W. Norton, 2013), 77.

21   Mayor's Committee on City Planning, *City Wide Studies: Part I; Basic Factors in the Planning of the City of New York*, 1940, 5. The percentage of the nation's manufacturing facilities located in New York City ranged from 13 percent to 15 percent between 1921 and 1935.

22   "Subway Complaints Pour In on M'avoy," *New York Times*, January 3, 1925; City Club of New York, "Subways or Children? Which or Both? A Letter to the Board of Estimate and Apportionment," January 12, 1927.

23   "Traffic Viaduct Urged by Enright," *New York Times*, November 28, 1922.

24   "Second Av. Chosen for Next Subway," *New York Times*, August 30, 1929; "Board Will Hasten East Side Subway," *New York Times*, January 27, 1930.

25   Board of Transportation, "More Subways Coming," press release, September 16, 1929; "100 Miles of Subway in New City Project; 52 of Them in Queens," *New York Times*, September 16, 1929.

26 "Manhattan Sales: Second Avenue Subway Project Causes 50% Rise in Prices,"
New York Times, September 2, 1929; "Second Av. Sales Feature Market," *New York Times*, October 11, 1929; "Civic Bodies Hail New Subway Plan," *New York Times*, April 6, 1929.

27 Alfred J. Doyle (senior electrical engineer), "Studies Made of the Second Avenue Trunk Line Project Subsequent to Jan. 1, 1931," office memorandum, August 28, 1952, author's possession; R. L. Duffus, "New York Speeds Up Labors for Transit Relief," *New York Times*, June 29, 1930.

28 Frederick A. Kramer, *Building the Independent Subway: The Technology and Intense Struggle of New York City's Most Gigantic Venture* (New York: Quadrant, 1990), 5.

29 "Showdown Looms on the 5-Cent Fare to Cut City's Costs," *New York Times*, January 9, 1932; "$70 Million Allowed for Subways in 1932," *New York Times*, August 28, 1931; Hood, *722 Miles*, 228; Lindsay Rogers, John Dickinson, and Joseph McGoldrick (Mayor's Committee on Taxation's Sub-Committee on Pricing of City Services), "Memorandum on the Cost of Rapid Transit to the City of New York: The Untermyer and Delaney Plans," May 1, 1931.

30 "New Links Planned for Subway System," *New York Times*, February 29, 1932; "Mayor Now Weighs Long Term Financing to Save on Subways," *New York Times*, July 18, 1932; "Debt Limit Curbs City Subway Plans," *New York Times*, May 15, 1935.

31 Hood, *722 Miles*, 299; Kramer, *Building the Independent Subway*, 44.

32 Hood, *722 Miles*, 239. Note that the Q train runs along both BMT and IND tracks.

33 William W. Hersey, "Parking Space Scarcity Called Car Sales Curb," *New York Herald Tribune*, February 29, 1948; R. L. Duffus, "A Rising Tide of Traffic Rolls over NY," *New York Times*, February 9, 1930.

34 Terry Golway, "W.P.A. Projects Left Their Stamp on the Region," *New York Times*, April 15, 2009.

35 "Moses Asks Start on Park Program," *New York Times*, October 8, 1945; Robert A. Caro, *The Power Broker: Robert Moses and the Fall of New York* (New York: Knopf, 1974), 896–97; Paul Goldberger, "Robert Moses, Master Builder, Is Dead at 92," *New York Times*, July 30, 1981.

36 "Last Trolleys Rolled in the City in 1957," *New York Times*, July 9, 1975.

37 Numbers obtained from Hickey, June 27, 2017.

38 Anthony Connors, "Then & Now an El of a Time," *Daily News*, February 21, 1999; Mayor's Committee on City Planning, *Report of a Study by the Works Progress Administration Project*, 1938, in Mayor's Committee on City Planning, *Community Studies: 1935 to 1938*, 6–16.

39 "Residential Trend on the East Side Enlarging the River Front Centres," *New York Times*, April 22, 1928; "Transit Links and Yorkville's Growth," *New York Times*, August 3, 1930; "City Urged to Speed 2d Av. Subway Plans," *New York Times*, January 5, 1930; "Many New Buildings Going Up in First Avenue," *New York Times*, August 31, 1930.

40 "Mrs. W.K. Vanderbilt to Live in Avenue A," *New York Times*, January 9, 1921; Christopher Gray, "Streetscapes/Sutton Place, Sutton Place South and One Sutton Place

North," *New York Times*, September 21, 2003; Mrs. Herbert L. Satterlee, letter to Mayor La Guardia, March 6, 1936, folder "Transit—Elevated Structures—Removal of 2nd & 3rd Ave Els," box 3896, La Guardia and Wagner Archives, LaGuardia Community College, Long Island City, New York; A. H. Vanderbilt (Mrs. W. K.), letter to La Guardia, February 21, 1936, folder "Transit—Elevated Structures."

41   Froman and Taubert Real Estate and Insurance, letter to La Guardia, February 19, 1936, folder "Transit—Elevated Structures"; "Elevated Razing Is Urged in 2nd Av.," *New York Times*, April 9, 1934; "Drive Opens to Raze 2d Av. Elevated Line," *New York Times*, February 24, 1936; Peter Kihss, "Our Changing City: Upper and Middle East Side," *New York Times*, July 1, 1955; Carolin Foster, letter to the editor, *New York Times*, April 11, 1934; "Would Use 2d Ave.," *New York Times*, September 9, 1934; Charles V. Bagli, "In Sutton Place's Backyard, Private Oasis on Public Land," *New York Times*, December 31, 2003.

42   Spencer Byard (mayor's law secretary), letter to Mrs. Ana W. Simpson, February 18, 1942; Lester Stone (mayor's executive secretary), letter to James F. Egan (public administrator, Hall of Records), January 2, 1942; La Guardia, handwritten response to a December 29, 1941, memo from Stone; Joseph B. Eastman (director of the Office of Defense Transportation), letter to J. Widman Bertch (chief of Special Projects Salvage Section), May 28, 1942; Donald M. Nelson (chair, War Production Board), letter to La Guardia, April 9, 1942, all from box 3896, La Guardia and Wagner Archives; "Move to Raze El on 2d Avenue Gains," *New York Times*, April 22, 1942; "Mayor Starts Demolition of 2d Ave. El," *New York Times*, July 8, 1942; Robert F. Dorr, *Air Combat: A History of Fighter Pilots* (New York: Caliber Books, 2006), 73; Cory Graff, "Unbreakable," *Air & Space Magazine*, November 2001.

43   Lawrence Stelter, "Analysis of Demolishing New York City Elevated Transit Lines," *Municipal Engineers Journal* 78, no. 2 (1990): 33.

44   David Gonzalez, "About New York; In 9th Ave. El's Shadow, a Symbol of Saner Times," *New York Times*, July 11, 1996; Bill Simmer, "New York Forum about Transport: Next Stop, the Bronx," *Newsday*, July 2, 1987; John F. McDonald, *Postwar Urban America: Demography, Economics, and Social Policies* (New York: Routledge, 2014), 137.

45   Fiorello La Guardia, "Text of Mayor La Guardia's Message to the New City Council at Its First Meeting," *New York Times*, January 6, 1944.

46   The figure of 781 miles is per "New Era in Transit," *New York Times*, May 27, 1940; 665 miles is per MTA, "Subways," accessed December 13, 2017, http://web.mta.info/nyct/facts/ffsubway.htm. The figure of 539 stations was calculated by taking the number of stations in 1945 (521), adding the 11 Second Avenue El stations closed in 1940, adding the 12 Second Avenue El stations closed in 1942, and then subtracting 5 stations added in 1941 on the Dyre Avenue line. The number of stations in 1945 (472) was found in Board of Transportation of the City of New York, *Report Including Analysis*, 14; and the figure of 437 miles, from 1940, is per "New Era in Transit."

2. An Empty Promise

1   Joseph B. Raskin, *The Routes Not Taken: A Trip through New York City's Unbuilt Subway System* (New York: Fordham University Press, 2014), 209.

2   Alexander Nobler Cohen, "Fallen Transit: The Loss of Rapid Transit on Second Avenue," *Third Rail*, July 2001, 15.

3   Maurice Zolotow, "Manhattan's Daily Riot," *Saturday Evening Post*, March 10, 1945, 22.

4   John Stanton, "New Dreams for Bagdad-on-the Subway," *New York Times*, May 14, 1944; Kenneth Jackson and David S. Dunbar, *Empire City: New York through the Centuries* (New York: Columbia University Press, 2005), 405.

5   Robert A. Caro, *The Power Broker: Robert Moses and the Fall of New York* (New York: Alfred A. Knopf, 1974), 757; Robert Moses, address before American Association of State Highway Officials, September 23, 1947, Waldorf-Astoria Hotel, box 29, series 1, Robert Moses Papers, Manuscripts and Archives Division, New York Public Library, New York.

6   George J. Lankevich, *American Metropolis: A History of New York City* (New York: New York University Press, 1998), 183; "O'Dwyer Indicates Moses' Retention," *New York Times*, November 2, 1945.

7   Robert Moses, *Report to Mayor O'Dwyer on Activities of the Office of City Construction Co-ordinator during the Year 1948*, box 90, series 4, Moses Papers.

8   Caro, *Power Broker*, 764–65.

9   William O'Dwyer, *Beyond the Golden Door*, ed. Paul O'Dwyer (New York: St. John's University, 1987), 228; "Text of O'Dwyer's Speech Asking 8-Cent Fare," *New York Times*, December 6, 1947.

10   Caro, *Power Broker*, 757; Lankevich, *American Metropolis*, 181.

11   Mason B. Williams, *City of Ambition: FDR, La Guardia, and the Making of Modern New York* (New York: W. W. Norton, 2013), 194; "O'Dwyer's First Budget," *New York Times*, April 7, 1946; Paul Crowell, "$252,398,094 Outlay Allocated for '47 by City Planners," *New York Times*, October 17, 1946.

12   O'Dwyer, *Beyond the Golden Door*, 233, 305, 314.

13   Moses, address before American Association of State Highway Officials; Robert Moses, "Let's Rebuild Our Cities," *This Week*, May 19, 1946.

14   Raskin, *Routes Not Taken*, 227.

15   Paul Crowell, "Subway Projects Found Too Costly," *New York Times*, September 2, 1955; Caro, *Power Broker*, 757.

16   William Reid, letter to O'Dwyer, n.d., in City of New York, *Three-Year Report, 1946–1949: Board of Transportation*, 1949, M45.95 ty no. 9, NYC Municipal Archives, New York.

17   "Gen. Gross Takes City Transit Post," *New York Times*, December 2, 1945; Caro, *Power Broker*, 757.

18   Robert J. Donovan, "Fare Hearing Is Latest Battle in 30-Year War," *New York Herald Tribune*, February 9, 1947; "They Certainly Squeeze That Nickel in Gotham," *Saturday Evening Post*, August 19, 1944; "City Sentiment Found to Be 3 to 1 against Subway Fare Increase," *New York Times*, March 27, 1945.

19   "O'Dwyer Program Asks 2% Sales Tax to Retain 5c Fare," *New York Times*, January 7, 1946; "Mayor's Sales Tax Rise Only to Aid Subways," *New York Times*, January 15, 1946; Caro, *Power Broker*, 758.

20 Caro, *Power Broker*, 761; Leo Egan, "New City Tax Plan in Dewey's Hands," *New York Times*, March 7, 1946.

21 "Text of O'Dwyer Letter," *New York Times*, March 12, 1946.

22 "City Fare and Public Works," *New York Times*, April 6, 1946; "Underground Problem," *New York Times*, November 9, 1947.

23 "O'Dwyer Program Asks 2% Sales Tax"; David Gelber, "Saving the Nickel Fare: The First 44 Years," *Village Voice*, September 16, 1971.

24 "O'Dwyer May Back Moses Fare Plea," *New York Sun*, April 15, 1946; "Mayor Is Turning to Transit Loans," *New York Times*, March 8, 1946.

25 City Construction Co-ordinator, *Report to the Mayor, Board of Estimate, City Planning Commission and City Council by the City Construction Co-ordinator on Progress and Proposed Revision in the Program of Essential Postwar Public Improvements*, April 15, 1946.

26 Paul Crowell, "City Transit Board Views 10-Cent Fare as Short of Needs," *New York Times*, July 15, 1946.

27 "The Mayor's First Year," *New York Times*, January 1, 1947; Caro, *Power Broker*, 757; "Text of O'Dwyer's Speech"; "City Transit Loss 1.7c on Each Rider," *New York Times*, March 11, 1946.

28 "Transit Needs Put at $92,498,775 More," *New York Times*, July 26, 1946; Crowell, "City Transit Board"; Moses, "The Public Works Problems of NYC," talk on *F. H. La Guardia Hour*, WJZ (AM radio), August 24, 1947, box 30, series 1, Moses Papers; Moses, *Report to Mayor O'Dwyer*; Moses, letter to O'Dwyer, December 20, 1946, box 90, series 4, Moses Papers.

29 Charles P. Gross, letter to the editor, *New York Times*, April 1, 1947; Moses, *Report to Mayor O'Dwyer*.

30 Moses, letter to O'Dwyer, October 7, 1949, box 90, series 4, Moses Papers.

31 Murray Schumach, "What's Wrong with the Subway? What Isn't?," *New York Times*, March 10, 1946; "City Urged to Ease Traffic Problems," *New York Times*, March 24, 1947.

32 "10c Fare without Delay Urged by Gross for City's Transit Lines," *New York Times*, September 12, 1946.

33 "Stand on Fare Rise Asked of O'Dwyer," *New York Times*, November 19, 1946; Paul Crowell, "Mayor Still Silent on Fare Increase," *New York Times*, July 7, 1947; Paul Crowell, "Mayor to Wage a Campaign for Fare Rise Referendum," *New York Times*, June 14, 1947; "Fare Rise Opposed, Tammany Men Say," *New York Times*, February 8, 1947; Paul Crowell, "Appeal to Albany; Amendment to Permit Action by Transit Board Is Sought," *New York Times*, November 7, 1947; Robert Potter, "To Start Monday: Public Discussions Will Continue Several Days If Need Arises," *New York Times*, February 4, 1947.

34 Jay Maeder, "You Get What You Pay For: Reconsidering the Nickel Ride," *Daily News*, September 18, 2000; Potter, "To Start Monday"; Crowell, "Appeal to Albany"; "Fare Rise Opposed."

35 Gelber, "Saving the Nickel Fare"; "Fare Rise Opposed"; "Disaster Unit Stands Idle at City Hall Fare Hearing," *New York Times*, February 11, 1947; William O'Dwyer, "Statements by Mayor and Borough President Hall on Transit Fare," *New York Times*,

February 13, 1947; "7 Radio Stations Will Broadcast Fare Hearings," *New York Herald Tribune*, February 8, 1947.

36 "State-Aid Plea Is Forecast for Fare Hearings," *New York Herald Tribune*, February 9, 1947; "10c-Fare Backers Charge O'Dwyer Staged Hearing to Get Funds at Albany," *New York Herald Tribune*, February 9, 1947; "What Were the Hearings For?," *New York Herald Tribune*, February 12, 1947.

37 Board of Estimate transit hearings, February 10 and 11, 1947, audio at WNYC, accessed January 4, 2017, http://www.wnyc.org/story/board-of-estimate-transit-hearings.

38 Board of Estimate transit hearings.

39 "The News of the Week in Review," *New York Times*, February 16, 1947; Board of Estimate transit hearings.

40 Stephen White, "Fare Orators Bandy Millions over a Nickel," *New York Herald Tribune*, February 11, 1947; David McConnell, "Mayor Leads Fight on Fare Rise," *New York Herald Tribune*, February 11, 1947; "City Board Rejects Transit Fare Rise as Tax on the Poor," *New York Times*, February 13, 1947; Lankevich, *American Metropolis*, 183.

41 Gelber, "Saving the Nickel Fare"; O'Dwyer, "Statements by Mayor"; Crowell, "Mayor to Wage a Campaign."

42 Gelber, "Saving the Nickel Fare."

43 Clifton Hood, *722 Miles: The Building of the Subways and How They Transformed New York* (Baltimore: John Hopkins University Press, 2004), 247.

44 "Text of O'Dwyer's Speech."

45 "The Issue," editorial, *New York Herald Tribune*, December 6, 1947; editorial, *Daily News*, December 6, 1947; "The Mayor's Program," editorial, *New York Times*, December 6, 1947.

46 Paul Crowell, "2d Avenue Subway Sought by Mayor," *New York Times*, December 8, 1947; David McConnell, "2d Ave. Subway Plan Is Drafted to Avert a Fare Rise above 8c," *New York Herald Tribune*, December 8, 1947; Cohen, "Fallen Transit," 15.

47 Crowell, "2d Avenue Subway"; Paul Crowell, "Subway Expansion to Cost $400,000 Proposed for City," *New York Times*, December 15, 1947; "The Mayor's Program," editorial, *New York Times*, December 6, 1947.

48 "O'Dwyer 8c-Fare Bill Due to Die," *New York Times*, March 9, 1948; "Mayor Requests Governor to Veto; Republican Bill to Raise City Fare," *New York Times*, March 25, 1948; "The Transit Bill Signed," *New York Times*, March 30, 1948.

49 Walter Arm, "Mayor Set to Raise Fare, A.F.L. and C.I.O. Agree," *New York Herald Tribune*, April 16, 1948; "Transit Board's Fare Rise Resolution," *New York Times*, April 21, 1948; "Fare Rise Praised by Trade Groups," *New York Times*, April 22, 1948; Gelber, "Saving the Nickel Fare."

50 Reid, letter to O'Dwyer.

51 "Former Mayor O'Dwyer Dead," *New York Times*, November 25, 1964.

52   Caro, *Power Broker*, 788; Robert D. McFadden, "Vincent Impellitteri Is Dead," *New York Times*, January 30, 1987; Sam Roberts, "Podcast: How Green Is My Book," *New York Times*, June 19, 2008, https://cityroom.blogs.nytimes.com/2008/06/19/podcast-how-green-is-my-book. (This story is not consistent with O'Dwyer, *Beyond the Golden Door*, 213.)

53   Caro, *Power Broker*, 791–95, 797.

54   "Backs Amendment 6: Bingham Urges Its Support to Improve Subways Here," *New York Times*, November 3, 1951; Douglas Dales, "Debt Issues Ready for State Ballot," *New York Times*, March 19, 1951; "Dewey Rounds Out Plan of School Aid," *New York Times*, February 7, 1950.

55   State of New York, Senate Committee on the Affairs of the City of New York, *First Interim Report on the Inquiry into the Public Transit System of NYC including Minority Report*, May 15, 1957; "2d Av. Subway Cost Estimated at Half Billion," *New York Herald Tribune*, August 31, 1929.

56   "Relief for the Needy," *Brooklyn Daily Eagle*, September 17, 1951; State of New York, Senate Committee, *First Interim Report*, Exhibit C.

57   "Budget Unit Backs Debt for Subway," *New York Times*, February 21, 1950; "Amendment 6—A New Subway," editorial, *New York Times*, November 1, 1951; "Backs Amendment 6"; State of New York, Senate Committee, *First Interim Report*, 18; New York State Unified Court System, "Votes Cast for and against Proposed Constitutional Conventions and Also Proposed Constitutional Amendments," accessed January 10, 2018, https://www.nycourts.gov/history/legal-history-new-york/documents/Publications_Votes-Cast-Conventions-Amendments.pdf.

58   Day & Zimmermann and Coverdale & Colpitts, *Joint Report of Engineers on the Organization, Methods and Procedures of the Board of Transportation and Its Various Departments, Its Facilities and Its Operations to the Board of Transportation of the City of New York*, N.Y., November 5, 1951, 273.

59   Day & Zimmerman and Coverdale & Colpitts, *Joint Report of Engineers*, 259.

60   Day & Zimmerman and Coverdale & Colpitts, *Joint Report of Engineers*, 165. (Note that the weekend ridership also included holiday ridership.)

61   George E. Spargo, letter to Moses, March 7, 1952, box 90, series 4, Moses Papers.

62   Leonard Ingalls, "2d Ave. Subway Plans Delayed by Rising Costs, Steel Shortage," *New York Herald Tribune*, January 16, 1952; Board of Transportation, "Communication to the Board of Estimate of the City of New York," July 8, 1952; "Banks' Gloom on City Credit Perils Subway," *World Telegram*, September 14, 1952; Paul Crowell, "Bankers Warn City of Risk in Building 2d Ave. Subway," *New York Times*, September 22, 1952; Blaine Littell, "Mayor Favors Going Ahead on 2nd Ave. Subway," *New York Herald Tribune*, September 22, 1952; City Construction Co-ordinator, *Report to Mayor Impellitteri on Activities of the Office of City Construction Co-Ordinator During the Year 1948*, May 15, 1951, box 90, series 4, Moses Papers; Ira Henry Freeman, "Rockaway Trains to Operate Today," *New York Times*, June 28, 1956; Daniel L. Kurshan (Citizens Budget Commission secretary), *Report to Members of the Board of Trustees of Citizens Budget Commission*, September 9, 1952, Office of Mayor, microfilm roll 50, Subject Files, NYC Municipal Archives.

63   "Mayor Calls for Launching of New $500 Million Subway," *Daily News*, September 16, 1952; "Mayor Surprises Self, Hints He'd Run Again," *New York Post*, September 15, 1952; "Mayor Spurns Warning, Asks 2nd Av. Subway," *New York Post*, September 15, 1952; Crowell, "Bankers Warn City."

64   Moses, letter to members of City Planning Commission, October 22, 1952, box 90, series 4, Moses Papers; Leonard Ingalls, "2d Ave. Subway Out of Budget," *New York Herald Tribune*, October 9, 1952; "'53 Capital Budget Omits 2d Ave. Line," *New York Times*, October 9, 1952.

65   "For a Transit Authority," editorial, *New York Times*, March 6, 1944; "For a Higher Subway Fare," *New York Times*, January 29, 1945; "2 Business Groups Urge Transit Unit," *New York Times*, September 12, 1952; David Wise, "City Receives 10-Cent Fare Ultimatum," *New York Herald Tribune*, March 6, 1953; "The City Manager Plan," *New York Herald Tribune*, March 14, 1953; Leonard Ingalls, "Legislature Passes Dewey Bills on City Transit and Adjourns," *New York Herald Tribune*, March 22, 1953.

66   New York City Transit Authority, *1st Annual Report: 1953–1954*, September 16, 1954, 34; Stanley Levey, "Dwindling Transit Funds," *New York Times*, January 17, 1957; Stanley Levey, "A 2d Ave. Subway Called Unlikely," *New York Times*, March 9, 1957.

67   Paul Crowell, "'54 Capital Budget to Set City Record," *New York Times*, October 9, 1953; "This Won't Wait," *New York Times*, May 15, 1953; New York City Transit Authority, *1st Annual Report*, 25; State of New York, Senate Committee, *First Interim Report*, 18–19; Paul Crowell, "Mayor Gets Report on Capital Budget," *New York Times*, September 2, 1949.

68   "Double-Cross Seen on 2d Ave. Subway," *New York Times*, January 6, 1956; "Want to Know What Wagner Did with 500 Million Bond Issue for Subways," *Leader-Observer* (Queens), September 20, 1956.

69   Levey, "Dwindling Transit Funds."

70   "Wider 3d Avenue Asked," *New York Times*, October 14, 1951; "Realty Interests Seek Quieter Third Avenue," *New York Times*, December 7, 1941; Andrew Sparberg, *From a Nickel to a Token: The Journey from Board of Transportation to MTA* (New York: Oxford University Press, 2014), 113; New York City Transit Authority, *1st Annual Report*, 29.

71   Nelson A. Rockefeller Institute of Government, "Motor Vehicle Registrations Issued, NYS: Selected Years 1930–91," Transportation section, New York State Statistical Yearbook, accessed April 18, 2019, https://rockinst.org/data-hub/new-york-data-sets; Michael R. Fein, *Paving the Way: New York Road Building and the American State, 1880–1956* (Lawrence: University Press of Kansas, 2008), 223.

72   Caro, *Power Broker*, 797; Moses, "Public Works Problems of NYC"; City of New York, *Progress Report, 1954–1955*, April 23, 1956, 20.

73   City of New York, *Progress Report*, 20; New York State Thruway Authority, "Overview of the Thruway System," accessed January 14, 2018, https://www.thruway.ny.gov/oursystem/overview.html.

74   Meyer Berger made the quip about the Upper East Side in Meyer Berger, *Meyer Berger's New York* (New York: Fordham University Press, 2004), xxiii.

75   Levey, "2d Ave. Subway Called Unlikely."

3. The Billionaire's Ambitions

1   Regional Plan Association (hereafter RPA), *The Region's Growth: A Report of the Second Regional Plan*, May 1967, 8, 81; RPA, "Rail Transit Plans," *Regional Plan News*, no. 71–72, December 1963.

2   "A Realistic Master Plan, the Here and Now: Step by Difficult Step," *New York*, December 1, 1969, 38; New York City Department of City Planning, "Gross Floor Area of Office Buildings Completed or under Construction in the Central Business District since 1947," *Newsletter*, November–December 1963, 2–3.

3   Vincent J. Cannato, *The Ungovernable City: John Lindsay and His Struggle to Save New York* (New York: Basic Books, 2009), 6.

4   RPA, "Rail Transit Plans"; Federal Highway Administration, "State Motor Vehicle Registrations, by Years, 1900–1995," accessed November 12, 2018, https://www.fhwa.dot.gov/ohim/summary95/mv200.pdf.

5   Greater New York Safety Council, *Mid-town Manhattan Parking Program: A Report of the Traffic and Transportation Division*, ca. 1959. Note that the number of vehicles increased from 249,000 to 736,000 between 1924 and 1956.

6   Richard P. Hunt, "Expressway Vote Delayed by City," *New York Times*, December 7, 1962; Joseph C. Ingraham, "3d Midtown Tube to Start Soon, Moses Says, Shelving Road Plan," *New York Times*, December 29, 1965.

7   Robert E. Niebuhr, "Where Are the Railroads and Subways Going," self-published, November 20, 1961, author's possession; Tri-State Regional Planning Commission, *Subway Overcrowding (1956–1976): Interim Technical Report*, November 1977; New York City Department of City Planning, "Better Rapid Transit for New York City," *Newsletter*, May 1963; Sylvester V. Pointkowski (director of public relations, New York City Transit Authority), letter to Charles R. Treuhold, April 9, 1962, folder 2 (Second Avenue Subway, 1994–2002), box 35, NYPIRG Straphangers Campaign Records: 1962–2007 (Bulk 1979–2006), Manuscripts and Archives Division, New York Public Library, New York.

8   Tri-State Regional Planning Commission, *Subway Overcrowding: 1956–1976*, 9–11; Richard Levine, "Seeking Bearable Level of Subway Discomfort," *New York Times*, October 10, 1987; New York City Department of City Planning, "Better Rapid Transit."

9   Emanuel Perlmutter, "City to Hear Plan for New Subway," *New York Times*, April 3, 1963; Emanuel Perlmutter, "New Subway Line to Bronx Asked for Rush Hours," *New York Times*, July 18, 1962; Clayton Knowles, "547 Million Asked for Transit Here," *New York Times*, May 3, 1963; R. W. Apple Jr., "Downtown Report Maps Vast Change in Next 25 Years," *New York Times*, November 21, 1963.

10   City Planning Commission, *Metropolitan Mobility: Proposals for Improved Transportation to Serve New York City*, November 1965, 9–10.

11   City Planning Commission, *Metropolitan Mobility*, 21–27.

12   RPA, "Transportation and the Manhattan Central Business District," policy statement, *Regional Plan News*, no. 82, February 1966.

13   Joseph P. Viteritti, ed., *Summer in the City: John Lindsay, New York, and the American Dream* (Baltimore: Johns Hopkins University Press, 2014), 256.

14   Richard Norton Smith, *On His Own Terms: A Life of Nelson Rockefeller* (New York: Random House, 2014), 400; "edifice complex" cited in Linda Greenhouse, "New Mall in Albany Beginning to Catch On," *New York Times*, January 31, 1977.

15   New York Temporary State Commission on Coordination of State Activities, *Staff Report on Public Authorities under New York State*, March 21, 1956, 43–57; Cary Reich, *The Life of Nelson A. Rockefeller: Worlds to Conquer, 1908–1958* (New York: Doubleday, 1996), 679; "Governor Calms Moses by Letter," *New York Times*, January 8, 1960; Robert A. Caro, *The Power Broker: Robert Moses and the Fall of New York* (New York: Alfred A. Knopf, 1974), 1071; Smith, *On His Own Terms*, 269–70.

16   State University Construction Fund, "History," accessed September 23, 2018, https://www.sucf.suny.edu/about/history.cfm; Smith, *On His Own Terms*, 374–76.

17   Charles Grutzner, "Three States Set Up Transportation Unit," *New York Times*, August 31, 1961; "Transit Administrator: William John Ronan," *New York Times*, August 19, 1968; Joseph E. Persico, *The Imperial Rockefeller: A Biography of Nelson Rockefeller* (New York: Simon and Schuster, 1982), 257.

18   John Sibley, "Report Rejects Rail Agency Plan," *New York Times*, January 16, 1964; Grutzner, "Three States"; Charles Grutzner, "Rockefeller Urges State Buy L.I.R.R. and Modernize It," *New York Times*, February 26, 1965.

19   Jay Kriegel (chief of staff and special counsel to Mayor John Lindsay), telephone interview with the author, March 14, 2016; Persico, *Imperial Rockefeller*, 57–58, 257; Smith, *On His Own Terms*, 269–70; "Governor Calms Moses."

20   John V. Lindsay, "A Modern Transportation System for New York City," campaign white paper, 1965, 1–2; Cannato, *Ungovernable City*, 94.

21   Lindsay, "Modern Transportation System," 3.

22   RPA, "Regional Plan Asks $1.5 Billion in Subway Improvements; Only Way to Speed Street Traffic, Association Observes," press release, February 3, 1966, Robert A. Olmsted Papers, City College Archives, New York.

23   Lindsay, "Modern Transportation System," 4.

24   Lindsay for Mayor press releases, October 1965, folder 212, "Traffic and Transit (Campaign Schedule & Press Releases)," box 103, John Vliet Lindsay Papers (MS 592), Manuscripts and Archives, Yale University Library, New Haven, CT.

25   Lindsay, "Modern Transportation System," 16–19.

26   "Stoppage of Trains Begins Smoothly," *New York Times*, January 2, 1966; Robert D. McFadden, "John V. Lindsay, Mayor and Maverick, Dies at 79," *New York Times*, December 21, 2000; Egbert Semple, "An Economic and Political Analysis of the Failure of the Second Avenue Subway Line" (master's thesis, Queens College, 1978), 35–41.

27   Mayor's Task Force, *The Threatened City: A Report on the Design of the City of New York*, February 7, 1967, 12, Internet Archive, https://archive.org/stream/threatenedcityre00newy/threatenedcityre00newy_djvu.txt.

28   Cannato, *Ungovernable City*, 99; Perkins, "personal and top confidential" memo to Lindsay, December 17, 1965, microfilm roll 45056, Office of the Mayor—Subject

Files 1966 to 1973, John V. Lindsay Collection, La Guardia and Wagner Archives, LaGuardia Community College, Long Island City, New York; Perkins, "personal and top confidential" memo to Lindsay, June 17, 1966, microfilm roll 45056.

29   "Lindsay Expecting Moses to Help Unify Transport," *New York Times*, January 18, 1966; Richard Witkin, "Transit Merger Decried by Moses," *New York Times*, January 21, 1966.

30   Caro, *Power Broker*, 1125, 1134; Arnold H. Lubasch, "Bank Will Fight Transit Merger," *New York Times*, March 13, 1966.

31   RPA, *Region's Growth*, summary page.

32   "Rockefeller Urges Abortion Review," *New York Times*, December 22, 1966.

33   Richard Witkin, "2.5-Billion Transit Bonds Voted in Major Victory for Governor, Bottom of Form," *New York Times*, November 8, 1967; State of New York, Office of the State Comptroller, *New Routes Capital Construction Program—New York City Transit Authority*, Audit Report NY-AUTH-30-79, February 7, 1980, 1–2; Richard Witkin, "Wide Gains Seen in Transit Unity," *New York Times*, January 6, 1967; Richard Madden, "Bond Issue Asked," *New York Times*, January 5, 1967.

34   Madden, "Bond Issue Asked"; letters, memos, and other materials documenting Rockefeller's efforts to secure support for the bond proposal, in Gov NAR, reel 110, Subject File: 1967 to 1970, Transportation, General Bond Issue, Nov. 9–14, 1967, Nelson A. Rockefeller Papers, Rockefeller Archive Center, Sleepy Hollow, NY; Richard Witkin, "$2.5 Billion Transportation Issue Has Top Billing," *New York Times*, October 29, 1967.

35   Caro, *Power Broker*, 1136.

36   Abrams, letter to Rockefeller, November 2, 1967, and Frank D. O'Connor (city council president), letter to Rockefeller, October 27, 1967, Gov NAR, reel 110, Subject File: 1967 to 1970, Transportation, General Bond Issue, Nov. 9–14, 1967, Rockefeller Papers.

37   Sydney H. Schanberg, "Transit Power Shift," *New York Times*, March 24, 1967; Richard E. Mooney, "Key to Increase in Transit Fares Lies in Politics and Public Policy," *New York Times*, January 1, 1968; Dan Tessler (assistant to the mayor), memo to administrators, commissioners, agency heads, assistants to the mayor, and all deputies, September 22, 1967, Gov NAR, reel 110, Subject File: 1967 to 1970, Transportation: General Bond Issue, Nov. 9–14, 1967, Rockefeller Papers; John Lindsay, "Transportation Bond Issue: JVL Remarks to Cabinet," September 15, 1967, box 360, Transportation, Lindsay Papers.

38   Persico, *Imperial Rockefeller*, 212; Smith, *On His Own Terms*, 389–90.

39   Ronald Maiorana, "Transit Program Sent to Governor," *New York Times*, April 1, 1967.

40   Sydney H. Schanberg, "Rockefeller Seeks Regional Agency to Direct Transit," *New York Times*, June 3, 1966; Fred C. Shapiro, "Wholly Ronan Empire," *New York Times*, May 17, 1970; Schanberg, "Transit Power Shift."

41   Jeffrey A. Kroessler, *New York Year by Year: A Chronology of the Great Metropolis* (New York: New York University Press, 2002), 303.

42   Metropolitan Transportation Authority (hereafter MTA), *2 Years: Transportation Progress*, March 1970, 1; Richard Witkin, "Routes Outlined for New Subways," *New York Times*, January 2, 1968.

43   Olmsted, letter to his parents from Luzon (Philippine Islands), September 5, 1945, Alan Olmsted's possession; Paul Crowell, "Board Asks Funds for 2d Ave. Subway," *New York Times*, August 25, 1945; Alan Olmsted (Bob Olmsted's son), interview with the author, Lower Manhattan, October 25, 2017.

44   Boris Pushkarev (retired RPA transportation planner), interview with the author, Cliffside Park, NJ, February 8, 2016; Olmsted, interview with the author.

45   New York City Transit Authority Engineering Department, *Transportation Study for 2nd Ave. Trunk Line with Connections in the Bronx and Queens*, March 1967; Coverdale & Colpitts, *Report to the Downtown-Lower Manhattan Association of a Study of an Additional Subway Line to Serve Downtown Manhattan via Water Street*, June 15, 1966.

46   Lindsay, letter to Ronan, December 18, 1967, microfilm roll 45056, Office of the Mayor—Subject Files 1966 to 1973, La Guardia and Wagner Archives.

47   Metropolitan Commuter Transportation Authority (hereafter MCTA), *Metropolitan Transportation: A Program for Action*, February 1968; Olmsted, interview with the author.

48   Schanberg, "Ronan Lays Transit Crisis to a 30-Year Lag in City," *New York Times*, August 25, 1968; Richard Witkin, "$2.9-Billion Transit Plan for New York Area Links Subways, Rail, Airports," February 29, 1968; "Better Transportation Ahead," editorial, *New York Times*, February 29, 1968.

49   T. W. Braun, "History of Events Immediately Prior to and Leading Up to Rockefeller's Decision and Statement of March 21, 1968," March 1968, attachment to letter from Braun to Ann Whitman (Office of the Governor), in Records: Counsel's Office, Rockefeller Papers.

50   *Supplementary Report on the NYC Rapid Transit Program*, subseries 12, Planning Series, Olmsted Papers.

51   MCTA, *Metropolitan Transportation*, 3 (cover letter from Ronan to Rockefeller).

52   MCTA, *Metropolitan Transportation*, 8–9; Bob Olmsted, memo to Ronan, October 21, 1968 (attached to memo from Olmsted to file, October 22, 1968), subseries 5, Planning Series, Olmsted Papers.

53   "Transport Plan Disputed on Cost," *New York Times*, November 5, 1967; Sydney H. Schanberg, "Governor Details 3-Part Program to Save 20c Fare," *New York Times*, March 9, 1967; "Ronan Says Area Faces a Crisis over Jetports," *New York Times*, April 24, 1967; Charles G. Bennett, "Transportation Funding Would Have 4 Sources," *New York Times*, February 29, 1968.

54   Cost per segment: Lower Bronx to 63rd Street, $150 million; 63rd Street to 34th Street, $70 million; 34th Street to Whitehall Street, $115 million; extension to Dyre Avenue, $60 million; connection to Upper Pelham line, $19 million. MCTA, *Metropolitan Transportation*, 31.

55   Coverdale & Colpitts, *Report to the Downtown-Lower Manhattan Association*, 4; Singstad & Kehart (consulting engineers), *Report on Construction Cost Estimates of the 8 Rapid Transit Subway Lines Proposed by the NYCTA*, August 6, 1968, 6.

56   Ronan, letter to Rockefeller, April 12, 1968, microfilm reel 9, Nelson A. Rockefeller Gubernatorial Records, Rockefeller Papers; New York City Department of City Planning, "Demand Higher Standards for New Subway," *Newsletter*, Summer 1968.

57   "Application of the City of New York Acting by the NYCTA for a Mass Transportation Facilities Grant under the Urban Mass Transportation Act of 1964, as Amended for Second Avenue Subway (Route 132A for the NYC Transit System)," ca. 1971.

58   Metropolitan Transportation Authority (hereafter MTA), "Testimony of Dr. William J. Ronan, Chairman, MTA, before the Board of Estimate of the City of New York: August 12, 1968," press release, August 12, 1968; Urban Mass Transit Administration, "Draft Environment Statement: Southern Extension of the Second Avenue Line for the NYC Transit System," January 1973.

59   Charles G. Bennett, "Ronan Warns City to Act on Transit Lest Funds Shrink," *New York Times*, August 13, 1968.

60   "Stop in Brooklyn Is Urged on Rail Line to Kennedy," *New York Times*, November 21, 1968; Seth S. King, "Expanded Subway Plans Urged by the 5 Borough Presidents and Lindsay," *New York Times*, September 19, 1968; Andrew Jacobs, "Whatever Happened to the Second Avenue Subway," *Our Town*, April 14, 1994.

61   Seth S. King, "Ronan Willing to Expand Subway Plans, and 'Happy' City Pays," *New York Times*, September 20, 1968; MTA, "Lower Second Avenue Route," *Regional Report*, Summer 1969; Richard Cohen, "Second Avenue Subway: Bumpy Road Ahead," *New York*, February 8, 1971, 36–39; Bob Olmsted, memo to Ronan, August 13, 1969, subseries 12, Planning Series, Olmsted Papers.

62   New York City Transportation Administration, City Planning Commission, and New York City Bureau of the Budget, *Standards of Rapid Transit Expansion: A Report to the Mayor and NYC Board of Estimate*, folder 200, "Transportation (Press Releases)," box 139, Lindsay Papers; William J. Ronan, letter to the editor, *Notes from Underground* (Committee for Better Transit publication), ca. 1973.

63   King, "Ronan Willing to Expand"; Seth S. King, "City Approves 2d Ave. Subway and 11 Other New Transit Lines," *New York Times*, September 21, 1968; "Cross-Midtown Rapid Transit," *New York Times*, March 25, 1968; "Go Signal on Transit," *New York Times*, August 23, 2018.

64   New York City Transit Authority (hereafter NYCTA), "Public Hearing in the Matter of Second Avenue Subway—Route 132A—East 34th Street to East 126th Street, Manhattan. Hunter College Assembly Hall, NY, NY, September 15, 1971, 7:30 o'clock p.m.," 18, 23–24.

65   Boris Pushkarev and Jeffrey Zupan, "Re: Station Spacing and Location of the Second Avenue Subway," September 25, 1970, office of the RPA, New York; Nancy Moran, "2d Avenue Subway to Get Just 3 Stops North of 57th," *New York Times*, August 28, 1970; NYCTA, "Public Hearing"; Frank J. Prial, "M.T.A. Adds a Stop, 72d St., to Its 2d Avenue Subway Plan," *New York Times*, August 28, 1971.

66   Boris Pushkarev, "RPA Working Paper: Preliminary, Not for Publication," February 1, 1968; RPA, news release, November 24, 1970, office of the RPA; Pushkarev, interview with the author; Urban Mass Transportation Administration, *Final Environmental Statement: Second Avenue (Project NY-UTG-44), 34th Street to 126th Street Manhattan*, May 1972, 28.

67   RPA, news release, November 24, 1970; John P. Keith, letter to RPA Board of Directors, October 15, 1970.

68   NYCTA, "Public Hearing," 77–100; Fred C. Shapiro, "Hearing," *New Yorker*, September 25, 1971; MTA, *1971 Annual Report*, ca. 1972, 21.

69   Cost per segment: 63rd Street to the Bronx, $150 million; 63rd Street to 34th Street, $70 million, per MCTA, *Metropolitan Transportation*, 54; NYCTA, press release, August 27, 1971, office of the RPA; Prial, "M.T.A. Adds a Stop."

70   MTA, "State Funds for Subway," *Regional Report*, November 1969.

71   First National City Bank, *Public Transportation in the New York Region*, 1970, 37; "Memo Prepared by Bureau of the Budget," September 2, 1970, folder 200 "Transportation (Press Releases)," box 139, Lindsay Papers.

72   Frank J. Prial, "News Analysis," *New York Times*, December 28, 1971; MTA, "Lawmakers Back Program," *Regional Report*, May 1969; Sydney H. Schanberg, "Albany Approves a Mortgage Tax Rise," *New York Times*, April 30, 1969.

73   MTA, "Dollar Dilemma," *Regional Report*, January 1970; MTA, *Transition: 1970 Annual Report*, ca. 1971, 10.

74   First National City Bank, *Public Transportation*, 14; MTA, *Transition*, 62; City of New York and NYCTA, "Application of the City of New York and the NYCTA, the Statutory Transit Construction and Operating Authority, for a Mass Transportation Facilities Grant under the Urban Mass Transportation Act of 1964, as Amended, for Southern Extension of the Second Avenue Line," January 1973, office of NYC Transit's Division of Operations Planning, New York; MTA, *1968-1973: The Ten-Year Program at the Halfway Mark*, 110.

75   First National City Bank, *Public Transportation*, 29; M. A. Farber, "Greater Woes Lie Ahead for City's Transit Riders," *New York Times*, July 30, 1984.

76   William E. Farrell, "Rockefeller Asks $2.5-Billion Bonds to Aid Transport," *New York Times*, March 21, 1971; "Items in Transportation Plan," *New York Times*, March 21, 1971; Frank Lynn, "Everybody Was for the Bond Issue except the People," *New York Times*, November 7, 1971.

77   Shapiro, "Wholly Ronan Empire"; Edward Hudson, "Subway Repairs Criticized Anew," *New York Times*, February 26, 1971.

78   John Lindsay, press release, January 30, 1970, box 360, Lindsay Papers; First National City Bank, *Public Transportation*, 13–19; Hudson, "Subway Repairs Criticized Anew."

79   Frank J. Prial, "IND Aide Suspended in Tunnel Incident," *New York Times*, August 20, 1971; "Graffiti Epidemic Strikes 7,000 Cars in Subway System," *New York Times*, October 21, 1972.

80   Edward M. Gramlich, "The New York City Fiscal Crisis: What Happened and What Is to Be Done?," *American Economic Review* 66, no. 2 (1976): 416.

81   "'Inherited' Deficit . . . ," *New York Times*, April 11, 1974; Jeff Nussbaum, "The Night New York Saved Itself from Bankruptcy," *New Yorker*, October 16, 2015; Roger Dunstan, "Overview of New York City's Fiscal Crisis," California Research Bureau, California State Library, 1995; Charles R. Morris, "Of Budgets, Taxes, and the Rise of a

New Plutocracy," in Viteritti, *Summer in the City*, 89–96; "Flawed Budget," *New York Times*, January 5, 1974: "Budgetary Shell Game," *New York Times*, February 19, 1974; Citizens Budget Commission, *New York City's Debt Problem*, July 1973, 1–2.

82   Citizens Budget Commission, *New York City's Debt Problem*, 3; Peter Kihssjan, "City Re-examines U.S. Relief Plan," *New York Times*, January 4, 1971; Congressional Budget Office, "The Causes of New York City's Fiscal Crisis," *Political Science Quarterly* 90 (1975): 670.

83   Marilyn Marks Rubin, *A Guide to New York City Taxes: History, Issues and Concerns*, PJ Solomon, December 2010, http://pjsc.magikcms.com/tax%20guides/CityGuideWeb.pdf.

4. Construction Begins and Construction Ends

1   "M'Clellan Motorman of First Subway Train," *New York Times*, October 28, 1904.

2   "Rapid Transit Tunnel Begun," *New York Times*, March 25, 1900.

3   Greg Sargent, "The Line That Time Forgot," *New York*, April 5, 2004; "MTA Groundbreaking Ceremony 103rd St. & 2nd Ave. Friday October 27, 1972. 9:30 AM. Final Draft J.E. Persico," October 20, 1972, Nelson A. Rockefeller Gubernatorial Records, Speeches, series 33, Nelson A. Rockefeller Papers, Rockefeller Archive Center, Sleepy Hollow, NY.

4   Metropolitan Transportation Authority (hereafter MTA), press release 65, October, 25, 1972, Robert A. Olmsted Papers, City College Archives, New York.

5   The $500 million contribution is discussed in the previous chapter; the $350 million assumed that the Second Avenue subway would cost $1 billion, with a $250 million contribution from the federal government and $100 million from the state. The MTA used a $1 billion cost estimate in its October 25, 1972, press release, while the mayor used an $850 million estimate in his remarks. John V. Lindsay, "Remarks by Mayor John V. Lindsay: Ground-Breaking for the Second Avenue Subway," October 27, 1972, Olmsted Papers; Lindsay, letter to Ronan, March 10, 1969, microfilm roll 45209, Office of Mayor—Confidential Subject Files, 1966 to 1973, La Guardia and Wagner Archives, LaGuardia Community College, Long Island City, New York.

6   "Press Questions of Governor NAR before 2nd Avenue Subway Groundbreaking, 103 St and 2nd Ave, NY, NY on October 27, 1972 at 9:45 A.M," Nelson A. Rockefeller, Vice Presidential, Joseph Persico, series 12, Nelson A. Rockefeller Record Group 26, Rockefeller Papers.

7   "Remarks of Governor NAR at 2nd Ave Subway Groundbreaking at 103 St and 2nd Ave, NY, NY on October 27, 1972 10:00 A.M.," Nelson A. Rockefeller, Vice Presidential, Joseph Persico, series 12, Nelson A. Rockefeller Record Group 26, Rockefeller Papers.

8   Traci Rozhon, "Turf: A Rockefeller Fixer-Upper," *New York Times*, October 14, 1999; Ralph Blumenthal, "Richard Nixon's Search for a New York Home," *New York Times*, July 30, 2008.

9   "Conversation No. 739–10," June 21, 1972, 12:38–1:22 p.m., White House Tapes, Richard Nixon Presidential Library and Museum, Yorba Linda, CA.

10   "Conversation No. 739–10"; Nick Thimmesch, "Whatever Happened to Richard Nixon?," *Los Angeles Times*, July 16, 1967.

11   Kenneth McKenna, "The Second Avenue Promises to Be Roomy, Cool and Elegant: But Will Enough Riders Use the New Line?," *Daily News*, August 29, 1974; New York City Transit Authority, "Public Hearing in the Matter of Second Avenue Subway—Route 132A—East 34th Street to East 126th Street, Manhattan, Hunter College Assembly Hall, NY, NY, September 15, 1971, 7:30 PM."

12   New York City Transit Authority, *Route 132-C Phase 1 Report, Second Avenue and Water Street Subway*, June 1973, chap. 2. Information about Brooklyn Bridge per Ed Plotkin, interview with the author, Dobbs Ferry, NY, January 17, 2016.

13   Urban Mass Transportation Administration (hereafter UMTA), *Final Environmental Impact Statement: Second Avenue (Project NY-UTG-44) 34th Street to 126th Street Manhattan*, May 1972, 17–27; UMTA, *Draft Environmental Statement: Southern Extension of the Second Avenue Line for the NYC Transit System*, January 1973, 30–47.

14   "City Planners Asking $252-Million for Big Water Tunnel to Queens," *New York Times*, December 11, 1969.

15   "Application of the City of New York and the New York City Transit Authority, the Statutory Transit Construction and Operating Authority, for a Mass Transportation Facilities Grant under the Urban Mass Transportation Act of 1964, as Amended, for Southern Extension of the Second Avenue Line," January 1973, A-2, office of NYC Transit's Division of Operations Planning, New York.

16   C. Sidamon-Eristoff (administrator), letter to William Ronan, July 26, 1972, microfilm roll 45209, Office of Mayor—Confidential Subject Files, 1966 to 1973, La Guardia and Wagner Archives.

17   UMTA, *Draft Environmental Statement*, 30–47.

18   Plotkin, interview with the author; Max H. Seigel, "Network of Uncharted Utility Lines Is Found in Digging for 2d Ave Subway," *New York Times*, February 18, 1973.

19   UMTA, *Final Environmental Impact Statement*, 21–23, 38–40; UMTA, *Draft Environmental Impact Statement, Second Avenue Subway Route 132-A: 34th Street to 126th Street, Manhattan*, August 27, 1971, 3.

20   Paul L. Montgomery, "2d Ave. Tunnelers Push On, despite Potential Futility," *New York Times*, January 10, 1975; "Subway Builder Is Killed; 2 Hurt as Walk Collapses," *New York Times*, April 11, 1974; "16 East Harlem Families Must Evacuate Buildings," *New York Times*, May 14, 1975.

21   J. Lee Rankin (NYC corporation counsel), memo to Lindsay, July 1, 1966, microfilm roll 45056, Office of the Mayor—Subject Files, 1966 to 1973, La Guardia and Wagner Archives; Rockefeller, letter to Lindsay, December 29, 1969, microfilm roll 45209, Office of Mayor—Confidential Subject Files, 1966 to 1973, La Guardia and Wagner Archives; Richard Witkin, "Subsidies to Save 20c Fare Studied by City and State," *New York Times*, February 16, 1967.

22   Lindsay, letter to Ronan, June 15, 1973, Office of the Mayor—(John V. Lindsay) Departmental Files, 1966–1973, Transit Authority to US Government, La Guardia and Wagner Archives; Max H. Siegel, "$10.3-Billion City Budget, with Realty-Tax Rise Held to 36 Cents, Is Agreed to by Leaders," *New York Times*, June 19, 1973 (the author's surname was misspelled by the newspaper; it was actually Seigel).

23   William J. Ronan, "Public Transportation Problems in Urban Areas," proceedings of a conference held by the Highway Research Board, Henniker, NH, July 9–14, 1972, *Transportation Research Board Special Report*, no. 144 (1974): 11.

24   Metropolitan Transportation Authority (hereafter MTA), board materials, July 9, 1973.

25   Edward C. Burks, "$6-Billion Transit Project Linked to Bond Approval," *New York Times*, October 6, 1973; Edward C. Burks, "Levitt Criticizes Transit Projects," *New York Times*, October 21, 1973.

26   Damon Stetson, "State A.F.L.-C.I.O. to Support $3.5-Billion Transit-Bond Issue," *New York Times*, September 7, 1973; Burks, "Levitt Criticizes Transit Projects"; Robert Lindsey, "Transit Bond Vote," *New York Times*, October 21, 1973; "Rockefeller Will Help City Raise Funds to Hold Fare," *New York Times*, July 25, 1973; Beame, letter to Warren Anderson, July 25, 1973, Office of the Mayor Abraham Beame, Subject Files, 1974–1977 (Mental Health & Retardation Svc D—NY Cultural Council—Appmt.), NYC Municipal Archives, New York.

27   Frank J. Prial, "News Analysis," *New York Times*, December 28, 1971.

28   Damon Stetson, "Jobs in City Down by 21,000 in 1973," *New York Times*, February 22, 1974; Alexander Cohen, "Is Padlocking a Peep Show Enough?," *New York Times*, August 13, 1972.

29   Charles R. Morris, "Of Budgets, Taxes, and the Rise of a New Plutocracy," in *Summer in the City: John Lindsay, New York, and the American Dream*, ed. Joseph P. Viteritti (Baltimore: Johns Hopkins University Press, 2014), 92–93; Richard Ravitch, *So Much to Do: A Full Life of Business, Politics, and Confronting Fiscal Crises* (New York: PublicAffairs, 2014), 79; John H. Allan, "City Bond Rating Upgraded Again," *New York Times*, December 15, 1973.

30   Office of Mayor John V. Lindsay, press release, October 24, 1973; Edward C. Burks, "Ground Is Broken for 2d Ave. Link," *New York Times*, October 25, 1973; Patrick Doyle, John Kelly, and Harry Stathos, "136 Hurt in Blaze on IRT Express," *Daily News*, October 26, 1973.

31   Edward C. Burks, "Ronan Expects Record Subway Construction in 1974," *New York Times*, November 11, 1973; Edward C. Burks, "Beame and Wilson Man the Jackhammers to Start 4th Segment of 2d Ave. Subway," *New York Times*, July 26, 1974; Montgomery, "2d Ave. Tunnelers Push On."

32   "Excerpts from the Debate between Rivals in the Democratic Mayoral Runoff," *New York Times*, June 15, 1973; Rudolph W. Giuliani, "Remarks at the Funeral Service for Mayor Abraham Beame," New York City Department of Records, February 13, 2001, http://www.nyc.gov/html/records/rwg/html/2001a/beame.html; Robert D. McFadden, "Abraham Beame Is Dead at 94," *New York Times*, February 11, 2001; Abe Beame, "Statement by Mayor Beame at Public Hearings before U.S. Senate Subcommittee on Transportation, Manhattan, March 4, 1974," Abraham D. Beame, Subject Files, 1974 Series: Deputy Mayor (Judah Gribetz), box 18, NYC Municipal Archives.

33   Linda Greenhouse, "Transit Subsidy Gaining Support," *New York Times*, January 13, 1974; Linda Greenhouse, "Wilson Signs Bill to Save City's 35c Transit Fare," *New York Times*, January 17, 1974.

34   Theodore Kheel, "The City's Best Weapon against Oil Blackmail," *New York*, November 5, 1973, 51–54.

35   Susan Friedwald, memo to Deputy Mayor Judah Gribetz, February 20, 1974, and City of New York, "Statement by Mayor Abraham D. Beame," press release, August 13, 1974, Abraham D. Beame, Subject Files, 1974 Series: Deputy Mayor (Judah Gribetz), box 18, NYC Municipal Archives; "President Richard Nixon's Daily Diary," Richard Nixon Presidential Library and Museum, February 6, 1974, https://www.nixonli brary.gov/sites/default/files/virtuallibrary/documents/PDD/1974/117%20Febru ary%201-15%201974.pdf; Richard D. Lyons, "President Offers $16-Billion Plan on Aid to Transit," *New York Times*, February 10, 1974; Edward C. Burks, "U.S. Aid Won't Save Fare, Beame Says," *New York Times*, February 1, 1974.

36   Fred Ferretti, "Beame Says He and Others Share Blame in City Crisis," *New York Times*, September 11, 1975; Ken Auletta, "Who's to Blame for the Fix We're In," *New York*, October 27, 1975, 40; David Yunich, letter to Governor Malcolm Wilson, August 19, 1974, office of the MTA Legal Department, New York.

37   Glenn Fowler, "Agencies Warned by Mayor to Curb Capital Spending," *New York Times*, November 2, 1974; Glenn Fowler, "Planner Assails City's Budgeting," *New York Times*, January 3, 1974.

38   Glenn Fowler, "Budget Experts Fear Rise of 13% in Property Tax," *New York Times*, January 12, 1974; Soma Golden, "Bankers Planning to Discuss Problems with Controller," *New York Times*, December 16, 1974.

39   Edward C. Burks, "Use of Lexington Ave. IRT, Busiest Line in City, Drops," *New York Times*, November 26, 1973.

40   "Dismissed Employee Settles with City for $19,000," *New York Times*, January 16, 1975; Murray Schumach, "Gimbels Will Build Entrances to Subway at Yorkville Store," *New York Times*, July 29, 1970; Robert E. Tomasson, "Gimbel, on M.T.A. Panel, Charged with Conflict," *New York Times*, May 27, 1970; Albert Scardino, "Gimbels at 86th: A Born Loser," *New York Times*, June 7, 1986.

41   Frank Lichtensteiger, "Protests Second Avenue Subway," commentary (op-ed), *Our Town*, November 8, 1974.

42   "Nixon Asks 50% Rise for Mass Transit," *New York Times*, January 31, 1974; Burks, "U.S. Aid Won't Save Fare"; Burks, "Beame and Wilson Man the Jackhammers."

43   Paul L. Montgomery, "5 M.T.A. Projects Postponed to '87," *New York Times*, November 8, 1974; "High-Cost Transit Delay," editorial, *New York Times*, November 7, 1974; Richard Witkin, "Stalled City Subway Expansion," *New York Times*, November 12, 1974.

44   Edward C. Burks, "2d Ave. Subway Is Delayed until 1986," *New York Times*, November 1, 1974; "Transit Bill Passes," *New York Times*, November 24, 1974.

45   The figure of $2.25 billion is per State of New York, Office of the State Comptroller (hereafter OSC), *New Routes Capital Construction Program: New York City Transit Authority*, Audit Report NY-AUTH-30-79, February 7, 1980, 10.

46   Richard Cohen, "Second Avenue Subway: Bumpy Road Ahead," *New York*, February 8, 1971, 38.

47   OSC, *New Routes Capital Construction Program*, 10–12; Ravitch, *So Much to Do*, 52.

48   OSC, *New Routes Capital Construction Program*, 11–12; Plotkin, interview with the author.

49   Bent Flyvbjerg, Mette Skamris Holm, and Soren Buhl, "Underestimating Costs in Public Works Projects: Error or Lie?," *Journal of the American Planning Association* 68, no. 3 (2002): 279–95; Bent Flyvbjerg, Massimo Garbuio, and Dan Lovallo, "Delusion and Deception in Large Infrastructure Projects: Two Models for Explaining and Preventing Executive Disaster," *California Management Review* 51, no. 2 (2009): 170–93.

50   Hugh Carey, "Text of Carey's State of the State Message as He Delivered It to the Legislature," *New York Times*, January 9, 1975; Jimmy Vielkind, "Gov. Hugh Carey: Role Model from a Past Fiscal Crisis," *Times Union* (Albany, NY), August 8, 2011.

51   "New York Debt Past and Present: A Talk with Gov. Hugh L. Carey," *Bond Buyer*, December 1, 2003; Donna E. Shalala and Carol Bellamy, "State Saves a City: The New York Case," *Duke Law Journal* 25, no. 6 (1977): 1119–22.

52   Congressional Budget Office, "The Causes of New York City's Fiscal Crisis," *Political Science Quarterly* 90, no. 4 (Winter 1975–76): 668; Edward M. Gramlich, "The New York City Fiscal Crisis: What Happened and What Is to Be Done?," *American Economic Review* 66, no. 2 (1976): 417–19.

53   Auletta, "Who's to Blame"; Ravitch, *So Much to Do*, chap. 4; "When Tuition at CUNY Was Free, Sort Of," *CUNY Matters*, October 12, 2011, http://www1.cuny.edu/mu/forum/2011/10/12/when-tuition-at-cuny-was-free-sort-of.

54   Roger Dunstan, "Overview of New York City's Fiscal Crisis," California Research Bureau, *CRB Note* 3, no. 1 (March 1, 1995): 3; Jeff Nussbaum, "The Night New York Saved Itself from Bankruptcy," *New Yorker*, October 16, 2015; Peter Goldmark, speech at "Governor Hugh L. Carey: The Legacy for New York State," Public Policy Forum, Rockefeller Institute, Albany, NY, October 3, 2011, Internet Archive, https://web.archive.org/web/20151013135625/http://www.rockinst.org/pdf/public_policy_forums/2011-10-03-Carey_Legacy.pdf.

55   Gerald Ford, "Federal Spending," *President Ford '76 Fact Book*, Gerald R. Ford Presidential Library & Museum, accessed July 2, 2017, https://fordlibrarymuseum.gov/library/document/factbook/fedspend.htm.

56   Peter Goldmark, telephone interview with the author, December 27, 2016; Dale Van Atta, *With Honor: Melvin Laird in War, Peace, and Politics* (Madison: University of Wisconsin Press, 2008), 285; "Testimony of Felix G. Rohatyn to the House Financial Services Committee," US House Committee on Financial Services, December 5, 2008, http://archives-financialservices.house.gov/hearing110/rohatyn120508.pdf.

57   Nussbaum, "The Night New York Saved Itself."

58   MTA, "Minutes of Meeting: Metropolitan Transportation Authority," December 13, 1974, office of the MTA Legal Department; Mayor's Policy Committee, *Transportation Policy and Programs: A Report of the Mayor's Policy Committee to Mayor Abraham D. Beame*, March 20, 1975, 7; Montgomery, "2d Ave. Tunnelers Push On"; Edward C. Burks, "Beame Trims Plans for New Subway," *New York Times*, March 21, 1975.

59   Burks, "Beame Trims Plans."

60   Edward C. Burks, "L.I.R.R. Terminal Delayed by M.T.A.," *New York Times*, January 19, 1975; "Statement by David L. Yunich (Chairman and Chief Executive Officer, Metropolitan Transportation Authority) before the Select Legislative Committee on Transportation, Albany, February 25, 1975," office of the MTA Legal Department.

61   Edward C. Burks, "M.T.A. Receives $87.5-Million Aid," *New York Times*, May 20, 1975; National Mass Transportation Assistance Act of 1974, Pub. L. No. 93-503, 88 Stat. 1565 (1974), http://uscode.house.gov/statutes/pl/93/503.pdf; Roy Ash (director of the Office of Management and Budget), memorandum for the president, November 25, 1974, folder "1974/11/26 S386 National Transportation Assistance Act of 1974 (1)," box 13, White House Records Office: Legislation Case Files, Gerald R. Ford Presidential Library, Ann Arbor, MI.

62   Ash, memorandum for the president; Martin Tolchin, "President Signs Mass-Transit Act," *New York Times*, November 27, 1974.

63   OSC, *New Routes Capital Construction Program*, 20–24; Edward C. Burks, "2d Ave. Subway Put Off Further," *New York Times*, December 14, 1974; City of New York and NYC Transit Authority, "Notice of Public Hearing: Request for Capital Grant Agreement Amendments to Permit Transfer of $74 Million of Previously Granted Federal UMTA Capital Funds from UMTA Project No. NY 03-0044, the Second Avenue Line in Manhattan (Route 132-A) to UMTA Project No. NY 03-0051, Archer Avenue Line in Queens (Route 131-D/133), and for the Temporary Use of 50 per Centum Thereof for the Payment of Operating Expenses," hearing date of June 3, 1975; Beame, letter to John Keith (RPA president), January 6, 1975, office of the RPA, New York.

64   Robert Olmsted, cover note to John Keith, January 8, 1975, attached to three-page paper titled "Summary of Reasons for Restoring the Construction of Three Miles of the Second Avenue Subway from 63rd Street North to 125th Street to High Priority Status," author's possession.

65   RPA Staff, memo to Board of Directors, February 19, 1975, office of the RPA; Keith, letter to Beame, December 20, 1974, office of the RPA; Ferretti, "New Construction Virtually Barred in Capital Budget," *New York Times*, December 4, 1974.

66   Boris Pushkarev, interview with the author, Cliffside Park, NJ, February 8, 2016; "Thirty Years in New York: Boris Pushkarev's Reflections on His RPA Career," Regional Plan Association, May 18, 2015, http://www.rpa.org/article/thirty-years-in-new-york-boris-pushkarevs-reflections-on-his-rpa-career; Boris S. Pushkarev with Jeffrey M. Zupan and Robert S. Cummea, *Urban Rail in America: An Exploration of Criteria for Fixed-Guideway Transit* (Bloomington: Indiana University Press, 1982).

67   Edward C. Burks, "Work Is Stopped on Subway Line," *New York Times*, September 26, 1975; Plotkin, interview with the author; Goldmark, telephone interview with the author, March 14, 2016.

68   Goldmark, telephone interview with the author, March 14, 2016; Goldmark, speech at "Governor Hugh L. Carey."

69   Nussbaum, "The Night New York Saved Itself"; Congressional Budget Office, "Causes of New York City's Fiscal Crisis"; Judith Cummings, "How to Seek City U. Tuition Assistance," *New York Times*, June 9, 1976.

70   John Darnton, "Unions and Banks Will Get Role in Governing of City," *New York Times*, November 19, 1975; "Conversation No. 739–10."

5. Saving the Subway

1   W. C. Hennessy (commissioner, New York State Department of Transportation), letter to R. Wayne Diesel (deputy state comptroller), attachment to State of New York, Office of the State Comptroller, *New Routes Capital Construction Program: New York City Transit Authority*, Audit Report NY-AUTH-30-79, February 7, 1980, app. C.

2   Stanley Levey, "A 2d Ave. Subway Called Unlikely," *New York Times*, March 9, 1957.

3   Costs that account for inflation were calculated based on James K. Cohen, "Capital Investment and the Decline of Mass Transit in New York City, 1945–1981," *Urban Affairs Quarterly* 23, no. 3 (1988): 383, table 6.

4   Norm Silverman, telephone interview with the author, December 7, 2015.

5   Charles G. Bennett, "A Record $250-Million Is Asked for Transit Expansion Here," *New York Times*, November 5, 1968; Mayor's Policy Committee, *Transportation: Policy and Programs; A Report of the Mayor's Policy Committee to Mayor Abraham D. Beame*, March 20, 1975, 13; Cohen, "Capital Investment," 380; Richard A. Chudd, David Schoenbrod, and Ross Sandler, *A New Direction in Transit: A Report to Mayor Edward I. Koch from Robert F. Wagner, Jr., Chairman, City Planning Commission*, December 1978, I–4. Inflation was calculated by using the US Bureau of Labor Statistics' consumer price index.

6   Paul Theroux, "Subway Odyssey," *New York Times*, January 31, 1982.

7   Theroux, "Subway Odyssey."

8   Metropolitan Transportation Authority (hereafter MTA) New York City Transit Authority (hereafter NYCTA), *Strategic Plan: 1985–1989*, December 1984, 3.

9   "Statement by David L. Yunich, Chairman and Chief Executive Officer, MTA, before the Assembly Committee on Transportation," January 22, 1976, office of NYC Transit's Division of Operations Planning, New York.

10   "Statement by David L. Yunich"; Richard Karp, "The Man Who Runs the Subways," *New York*, April 9, 1979, 36–48; MTA, *1978 Annual Report*, 1979, 3; Steve Polan, telephone interview with the author, January 18 and 19, 2017; Ross Sandler, telephone interview with the author, January 20, 2017.

11   Polan, telephone interview with the author; "Wrong Way on Westway," editorial, *New York Times*, December 15, 1978; "The Real Dimensions of Westway," editorial, *New York Times*, February 16, 1981; "Hang On to Westway," editorial, *New York Times*, September 12, 1982; Edward C. Burks, "Issue and Debate," *New York Times*, February 3, 1975.

12   Steven R. Weisman, "Koch Calls Westway a Disaster and Vows It Will Never Be Built," *New York Times*, October 28, 1977; Karp, "Man Who Runs the Subways," 37; Richard J. Meislin, "Westway Report Estimates a Loss of 10,000 New Jobs with Trade-In," *New York Times*, December 24, 1977.

13   Weisman, "Koch Calls Westway a Disaster"; Leslie Maitland, "Carey Did Not Apply for Transit Funds, U.S. Officials Assert," *New York Times*, September 23, 1979; Mort Downey, telephone interview with the author, July 14, 2017.

14   Tony Schwartz, "The Subway: City's Lifeline for 75 Years," *New York Times*, April 4, 1980; Polan, telephone interview with the author ; MTA's annual reports from 2011, 2012, and 2013; Chudd, Schoenbrod, and Sandler, *New Direction in Transit*, 3.

15   MTA, *10 Year Capital Needs: MTA*, July 1977, folder 198, box 12, NYC Municipal Archives, New York; Robert Rickles and Harold Holzer, "The Light at the End of the Subway Tunnel," *New York*, February 1, 1982, 23; Chudd, Schoenbrod, and Sandler, *New Direction in Transit*, III-3–III-4.

16   Judith Cummings, "Subway Riders Frazzled by Delays and Crowding," *New York Times*, January 27, 1981; Richard E. Rieder, "New York's Subway Loses a Customer," letter to the editor, *New York Times*, January 23, 1981 (letter dated January 9, 1981).

17   Judith Cummings, "Subway Derailment Adds to Strain on Transit Lines," *New York Times*, January 13, 1981.

18   Cummings, "Subway Riders Frazzled"; Daniel Machalaba, "Train Master: Underneath New York, David Gunn Tackles a Monumental Task," *Wall Street Journal*, April 25, 1984.

19   Machalaba, "Train Master"; Chudd, Schoenbrod, and Sandler, *New Direction in Transit*, V-2–V-5; Mark Seaman, Allison L. C. de Cerreño, and Seth English-Young, "From Rescue to Renaissance: The Achievements of the MTA Capital Program 1982–2004," Rudin Center for Transportation Policy and Management, 2004, 1–2; MTA, *10 Year Capital Needs*.

20   MTA, *10 Year Capital Needs*.

21   Albert Samaha, "The Rise and Fall of Crime in New York City: A Timeline," *Village Voice*, August 7, 2014; Christina Sterbenz, "New York City Used to Be a Terrifying Place," *Business Insider*, July 12, 2013; NYCTA, *Strategic Plan*, 6; Seaman, de Cerreño, and English-Young, "From Rescue to Renaissance," 2; "Subway Crime, Union Mischief," *New York Times*, March 20, 1979.

22   Theroux, "Subway Odyssey."

23   Theroux, "Subway Odyssey."

24   Paul Goldberger, "Capital Subway: Grace amid Monuments," *New York Times*, February 6, 1978; Sandy Hornick (former deputy executive director, NYC Department of City Planning), telephone interview with the author, July 10, 2017; Zachary M. Schrag, *The Great Society Subway: A History of the Washington Metro* (Baltimore: Johns Hopkins University Press, 2014), 69.

25   Chudd, Schoenbrod, and Sandler, *New Direction in Transit*, I-3, III-9–III-10; Permanent Citizens Advisory Committee to the MTA (hereafter PCAC), *MTA Performance: A Statistical Study, 1975–1980*, February 1981, 1–2, office of PCAC, New York; Seaman, de Cerreño, and English-Young, "From Rescue to Renaissance," 1–2.

26   Jack Bigel, *Financing New York's Public Transit System: A Report Presented to the MTA Forum*, January 30, 1981, 8, 43; MTA, *1980 Annual Report*, 1981.

27   PCAC, *The Metropolitan Transportation Authority's Capital Program: Part I, Comparison with the Staff Report of Capital Revitalization for the 1980's and Beyond*, April 1984, 1–6, office of PCAC; MTA, *10 Year Capital Needs*; John D. Caemmerer (chair), *A*

Report to the Governor and the Legislature by the New York State Legislative Commission on Critical Transportation Choices: Annual Report, 1979–1980, 1981, 154.

28   Sandler, telephone interview with the author.

29   Robert F. Wagner Jr., "Mayor Koch and the Politics of Mass Transit," letter to the editor, *New York Times*, July 15, 1981; Sandler, telephone interview with the author; Chudd, Schoenbrod, and Sandler, *New Direction in Transit*, 9; Maurice Carroll, "Planners Urge Spending More on Fixing Subways," *New York Times*, December 29, 1978.

30   Carroll, "Planners Urge Spending More."

31   "John Caemmerer, Chairman of State Senate Transit Panel," *New York Times*, February 8, 1982.

32   Caemmerer, *Report to the Governor*, 153–55.

33   Jimmy Carter, "Remarks at the Annual Convention of the American Public Transit Association," New York, September 25, 1979, in *Public Papers of the Presidents of the United States: Jimmy Carter, June 23 to December 31, 1979* (Washington, DC: Government Printing Office, 1980), 1739.

34   Leslie Maitland, "Yunich Quits as M.T.A. Chairman," *New York Times*, December 31, 1976; Leslie Maitland, "Fisher Resigns as M.T.A. Head," *New York Times*, October 6, 1979; "Daily Diary of President Jimmy Carter," September 25, 1979, Jimmy Carter Presidential Library and Museum, https://www.jimmycarterlibrary.gov/assets/docu ments/diary/1979/d092579t.pdf.

35   Bigel, *Financing New York's Public Transit System*, 2–3.

36   James Lardner, "Painting the Elephant," *New Yorker*, June 25, 1984, 41–42; "Conversation No. 739–10," June 21, 1972, 12:38–1:22 p.m., White House Tapes, Richard Nixon Presidential Library and Museum, Yorba Linda, CA.

37   Richard Ravitch, *So Much to Do: A Full Life of Business, Politics, and Confronting Fiscal Crises* (New York: PublicAffairs, 2014), 132; "Ravitch Hopes He'll Find the Silver Lining in Albany," *New York Times*, February 1, 1981; David A. Andelman, "Half-Fare Setup on City Transit Sharply Curbed," *New York Times*, March 15, 1980; David A. Andelman, "M.T.A. May Face Deficit Next Year of $200 Million," *New York Times*, November 21, 1979; Richard J. Meislin, "Measure to Aid Transit Systems Signed by Carey," *New York Times*, June 20, 1980.

38   Ari L. Goldman, "Koch Asked to Stop New Construction, Close 200 Schools," *New York Times*, April 9, 1979.

39   *Socioeconomic Factors Associated with Hunger and Poverty in Urban America: Hearing before the Select Committee on Hunger*, 99th Cong., First Session 76 (1985), hearing held in Brooklyn, NY, November 8, 1985; Joe Flood, "Why the Bronx Burned," *New York Post*, May 16, 2010; Mario Maffi, *Gateway to the Promised Land: Ethnic Cultures on New York's Lower East Side* (New York: New York University Press, 1995), 60; Alan S. Oser, "Rental Construction for Upper East Side," *New York Times*, February 15, 1980.

40   David A. Andelman, "Tunnel Project, Five Years Old, Won't Be Used," *New York Times*, October 11, 1980.

41 Rickles and Holzer, "Light at the End," 22; E. J. Dionne Jr., "Carey Names Ravitch to Head M.T.A.," *New York Times*, October 18, 1979.

42 Ravitch, *So Much to Do*, 131–32; John M. Kaiser, "New York Metropolitan Transportation Authority Infrastructure Program," *Annals of the New York Academy of Sciences* 431, no. 1 (1984): 334; Richard Ravitch, interview with the author, Waterside Plaza, NY, April 24, 2017.

43 MTA, *1980 Annual Report*; Seaman, de Cerreño, and English-Young, "From Rescue to Renaissance," 4.

44 MTA, *Staff Report of Capital Revitalization for the 1980's and Beyond and a Statement by Richard Ravitch*, November 25, 1980, 1–15; Seaman, de Cerreño, and English-Young, "From Rescue to Renaissance," 6; Judith Cummings, "M.T.A. Proposes 5 Ways to Raise Funds to Combat Physical Decline," *New York Times*, November 26, 1980.

45 MTA, *Staff Report*, 6–7.

46 Ravitch, interview with the author; Lardner, "Painting the Elephant," 59–60; Robin Herman, "Ravitch Assails Proposal to Halt U.S. Tax Benefit," *New York Times*, February 22, 1982.

47 Steve Polan, interview with the author, New York, March 10, 2017.

48 Lardner, "Painting the Elephant," 44; Edward C. Burks, "Issue and Debate," *New York Times*, February 3, 1975; Polan, telephone interview with the author.

49 Lardner, "Painting the Elephant," 44–57; Ravitch, interview with the author; MTA, *1980 Annual Report*.

50 PCAC, *MTA Performance*, 3, 38.

51 Hugh L. Carey, *The NYS Economy in the 1980's: A Program for Economic Growth*, January 26, 1981, 1; PCAC, *A Review of MTA Chairman Richard Ravitch's Statement on Funding Sources for Capital Revitalization*, February 1981, 3, 21, office of PCAC; Glenn Fowler, "Capital Budget of 1 Billion Has Renewal as Aim," *New York Times*, April 27, 1979.

52 "Ravitch Hopes He'll Find the Silver Lining"; Judith Cummings, "January Subway Service Assailed as the Worst in the Lines' History," *New York Times*, February 9, 1981.

53 Polan, telephone interview with the author; Judith Cummings, "Transit Decline Poses a Threat to Jobs in City," *New York Times*, April 5, 1981.

54 Polan, telephone interview with the author; Richard J. Meislin, "Higher Fare Looms at the End of the Transit Tunnel," *New York Times*, March 22, 1981; Paul Burton, "MTA Funding Dance Looks Familiar," *Bond Buyer*, October 19, 2015.

55 Richard J. Meislin, "M.T.A. Improvements Totaling $5 Billion Proposed by Carey," *New York Times*, March 3, 1981; Richard J. Meislin, "Carey's Plan to Aid M.T.A.," *New York Times*, March 5, 1981; Richard J. Meislin, "2 Democratic Leaders Ask Carey to Explore Trade-In on Westway," *New York Times*, March 4, 1981.

56 Polan, telephone interview with the author; Ravitch, *So Much to Do*, 130–31.

57 PCAC, *Review of MTA Chairman*, 7; Gene Russianoff, "Rebuilding Our Transit," *New York Times*, April 29, 1981.

58   NYPIRG Straphangers Campaign Records: 1962–2007 (Bulk 1979–2006), Manuscripts and Archives Division, New York Public Library.

59   Polan, telephone interview with the author.

60   "Highway Chief Asks a Westway Decision," *New York Times*, May 13, 1981; Meislin, "2 Democratic Leaders"; Meislin, "M.T.A. Improvements"; Wagner, "Mayor Koch."

61   Frank Lynn, "Politics and Transit Fares in New York," *New York Times*, March 25, 1981; Meislin, "Carey's Plan to Aid M.T.A."

62   "There's No Blinking at Medicaid," *New York Times*, April 30, 1981; Robin Herman, "Just Another Budget Deadline, Albany Shrugs," *New York Times*, April 19, 1981; Sydney H. Schanberg, "New York: A Record for Albany Delinquents," *New York Times*, May 9, 1981; Ernest Holsendolph, "Reagan Plan Stirring Fear of Mass Transit Cutbacks," *New York Times*, April 9, 1981.

63   "Carey Defends Westway as Part of Mass Transit," *New York Times*, April 16, 1981; Deblina Chakraborty, "When Times Square Was Sleazy," CNN, April 18, 2016, https://www.cnn.com/2016/04/18/us/80s-times-square-then-and-now/index.html; Joyce Purnick, "Builders Are Urged to Forge One Plan for Times Square," *New York Times*, June 5, 1981.

64   Michael Kramer, "Carey in Love," *New York*, April 13, 1981, 21–23; Elisabeth Bumiller, "The Big Apple Kiss," *Washington Post*, April 13, 1981; Deirdre Carmody, "Marriage Is Wife's Fourth, Carey's Office Confirms," *New York Times*, April 15, 1981.

65   Richard Ravitch, "Text of Letter by Ravitch to Carey, Koch and Legislative Leaders," *New York Times*, May 14, 1981; Judith Cummings, "Ravitch Says Fare Will Go Up to 75 Cents," *New York Times*, July 1, 1981; Richard Levine, Don Wycliff, and Carlyle C. Douglas, "The Region in Summary: Ravitch and Friends Break Transit Logjam," *New York Times*, July 5, 1981; Judith Cummings, "City's Fare Rises to 75 Cents and Rails Increase by 25%," *New York Times*, July 3, 1981.

66   Lardner, "Painting the Elephant," 50–57; Richard J. Meislin, "A Toll on Politicians," *New York Times*, July 10, 1981; Ravitch, *So Much to Do*, 139.

67   MTA, *1981 Annual Report*, 1982, 5.

68   Rickles and Holzer, "Light at the End," 22; Richard Ravitch, keynote remarks, "New York's Infrastructure" (Speaker Seminars on the 1980s, Legislative Office Building, Albany, NY, September 16–17, 1981); Raymond Hernandez, "Stanley Fink, Assembly Speaker, 61, Is Dead," *New York Times*, March 6, 1997; Richard J. Meislin, "Higher Taxes to Finance M.T.A. Suggested by Senator in Albany," *New York Times*, May 22, 1981; Ravitch, *So Much to Do*, 62, 139–40.

69   Meislin, "Toll on Politicians"; Robin Herman, "Five Taxes Voted in Albany to Give Mass-Transit Aid," *New York Times*, July 10, 1981; Robin Herman, "Assembly Passes $5.6 Billion Plan for M.T.A. Aid," *New York Times*, June 23, 1981.

70   Ravitch, *So Much to Do*, 154.

71   Polan, interview with the author.

72   Lardner, "Painting the Elephant," 59; Herman, "Ravitch Assails Proposal."

73 Polan, telephone interview with the author; Lardner, "Painting the Elephant," 60; Ravitch, *So Much to Do*, 146.

74 Ari L. Goldman, "Plan to Improve Transit Receives Final Approval," *New York Times*, December 23, 1981; PCAC, *MTA's Capital Program*, 5–6.

75 Sandler, telephone interview with the author; Lardner, "Painting the Elephant," 41.

76 Ravitch, *So Much to Do*, 156–57; Ravitch, interview with the author; Polan, telephone interview with the author.

77 New York State Department of Transportation in cooperation with the MTA and the City of New York, *Management Study of the Metropolitan Transportation Authority: Planning Document*, April 1976, 10; Ravitch, interview with the author.

78 Ravitch, *So Much to Do*, 158; Ravitch, interview with the author.

79 Ravitch, *So Much to Do*, 158.

80 Seaman, de Cerreño, and English-Young, "From Rescue to Renaissance," 7; Ravitch, interview with the author; Machalaba, "Train Master."

81 NYCTA, *Strategic Plan*, 12–13; Mysore Nagaraja, interview with the author, Paramus, NJ, October 2, 2017.

82 NYCTA, *Strategic Plan*, 12–20; Machalaba, "Train Master."

83 M. A. Farber, "Greater Woes Lie Ahead for City's Transit Riders," *New York Times*, July 30, 1984; Machalaba, "Train Master."

84 Machalaba, "Train Master"; Thomas Prendergast, "A Celebration of the Life of Robert R. Kiley, September 16, 1935–August 9, 2016," University Club, New York, September 30, 2016; Farber, "Greater Woes Lie Ahead."

85 Office of Inspector General, press release, February 10, 1985; Maurice Carroll, "A New Inspector General Set for M.T.A. by the Governor," *New York Times*, December 15, 1984; Suzanne Daley, "Transit System Fighting Flaws in 5-Year Plan," *New York Times*, May 28, 1985; Mysore Nagaraja, interview with the author, Paramus, NJ, October 9, 2017.

86 NYCTA, *Strategic Plan*, 15–16; Machalaba, "Train Master"; Daniel Machalaba, "On Track: Transit Manager Shows New York Subway Isn't Beyond Redemption," *Wall Street Journal*, October 14, 1988.

87 Fox Butterfield, "On New York Walls, the Fading of Graffiti," *New York Times*, May 6, 1988; Ari L. Goldman, "Dogs to Patrol Subway Yards," *New York Times*, September 15, 1981; Jonathan Soffer, *Ed Koch and the Rebuilding of New York City* (New York: Columbia University Press, 2010), 96.

88 "Koch: When He Talks Transit, He Talks Tough," *Mass Transit*, January 1978, 11; Clyde Haberman, "City Hall Notes: Koch's Name Is Doin' Fine on Releases," *New York Times*, May 9, 1982; Randy Kennedy, "Tunnel Vision: Here You Can't Tell the Future from a Hole in the Ground," *New York Times*, October 21, 2003; Ari L. Goldman, "For Rnt by M.T.A.: 2 Tunls, Need Wrk, No Vu," *New York Times*, August 2, 1982; Richard Haitch, "Follow-Up on the News: 'Subway' for Rent," *New York Times*, September 26, 1982; "Paul D. Catalano; Executive, 60," *New York Times*, January 31, 1991; Ronay Menschel, telephone interview with the author, January 9, 2017.

89   Patricia Hurtado, "Subway Link to N.J. Urged by Planners," *Newsday*, March 21, 1986.

90   Clifford D. May, "Federal Funds Hard to Spend, New York's Lawmakers Find," *New York Times*, March 17, 1989.

91   May, "Federal Funds Hard to Spend."

92   Michael Oreskes, "Key Question on Bond Issue," *New York Times*, November 1, 1983; Frank Lynn, "New York's Voters Give Approval to $1.25 Billion State Bond Issue," *New York Times*, November 9, 1983; "N.Y.C., 2000," *New York*, December 22–29, 1986, 56.

93   MTA, *Report to the Governor: 1991*, 1992, 14–27; Machalaba, "On Track."

94   Donatella Lorch, "The 'Subway to Nowhere' Now Goes Somewhere," *New York Times*, October 29, 1989.

95   MTA, *Report to the Governor: 1989*, 1990, 3–4, 17; Independent Budget Office of the City of New York, *New York City Transit's Fiscal Condition*, August 18, 1999, https://ibo.nyc.ny.us/iboreports/transitbrief.html; PCAC, *The Road Back: A Historic Review of the MTA Capital Program*, May 2012, 4.

96   MTA, *1981 Annual Report*, 15, 28, 99 (the debt level included MTA, TBTA, and NYCTA outstanding debt; it did not include $200 million in debt that the TBTA issued on behalf of the state to build a convention center, which the state was repaying); MTA, *Report to the Governor: 1991*, 1992, 121–34; MTA, *1992 Annual Report*, 1993, 151–57.

97   MTA, *MTA Capital Needs & Opportunities, 1992–2011*, May 25, 1990, 5.

6. Planning from the Bottom Up

1   Jon Melnick, telephone interview with the author, May 5, 2017; Rapid Transit Service Design, "Brilliant Capital Ideas for the Future," September 27, 1988, notes from meeting, office of NYC Transit's Division of Operations Planning, New York (hereafter NYCT Office).

2   Howard Benn (assistant vice president, Operations Planning, New York City Transit Authority) to Operations Planning Section Directors, September 22, 1988, NYCT Office.

3   John G. Gaul, memo to CK (Chuck Kirchner), "Subject: Capital Program," October 7, 1988, NYCT Office.

4   NYC Transit Authority (hereafter NYCTA), Operations Planning Department, Service Planning, "Twenty (20) Year Capital Needs Analysis: Problem; Six (6) Over Capacity Lines," internal document, January 10, 1989, NYCT Office.

5   NYCTA, "Twenty (20) Year Capital Needs Analysis."

6   Rapid Transit Service Design, "Brilliant Capital Ideas."

7   Kirk Johnson, "Officials Debate How to Get Homeless Out of the Subways," *New York Times*, September 5, 1988; Melnick, telephone interview with the author.

8   Metropolitan Transportation Authority (hereafter MTA), *MTA Capital Needs & Opportunities, 1992–2011*, May 25, 1990, 18–19.

9   MTA, *MTA Capital Needs*, 5.

10   MTA, *MTA Capital Needs*, 11–13.

11   Richard Levine, "As Gridlock Mounts, Region Buys More Cars," *New York Times*, April 10, 1990; MTA, *MTA Capital Needs*, 8–10.

12   Sam Roberts, "The Eternal Aim to Make Cities More Livable," Metro Matters, *New York Times*, April 2, 1990; Alan Finder, "Tunnel Waiting Two Decades for a Train: Shafts for the Second Avenue Subway Are Maintained, in Case the Line Is Ever Built," *New York Times*, April 19, 1994.

13   Jon Melnick, memo to files, August 23, 1991; Kevin Desmond (chief of operations planning), memo to Jack Lusk (senior vice president), "Re: Capital Program Planning Studies," August 18, 1992; Edward Sernier, memo to Andrew Bata, James Chin, and Norm Silverman, February 17, 1989; *Capital Project Summary (for Second Avenue Subway Study)*, Planning No. EN12-4410, ca. 1990; *Capital Project Summary (for Second Avenue Design)*, Planning No. EN12-4411, ca. 1990. All of these documents were found in NYCT Office).

14   Emily Sachar, "The Giuliani Budget: No Free Ride for Rudy," *Newsday*, February 6, 1994; Alan Finder, "Tunnel Waiting Two Decades for a Train," *New York Times*, April 19, 1994; Permanent Citizens Advisory Committee to the MTA, *The Road Back: A Historic Review of the MTA Capital Program*, May 2012, 15.

15   Alan Altshuler and David Luberoff, *Mega-Projects: The Changing Politics of Urban Public Investment* (Washington, DC: Brookings Institution, 2003), 27–42.

16   Don H. Pickrell, *Urban Rail Transit Projects: Forecast versus Actual Ridership and Costs*, 1989, vi–vii; American Public Transit Association, *ISTEA and TRANSIT: A Topical Guide to Funding Provisions of the Intermodal Surface Transportation Efficiency Act and Related Laws, including FY 1998 Appropriation Act and FY 1998 Six-Month ISTEA Extension Act*, February 9, 1998, 5; Daniel Duff, Edward J. Gill Jr., and G. Kent Woodman, "Legal Handbook for the New Starts Process," *TCRP Legal Research Digest* 30 (February 2010), 9–12.

17   Bernard Cohen, memo to Daniel Scannell, "Re: Long Range Planning," June 18, 1993, author's possession.

18   The request for proposals was issued in 1994 and the contract was awarded in the beginning of 1995, per Tom Harknett (project manager for consultants), telephone interview with the author, April 26, 2017; Todd DiScala, telephone interview with the author, April 19, 2017.

19   Federal Transit Administration, "Supplemental Draft Environmental Impact Statement on the Manhattan East Site Alternatives Project—Second Avenue Subway," *Federal Register*, March 22, 2001, 16093–94.

20   Peter Cafiero, interview with Peter Derrick and Patrizia Nobbe, New York, October 28, 2014, audio recording in author's possession.

21   Vollmer Associates, SYSTRA Consulting, and Allee King Rosen & Fleming, prepared for MTA New York City Transit, *Manhattan East Side Transit Alternatives (MESA)/Second Avenue Subway Summary Report* (hereafter *MESA Summary Report*), October 2001, 4; Federal Transit Administration and MTA/NYC Transit, *Manhattan East Side Alternatives Study: Draft Environmental Impact Statement* (hereafter *MESA Draft EIS*), August 1999, chap. 9B, p. 1; chap. 4, p. 2.

22   DiScala, telephone interview with the author, April 19, 2017.

23   Harknett, telephone interview with the author; *MESA Draft EIS*, chap. 1, p. 6; chap. 9D.

24   *MESA Draft EIS*, chap. 9D.

25   *MESA Summary Report*, 4.

26   Todd DiScala, telephone interview with the author, May 11, 2017; Federal Transit Administration and MTA NYC Transit, *Manhattan East Side Transit Alternatives Study: Major Investment Study/Draft Environmental Impact Statement Scoping Document* (hereafter *MIS/DEIS Scoping Document*), June 1995, 1–4. Note that the word *Transit* was subsequently eliminated from the title of this study, so the title of the environmental impact statement refers to the *Manhattan East Side Alternatives Study*.

27   *MIS/DEIS Scoping Document*, 11–17; *MESA Summary Report*, 10; DiScala, telephone interview with the author, May 11, 2017.

28   Todd DiScala, telephone interview with the author, April 22, 2017; Peter Cafiero, interview with the author, New York, December 24, 2015; Cafiero, interview with Derrick and Nobbe.

29   Richard Pérez-Peña, "M.T.A. Expected to Retreat Only a Little on Service Cuts," *New York Times*, August 10, 1995; Cafiero, interview with Derrick and Nobbe.

30   Clifford Krauss, "1996 Data Show Crime Rates Are Still Falling in New York," *New York Times*, July 3, 1996.

31   Dennis Hevesi, "Market-Rate Rents in Manhattan," *New York Times*, July 14, 1996.

32   DiScala, telephone interview with the author, May 11, 2017; *MIS/DEIS Scoping Document*, 10–13, 17.

33   *MESA Draft EIS*, chap. 20, p. 4.

34   *MESA Draft EIS*, chap. 16, p. 2.

35   Boris Pushkarev, interview with the author, Cliffside Park, NJ, February 8, 2016; Cafiero, interview with Derrick and Nobbe.

36   Peter Cafiero, memo to William Wheeler, Lawrence Fleischer, and Jack Dean, "Subject: Long Range Planning Framework Meetings," April 16, 1988, author's possession.

37   George E. Pataki, *Pataki: An Autobiography*, with Daniel Paisner (New York: Viking, 1998), 187.

38   Bob Yaro, telephone interview with the author, May 17, 2017; Maryanne Gridley (senior aide to Pataki) used the word "twist" in a telephone interview with the author, August 5, 2011; Bob Liff, "Pataki Lets Fly on Transit Plan for Airports, Subways, LIRR," *Daily News*, May 3, 1996.

39   Gridley, telephone interview with the author; "Vote Cast for Governor and Lieutenant Governor by Party of Candidates: New York State by County—November 8, 1994," New York State Board of Elections, accessed July 14, 2018, https://www.elections.ny.gov/NYSBOE/elections/1994/gov94.pdf.

40 Liff, "Pataki Lets Fly"; George Pataki, interview with the author, New York, December 14, 2011.

41 George Pataki, "Master Links: A Regional Transportation Vision for the 21st Century," ca. 1996, 1–12, author's possession; MTA planner, interview with the author, April 26, 2017.

42 Pataki, interview with the author; Pataki, "Master Links," 14; Ian Fisher, "Man in the News: For the M.T.A., a Pataki Loyalist; E. Virgil Conway," *New York Times*, April 22, 1995.

43 MTA, *Capital Program: 1995–1999*, approved by the Capital Program Review Board in March 1999, 1–2; Richard Pérez-Peña, "Plan Edges L.I.R.R. Closer to a Grand Central Link," *New York Times*, April 25, 1996; "Whose Mega-Project?—Planners Say LIRR-Grand Central Project Folly without Better East Side Transit," *Mobilizing the Region*, May 2, 1997; Transportation Equity Act for the 21st Century, Pub. L. No. 105-178 (1998), Sec. 3030(c), https://www.fhwa.dot.gov/tea21/tea21.pdf.

44 DiScala, telephone interview with the author, April 19, 2017; Henry Alford, "Step Aside? Who, Me?," *New York Times*, November 18, 1996.

45 DiScala, telephone interview with the author, April 19, 2017; Norm Silverman, letter to Jeff Zupan, March 31, 1997, author's possession.

46 Jack Dean, interview with the author, Newark, NJ, June 27, 2017.

47 Cafiero, interview with Derrick and Nobbe; Todd DiScala, telephone interview with the author, May 4, 2017; Silverman to Zupan, March 31, 1997.

48 Lincoln Anderson, "Second Ave. Subway Talks Renewed," *Our Town*, March 27, 1997.

49 *MESA Draft EIS*.

50 Silverman to Zupan, March 31, 1997; Silverman, letter to Zupan, May 28, 1997.

51 Philip Mark Plotch, *Politics across the Hudson: The Tappan Zee Megaproject* (New Brunswick, NJ: Rutgers University Press, 2015), 63–67; Pataki, "Master Links," 8; STV Incorporated (prepared for MTA/LIRR), *Major Investment Study for the Long Island Transportation Corridor: LIRR East Side Access Project*, March 1998, 7-7; MTA official, interview with the author, 2012.

52 DiScala, telephone interview with the author, April 19, 2017.

53 David R. Francis, "What Reduced Crime in New York City," National Bureau of Economic Research, accessed May 8, 2017, http://www.nber.org/digest/jan03/w9061.html.

54 Virgil Conway, interview with the author, New York, April 5, 2011; ridership numbers obtained from Robert Hickey (NYC Transit's Operations Planning Department), June 27, 2017.

55 Bruce Schaller, "Mode Shift in the 1990s: How Subway and Bus Ridership Outpaced the Auto in Market Share Gains in New York City," Schaller Consulting, August 8, 2001, 7–12, http://www.schallerconsult.com/pub/modeshft.pdf; Thomas J. Lueck, "New York's Bus Ridership Surges after Long Decline," *New York Times*, December 22, 1998; New York City Independent Budget Office, *New York City Transit's Fiscal Condition*, August 18, 1999, https://ibo.nyc.ny.us/iboreports/transitbrief.html.

56   Garry Pierre-Pierre, "Subway and Bus Rides Up by a Million a Day," *New York Times*, February 20, 1999; Fred Kaplan, "Subway Riders Losing Their Angst," *Boston Globe*, March 14, 1999.

57   DiScala, telephone interview with the author, April 19, 2017; New York City Transit official, interview with the author, 2016; Pataki, interview with the author.

58   "MTA Pours Cold Water on Subway Plan," *Mobilizing the Region*, February 5, 1999; New York City Transit official, interview with the author.

59   "MTA Chairman Returns to Work," *Crain's New York Business*, May 18, 1998.

60   "NYC Debates Gridlock and Subway Plans," *Mobilizing the Region*, August 20, 1999; Harknett, telephone interview with the author.

61   Lee Sander, interview with the author, New York, May 18, 2017. Sander was executive director of the Center for Transportation Policy and Management (later known as the Rudin Center for Transportation Policy and Management) at NYU, and an executive at Frederic R. Harris.

62   Yaro, telephone interview with the author; Sander, interview with the author; Gene Russianoff, telephone interview with the author, May 17, 2017.

63   Regional Plan Association (hereafter RPA), "Campaign Plan—2nd Avenue Subway (Confidential Discussion Document)," ca. February 1998, 1–2, office of the RPA, New York.

64   Steven Weber, telephone interview with the author, November 30, 2015; Albert Appleton, interview with the author, February 10, 2016.

65   Weber, telephone interview with the author.

66   Russianoff, telephone interview with the author; James Rutenberg, "Riders Stuffed like Sardines and Some Transit Experts Fear Crowding Will Get Even Worse," *Daily News*, May 13, 1998.

67   Russianoff, telephone interview with the author.

68   Russianoff, telephone interview with the author.

69   Yaro, telephone interview with the author; Lee Sander, interview with Patrizia Nobbe, August 12, 2012, audio recording in author's possession; Tina Kelley, "Officials Urge M.T.A. to Build Full Second Ave. Subway Line," *New York Times*, September 9, 2017; Thomas J. Lueck, "M.T.A. to Propose Spending Billions on Rail Expansion," *New York Times*, September 26, 1999.

70   Jeff Zupan, interview with the author, New York, January 19, 2016.

71   Weber, telephone interview with the author; Lou Sepersky (Community Board 6), telephone interview with the author, April 21, 2017. Numerous consultants, government officials, and transportation advocates discussed working with Olmsted in interviews with the author between 2016 and 2018.

72   Weber, telephone interview with the author; Zupan, interview with the author; Jeff Zupan, telephone interview with the author, May 12, 2017; RPA, *MetroLink: New Transit for New York*, January 1999; Jeffrey M. Zupan, "Robert A. Olmsted: An Appreciation," Regional Plan Association, September 7, 2010, http://www.rpa.

org/spotlight/robert-olmsted-appreciation; Jeff Zupan, telephone interview with the author, May 11, 2017.

73   Silverman to Zupan, May 28, 1997; Silverman to Zupan, March 31, 1997; Zupan, letter to Silverman, April 21, 1997; Zupan, memo to H. Claude Shostal, Bob Yaro, Al Appleton, and Steven Weber, February 15, 1999; all in author's possession.

74   RPA, *MetroLink*, 2.

75   Brian Mackle, "2001: A Subway Odyssey," *Our Town*, February 11, 1999; Sander, interview with the author.

76   Thomas J. Lueck, "Officials Cite Costly Hurdles to Second Avenue Subway Plan," *New York Times*, March 12, 1999; Appleton, interview with the author; Lou Sepersky's comment about watching grass grow per Keith Meatto, "Slow Train Coming," *Our Town*, December 16, 1998; Mackle, "2001: A Subway Odyssey."

77   Mackle, "2001: A Subway Odyssey"; Weber, telephone interview with the author; Russianoff, telephone interview with the author.

78   "The Cops Are Your Enemy," editorial, *New York Daily News*, December 2, 1997; Weber, telephone interview with the author; Lee Sander, email to the author, April 25, 2017.

79   Lueck, "Officials Cite Costly Hurdles"; James Rutenberg, "13B Rail Plan Offers New Second Ave. Line," *New York Daily News*, January 27, 1999; Weber, telephone interview with the author. All MTA board members are nominated by the governor, with six (including the chair) recommended by the governor, four by the mayor, and three by the county executives from Long Island and Westchester County. Four other members cast one collective vote. All members must be confirmed by the state senate.

80   RPA, *MetroLink*, 24; Neil MacFarquhar, "Straphangers Assail Plan to Ease East Side Crush," *New York Times*, August 17, 1999; "Transit Gridlock? Yes, NYC Needs a Full-Length 2nd Avenue Subway, but It Also Needs a Timely State Budget," *Newsday*, March 16, 2000; "An Investment Strategy for the Subways," editorial, *New York Times*, February 16, 1999.

81   Bill Varner, "2nd Ave. Subway Plan Gets Boost at Senate Hearing," *Journal News* (White Plains, NY), March 12, 1999; Goodman, letter to Gene Russianoff, February 18, 1999, folder 2 (Second Avenue Subway, 1994–2002), box 35, NYPIRG Straphangers Campaign Records: 1962–2007 (Bulk 1979–2006), Manuscripts and Archives Division, New York Public Library; "Opening Statement by Senator Roy M. Goodman, Chairman, State Senate Investigations Committee, at Hearing to Examine the Feasibility and Importance of Constructing a 2nd Avenue Subway Line," press release, March 11, 1999, folder 2, box 35, Straphangers Campaign Records.

82   "Testimony of Various Community Leaders at State Senate Committee Investigation Hearings regarding the Second Avenue Subway," March 11, 1999, office of Carolyn Maloney, New York; Lueck, "Officials Cite Costly Hurdles"; James Rutenberg, "Mayor Seeks Millions for 2nd Ave. Subway," *Daily News*, March 12, 1999.

83   "Testimony of Gene Russianoff (Staff Attorney, NYPIRG Straphangers Campaign) at the NYS Senate Hearing on a Second Avenue Subway, NYC, March 11, 1999," folder 2, box 35, Straphangers Campaign Records; Robert Paaswell, "NYS Senate Committee on Investigation: Comments on the Second Avenue Subway," March 11, 1999, folder 2, box 35, Straphangers Campaign Records.

84   "Testimony of Various Community Leaders"; Raymond Hernandez, "Coal Furnaces at 18 Schools to Be Replaced," *New York Times*, April 11, 1997.

85   "Testimony of Various Community Leaders."

86   Sepersky, telephone interview with the author; C. Virginia Fields, interview with the author, New York, November 19, 2015; Mackle, "2001: A Subway Odyssey."

87   The term "stubway" was first used by Maloney and Zupan at Maloney's panel on March 30, 1999, per Zupan, telephone interview with the author and follow-up email to the author, May 12, 2017; "Grand Project," editorial, *Newsday*, September 30, 1999; DiScala, telephone interview with the author, April 19, 2017.

88   DiScala, telephone interview with the author, May 4, 2017; 2000 census data per Federal Transit Administration (hereafter FTA) and MTA NYC Transit, *Second Avenue Subway in the Borough of Manhattan (New York County, New York): Final Environmental Impact Statement and Final Section 4(F) and Section 6(F) Evaluation*, April 2004, chap. 6, p. 4, table 6-1.

89   Fields, interview with the author; Russianoff, telephone interview with the author; "Second Avenue Subway Task Force Education Working Group Meeting Notes," meeting on February 23, 1999, folder 2, box 35, Straphangers Campaign Records; Nina Siegal, "Neighborhood Report: New York Up Close; Supporters Use Sardines to Fish for a New Subway," *New York Times*, June 27, 1999; FTA and MTA, *Second Avenue Subway*, app. O, p. O-5.

90   Carl Campanile, "MTA Is Pushing V. Subway to Side Track," *New York Post*, June 27, 1999; Bob Kulikowski (Office of the Manhattan Borough President), memo to 2nd Avenue Subway Task Force Members, July 28, 1999, office of Carolyn Maloney; Romy Varghese, "No Breathing Room in MTA's Draft Budget," *Our Town*, July 8, 1999.

91   *MESA Draft EIS*, chap. 23, pp. 1, 2; S-15, table S-1.

92   New York City Council, Committee on Transportation, "Resolution No. 946," September 8, 1999, folder 2, box 35, Straphangers Campaign Records; Gene Russianoff, "Testimony of Gene Russianoff (Staff Attorney, NYPIRG Straphangers Campaign) before the NYC Council Committee on Transportation Hearing on a Second Avenue Subway, September 8, 1999," folder 2, box 35, Straphangers Campaign Records; James Rutenberg, "Moguls: Add Subway Lines," *Daily News*, March 11, 1999; Lou Tomson, telephone interview with the author, August 5, 2011.

93   Bob Yaro, telephone interview with the author, May 19, 2017; "Making a Transit Wish List Real," editorial, *New York Times*, August 22, 1999; "The Full Second Avenue Subway," editorial, *New York Times*, September 10, 1999.

94   Cafiero, interview with the author; FTA and MTA, *Second Avenue Subway*, app. O.

95   MTA, *Capital Program 2000–2004*, as submitted to the Capital Program Review Board, October 1999, 101; Lueck, "M.T.A. to Propose Spending Billions."

96   Thomas J. Lueck, "T.A.'s Capital Plan Goes Beyond Second Ave. Subway," *New York Times*, October 3, 1999; Thomas J. Lueck, "Work Is Proposed on 2d Ave. Subway," *New York Times*, September 29, 1999; Carl Campanile and Maggie Haberman, "MTA OKs $700m for Stubway," *New York Post*, September 30, 1999; Ellis Henican, "Chapter 10: Getting There from Here," *Newsday*, October 24, 1999.

97   Lueck, "Work Is Proposed"; "MESA Not a Beaut," *Mobilizing the Region*, September 17, 1999; Jeff Zupan, "State of RPA: MTA Board of Directors, MTA Capital Program, September 29, 1999," folder 11 (63rd Street Tunnel—Second Avenue Subway), box 17, Straphangers Campaign Records.

98   Peter Donohue and Bob Kappstatter, "Straphangers Have a Cow: Protesting Herd Seeks Full 2nd Ave. Line," *New York Daily News*, December 1, 1999; Mark Green and C. Virginia Fields, letter to colleague, November 16, 1999, folder 11, box 17, Straphangers Campaign Records.

99   Carl Campanile, "Poll: Subway Should Go the Distance—If We Don't Pay," *New York Post*, October 22, 1999.

100 Conway, interview with the author.

101 Lueck, "M.T.A. to Propose Spending Billions"; Sander, interview with the author; Raymond Hernandez, "Albany Misses Budget Deadline Again," *New York Times*, April 1, 2000; "NY Senate Demands Transit-Highway Funding Parity," *Mobilizing the Region*, December 30, 1999; "Senate Republicans Block Transit Plan," *New York Times*, December 22, 1999; Richard Pérez-Peña, "New 5-Year Transit Plan Must Serve Many Masters," *New York Times*, September 30, 1999; Carl Campanile, "MTA's Subway Plan Sparks Controversy," *New York Post*, September 26, 1999; Lueck, "Work Is Proposed"; Richard Pérez-Peña, "Assembly Speaker Links Subway to Budget Vote," *New York Times*, March 15, 2000; Thomas J. Lueck, "M.T.A. Chief Won't Rule Out Higher Fare to Pay for Expansion Plan," *New York Times*, November 4, 1999; Sheldon Silver, *NYC Transit Needs: A Report on the MTA's 2000–2004 Capital Program*, February 2000, 7; Carl Campanile, "Silver Won't Accept 2nd Best on E. Side Subway," *New York Post*, September 22, 1999.

102 Robert D. McFadden, "M.T.A. Rejects Ad Criticizing Packed Trains," *New York Times*, March 7, 2000; "Censors in the Subway," editorial, *New York Times*, March 10, 2000; Christopher Dunn, "The Subway as Savage Soapbox," *New York Law Journal*, October 4, 2012, https://www.nyclu.org/en/publications/column-subway-savage-soapbox-new-york-law-journal; Dennis Duggan, "The Subway Sardines Speak Up," *Newsday*, March 17, 2000; "Underground Campaigning," editorial, *New York Post*, March 11, 2000.

103 Richard Pérez-Peña, "Plans Advance for Building a 2nd Avenue Subway the Length of Manhattan," *New York Times*, April 5, 2000; Andy Newman, "New Subway Line in Transit Budget," *New York Times*, April 20, 2000; "M.T.A.'s Capital Plan Wins Final Approval," *New York Times*, May 5, 2000.

7. A Twenty-First-Century Subway

1   "Show Us the Money: MTA's Grand Transit Plan Needs Realistic Financing," editorial, *Newsday*, April 22, 2000; Tom McGinty, "MTA Money Matters: On Borrowed Time, Billions, It Should Be the Best of Times for Public Transit," *Newsday*, June 5, 2005; "The MTA's Road to Ruin," editorial, *New York Post*, April 10, 2000.

2   Richard Pérez-Peña, "M.T.A.'s Plan Spawns Warnings of a Debt Crisis and Higher Fares," *New York Times*, April 3, 2000; Permanent Citizens Advisory Committee to the MTA (hereafter PCAC), *The Road Back: A Historic Review of the MTA Capital Program*, May 2012, 15.

3   Diana Fortuna and Charles Brecher, "Judging the MTA Capital Plan," *New York Post*, April 23, 2000; Pérez-Peña, "M.T.A.'s Plan Spawns Warnings"; Richard Pérez-Peña and Randy Kennedy, "Private Promoter for Transit Debt," *New York Times*, May 1, 2000; Brian M. Rosenthal, Emma G. Fitzsimmons, and Michael Laforgia, "How Politics and Bad Decisions Starved New York's Subways," *New York Times*, November 18, 2017; "MTA's Road to Ruin"; Andy Newman, "New Subway Line in Transit Budget," *New York Times*, April 20, 2000.

4   Richard Ravitch, interview with the author, New York, February 28, 2012.

5   Randy Kennedy, "$3.8 Billion Transportation Bond Act Flying below New York Voters' Radar," *New York Times*, November 6, 2000; Philip Lentz, "$3.8 Billion Bond Act Could Derail," *Crain's New York Business*, July 17, 2000; Eric Lipton, "Supporters of Transportation Bond Act Finally Have the Mayor on Board," *New York Times*, October 12, 2000.

6   Lipton, "Supporters of Transportation Bond Act"; Sidney Schaer, "A Weekly Guide to the Roads & Rails on Long Island," *Newsday*, November 5, 2000; Lentz, "$3.8 Billion Bond Act"; Bob Yaro, telephone interview with the author, May 19, 2017.

7   Mark Nachbar, fax to Senator Caesar Trunzo, November 28, 2000, author's possession; Jay Gallagher, "Easier Ride Plum for New State Debt," *Poughkeepsie Journal*, April 30, 2000; "Bond Defeat a Wise Move," editorial, *Plattsburgh Press Republican*, November 15, 2000; Jordan Rau, "Pataki Supportive of Bond Act," *Newsday*, September 19, 2000; Robert Polner, "Mayor Undecided on Transit Bond," *Newsday*, October 2, 2000; Jordan Rau, "Lukewarm Response for Bond Proposal," *Newsday*, October 18, 2000; Fredric U. Dicker and Tom Topousis, "Gov. Has '2nd' Thoughts on E. Side Line," *New York Post*, April 6, 2000; Matthew Cox, "Pataki Defers on Bond," *Newsday*, April 6, 2000.

8   Kennedy, "$3.8 Billion Transportation Bond Act"; Sewell Chan, "Transportation Bond Proposal Will Be on November Ballot," *New York Times*, July 18, 2005.

9   Matthew Schuerman, "Will M.T.A. Derail?," *New York Observer*, November 7, 2005; "November 7, 2000, General Election: Proposal Number One; A Proposition; Transportation Infrastructure Bond Act of 2000," New York State Board of Elections, accessed April 22, 2017, http://www.elections.ny.gov/NYSBOE/elections/2000/wbprop2000.pdf.

10   Kenneth Lovett, Fredric U. Dicker, and Tom Topousis, "MTA: Key Transit Plans on $haky Track," *New York Post*, January 24, 2001; Tom Topousis and Kenneth Lovett, "Gov $queezing PA as It Goes Tolling for Dollars," *New York Post*, January 16, 2001.

11   Joe Williams and Pete Donohue, "Transit Chief Conway to Leave Post in March," *Daily News*, January 24, 2001; Joe Mahoney, "Gov Picks Kalikow as New MTA Chief," *Daily News*, January 31, 2001; Robin Finnmay, "A Mass Transit Chief Who Runs with the Ferraris," *New York Times*, May 6, 2005; Greg Sargent, "The Line That Time Forgot," *New York*, April 5, 2004.

12   Lee Sander, email to the author, April 25, 2017; Yaro, telephone interview with the author; Finnmay, "Mass Transit Chief."

13   Federal Transit Administration (hereafter FTA), *Annual Report on Funding Recommendations: Fiscal Year 2003*, 2002, introduction, table 1A; Kate Lowe and Sandra

Rosenbloom (Urban Institute), *The Federal New Starts Program: What Do New Regulations Mean for Metropolitan Areas?*, March 2014, 2–3.

14   Alan Treffeisen, New York City Independent Budget Office, *How Much Would the City's Annual Contribution Be Today If Aid for the Metropolitan Transportation Authority's Capital Projects Had Kept Pace with Inflation?*, January 22, 2015.

15   Christopher (Chris) Boylan, draft letter to Letitia Thompson (FTA), July 24, 2001, author's possession; MTA NYC Transit, *Draft Scope of Work: Supplemental Draft/ Final EIS: Manhattan East Side Transit Alternatives Study*, April 5, 2001, 1–2, 15–16.

16   FTA, *Annual Report on Funding Recommendations: Fiscal Year 2001*, 2000.

17   "Second Avenue Subway: Question and Answers," Metropolitan Transportation Authority (hereafter MTA) internal document, October 28, 2002, author's possession; Jack Dean, email to Lawrence Fleischer and William Wheeler, "FTA Tour Thoughts," July 10, 2001, author's possession.

18   Christopher Boylan, telephone interview with the author, July 12, 2017; Sewell Chan, "If Federal Transit Bill Is a Smorgasbord, the City Is in Line," *New York Times*, March 13, 2005; Carolyn Maloney, "Our Two Senators Deliver for New York," press release, July 12, 2001.

19   Christopher Boylan, interview with the author, New York, January 5, 2016; Ronald Smothers, "Leasing of Trade Center May Help Transit Projects, Pataki Says," *New York Times*, July 25, 2001.

20   FTA, "Major Investment Study/Environmental Impact Statement on the Lower Manhattan Access Alternatives Study in New York County, NY," *Federal Register*, June 4, 1998, 30558–59; Jack Dean, interview with the author, Newark, NJ, June 27, 2017.

21   Dean, interview with the author; "Larry and Chris and Jack Comments on Water Street," MTA internal document, ca. 2001, author's possession; FTA and MTA NYC Transit, *Second Avenue Subway in the Borough of Manhattan (New York County, New York): Final Environmental Impact Statement and Final Section 4(F) and Section 6(F) Evaluation*, April 2004, app. B.

22   Peter Cafiero, interview with Peter Derrick and Patrizia Nobbe, New York, October 28, 2014, audio recording in author's possession.

23   National Commission on Terrorist Attacks upon the United States, *The 9/11 Commission Report*, Executive Summary, July 2004, 1; H. Carl McCall (New York State comptroller), *The Impact of the World Trade Center Tragedy on the Metropolitan Transportation Authority*, Report 9-2002, December 2001, 1.

24   Tri-State Transportation Campaign, *Metropolitan Transportation since September 11: A Media Source-Book*, September 3, 2002, 5, http://www.tstc.org/reports/9-11 sourcebook.pdf.

25   Thomas P. DiNapoli (New York State comptroller), *Progress Report: The MTA Capital Security Program*, January 2008, 1; MTA, *2001 Annual Report*, 2002, 13–14; FTA, *Annual Report on Funding Recommendations: Fiscal Year 2005*, 2004, B-32; Dean, interview with the author.

26   Dwight D. Eisenhower, "Remarks at the National Defense Executive Reserve Conference," November 14, 1957, American Presidency Project, https://www.presidency. ucsb.edu/documents/remarks-the-national-defense-executive-reserve-conference.

27   Lou Tomson, telephone interview with the author, August 5, 2011; Peter S. Kalikow, "If You Build It, Riders Will Come," draft letter to the editor, December 9, 2001, author's possession.

28   Dan Mangan, "2nd Ave. Subway Fast-Tracked," *New York Post*, October 7, 2001.

29   Jack Dean, "SAS September 26, 2001 Coordination Meeting Notes," author's possession.

30   William Neuman, "His Job: Make the Train System Expand on Time," *New York Times*, December 29, 2006; Mysore Nagaraja, interview with the author, Paramus, NJ, September 11, 2017.

31   Nagaraja, interview with the author, September 11, 2017.

32   Sheldon Fialkoff, telephone interview with the author, June 26, 2017.

33   Fialkoff, telephone interview with the author; Ed Plotkin, interview with the author, Dobbs Ferry, NY, January 17, 2016; Don Phillips, interview with the author, New York, January 15, 2016.

34   Fialkoff, telephone interview with the author.

35   Fialkoff, telephone interview with the author; MTA, *2001 Annual Report*, 15; Dan Mangan, "Second Ave. Subway Clears $200m Hurdle," *New York Post*, November 16, 2001; Anil Parikh, email to the author, July 5, 2017; Alan J. Wax, "1st Tenant Moves Downtown since 9/11," *Newsday*, March 19, 2002.

36   John Cichowski, "Whose Bright Idea?," *The Record* (Hackensack, NJ), April 13, 2006.

37   Nagaraja, interview with the author, September 11, 2017; Fialkoff, telephone interview with the author.

38   William Langewiesche, "What Lies Beneath," *Vanity Fair*, October 25, 2013.

39   FTA and MTA NYC Transit, *Final EIS*, April 2004, S-12.

40   Christopher K. Bennett (DMJM Harris/AECOM), *Second Avenue Subway—A Status Report*, June 13, 2008, sec. 2, https://www.arema.org/files/library/2008_Conference_Proceedings/Second_Avenue_Subway-A_Status_Report_2008.pdf. The platform at the Wall Street station on the Lexington Avenue line is approximately seven feet wide.

41   Kevin Smith, "Delivering a New York City Mega-Project," *International Railway Journal*, April 18, 2017, https://www.railjournal.com/in_depth/delivering-a-new-york-city-mega-project; Alexandra Lange, "In the Second Avenue Subway, Art and Architecture Are at Odds," *Curbed New York*, February 28, 2017, https://ny.curbed.com/2017/2/28/14749752/second-avenue-subway-nyc-transit-architecture.

42   Mysore Nagaraja, interview with the author, Paramus, NJ, October 9, 2017.

43   Phillips, interview with the author.

44   FTA and MTA NYC Transit, *Final EIS*, 2–13; Bennett, *Second Avenue Subway*, secs. 1 and 2.

45   "The Cost of the Second Avenue Subway," MTA internal document, ca. 2002, author's possession.

46   City of New York, "Zoning Resolution of the City of New York," Article IX: Special Purpose Districts, chap. 5: Special Transit Land Use District, established

November 7, 1974, and most recently amended November 30, 2017; Clemente Lisi, "Hey, Wait a 2nd—Shops in Subway's Path Face Eviction," *New York Post*, May 24, 2004; Cafiero, interview with Derrick and Nobbe.

47 Fialkoff, telephone interview with the author; Peter Cafiero, interview with the author, New York, January 21, 2016.

48 FTA and MTA NYC Transit, *Final EIS*, chap. 2, pp. 15–20; MTA government and community affairs officer, telephone interview with the author, January 26, 2016.

49 Timothy Forker and Donald Tsang (NYC Transit's Department of Subways), email to eleven other NYC Transit employees, May 3, 2002, author's possession.

50 Phillips, interview with the author; Nagaraja, interview with the author, October 9, 2017.

51 New York City Transit, *Second Avenue Subway / Manhattan East Side Transit Alternatives Study: Application to Commence Preliminary Engineering*, October 2001, chap. 1, p. 3; chap. 2, p. 12.

52 "Cost of the Second Avenue Subway"; "Rough Draft of SAS Costs," MTA internal document, March 2002, author's possession; *Oversight Hearing on the Boston Central Artery/Tunnel Project, Hearing before the Committee on Commerce, Science, and Transportation*, US Senate, 106th Cong., 2nd sess. (May 3, 2000) (statement of Senator John McCain).

53 Dean, interview with the author; William (Bill) Woodford, letter to Cafiero, August 19, 2003, author's possession.

54 Jean Banker, email to Sharon Lubitz, "FTA Section 5309 submission—Financial Capacity Analysis," August 19, 2004, author's possession.

55 In the FTA's annual reports on funding recommendations for the fiscal years 2003, 2004, and 2005, the section titled "Project Evaluation and Rating Process" explains the evaluation criteria, and the section "Summary of New Starts Project Ratings" lists all of the proposed projects and funding requests. The median request was approximately $123 million.

56 MTA planners revisited Bob Olmsted's proposal from the 1960s to run service from Queens through the 63rd Street tunnel and down Second Avenue. They found that this would not work, however, because of subway capacity constraints both in Queens and on Second Avenue. Dean, interview with the author; FTA and MTA NYC Transit, *Final EIS*, app. O, response to comment 4, and chap. 2, 2–14.

57 Dean, interview with the author; Bill Woodford, interview with the author, July 8, 2017.

58 Dean, interview with the author; Woodford, interview with the author; US General Accounting Office, Mass Transit: *FTA Needs to Better Define and Assess Impact of Certain Policies on New Starts Program*, June 2004, 15–16; "Second Avenue Subway Plan Shapes Up," *Mobilizing the Region*, April 14, 2002.

59 Phasing information comes from interviews with MTA and FTA officials as well as the following documents in the author's possession: "Phasing Impacts: Changes from SDEIS to FEIS," September 12, 2003; DMJM Harris/Arup (for MTA Capital Construction), "Second Avenue Subway Construction Phasing Plan," ca. 2003; "Overview

of Construction Sequencing Options," prepared for Katie Lapp, ca. September 23, 2003; "DMJM Harris/Arup, Project Implementation Plan," presentation to Technical Advisory Committee, December 8, 2003; "Fact Sheet for Bill," October 2003; Mysore Nagaraja, "Second Avenue Subway Project," presentation to Peter Kalikow, February 18, 2003.

60   Nagaraja, interview with the author, September 11, 2017.

61   Nagaraja, interview with the author, September 11, 2017; Anil Parikh, memo to Second Avenue Subway Project Team (MTA, NYC Transit, and DMJM Harris/ARUP staff), August 22, 2001, office of NYC Transit's Division of Operations Planning, New York; "Fact Sheet," MTA internal document, October 2003, author's possession.

62   Nagaraja, interview with the author, September 11, 2017.

63   Boylan, telephone interview with the author; Mort Downey, telephone interview with the author, July 14, 2017.

64   FTA, *Annual Report on Funding Recommendations: Fiscal Year 2006*, 2005, Project Justification Rating and table 2C.

65   FTA and MTA NYC Transit, *Final EIS*, chap. 9.

66   Raymond Gearity, letter to Douglas Sussman (MTA), "Written Comments on SDEIS," June 6, 2003, author's possession.

67   Fialkoff, telephone interview with the author.

68   FTA and MTA NYC Transit, *Final EIS*, chaps. 2 and 15.

69   "Second Avenue Subway: MTA / NYC Transit / FTA—Coordination Meeting, Highlights of FTA Second Avenue Meeting on July 17th, 2002," MTA internal document, August 12, 2002; Anthony Semancik, "EIS Length Whitepaper v2," ca. 2002, author's possession; Philip Plotch, "August 15, 2002 Meeting to Discuss Cutting Down the 2nd Avenue Subway SDEIS," ca. 2002; Christopher Boylan, letter to Letitia Thompson, October 16, 2002; "Summary of Revisions Made to Second Avenue Subway: October 2002 Preliminary SDEIS," MTA internal document, n.d.; MTA, "EIS Printing Costs for Second Ave. Subway," n.d.; all in author's possession. Note that the author worked in the MTA Planning Department at the time.

70   Pete Donohue, "No Second Thoughts on Subway," *Daily News*, May 13, 2003; Bobby Cuza, "Public Hearings Begin on Second Avenue Subway," NY1, May 12, 2003, https://www.ny1.com/1-all-boroughs-news-content/30127/public-hearings-begin-on-second-avenue-subway (article no longer viewable on NY1 website); Matthew Sweeney, "Support for Second Avenue Subway," *New York Sun*, May 13, 2003.

71   "M.T.A. Presents Early Plans for Second Ave. Subway," *Downtown Express*, May 20–26, 2003.

72   Bennett, *Second Avenue Subway*, sec. 2.

73   Clemente Lisi, "E. Siders Rail against Subway Plan," *New York Post*, September 23, 2003; Pete Donohue, "2nd Thoughts on 2nd Ave. Line," *Daily News*, September 23, 2003.

74   Philip Plotch, email to Larry Fleischer, September 23, 2003, author's possession; Barry Schneider, interview with the author, New York, June 15, 2017; "Community

Boards: Second Ave. Subway Land Seizures Have U.E.S. Residents Up in Arms," *New York Observer*, August 4, 2003; Donohue, "2nd Thoughts"; David Novarro, "Lawsuit Filed over 2nd Ave Subway Entrance," WABC-TV Channel 7 *Eyewitness News*, February 16, 2011; Yorkshire Towers Company v. US Department of Transportation, US District Court (Southern District of New York), December 1, 2011, https://environment.transportation.org/clue/view_file.aspx?fileID=1100,1.

75   Plotch to Fleischer; Cafiero, interview with Derrick and Nobbe; Alissa Kosowsky (assistant director, government and community relations, NYC Transit), letter to Elizabeth McKee (district manager, Community Board 8), May 5, 2004, author's possession.

76   Kosowsky to McKee; Cafiero, interview with Derrick and Nobbe.

77   Michael Luo, "M.T.A. Expected to Ask for Proposals to Build First Stage of 2nd Ave. Subway," *New York Times*, April 27, 2004; Ray Sanchez, "In the Subways: Waiting for a Train That Never Comes," *Newsday*, April 29, 2004; Caren Halbfinger, "Clear the Track," *Journal News* (White Plains, NY), April 27, 2004.

78   Lee Sander, interview with the author, New York, May 18, 2017; Joyce Purnick, "A Subway Line Is Suddenly a Bandwagon," Metro Matters, *New York Times*, April 29, 2004; DMJM Harris/Arup executive, telephone interview with the author, July 11, 2017; "Chronology: SAS Cost and Schedule Growth," MTA Capital Construction internal document, May 2011, author's possession.

79   Sandy Hornick, telephone interview with the author, July 10, 2017; "Mayor Says Funding #7 Extension Will Compete with Other Projects," *Mobilizing the Region*, June 16, 2003.

80   Charles Bagli, "East Side, West Side: 7 Line's Fate Pits City against State," *New York Times*, March 19, 2004.

81   MTA, *Fulton Street Transit Center—Fact Sheet*, May 2004.

82   Philip Lentz, "Business Groups Split on WTC Plan," *Crain's New York Business*, July 15, 2002; State of New York Executive Chambers, "Governor Pataki Announces Results of Joint Study on Lower Manhattan to Long Island and JFK Rail Link," press release, May 5, 2004.

83   Philip Mark Plotch, *Politics across the Hudson: The Tappan Zee Megaproject* (New Brunswick, NJ: Rutgers University Press, 2015), 73–74.

84   New York State Department of Transportation, *2009 New York State Rail Plan: Strategies for a New Age*, 2009, 43, 53–54; Jerry Nadler, "Top NY POLS Back Rail Freight Tunnel," press release, April 13, 2003.

85   Charles V. Bagli and Randy Kennedy, "Old or New? Debate Rages over Transit Downtown," *New York Times*, October 12, 2002; John Toscano, "N Train Extension to LaG Scrapped," *Queens Gazette*, July 16, 2003.

86   Partnership for New York City, *Transportation Choices and the Future of the New York City Economy*, 2003/2004, 1; Charles Schumer, "Building Transportation for the Next Century: We Can Do It All," *Gotham Gazette*, April 26, 2004.

87   "Puffy: A Naked Wedding Guest," *New York Post*, December 5, 2001; Michael Cooper, "Pataki Proposes Allowing Private Companies to Lease Roads and Bridges," *New York Times*, January 26, 2005.

88 Michael Luo, "On Transit Map, All Roads Lead to Politics," *New York Times*, January 25, 2004; Bagli and Kennedy, "Old or New?"

89 Kathryn Wylde, telephone interview with the author, July 17, 2017; Partnership for New York City, *Transportation Choices*, 1–2.

90 Partnership for New York City, *Transportation Choices*, 1–2; Wylde, telephone interview with the author; Stephen Jacob Smith, "Dan Doctoroff and John Zuccotti Don't Think the East Side Needs Another Subway," *New York Observer*, July 31, 2013.

91 Pete Bowles, "Report Sees 2nd Ave. Subway as Economic Boon," *Newsday*, December 20, 2003; Sheldon Silver, "For a Full 2nd Avenue Subway," letter to the editor, *New York Post*, December 13, 2003.

92 Sander, interview with the author; Yaro, telephone interview with the author; Joseph Berechman, telephone interview with the author, June 29, 2017; Wylde, telephone interview with the author.

93 Craig Horowitz, "Underground Man," *New York*, April 5, 2004.

94 Richard Pérez-Peña, "In Transit Crisis, a Cash Bind Many Foresaw," *New York Times*, October 25, 2004.

95 Joshua Robin and Joie Tyrrell, "Transit Troubles, MTA's Time to Pay," *Newsday*, August 22, 2004; McGinty, "MTA Money Matters"; PCAC, *Road Back*, 17; Citizens Budget Commission, *How to Balance the MTA's Budget: A Report of the Citizens Budget Commission*, June 27, 2006, 21, table 7; MTA, *2004 Annual Report: Comprehensive Annual Financial Report for the Year Ended December 31, 2004*, 2005, 20, 27.

96 Michael Luo, "M.T.A.'s Budget: Nonstop Need for More," *New York Times*, October 3, 2004; Preston Niblack, "Tunnel Vision," *New York Times*, December 19, 2004; Robin and Tyrrell, "Transit Troubles"; McGinty, "MTA Money Matters."

97 State of New York Comptroller, *Review of the Proposed Financial Plan and Capital Program for the Metropolitan Transportation Authority*, Report 7-2005, October 2004, 4; Michael Luo, "M.T.A. Offers Capital Plan," *New York Times*, September 30, 2004; Caren Halbfinger, "MTA Wants to Spend $27.3B on Capital Projects in 5 Years," *Journal News*, July 30, 2004.

98 Chuck Ryker (NYC Transit), "Manhattan East Side Transit Study: Water Street Alignment," ca. 2001, author's possession; Philip Plotch, "Second Avenue Subway Info for Bill," July 1, 2003, author's possession.

99 State of New York Comptroller, *Review of the Proposed Financial Plan*, 4, 36–37; Sewell Chan, "M.T.A. Expansion Plans in Jeopardy, Chief Says," *New York Times*, December 22, 2004; Joshua Robin, "MTA Chairman's Plea: Hey Boss, Send Money," *Newsday*, December 22, 2004; Pérez-Peña, "In Transit Crisis."

100 Joshua Robin, "Pataki Allots Less Than MTA Sought," *Newsday*, January 19, 2005; Robin, "MTA Chairman's Plea."

101 Robin, "MTA Chairman's Plea"; Marcus Baram, "Kalikow Says He Won't Budge on MetroCard," *New York Observer*, December 6, 2004; Chan, "M.T.A. Expansion Plans in Jeopardy"; Sewell Chan, "Transit Chief Shows Signs of Political Independence," *New York Times*, February 26, 2005.

102 Luo, "On Transit Map"; Sargent, "Line That Time Forgot"; Matthew Schuerman, "Second Avenue Subway Convert Protects First Leg of Biggest Dig," *New York Observer*, April 16, 2007; Finnmay, "Mass Transit Chief."

103 Robin, "MTA Chairman's Plea"; Baram, "Kalikow Says He Won't Budge."

104 Sewell Chan, "State Review Board Rejects M.T.A.'s 5-Year Spending Plan," *New York Times*, December 23, 2004.

105 Sander, interview with the author; Sander, email to the author; Greg Clary, "Coalition Revs Up Fight for Transit Funds," *Journal News*, February 9, 2005.

106 Downey, telephone interview with the author; Larry Penner (former FTA planner), telephone interview with the author, July 12, 2017.

107 Joshua Robin, "MTA Money Matters: MTA Urged to Pick Long-Term Gain," *Newsday*, June 6, 2005; State of New York, "Governor and Legislature Announce Local Projects Supported by State's Five-Year State Transportation Plan," press release, July 17, 2015.

108 Sewell Chan, "Bond Act Needed, M.T.A. Chairman Says," *New York Times*, June 10, 2005; Al Baker, "Accord Reached on Transportation Spending Plan," *New York Times*, July 14, 2005; Sander, interview with the author; "Construction of Part of Second Avenue Subway Route 132A Tunnels—92nd to 63rd Streets, Borough of Manhattan," Contract No. C-26002, advertisement, *NYS Contract Reporter*, December 20, 2006; D. Caiden, J. Sankar, A. Parikh, and R. Redmond, "Rock Tunnels for the Second Avenue Subway," in *North American Tunneling 2006*, ed. Levent Ozdemir (London: Taylor and Francis, 2006), 13–20.

109 Stephen Morgan, telephone interview with the author, June 27, 2017.

110 New York State Laborers, "Transportation Bond Act Passes," *Tri-Fund*, Spring 2006, 10–11; Morgan, telephone interview with the author.

111 Sewell Chan, "Lack of Interest by Voters Is Concern on Bond Measure," *New York Times*, November 8, 2005; Nick Reisman, "Pataki, Construction Groups Support Transportation Bond," *Star-Gazette* (Elmira, NY), September 18, 2005; Sewell Chan, "Transportation Bond Proposal Will Be on November Ballot," *New York Times*, July 18, 2005; Schuerman, "Will M.T.A. Derail?"; Sewell Chan, "Stakes High for M.T.A. and City in Vote on $2.9 Billion Bond Act," *New York Times*, October 25, 2005; Sewell Chan, "Voters Approve Transit Bonds for $2.9 Billion," *New York Times*, November 9, 2005.

112 Cathy Woodruff, "State Makes Drive for Transportation Funds," *Times Union* (Albany, NY), October 20, 2005; Reisman, "Pataki, Construction Groups"; George Pataki, Sheldon Silver, and Joseph Bruno, "2005 Transportation Memorandum of Understanding," July 13, 2017.

113 New York State Laborers, "Transportation Bond Act Passes," 10–11; Chan, "Lack of Interest by Voters"; Morgan, telephone interview with the author.

114 Chan, "Voters Approve Transit Bonds"; Chan, "Stakes High for M.T.A."; Rich Calder, "MTA Makes Raily Big Push for $2.9b Bond," *New York Post*, September 14, 2005; Joshua Robin, "MTA to Push Its Riders to Vote," *Newsday*, September 14, 2005.

115 Tom Madison, email to the author, July 9, 2017.

116 Madison, email to the author.

117 Chan, "Voters Approve Transit Bonds"; Bill Sanderson, "2nd Ave. Back on Track," *New York Post*, November 10, 2005.

118 Mysore Nagaraja, letter to Nancy Shevell Blakeman (chair of the MTA board's Capital Construction, Planning, and Real Estate Committee), November 2005, author's possession; Sewell Chan, "Transit Agency Authorizes Funds for 2nd Avenue Line," *New York Times*, November 16, 2005; J. Jioni Palmer, "Second Ave. Line in Final Design Stage," *Newsday*, April 18, 2006.

119 Bagli, "East Side, West Side."

8. Building a Subway and Unleashing the Plagues

1 Carolyn Maloney, interview with the author, New York, July 20, 2015; Chris Boylan, interview with the author, New York, January 5, 2016.

2 Boylan, interview with the author.

3 Maloney, interview with the author.

4 Mort Downey, telephone interview with the author, July 14, 2017; William Neuman, "U.S. Approves $1.3 Billion for 2nd Avenue Subway," *New York Times*, November 19, 2007; Jeremy Olshan, "MTA to $uffer If Train 'Stalls'—Could Lose Feds' 'Second' Helping," *New York Post*, November 20, 2007.

5 Audrey Dutton, "Spitzer Meets with Democrats in D.C.," *Newsday*, December 7, 2006.

6 Pete Donohue, "Second Ave. Subway Plan Picks Up Speed," *Daily News*, October 24, 2006; Chuck Bennett, "MTA Chief Hopeful Named to Panel," *Newsday*, November 17, 2006; Jeremy Olshan, "MTA's Kalikow to Depart Next Spring," *New York Post*, December 1, 2006; Matthew Schuerman, "Second Avenue Subway Convert Protects First Leg of Biggest Dig," *New York Observer*, April 16, 2007.

7 Schuerman, "Second Avenue Subway Convert."

8 Chuck Bennett, "Dig Date Set for 2nd Ave. Subway Line," *Newsday*, March 12, 2007; Caren Halbfinger, "MTA Signs First Contract for 2nd Avenue Subway," *Journal News* (White Plains, NY), March 21, 2007; William Neuman, "Was There a Ghost? No, Just a Tunnel at the Latest Subway Groundbreaking," *New York Times*, April 13, 2007; Jeremy Olshan, "City Goes Back for Seconds," *New York Post*, April 13, 2007.

9 Olshan, "City Goes Back for Seconds"; herenthere, "Groundbreaking for NYC Second Avenue Subway," WABC-TV Channel 7 *Eyewitness News*, YouTube video, 1:37, April 12, 2007, https://www.youtube.com/watch?v=41IywEP-JJk.

10 Alan Olmsted, interview with the author, October 25, 2017.

11 Peter Cafiero, email to the author, August 2, 2017; Peter Cafiero, interview with the author, New York, August 15, 2017; Olmsted, interview with the author; Robert A. Olmsted, "Rail Transit in New York: The Next 25 Years," September 15, 2007, author's possession.

12 Clyde Haberman, "Could It Be? A Miracle on 2nd Ave.," *New York Times*, April 13, 2007.

13   Sewell Chan, "M.T.A. Director Calls for Ambitious Expansion," *New York Times,* March 3, 2008.

14   William Neuman, "Bleaker Budget for M.T.A. Likely Means Severe Cuts," *New York Times,* November 10, 2008; William Neuman, "M.T.A. Plan Shows Less Help from Congestion Pricing," *New York Times,* February 28, 2008.

15   Tri-State Transportation Campaign, "July 2008: The MTA Capital Program Amendment, Examined," *Mobilizing the Region,* July 3, 2008, http://blog.tstc. org/2008/07/03/the-mta-capital-program-amendment-examined; William Neuman, "M.T.A. Cuts Delay Some Big Projects until 2010," *New York Times,* June 24, 2008; Chuck Bennett, "Work Running Late, Audit: Repairs in Subway Taking Decades Longer Than Planned," *Newsday,* February 2, 2007.

16   Metropolitan Transportation Authority (hereafter MTA), *2008 Annual Report,* 2009, 54; MTA, "Schedule K: Ratification of Completed Procurement Actions," *MTA Board Action Items,* September 2013, 160; MTA, "List of Competitive Procurements for Board Approval," *MTA Board Action Items,* April 2013, 100.

17   Christopher K. Bennett (DMJM Harris/AECOM), *Second Avenue Subway—A Status Report,* June 13, 2008, sec. 4.3, https://www.arema.org/files/library/2008_ Conference_Proceedings/Second_Avenue_Subway-A_Status_Report_2008.pdf; construction team member, telephone interview with the author, September 28, 2017; Mysore Nagaraja, interview with the author, Paramus, NJ, October 2, 2017.

18   WSP Parsons Brinckerhoff, "New York Opens Its Second Avenue Subway," Insights, January 25, 2017, https://www.wsp.com/en-US/insights/new-york-opens-its-second-avenue-subway.

19   Halbfinger, "MTA Signs First Contract"; Vincent Tirolo, Thomas Maxwell, and Anil Parikh, "Construction of a TBM Launch Box in a Complex Urban Environment," *Mining Engineering,* March 2013, 50.

20   MTA, exhibit at Second Avenue subway Community Information Center, 125th Street, New York, December 5, 2017; Ed Plotkin, interview with the author, Dobbs Ferry, NY, January 17, 2016; Emily Rueb, "Why Are the Streets Always Torn Up?," *New York Times,* August 21, 2016; New York City Department of Transportation (hereafter DOT) senior official, telephone interview with the author, October 26, 2017; Don Phillips, interview with the author, New York, January 15, 2016.

21   Tom Namako, "Hole-Y Wow for 2nd Ave.—Huge Subway Tunnel Dig Finally Starts," *New York Post,* May 15, 2010; John Miksad (Con Edison), letter to Douglas Sussman (MTA), written comments, Supplemental DEIS, June 9, 2003, author's possession; Alaeden Jlelaty, telephone interview with the author, June 28, 2017.

22   Pablo LeMus (project engineer, E. E. Cruz & Company), telephone interview with the author, June 22, 2018.

23   MTA Capital Construction, *Second Avenue Subway: March 2014 Public Workshop Follow-Up Report,* June 2014, 20.

24   Alfonso Castillo, "This Project Boring in Name Only," *Newsday,* May 15, 2010; MTA Capital Construction, "Tunnel Boring Machine Delivery Notice," April 12, 2010; Andrew Grossman, "City Grinds Out a Market for Muck," *Wall Street Journal,* December 22, 2011; Regional Plan Association, *Building Rail Transit Projects Better for Less:*

A Report on the Costs of Delivering MTA Megaprojects, February 2018, 42–44; Benjamin Kabak, "Building a Subway Most Expensive," *2nd Ave. Sagas*, November 9, 2011, http://secondavenuesagas.com/2011/11/09/building-a-subway-most-expensive.

25   Jim Rush, "Innovations in Ground Improvement Award," *TBM: Tunnel Business Magazine*, April 20, 2015, 40; Julie Freitas, telephone interview with the author, August 30, 2017.

26   Cathy Cunningham, "Second Coming: The East Side Awaits the Second Avenue Subway," Commercial Observer, July 27, 2016, https://commercialobserver.com/2016/07/second-coming-the-east-side-awaits-the-second-avenue-subway; Kim Tingley, "Tunneling below Second Avenue," *New York Times*, August 1, 2012; Maile Bucher, "Project Update: Second Avenue Subway," Mass Transit, August 15, 2016, https://www.masstransitmag.com/rail/article/12227191/project-update-second-avenue-subway; MTA, "Tunneling for Second Avenue Subway," press release, September 22, 2011; MTA, "Excavation of West Tunnel for Second Avenue Subway Complete," press release, February 7, 2011.

27   Wynton Habersham, interview with the author, New York, May 14, 2018.

28   MTA, "Second Av Subway Ridership Growing Rapidly," press release, February 1, 2017; Nagaraja, interview with the author, October 2, 2017; Bucher, "Project Update"; Dan Rivoli, "Fall of the Muck House," *AM New York*, June 10, 2013; Guido Schattanek, Helen Ginzburg, and John Faeth (Parsons Brinckerhoff consultants for MTA Capital Construction), *Air Monitoring Study to Evaluate Pollution Effects of Subway Construction in New York City*, AWMA Paper 2012-A-278, 2012, 2–4; Grossman, "City Grinds Out a Market"; Tingley, "Tunneling below Second Avenue"; Ilya Marritz, "Underground Economy: Cashing In on Rubble from the 2nd Avenue Subway," *WNYC News*, August 23, 2011, https://www.wnyc.org/story/154040-underground-economy-how-subway-tunnel-rubble-turned-cash.

29   Bennett, *Second Avenue Subway*, sec. 3.2; Nagaraja, interview with the author, October 2, 2017; DOT senior official, telephone interview with the author; MTA, "Determination and Findings Pursuant to Article 2 of the New York Eminent Domain Procedure Law: Second Avenue Subway Project," *MTA Board Action Items*, June 2010, 40–42; Michael Horodniceanu, "Lessons from the Second Avenue Subway and Other Megaprojects," slide presentation, CityLaw Breakfast, New York, April 6, 2017.

30   Jlelaty, telephone interview with the author.

31   Jlelaty, telephone interview with the author; DOT senior official, telephone interview with the author.

32   Jlelaty, telephone interview with the author.

33   Lisa Riordan Seville and Jennifer Fermino, "Sweet Subway Silence—2nd Ave. Curfew," *New York Post*, August 16, 2011; Horodniceanu, "Lessons from the Second Avenue Subway"; Christine Haughney, "2 Views on Subway Project: Delay Work to Clear Air, or Carry On and Profit Sooner," *New York Times*, November 23, 2011; Kevin Sheehan and Jennifer Fermino, "MTA 2nd Ave. House Calls," *New York Post*, February 22, 2012.

34   Colin Mixson and Jennifer Fermino, "Second Avenue Subway Causes a Dust Storm," *New York Post*, June 24, 2011; Jennifer Maloney and Andrew Grossman, "Air Quality Worries Halt Subway Blasts," *Wall Street Journal*, November 23, 2011; Jeane

MacIntosh, "Second Ave. Subway Dust Harmless, Says MTA," *New York Post*, September 27, 2011; Richard Bass, telephone interview with the author, June 5, 2017.

35   Joseph Berger, "Mistake in Second Avenue Subway Work Cuts Gas Off," *New York Times*, October 14, 2010; Jessica Simeone and Tom Namako, "Now It's Second Avenue Floodway," *New York Post*, October 30, 2009; "End of the Line: For Second Avenue Shop Owners, It's a Subway to Hell," *New York*, February 10, 2008.

36   Michael M. Grynbaum, "Learning the Hard Way about Life across Town," *New York Times*, December 16, 2010; Andrew Grossman, "Rats Mob the Upper East Side," *Wall Street Journal*, April 24, 2010; "The Most Rat-Infested Block on the Upper East Side," *NY Press*, August 21, 2013; Edmund Demarche and Tom Namako, "Plagues of 2nd Ave.," *New York Post*, October 18, 2010.

37   Shannon Ho, "Throughout 2nd Avenue Subway Build, Local Businesses See Fewer Customers, No Aid," *Gotham Gazette*, February 23, 2015; Katherine Romero and Tom Namako, "Second Avenue $ubpar," *New York Post*, August 19, 2009; Heather Haddon, "Cup of Woe on 2nd Ave.," *AM New York*, June 15, 2010.

38   Kevin Fasick, Dan Kadison, and Patrick Gallahue, "Storeowner Complaints: Trouble in 'Store' from 2nd Ave. Subway," *New York Post*, December 31, 2007; Kira Bindrim, "Subway Derails 2nd Ave.," *Crain's New York Business*, January 26, 2009; Jennifer Bleyer, "Clobbered by a Train They Didn't See Coming," *New York Times*, January 27, 2008; Haddon, "Cup of Woe"; Isabel Vincent and Melissa Klein, "2nd Ave. $nubway on Damage Claims," *New York Post*, September 25, 2011.

39   David Seifman and Tom Namako, "Mike Takes a Big Dig at 2nd Ave. Subway," *New York Post*, February 20, 2009; Dan Quart (assemblyman), interview with the author, New York, September 27, 2017.

40   Maggie Clark (community planning fellow, Fund for the City of New York), "2nd Avenue Business Analysis: Manhattan Community Board 8," June 2017; Quart, interview with the author; Adrianne Pasquarelli, "Second Avenue Businesses Not Digging Subway," *Crain's New York Business*, June 21, 2010.

41   Christine Haughney and Michael M. Grynbaum, "M.T.A. Halts Blasting for 2nd Ave. Subway around 72nd St.," *New York Times*, November 22, 2011; Plotkin, interview with the author.

42   Candace Taylor, "Manhattan Home Prices Double since Start of Decade, Report Says," Real Deal, February 2, 2011, https://therealdeal.com/2011/02/02/candy-shell; Brown Harris Stevens, *Manhattan Residential Market Report, Third Quarter 2010*, http://media.bhsusa.com/pdf/BHS3Q10_Market_Report.pdf; "Average Sales Price of Houses Sold for the United States," Federal Reserve Bank of St. Louis, accessed October 24, 2018, https://fred.stlouisfed.org/series/ASPUS; DOT senior official, telephone interview with the author.

43   Naomi Doerner, telephone interview with the author, October 17, 2017; MTA official, telephone interview with the author, January 26, 2016.

44   Construction team member, telephone interview with the author, January 22, 2016; Guido Schattanek, telephone interview with the author, August 9, 2017.

45   Horodniceanu, "Lessons from the Second Avenue Subway"; William E. Goodrich, "Second Avenue Subway Project: Managing Construction and Its Challenges in One

of the Country's Densest Urban Environments" (presentation, APTA Rail Conference, June 2013), https://www.apta.com/previousmc/rail/previous/2013/program/Documents/GoodrichW_MTA-new-yorks-second-ave.pdf.

46   Tom Namako, telephone interview with the author, October 27, 2017.

47   Namako, telephone interview with the author; Thomas S. Hines, "A Star Is Built," *New York Times*, March 19, 1995.

48   Barry Schneider, interview with the author, New York, June 15, 2017; Craig Lader, interview with the author, New York, June 15, 2017.

49   Outreach team member, telephone interview with the author, October 2, 2017; Schneider, interview with the author; Marc Beja, "We Hear UES Complaints," *AM New York*, April 9, 2012.

50   CB8 Speaks, "M. Barry Schneider from the Second Ave. Subway Task Force Is the Guest," interview with David Rosenstein, Manhattan Neighborhood Network, May 2, 2010, YouTube video, 27:54, September 14, 2016, https://www.youtube.com/watch?v=V_bMwC3tyR0; Schneider, interview with the author; outreach team member, telephone interview with the author, October 2, 2017.

51   "Subway Construction Raises Blasting, Rodent Questions," *Our Town*, March 31, 2010; Schneider, interview with the author; City of New York Manhattan Community Board 8, Second Avenue Subway Task Force, minutes from meeting, March 24, 2010.

52   Outreach team member, telephone interview with the author, September 19, 2017.

53   Jay Walder, presentation to the New York State Senate Standing Committee on Corporations, Authorities and Commissions, New York City, nysenateuncut, "Public Hearing: The Second Avenue Subway Construction Part 1," YouTube video, 1:38:06 (Walder's presentation begins at 11:50), November 30, 2010, https://www.youtube.com/watch?v=C9TYe0Ibucg.

54   NYC Transit official, interview with the author, January 26, 2016.

55   Lois Tendler, telephone interview with the author, October 19, 2017. In February 2012, the storefront vacancy rates were as follows: 1st Ave., 11 percent; 2nd Ave., 10 percent; and 3rd Ave., 8 percent, not including properties that were purchased by the MTA. MTA, *Upper East Side Store Report*, no. 10, January 12, 2011–February 11, 2012.

56   Tendler, telephone interview with the author.

57   Namako, telephone interview with the author.

58   Schneider, interview with the author; Michael Horodniceanu, telephone interview with the author, September 8, 2017.

59   Doerner, telephone interview with the author.

60   Walder, presentation.

61   Tendler, telephone interview with the author; Doerner, telephone interview with the author; outreach team member, telephone interview with the author, October 2, 2017.

62   Michael Porto, interview with the author, New York, January 6, 2016; Doerner, telephone interview with the author; Bucher, "Project Update."

63   Porto, interview with the author; outreach team member, interview with the author, New York, May 30, 2017.

64   Schneider, interview with the author; Porto, interview with the author; MTA Capital Construction, *Second Avenue Subway: Public Workshop, November 2011 Follow-Up Report*, February 2012, 7–11.

65   MTA, "Staff Summary" of legal agreement, *MTA Board Action Items*, July 2012, 71–72; outreach team member, telephone interview with the author, October 2, 2017; Doerner, telephone interview with the author.

66   Doerner, telephone interview with the author.

67   Beja, "We Hear UES Complaints."

68   Ben Heckscher, telephone interview with the author, June 13, 2017.

69   William Langewiesche, "What Lies Beneath," *Vanity Fair*, October 25, 2013.

70   Goodrich, "Second Avenue Subway Project"; Horodniceanu, "Lessons from the Second Avenue Subway"; MTA, "A Note from the SAS Community Outreach Team," *Second Avenue Subway Newsletter*, January/February 2017; Tingley, "Tunneling below Second Avenue."

71   Porto, interview with the author; Kevin Fasick and Gary Buiso, "Deep Peek at 2nd Ave. Subway, Shaken Residents Unswayed," *New York Post*, January 22, 2012.

72   Construction team member, telephone interview with the author, January 22, 2016; design team official, telephone interview with the author, July 11, 2017; Bass, telephone interview with the author.

73   Namako, telephone interview with the author; Schneider, interview with the author; Jennifer Fermino, "UES Subway Tunnel of Love," *New York Post*, March 10, 2012.

74   Tendler, telephone interview with the author.

75   Seifman and Namako, "Mike Takes a Big Dig."

76   Nancy Ploeger, telephone interview with the author, June 5, 2017; MTA Capital Construction, "Enhanced Pedestrian Safety Measures," November 19, 2012; Tom Namako, "Subway Salvation—Prettying-Up for 2nd Ave. Dig," *New York Post*, October 23, 2010; Porto, interview with the author; Stephen Goldsmith and Susan Crawford, *The Responsive City: Engaging Communities through Data-Smart Governance* (New York: John Wiley and Sons, 2014), 95–96.

77   Lisa Riordan Seville and Jennifer Fermino, "Sweet Subway Silence—2nd Ave. Curfew," *New York Post*, August 16, 2011; Maura O'Connor and Jennifer Fermino, "E. Siders Blast MTA Night Blasting," *New York Post*, August 6, 2011.

78   Haughney and Grynbaum, "M.T.A. Halts Blasting"; Jennifer Fermino, "2nd Ave. Blasts on Hold," *New York Post*, November 23, 2011; Pete Donohue, Kerry Wills, and Bill Hutchinson, "Silence on 2nd Ave.," *Daily News*, November 23, 2011; construction team member, telephone interview with the author, January 22, 2016; Horodniceanu, telephone interview with the author.

79   Schattanek, Ginzburg, and Faeth, *Air Monitoring Study*, 5–7; Schattanek, interview with the author.

80   Schattanek, Ginzburg, and Faeth, *Air Monitoring Study*, 1; construction team member, telephone interview with the author, January 22, 2016.

81   Construction team member, telephone interview with the author, January 22, 2016; Parsons Brinckerhoff (prepared for MTA Capital Construction), *Air Quality Monitoring Study of Construction Activities between 69th and 87th Street on Second Avenue*, January 17, 2012, 18.

82   Brinckerhoff, *Air Quality Monitoring Study*, 17–18; construction team member, telephone interview with the author, January 22, 2016.

83   MTA Capital Construction, "Schedule K: Ratification of Completed Procurement Actions," *MTA Board Action Items*, May 2012, 78; MTA Capital Construction, "Schedule K: Ratification of Completed Procurement Actions," *MTA Board Action Items*, September 2012, 88; MTA Capital Construction, "Schedule K: Ratification of Completed Procurement Actions," *MTA Board Action Items*, April 2013, 126; MTA Capital Construction, *Quarterly Report: Second Avenue Subway Phase 1; July, August and September 2012*, n.d.

84   Marc Beja, "Worker Banned for Rail Blast," *AM New York*, September 14, 2012; Jennifer Fermino, Kirstan Conley, and Don Kaplan, "2nd Ave. Blast Blame," *New York Post*, August 23, 2012; Andy Newman and Vivian Yee, "Explosion on 2nd Avenue Subway Project Breaks Windows at Street Level," *New York Times*, August 22, 2012; Ted Mann, "Deep Blast, Big Mess: Construction Work on Second Avenue Subway Rains Debris on East 72nd Street," *Wall Street Journal*, August 22, 2012.

85   Freitas, telephone interview with the author; Schattanek, interview with the author; Sean Manning, "Sandhogs Tunneling under Second Avenue," *Village Voice*, April 11, 2012.

86   Carmen Bianco, telephone interview with the author, December 15, 2015.

87   Bianco, telephone interview with the author; Habersham, interview with the author.

88   Bianco, telephone interview with the author; Tom Prendergast, interview with the author, New York, August 24, 2017.

89   "MTA New York City Transit Continues to Move Ahead at Sandy Plus Three," MTA, accessed October 24, 2017, http://web.mta.info/sandy/nyct_girds.htm; "MTA River Crossings Damaged by Superstorm Sandy," MTA, accessed October 24, 2017, http://web.mta.info/sandy/images/MTA%20River%20Crossing%20Dam age_Superstorm%20Sandy.pdf; "MTA: Sandy Is Worst Subway Disaster in 108-Year History," News 12, October 30, 2012, http://brooklyn.news12.com/story/34777184/mta-sandy-is-worst-subway-disaster-in-108-year-history; Mysore Nagaraja, interview with the author, Paramus, NJ, September 11, 2017; Bianco, telephone interview with the author.

90   Federal Transit Administration and MTA NYC Transit, *Second Avenue Subway in the Borough of Manhattan (New York County, New York): Final Environmental Impact Statement and Final Section 4(F) and Section 6(F) Evaluation*, April 2004, S-15; Nagaraja, interview with the author, October 2, 2017.

91   MTA Capital Construction, "Chronology: SAS Cost and Schedule Growth," internal document, May 2011, author's possession.

92   Federal Transit Administration and MTA/NYC Transit, *Manhattan East Side Alternatives Study: Draft Environmental Impact Statement*, August 1999, 23-1, 23-2, S-15, table S-1; Nagaraja, interview with the author, September 11, 2017; MTA Capital Construction, "Chronology"; Nagaraja, interview with the author, October 2, 2017.

93   Bucher, "Project Update"; Horodniceanu, telephone interview with the author; MTA Capital Construction, "Chronology"; MTA Capital Construction, "Results of Comprehensive Project Reviews: Second Avenue Subway & East Side Access," PowerPoint presentation to MTA Capital Construction, Planning and Real Estate Committee, July 22, 2009; Pete Donohue, "MTA Construction Chief Says That 2nd Ave. Subway Delays Are Over," *Daily News*, July 22, 2009.

94   Outreach team member, telephone interview with the author, October 2, 2017.

9. Andrew Cuomo's Finish Line

1   Jimmy Vielkind and James M. Odato, "Cuomo Control of Information Includes Screening, Redaction of Records at State Archives," *Times Union* (Albany, NY), July 23, 2012; Jonathan Mahler, "The Making of Andrew Cuomo," *New York Times*, August 11, 2010; Celeste Katz, "Eliot Spitzer: Everyone Knows Andrew Cuomo's the Dirtiest, Nastiest Political Player Out There," *Daily News*, September 23, 2010; Jeremy Smerd and Daniel Massey, "Cuomo: The Boss; Nothing Gets Done in This State without His Say," *Crain's New York Business*, March 25, 2012.

2   Philip Mark Plotch, *Politics across the Hudson: The Tappan Zee Megaproject* (New Brunswick, NJ: Rutgers University Press, 2015), 143–55.

3   Joan McDonald, interview with the author, New York, February 21, 2017.

4   "Under Second Avenue with Governor Cuomo, Part 1," NY1, December 15, 2016, http://www.ny1.com/nyc/all-boroughs/inside-city-hall/2016/12/14/ny1-online-- under-second-avenue-with-governor-cuomo--part-1.html; Lois Tendler, telephone interview with the author, October 19, 2017; Jim Brennan, telephone interview with the author, September 29, 2017.

5   Former MTA executive, telephone interview with the author, August 30, 2017.

6   Jessica Newman, "Driscoll Will Be the Sixth Thruway Authority Leader in Seven Years," *City and State New York*, August 26, 2017, https://www.cityandstateny.com/ articles/policy/infrastructure/driscoll-sixth-official-to-lead-thruway-authority- turnover; senior state transportation official, interview with the author, New York, September 17, 2017; New York state assemblyman, interview with the author, legislator's office, 2017.

7   Josh Benson, "Jay Walder Won't Be Answering to Andrew Cuomo Anymore, and Maybe That's the Point," *Politico*, July 22, 2011, https://www.politico.com/states/ new-york/city-hall/story/2011/07/jay-walder-wont-be-answering-to-andrew- cuomo-anymore-and-maybe-thats-the-point-000000; former MTA executive, telephone interview with the author.

8   Former MTA executive, telephone interview with the author; Michael M. Grynbaum, "Three Leaders, All Comfortable, Put Three Different Faces on Storm Response," *New York Times*, October 29, 2012; "Heard around Town," *City and State New York*, August 30, 2011.

9   NYC Mayor's Office, "The Money for the MTA's Subway Crisis Plan Is in Governor Cuomo's Budget," press release, July 27, 2017; Jim Brennan, "Cuomo Gave MTA Chump Change from State's $9.9 Billion Windfall in Settlements with Wall Street Badguys," Jim Brennan's Commentaries, June 8, 2017, https://jimbrennanscommentaries.com/2017/06/08/cuomo-gave-mta-chump-change-from-states-9-9-billion-windfall-in-settlements-with-wall-street-badguys; State of New York, *FY 2017 Enacted Capital Program and Financing Plan*, May 2016, 10; Andrew M. Cuomo and Robert F. Mujica Jr. (budget director), *FY 2018 Executive Budget Financial Plan*, 2017, 151–52.

10   Jim Brennan, "The Governor Cannot Duck Reckoning for Mass Transit Decline," Gotham Gazette, June 23, 2017, http://www.gothamgazette.com/columnists/other/130-opinion/7023-the-governor-cannot-duck-reckoning-for-mass-transit-decline; Brennan, telephone interview with the author.

11   William Vantuono, "Railway Age Railroader of the Year: Tom Prendergast," YouTube video, 34:58, January 12, 2017, https://www.youtube.com/watch?v=obGxUx3miik; Thomas Prendergast, interview with the author, New York, August 24, 2017.

12   Vantuono, "Railway Age Railroader of the Year"; "New Head of L.I.R.R. Is Selected," *New York Times*, August 11, 1994.

13   Prendergast, interview with the author; Emma G. Fitzsimmons, "Chief of Transportation Authority Must Wage a Political Battle for Funding," *New York Times*, July 28, 2015.

14   Metropolitan Transportation Authority (hereafter MTA), *Capital Program: 2015–2019 (as Proposed to the Board)*, September 24, 2014; Madeline Marvar, "2014: MTA Capital Program Highlights Dire Need for Sustainable Funding Sources," Mobilizing the Region, September 24, 2014, http://blog.tstc.org/2014/09/24/mta-capital-program-highlights-dire-need-for-sustainable-funding-sources; Federal Transit Administration, *Annual Report on Funding Recommendations: Fiscal Year 2018 Capital Investment Grant Program*, May 2017, table 2C.

15   Jorteh Senah, "State Review Board Nixes MTA Capital Program," Transportation Nation, WNYC, October 3, 2014, https://www.wnyc.org/story/state-transportation-department-pulls-stop-sign-mta-capital-program; Jimmy Vielkind, "Cuomo: M.T.A. Capital Plan Is Bloated," *Politico*, October 7, 2014, https://www.politico.com/states/new-york/albany/story/2014/10/cuomo-mta-capital-plan-is-bloated-016387; Prendergast, interview with the author; Emma G. Fitzsimmons, "Hope Fades for State Help on M.T.A. Capital Budget as Legislative Session Nears End," *New York Times*, June 10, 2015.

16   Jim Dwyer, "Mayor de Blasio and Governor Cuomo Point Fingers, but There's Enough Blame for Both," *New York Times*, July 2, 2015; Josh Dawsey, "New York City Mayor Bill de Blasio Lashes Out at Gov. Andrew Cuomo," *Wall Street Journal*, June 30, 2015; Michael Gartland and Leonard Greene, "Raging Bill—Shocking Attack at 'Vendetta' Gov," *New York Post*, July 1, 2015; Michael M. Grynbaum, "Patience Spent, de Blasio Accuses Cuomo of Hurting New York City Out of 'Revenge,'" *New York Times*, June 30, 2015.

17   Alan Treffeisen, New York City Independent Budget Office, *How Much Would the City's Annual Contribution Be Today If Aid for the Metropolitan Transportation*

Authority's Capital Projects Had Kept Pace with Inflation?, January 22, 2015; Paul Burton, "Ravitch Calls MTA Funding Dilemma a Mess," *Bond Buyer*, August 11, 2015; Emma G. Fitzsimmons and Alexander Burns, "New York City and State Reach Agreement on M.T.A. Capital Plan," *New York Times*, October 10, 2015.

18   Emma G. Fitzsimmons, "M.T.A. Approves Budget, but Deal Cuts 2nd Ave. Line Funding," *New York Times*, October 28, 2015; Robert J. Rodriguez (assemblyman), "Elected Officials and Transit Advocates Ask MTA to Restore Funding for Second Avenue Subway Extension to 125th Street," press release, November 3, 2015; Brennan, telephone interview with the author.

19   Brennan, telephone interview with the author; Emma G. Fitzsimmons, "De Blasio Joins in Criticism of 2nd Avenue Subway Cuts," *New York Times*, November 4, 2015.

20   Brennan, telephone interview with the author; MTA, "Statement from MTA Chairman and Chief Executive Officer Thomas F. Prendergast on Second Avenue Subway," press release, November 12, 2015; MTA, *MTA Capital Program: 2015–2019 (as Approved by the MTA Board April 20, 2016, as Approved by the CPRB May 23, 2016)*, 41.

21   Former MTA executive, telephone interview with the author; NYC Transit official, interview with the author, New York, December 18, 2017.

22   Fredric U. Dicker, telephone interview with the author, September 21, 2017; Fredric U. Dicker, "Cuomo's Former Chief of Staff Still on Payroll," *New York Post*, February 22, 2015; Phil Reisman, "Do You Know Where Larry Schwartz Works? Ask Cuomo," *Journal News* (White Plains, NY), February 23, 2015.

23   Senior MTA officials, interviews with the author, 2017.

24   Senior state transportation official, interview with the author.

25   Patrick McGeehan, "Czar of Infrastructure Embraces Role as Pillar for Port Authority," *New York Times*, August 13, 2017.

26   NYC Transit senior official, telephone interview with the author, August 10, 2017.

27   Governor's Press Office, "Governor Cuomo Unveils Design of Reimagined MTA Subway Cars and Details Ambitious Plan to Enhance Subway Stations," press release, July 18, 2016; Dana Rubinstein, "Cuomo Lays Out Mass Transit Plan for the Future," *Politico*, January 8, 2016, https://www.politico.com/states/new-york/albany/story/2016/01/cuomo-lays-out-mass-transit-plan-for-the-future-000000; Governor's Press Office, "Governor Cuomo Announces Transformational Plan to Reimagine New York's Bridges and Tunnels for 21st Century," press release, October 5, 2016; Governor's Press Office, "8th Proposal of Governor Cuomo's 2016 Agenda: Bring the MTA into the 21st Century to Dramatically Improve the Travel Experience for Millions of New Yorkers and Visitors," press release, January 8, 2016.

28   Governor's Press Office, "Governor Cuomo Announces Transformational Plan"; Dana Rubinstein, "Tunnel Towers Give Rise to Questions about MTA Board," *Politico*, September 14, 2017, https://www.politico.com/states/new-york/albany/story/2017/09/11/architectural-tunnel-towers-rise-so-do-questions-about-the-mta-board-114410; Joe Anuta, "Guv's Tweaks Delay Penn Station Upgrade," *Crain's New York Business*, January 30, 2017; Nick Paumgarten, "The Second Avenue Subway Is Here!," *New Yorker*, February 13 and 20, 2017.

29   Citizens Budget Commission, "Misplaced Priorities in the MTA's Capital Plan," policy brief, October 2014.

30   Paumgarten, "Second Avenue Subway."

31   Michael Horodniceanu, telephone interview with the author, September 8, 2017.

32   Rick Cotton, speech at 141st CityLaw Breakfast, Center for New York City Law at New York Law School, April 6, 2017, http://www.citylandnyc.org/citylaw-breakfas t-michael-horodniceanu-mta-construction.

33   Outreach team member, interview with the author, New York, May 30, 2017.

34   Vantuono, "Railway Age Railroader of the Year"; Frommer's, "Getting Around in New York City," https://www.frommers.com/destinations/new-york-city/getting-around. This language appeared on the Frommer's site in 2015 and 2016, per the Internet Archive Wayback Machine, accessed November 3, 2018, https://archive.org/web.

35   Prendergast, interview with the author.

36   Prendergast, interview with the author.

37   Prendergast, interview with the author.

38   Prendergast, interview with the author; MTA, "The MTA Network: Public Transportation for the New York Region," accessed November 11, 2017, http://web.mta. info/mta/network.htm; American Public Transportation Association, 2015 Public Transportation Fact Book, November 2015, 8.

39   Emma G. Fitzsimmons and Jesse McKinley, "Amid Subway Crisis, Cuomo Taps an Old Hand to Head M.T.A.," New York Times, June 22, 2017; Veronica Vanterpool, telephone interview with the author, August 11, 2017; Prendergast, interview with the author.

40   Richard Ravitch, interview with the author, Waterside Plaza, NY, April 24, 2017; former MTA executive, interview with the author.

41   Senior state transportation official, interview with the author.

42   Prendergast, interview with the author; Vincent Barone, "Second Avenue Subway Faces Delays before Dec. 31 Opening," Newsday, October 3, 2016.

43   MTA Capital Construction, Quarterly Report: Second Avenue Subway Phase 1; October, November and December 2015, 3–6.

44   NYC Transit, "UP64 Rev4 Status DD 01-Nov-11 Update r0 (Update as of 11-28-11 Final) SAS Integrated Project Schedule Remaining Work as of 01-Nov-11," internal document, November 30, 2011, author's possession.

45   Salvatore DeMatteo, telephone interview with the author, October 14, 2017; Dana C. Nifosi (FTA), letter to Thomas Prendergast, "Re: Buy America Investigation Decision: Second Avenue Subway Project's Water Mist Fire Suppression System," January 6, 2015.

46   Oversight team member, telephone interview with the author, September 28, 2017.

47   NYC Transit, "SAS Schedule Compression and Its Effect on NYCT Resources," internal document, ca. 2011, author's possession; Barry L. Kluger (MTA inspector general),

Improving Structural Inspections at MTA New York City Transit, MTA/OIG Report #2012-11, April 2013, 8–18; Barry L. Kluger, *Improving Inspections of NYC Transit Stations,* MTA/OIG Report #2010-05, June 2010, 1–3.

48 DeMatteo, telephone interview with the author; NYC Transit, "UP64 Rev4 Status DD 01-Nov-11 Update r0."

49 DeMatteo, telephone interview with the author.

50 Oversight team member, telephone interview with the author; DeMatteo, telephone interview with the author.

51 Pete Donohue, "MTA Construction Chief Says That 2nd Ave. Subway Delays Are Over," *Daily News,* July 22, 2009; Prendergast, interview with the author.

52 Vanterpool, telephone interview with the author; William Murphy, "MTA to Award Additional $66M to Second Avenue Subway Project," *Newsday,* February 23, 2016; MTA Capital Construction, "Staff Summary: Second Avenue Subway Accelera-tion Agreements," February 18, 2016, in MTA, *MTA Board Action Items,* Febru-ary 2016, 1–2.

53 Senior construction manager, telephone interview with the author, August 23, 2017; MTA Capital Construction, "Schedule K: Ratification of Completed Procurement Actions," for E. E. Cruz/Tully Construction Co., in MTA, *MTA Board Action Items,* March 2016, 110.

54 MTA Capital Construction, "Staff Summary," 1–2; "Local 3 Helps Unveil New 2nd Avenue Subway," Local Union No. 3 IBEW, February 2017, https://www.local3i bew.org/news/local-3-helps-unveil-new-2nd-avenue-subway; NYC Office of the Comptroller, "§220 Prevailing Wage Schedule: Effective Period: July 1, 2016 through June 30, 2017," July 1, 2016; Bob DeThomasis, telephone interview with the author, August 2, 2017.

55 Don Phillips, interview with the author, New York, January 15, 2016; Alaeden Jlelaty, telephone interview with the author, June 28, 2017; Pablo LeMus, telephone inter-view with the author, June 22, 2018.

56 Wynton Habersham, interview with the author, New York, May 14, 2018; MTA Capital Construction, *Quarterly Report,* 16.

57 Larry Reuter, telephone interview with the author, June 22, 2018.

58 Prendergast, interview with the author; DeMatteo, telephone interview with the author.

59 Construction supervisor, telephone interview with the author, August 21, 2017; over-sight team member, telephone interview with the author.

60 Construction supervisor, telephone interview with the author.

61 DeMatteo, telephone interview with the author; Governor's Office, "Schedule of the Office of the Governor of New York," December 2016; senior construction manager, telephone interview with the author; "Under Second Avenue with Governor Cuomo."

62 Senior construction manager, telephone interview with the author; Paumgarten, "Sec-ond Avenue Subway"; DeMatteo, telephone interview with the author.

63 Construction officials, telephone interviews with the author, 2017; DeThomasis, telephone interview with the author; DeMatteo, telephone interview with the author.

64 Prendergast, interview with the author.

65 Prendergast, interview with the author; DeMatteo, telephone interview with the author; DeThomasis, telephone interview with the author.

66 DeMatteo, telephone interview with the author; senior construction manager, telephone interview with the author; Alphonse Calvanico, telephone interview with the author, September 7, 2017.

67 Randi F. Marshall, "Talking Point: Laser-Focused on East Side Access," *Newsday*, September 6, 2018; Mark Chiusano, "Cuomo Talks Second Avenue Subway with Newsday/amNewYork Editorial Board," *AM New York*, September 5, 2018; senior construction manager, telephone interview with the author; Horodniceanu, telephone interview with the author.

68 DeThomasis, telephone interview with the author.

69 DeThomasis, telephone interview with the author.

70 DeThomasis, telephone interview with the author.

71 Outreach team member, interview with the author; DeThomasis, telephone interview with the author.

72 DeThomasis, telephone interview with the author.

73 Emma G. Fitzsimmons, "With Second Ave. Subway, Cuomo Has Hands-On Role and Eye on the Future," *New York Times*, December 13, 2016; Amanda Mikelberg, "Second Avenue Subway's December Deadline Imperiled: Testing Is Underway as Workers Complete Infrastructure," *Metro*, November 18, 2016.

74 "Under Second Avenue with Governor Cuomo"; Governor's Press Office, "Video, Photos & Rush Transcript: Governor Cuomo Debuts New 86th Street Subway Station and New Entrance at 63rd Street Subway Station," press release, December 30, 2016.

75 NYGovCuomo, "Governor Cuomo Debuts New 86th Street Subway Station and New Entrance at 63rd Street Subway Station," YouTube video, 12:57, December 30, 2016, https://www.youtube.com/watch?v=luQ1pO1t6cQ.

76 Ben Heckscher, telephone interview with the author, June 13, 2017; "Under Second Avenue with Governor Cuomo"; Governor's Press Office, "Video, Photos & Rush Transcript."

77 Stephen Nessen, "New York's Long-Awaited Second Avenue Subway Finally Leaves the Station," *All Things Considered*, National Public Radio, January 2, 2017, https://www.npr.org/2017/01/02/507898727/new-yorks-long-awaited-second-avenue-subway-finally-leaves-the-station; "Under Second Avenue with Governor Cuomo."

78 "NYC Welcomes Second Avenue Subway," *CBS This Morning*, CBS, January 2, 2017, https://www.cbsnews.com/news/nyc-welcomes-second-avenue-subway; "Take a Ride on NYC's New Second Ave. Subway Line with Gov. Cuomo," *Today Show*, NBC, December 30, 2016, https://www.today.com/video/take-a-ride-on-nyc-s-new-second-

ave-subway-line-with-gov-cuomo-844494915539; "Under Second Avenue with Governor Cuomo."

79   Nessen, "New York's Long-Awaited Second Avenue Subway"; Paumgarten, "Second Avenue Subway"; Mort Downey, telephone interview with the author, July 14, 2017.

80   Stephen Nessen, "A Better Sounding Subway," *WNYC News*, May 15, 2017, https://www.wnyc.org/story/better-sounding-subway; Nessen, "New York's Long-Awaited Second Avenue Subway"; Amy Plitt, "Second Avenue Subway Gets Its Historic Inaugural Ride on New Year's Eve," Curbed New York, January 1, 2017, https://ny.curbed.com/2017/1/1/14139394/second-avenue-subway-first-ride-governor-cuomo.

81   Ralph Gardner Jr., "Ralph Gardner Jr: The Second Avenue Subway," *Midday Magazine*, WAMC, January 14, 2017, https://www.wamc.org/post/ralph-gardner-jr-second-avenue-subway.

82   Paumgarten, "Second Avenue Subway"; Shaye Weaver, "See: Photos and Video of the 96th Street Second Avenue Subway Station," DNA Info, December 22, 2016, https://www.dnainfo.com/new-york/20161222/upper-east-side/second-avenue-subway-tour-96th-street-station.

83   Governor's Press Office, "Governor Cuomo Presents Largest Permanent Public Art Installation in New York History Ahead of Second Avenue Subway Opening," press release, December 19, 2016.

84   DeMatteo, telephone interview with the author; senior construction manager, telephone interview with the author.

85   Peter Cafiero, interview with the author, New York, August 15, 2017; Alan Olmsted, interview with the author, New York, October 25, 2017; Peter Cafiero, email to Alan Olmsted, December 30, 2016, author' possession.

86   New York City Department of Transportation, "2nd Avenue Safety and Mobility Improvements," presentation to Community Board 8, New York, January 6, 2016.

87   Kate King, "Riders and Residents Greet Second Avenue Subway's Opening," *Wall Street Journal*, January 2, 2017; Charmaine P. Rice, "Bye-Bye Barricades," *New York Press*, January 3, 2017.

Conclusion

1   Mariela Quintana, "How the Second Avenue Subway Has Affected Yorkville Homes," StreetEasy, January 12, 2018, https://streeteasy.com/blog/second-avenue-subway-yorkville-impact-one-year-in; Anna Sanders, "Second Avenue Subway Gave a Big Boost to Nearby Businesses," *New York Post*, December 30, 2017.

2   Peter Cafiero, interview with the author, New York, August 15, 2017; Metropolitan Transportation Authority (hereafter MTA), *Second Avenue Subway Newsletter*, April 2017, 2; Dan Rivoli, "Second Ave. Subway Takes Pressure off Lexington Line," *Daily News*, July 13, 2018.

3   Alon Levy, "US Rail Construction Costs," *Pedestrian Observations* (blog), May 16, 2011, https://pedestrianobservations.com/2011/05/16/us-rail-construction-costs; "New York's Second Coming," editorial, *Wall Street Journal*, January 3, 2017; Urban Engineers of New York (prepared for the Federal Transit Administration), *PMOC*

Monthly Report: Second Avenue Subway Phase 1 Project, report period for December 2017, 13. The Federal Transit Administration's project management oversight consultant (PMOC) issued monthly reports for the first phase of the Second Avenue subway.

4   Urban Engineers of New York, *PMOC Monthly Report*, January 2017, secs. 1.0, 4.0.

5   Urban Engineers of New York, *PMOC Monthly Report*, February 2017, secs. 1.0, 7.0.

6   Urban Engineers of New York, *PMOC Monthly Report*, October 2017, 5; NYC Transit official, telephone interview with the author, August 10, 2017.

7   MTA Capital Construction, *Quarterly Review Report—4th Quarter 2016*, 10–20; fire safety officer, interview with the author, New York, October 9, 2017; Emma G. Fitzsimmons, "Months after Second Avenue Subway Opening, Safety Testing Is Not Finished," *New York Times*, September 20, 2017; Urban Engineers of New York, *PMOC Monthly Report*, October 2017, 3, 8–10.

8   MTA, "Transit & Bus Committee Meeting: May 2017"; MTA, "Transit & Bus Committee Meeting: June 2017"; Shaye Weaver, "2nd Ave. Subway's 83rd St. Entrance Closed Due to Broken Escalators," DNA Info, May 17, 2017, https://www.dnainfo.com/new-york/20170516/yorkville/second-avenue-subway-83rd-street-entrance-exit-closed-escalator-repairs; "Power Outage Shuts Down Stretch of 2nd Avenue Subway on Upper East Side," WABC-TV, June 2, 2017, https://abc7ny.com/traffic/power-outage-shuts-down-stretch-of-2nd-avenue-subway/2062364; Linda Schmidt, "Broken Subway Elevators Cause Commuter Confusion," FOX 5, March 28, 2017, http://www.fox5ny.com/news/broken-subway-elevators-cause-commuter-confusion; NYC Transit official, telephone interview with the author; MTA official, email to the author, August 11, 2017.

9   MTA official, interview with the author, New Jersey, August 22, 2017; NYC Transit official, telephone interview with the author.

10   Thomas Prendergast, interview with the author, New York, August 24, 2017.

11   Samuel Wong, telephone interview with the author, October 23, 2017; Larry Reuter, telephone interview with the author, June 22, 2018; Wynton Habersham, interview with the author, New York, May 14, 2018.

12   Habersham, interview with the author.

13   Wong, telephone interview with the author.

14   Habersham, interview with the author; Office of the New York State Comptroller, *Metropolitan Transportation Authority—New York City Transit Selected Safety and Security Equipment at Subway Stations*, April 12, 2018, 1–2.

15   Emma G. Fitzsimmons and J. David Goodman, "As Subway Riders Fume, City and State Leaders Are Mostly Mum," *New York Times*, May 15, 2017; Brian M. Rosenthal, Emma G. Fitzsimmons, and Michael Laforgia, "How Politics and Bad Decisions Starved New York's Subways," *New York Times*, November 18, 2017; Quinnipiac University Poll, "More NYC Voters Blame Cuomo for Poor Subways, Quinnipiac University Poll Finds," press release, July 27, 2017.

16   Aaron Short, "Three-Quarters of City's Subway Lines Plagued by Chronic Delays," *New York Post*, June 17, 2017.

17   "New York Leaders Are Failing Its Subway Riders," editorial, *New York Times*, January 7, 2018; "How Cuomo Can Lead the Way to Saving the Subway," editorial, *New York Post*, June 20, 2017; "Fair Is Fare, Mr. Mayor, So Help Pay to Fix the Subways," editorial, *Daily News*, July 24, 2017; "Cuomo Grabs the Throttle to Take Solo Control of the MTA," editorial, *Daily News*, June 21, 2017; Erin Durkin and Dan Rivoli, "Mayor de Blasio Plans to Push MTA to Take Responsibility, Fix Troubled Subway System," *Daily News*, July 26, 2017.

18   Andrew Liptak, "All NYC Subway Stations Will Have Cellular and Wi-Fi Service Tomorrow," The Verge, January 8, 2017, https://www.theverge.com/2017/1/8/14207230/nyc-subway-stations-cellular-wifi-service-mta-transit-wireless-new-york.

19   Emma G. Fitzsimmons and Michael Laforgia, "How Cuts in Basic Subway Upkeep Can Make Your Commute Miserable," *New York Times*, December 20, 2017; Rosenthal, Fitzsimmons, and Laforgia, "How Politics and Bad Decisions Starved New York's Subways"; Office of the State Comptroller, *Financial Outlook for the Metropolitan Transportation Authority: Report 7-2018*, November 2017, 4.

20   Zack Fink, "Cuomo's Attempt to Put Subway Responsibility on City a Bit of an About-Face," NY1, July 24, 2017, https://www.ny1.com/nyc/all-boroughs/transit/2017/07/24/state-and-city-fight-over-subway-responsibility; Nathan Tempey, "Cuomo Denies Controlling the MTA despite Controlling the MTA," Gothamist, May 19, 2017, http://gothamist.com/2017/05/19/mta_cuomo_subway_broken.php.

21   Danielle Furfaro and Natalie Musumeci, "Subway Derailment Causes System-Wide Chaos a Day Later," *New York Post*, June 28, 2017; State of New York Executive Chamber, "Declaring a Disaster Emergency in the Five Boroughs of New York City and the Counties of Dutchess, Nassau, Orange, Putnam, Rockland, Suffolk and Westchester That Incorporate the MTA Region in the State of New York," Executive Order No. 168, June 29, 2017; Governor's Press Office, "Video, Photos & Rush Transcript: Governor Cuomo Announces $1 Billion in New MTA Funding and Declares State of Emergency to Speed Up Subway Repairs," June 29, 2017.

22   Dan Rivoli, "MTA Brass Pushed Link between Subway Delays and Power Problems," *Daily News*, January 21, 2018; Urban Engineers of New York, *PMOC Monthly Report*, June 2017, 6; and *PMOC Monthly Report*, July 2017, 6.

23   Thomas J. Lueck, "After 24 Years, Subway Line for Second Avenue Gets Another Look," *New York Times*, January 27, 1999; Jen Kirby, "What Is Wrong with the MTA—and Can It Be Fixed?," *New York*, June 29, 2017.

24   The total cost of construction, real estate, and contractors' equipment for the 1904 subway was approximately $60 million (or $2.1 million per station), according to *The New York Subway Souvenir* (New York: Burroughs and Company, 1904), 10; and Clifton Hood, *722 Miles: The Building of the Subways and How They Transformed New York* (Baltimore: John Hopkins University Press, 2004), 71.

25   MTA Capital Construction, *Second Avenue Subway Project Report: April, May and June 2017*, 5; MTA, "Staff Summary: Construction Services for 301–303 E 83rd Street," *MTA Board Action Items*, June 2011, 47; Anil Parikh and Manan Garg, "Staff Summary: Construction Services for 250 E. 87th Street (Block 1532, Lot 22)," *MTA Board Action Items*, July 2011, 57–58.

26   Tom Namako and Irene Plagianos, "2nd Avenue Subway, Second Avenue Evacuation," *New York Post*, June 30, 2009; Jessica Simeone and Tom Namako, "Second Ave. on Snail Rail," *New York Post*, September 26, 2009; Tom Namako, "Bracing for 2nd Ave. Subway," *New York Post*, October 22, 2009; Tom Topousis, "Rail Shaky Ground—2nd Ave. Bldgs. Must Be Shored Up," *New York Post*, October 26, 2010; MTA, "Schedule K: Ratifications of Completed Procurement Actions; S3 Tunnel Constructors," *MTA Board Action Items*, January 2010, 164; Jennifer Gould Keil, Rebecca Rosenberg, and Tom Namako, "2nd Ave. Subway Exiles $core Big," *New York Post*, June 22, 2010.

27   Cafiero, interview with the author.

28   DMJM Harris/Arup executive, telephone interview with the author, July 11, 2017; Urban Engineers of New York, *PMOC Monthly Report*, December 2017, 12.

29   Arcadis, "Currency Commodities and International Construction Costs," press release, December 9, 2015; Turner and Townsend, *International Construction Market Survey 2015*, 2015, 9; City of New York, Office of the Comptroller, "§220 Prevailing Wage Schedule: Effective Period: July 1, 2015 through June 30, 2016," January 11, 2016.

30   Michael Horodniceanu, telephone interview with the author, September 8, 2017.

31   Horodniceanu, telephone interview with the author.

32   Brian M. Rosenthal, "The Most Expensive Mile of Subway Track on Earth," *New York Times*, December 28, 2017; construction official, telephone interview with the author, August 25, 2017; senior construction manager, telephone interview with the author, August 23, 2017.

33   General Contractors Association—Metallic Lathers, "Agreement between General Contractors Association of New York, Inc. and Local #46 Metallic Lathers Union and Reinforcing Iron Workers New York and Vicinity: July 1, 2008 to June 30, 2014"; Rosenthal, "Most Expensive Mile"; General Contractors Association—Tunnel Workers, "Agreement between the Compressed Air and Free Air Tunnel Workers Union Local 147, LIUNA and the General Contractors Association of New York, Inc.: July 1, 2014–June 30, 2018."

34   Agreements between the members of the General Contractors Association of New York, Inc., and the District Council of Carpenters (for the period July 1, 2011–May 31, 2017), the International Union of Operating Engineers (for the period July 1, 2014–June 30, 2018), and the Timbermen (for the period July 1, 2011–May 31, 2017).

35   Mysore Nagaraja, interview with the author, Paramus, NJ, October 2, 2017.

36   New York City Department of Transportation senior official, telephone interview with the author, October 26, 2017; Shannon Ayala, "Second Avenue Subway Brings Fear-Inducing LED Streetlights," Curbed New York, April 24, 2015, https://ny.curbed.com/2015/4/24/9967188/second-avenue-subway-brings-fear-inducing-led-streetlights.

37   Michael Horodniceanu, letter to Michael L. Culotta (FTA), September 11, 2013, author's possession.

38   Horodniceanu to Culotta.

39   MTA, "MTA Utilization Plan," accessed February 18, 2018, http://web.mta.info/mta/procurement/utilplan.html.

40 Richard Barone (Regional Plan Association), interview with the author, New York, May 9, 2018; Pablo LeMus (project engineer, E. E. Cruz), telephone interview with the author, June 22, 2018.

41 Rosenthal, "Most Expensive Mile"; Alon Levy, "Why We Can't Have Nice Things," *American Interest*, February 10, 2017.

42 Nagaraja, interview with the author; Regional Plan Association, *Building Rail Transit Projects Better for Less: A Report on the Costs of Delivering MTA Megaprojects*, February 2018, 37–39.

43 MTA, "Capital Program Oversight Committee Meeting," December 2017.

44 Alaeden Jlelaty, telephone interview with the author, June 28, 2017.

45 Rick Cotton, speech at 141st CityLaw Breakfast, Center for New York City Law at New York Law School, April 6, 2017, http://www.citylandnyc.org/citylaw-breakfast-michael-horodniceanu-mta-construction.

46 MTA, "Capital Program Oversight Committee Meeting," December 2017.

47 Nagaraja, interview with the author.

48 Peter Hall, *Great Planning Disasters* (Berkeley: University of California Press, 1982), 109, 138.

49 Office of the State Comptroller, *Financial Outlook*, 1.

50 Ronnie Lowenstein (director, Independent Budget Office of the City of New York), letter to Gale Brewer (Manhattan Borough President), June 11, 2017, http://www.ibo.nyc.ny.us/iboreports/mta-service-delays-disruptions-letter-2017.pdf.

51 Prendergast, interview with the author; Emma G. Fitzsimmons, "Key to Improving Subway Service in New York? Modern Signals," *New York Times*, May 1, 2017.

52 Reuter, telephone interview with the author; Adam Forman (Center for an Urban Future), testimony at city council hearing, June 18, 2014, https://nycfuture.org/research/testimony-aging-infrastructure-new-york-citys-gas-steam-and-water-infra stru; Sewell Chan, "Why the Subways Flood," *New York Times*, August 8, 2007.

53 Terese Loeb Kreuzer, "Old South Ferry Subway Station to Reopen Next Month," *Downtown Express*, March 12, 2013; Dan Rivoli, "Renovated South Ferry Station Reopens after Hurricane Sandy Shuttered It for Nearly Five Years," *Daily News*, June 27, 2017.

54 Habersham, interview with the author.

55 Office of the State Comptroller, *Financial Outlook*, 14–15.

56 Eyewitness News ABC7NY, "30 Percent MTA Fare Hike? Cuomo Says Could Happen without Congestion Pricing," WABC-TV Channel 7 *Eyewitness News*, YouTube video, 2:01, February 8, 2019, https://www.youtube.com/watch?v=DyuwJ8pJEa0; Emma G. Fitzsimmons, "Cuomo Warns of a 30 Percent Fare Hike If Congestion Pricing Fails," *New York Times*, February 7, 2019; Laura Bliss, "How New York Finally Passed Congestion Pricing," City Lab, March 27, 2019, https://www.citylab.com/transpor tation/2019/03/congestion-pricing-nyc-travel-tips-subway-manhattan-driving/585781.

57   "Mayor Now Weighs Long Term Financing to Save on Subways," *New York Times*, July 18, 1932; Fiorello La Guardia, "Text of Mayor La Guardia's Message to the New City Council at Its First Meeting," *New York Times*, January 6, 1944; Edward C. Burks, "Beame Trims Plans for New Subway," *New York Times*, March 21, 1975; "New York's David Yunich," *Railway Age*, October 11, 1976, 16–18.

Page numbers in *italics* indicate maps and illustrations. Numbers followed by *n* refer to endnotes.

Abrams, Robert, 59
accessibility, 168, 234, 257
accountability, 218, 234, 238–40, 259
acoustics, 168–69, 214. *See also* noise
  mitigation
advertisements, 42, 155, 189–90
advocacy, 141–55, 189–91, 205, 266
advocacy groups, 58–59. *See also* Automotive
  Club of New York; Citizens Budget
  Commission; Citizens Transit Committee;
  City Club of New York; Empire State
  Transportation Alliance; Greater New
  York Safety Council; Guardian Angels;
  Metropolitan Housewives' League;
  Natural Resources Defense Council; New
  York Roadway Improvement Coalition;
  Regional Plan Association (RPA);
  Second Avenue Business Association;
  Straphangers Campaign
aesthetics, 227
affirmative action, 258
air-conditioning, 62, 75–76
air pollution, 129, 205, 213–14
Albert, Andrew, 235
Allen, Woody, 80
ambitions, 49–72
American Airlines, 94
American Express, 2
American Federation of Labor, 36–37
American Labor Party, 38

Amtrak, 102, 182, 262
Anderson, Warren, 110, 114
Appleton, Albert (Al), 146–47
architecture, 168–69
artwork, 169, 236, 241–42, *245*, 257
asbestos, 254
Astoria, 148
automated (electronic) fare cards, 117–18,
  128–29, 142, 265
automobiles: congestion pricing, 266–67,
  275; traffic congestion, 17, 28, 129,
  134; traffic management, 14, 20, 22,
  45–47, 50, 55, 201–2, 213, 263.
  See also highways
Automotive Club of New York, 146

Bananas, 80
Barone, Richard, 253
BART, 262–63
Bass, Richard, 212
Beame, Abe, 45–46, 56, 70–71, 81–84,
  89–93, 97, 180–81, 268
Beame Shuffle, 91
Beijing, China, 5
Bellamy, Carol, 112
Bianco, Carmen, 216–17
Big Dig, 172
blasting and explosives, 210, 213–16, *215*
Bloomberg, Michael, 181–82, 189, 195,
  212, 223

BMT (Brooklyn–Manhattan Transit
    Corporation), 14, 20, 32
Board of Estimate, 33–38, 64–66, 161
Board of Transportation, 16, 20, 34–36, 42,
    42–43, 60–61
bonds: long-term, 70–71; municipal,
    54, 82–85, 90, 157–58; performance
    and payments, 196; short-term, 84;
    transportation, 45–46, 56–60, 63, 69,
    73–74, 80–82, 92, 108, 111, 114, 155,
    158–59, 188–91, 266; underwriting
    fees, 158
Boston, Massachusetts, 172
Boylan, Chris, 162, 176, 192
bridges, 21, 108. *See also* Tappan Zee Bridge;
    Triborough Bridge and Tunnel Authority
    (TBTA)
Brodsky, Richard, 182
Broer, Steve, 213
Bronx, 18, 40, 42, 56, 63, 67–68, 86, 106,
    132–33, 178, 199
Bronx Board of Trade, 18
Brooklyn, 15, 18, 27, 40, 42, 51, 56, 62–63,
    86–87, 138, 146, 195
Brooklyn Daily Eagle, 42
Brooklyn Rapid Transit Company (BRT),
    13–14
Brooklyn–Battery Tunnel, 61
Brooklyn–Manhattan Transit Corporation
    (BMT), 14, 20, 32
Brown, Henry Collins, 14–15
BRT (Brooklyn Rapid Transit Company),
    13–14
Buckley, James, 94
bureaucracy, 128–32, 209, 240, 259
bus lanes, 140
buses, 44–45, 98, 134, 142, 226
business owners, 94, 204–6
Buy America rules, 258

Caemmerer, John D., 104, 114
Cafiero, Peter, 124–25, 129–31, 146–47,
    153–55, 163, 174–76, 179, 194, 243;
    *Manhattan East Side Transit Alternatives
    Study*, 132–43, 152, 161
Calvanico, Alphonse, 238–39
Cantaloup Kids, 205
Carey, Hugh, 86–90, 98–99, 105, 109–114,
    116, 123
Caro, Robert, 41
carpenters' union, 256
Carter, Jimmy, 104, 107
Castelbuono, A. J., 159
CBS, 241

cell phone service, 227, 251
Chambers Street station, 269
Chase Manhattan Bank, 57, 59–60
Chicago, Illinois, 2
Chicago Transit Authority, 115
Chinatown, 269, 274
Chrystie Street (Manhattan), 51
Citizens Budget Commission, 44, 228
Citizens Transit Committee, 32
City Club of New York, 17
City University, 89, 94
climate change issues, 217, 264–65
Clinton, Hillary, 159
Cohen, Alexander, 81
collective bargaining, 118
Colt Industries, 94
communication systems, 233–34, 250–51
Communist Party, 36, 38
Community Board 8, 204–9
community relations, 78, 87, 209–214
Con Edison, 13, 197, 199, 217, 236–39
Coney Island, 118
Coney Island Creek, 177
congestion pricing, 5, 266–67, 275
construction: cut-and-cover, 77–78, 169,
    198–99; tunnel boring, 169, 198, 200,
    253, 256
construction costs, 4, 6, 11, 19, 39, 42, 44,
    47, 51, 61, 63, 141, 148, 152 169–73,
    196–97, 214, 217–18, 252–60, 265
construction unions, 254–57
consulting services, 195–96
Conway, Virgil, 135–39, 142–44, 149–50,
    154–57, 187
corporate taxes, 113
corruption, 28–29, 40–41, 224
cost effectiveness, 131, 139, 163, 172–76
cost estimates. *See* construction costs
Cotton, Rick, 227, 229, 237, 261
countdown clocks, 227, 251
crane oilers, 256
crime, 101, 105, 121–22, 135, 141
crowding. *See* New York City subway:
    passenger conditions
Crowe, Eddie, 204
Cuomo, Andrew, 116, 205, 218, 221–45,
    245, 252, 266–68; key dates, 275;
    priorities, 227–29, 249, 251; tactics, 239
Cuomo, Madeline, 205
Cuomo, Mario, 116, 157, 223
#CuomosMTA, 252
customer-friendly initiatives, 228
cut-and-cover construction, 77–78, 169,
    198–99

Daily News, 39, 90, 178–79, 225, 251–52
D'Amato, Alfonse, 120–21, 137–38, 141
de Blasio, Bill, 224–26, 252
deadlines, 229, 236, 240
Dean, Jack, 161
deception, 41–48, 62–63, 68–69, 71, 74, 84, 88
Del Giudice, Michael, 116
DeMatteo, Salvatore, 233–34, 236–38
Democratic Party, 28–29, 36–37, 41, 192–93
derailments, 100, 110, 251–52
design issues, 165–71, 190–93, 196, 217, 236, 241; costs of, 260–61; tile colors, 226
DeThomasis, Bob, 239–40
Dewey, Thomas, 32–33, 45
Dicker, Fred, 226
disadvantaged business enterprises, 258
DiScala, Todd, 146–47; *Manhattan East Side Transit Alternatives Study*, 132–43, 152, 161
DMJM Harris/Arup, 166, 180, 196
Doctoroff, Dan, 4, 183
Dorn, Jennifer, 188
Douglass, Bob, 54
Dow Jones Industrial Average, 141
Downey, Mort, 176, 193
Downtown-Lower Manhattan Association, 51, 61, 63
dust control, 199, 203–5, 210–16, 257

easements, 170
East Harlem, 106, 133, 142, 151, 171, 260–62, 274
East Midtown, 133
East River tunnel, 121
East Side, 3, 15, 49–51, 178–79; *Manhattan East Side Transit Alternatives Study*, 132–43, 152, 161; Master Links plan, 138. *See also* East Village; Lower East Side; Upper East Side
East Side Access. *See* Grand Central Terminal: Long Island Rail Road connection
East Village, 93, 274
economic development, 112, 129, 183–85
economic recession, 84, 208, 223
edifice complex, 62
E. E. Cruz & Company, 258–59
Eighth Avenue subway, 18, 23, 87
Eisenhower, Dwight, 164–65
electrical power, 13, 236–37
electricians, 69, 235, 255

electronic (automated) fare cards, 117–18, 128–29, 142, 265
electronic signs, 6, 233–34, 263
electronics maintenance, 250–51
elevated lines (Els), 10–13, *12*, 19–24
elevators, 249, 256
emergency, state of, 110, 249–52, 266–67
eminent domain, 170
emissions monitoring, 214
Empire State Transportation Alliance, 144–48, 152–55, 158–60, 188–89
energy crisis, 83
Engel, Eliot, 193
engineering, 165–71, 180
environmental analysis, 176–80
environmental impact statements, 130–31, 140–41, 155, 177–78, 180
environmental issues, 78, 120, 130, 213–14
Environmental Protection Agency (EPA), 213–14
equipment, 43–45, 70, 216–17, 263
escalators, 50–51, 75–76, 169, 237, 240, 248–49
Esnard, Robert, 120
evacuations, 70

false expectations: about federal funding, 74, 88; about low fares, 13, 40; about transportation improvements, 1–3, 7, 13, 59, 182, 267. *See also* deception
fan plants, 195
fare cards, electronic (automated), 117–18, 128–29, 142, 265
fares, 5, 13–14, 19, 32–34, 68–71, 114; efforts to avoid hikes, 36–39, 90–94, 97, 102–3, 109, 155–57, 181, 249, 267; false expectations for low fares, 13, 40; half-fare programs, 106; increases, 39, 43, 94, 105, 113, 117, 186; student discounts, 79; two-fare zones, 142
Farley Post Office building, 182–83
Federal Communications Commission (FCC), 37
federal funding, 31–32, 52, 56, 68–74, 84, 107–8, 115, 120, 130, 143, 148, 187; applications for, 151–52, 171–76; Beame Shuffle, 91; competition for, 142–43, 160; false expectations, 74, 88; New Starts, 160–62, 172–76, 182, 188, 192–93, 226; requirements for, 66, 160, 258; for Second Avenue subway, 93, 193, 241; for Westway, 111–12
Federal Reserve of New York, 110

Federal Transit Administration (FTA), 131, 152, 160, 224, 258; key dates, 275; New Starts program, 160–62, 172–76, 182, 188, 192–93, 226
Ferrante, Carol, 179
Fialkoff, Sheldon, 144, 167
Fields, C. Virginia, 150–51
financing public transportation, 3, 6–7, 84, 112, 238–39. *See also* bonds; federal funding
Fink, Stanley, 114, *123*
fire(s), 82, 110, 121, 251, 265
fire-protection systems, 234, 248
fire-safety standards, 248, 257
First Avenue (Manhattan), 140, 208
First Avenue Association, 22
Fisher, Harold, 98–99, 102, 104
flooding, 217, 264–65, *268*
floor space, 51, 125. *See also* New York City subway: passenger conditions
Ford, Gerald, 86, 89–91
Freitas, Julie, 216
Frommer's, 230
FTA. *See* Federal Transit Administration
Fulton Street Transit Center, 168, 174–75, 180–81, 185

Gardner, Ralph, Jr., 242
garment industry, 17
gentrification, 21–23, 147–48
geological differences, 78, 197
German immigrants, 197–98
Gimbels, 85
Giuliani, Rudy, 130, 135, 148, 154–55, 164, 182
goal setting, 218, 227, 240
Godey, John, 80
Goldberger, Paul, 102
Goldman Sachs, 2
Goldmark, Peter, 93–94
Goldsmith, Steven, 212–13
good repair, state of, 107–110, 186–87, 195, 228–30, 252, 263
Goodman, Roy, 67, 149–50
Gopstein, Doron, 179
Gothamist, 252
Gouletas, Evangeline, 112–13
Gracie Mansion, 212
graffiti, 70, *95*, 97, 100, 119, *122*
Grand Central subway station, 11, 125, 133–34, 154, 260
Grand Central Terminal, 17, 46–49, *48*, 133–34; Long Island Rail Road connection, 131–32, 138–43, 153–55,

180–81, 186–88, 191–95, 218, 229, 260–62; Master Links plan, 138; Penn Station connection, 182
Grannis, Pete, 151–52
Great Depression, 19–20
Greater New York Safety Council, 50
Green, Bill, 121
Green, Mark, 154
Green Guerillas, 106
Griffin, Kenneth, 168–69
Gross, Charles, 31, 36
Guardian Angels, 101
Gunn, David, 117–18, 128

Habersham, Wynton, 216, 250
Hall, Peter, 262–63
Harkness, LeRoy T., 14
Hearst, William Randolph, 14
Heastie, Carl, 226
heat detectors, 234
heat issues, 168, 265
Heckscher, Ben, *127*, *200*, *201*, 211
Hellcat fighter planes, 23
Herald Tribune, 39
Hewitt, Abram, 11
highways, 21, 31–34, 45–47, 50–52, 129–30, 180. *See also specific highways*
history: before WWII, 10–26; 1940s and 1950s, 27–48; 1960s–1972 ambitions, 49–72; 1970s and 1980s (saving the subway), 96–123; 1972–76 (construction), 73–95; 1990s (planning), 124–56; 2000–2005 (twenty-first-century subway), 157–91; 2006–14 (construction), 192–220; 2015–16 (Cuomo's finish line), 221–45; key dates, 273–75; turning points, 266–68
homelessness, 128
Horodniceanu, Michael, 197–98, 202, 205, 208–212, 214, 217–18, 220, 229, 234, 237, 240, *245*, 255
Hudson River Tunnel, 181–82, 191, 262
Hunter College, 209
Hurricane Sandy, 217, 223, 251–52, 265, *268*
Hylan, John, 14, 16–17, 59, 266–67, 273

Impellitteri, Vincent, 41, 44, 47
Independent (IND) subway, 16–20, 266
inflation, 63, 87
information centers, 210, 262
information screens, 228
Interborough Rapid Transit Company (IRT), 11–14, 20, 32

Iranian Revolution, 103
IRT (Interborough Rapid Transit Company),
    11–14, 20, 32

Jacob Ruppert Brewing Company, 198
Javits, Jacob, 94–95
JFK Airport, 86–87
Jlelaty, Alaeden, 196, 198, 201–2, 235, 260
Johnson, Lyndon B., 89
Joseph, Lazarus, 41, 44
J train, 163

Kalikow, Peter, 159–60, 163–65, 171–74,
    180, 185–90, 193–94, 202
Keith, John, 92
Kennedy International Airport, 65, 181
Kheel, Theodore, 83–84
Kiley, Robert, 117–18, 128–29, 143, 158, 266
Kirchner, Chuck, 124
Koch, Edward (Ed), 91, 99, 103–4, 110–16,
    119, 122–23
Kone, 237

La Guardia, Fiorello, 19–23, 26, 27–32, 67,
    91, 266, 268
labor costs, 35, 81, 98, 235, 255
labor strikes, 56, 105–6
labor unions, 34, 118, 154–55, 166, 235,
    249, 254–57
Laborers' Local Union No. 147 (sandhogs),
    215–16
LaGuardia Airport: subway extension to,
    148, 153–55, 182, 191, 222, 229
Lapp, Katie, 180
Lazio, Rick, 159
leadership, 6–7, 94, 266
LED lights, 227–28
legislation, 113, 130
LeMus, Pablo, 236
Levitt, Arthur, 81
Lexington Avenue subway, 3, 23, 75;
    construction, 25; express tracks,
    125; express trains, 134; on-time
    performance, 251; passenger conditions,
    51, 133–34, 225–26, 251; platforms,
    50–51; ridership, 21, 85, 142, 247; "Step
    Aside, Speed Your Ride" program, 139;
    ten-car trains, 50–51; before WWII,
    11–16, 21
Lhota, Joe, 217, 251–52
Liberal Party, 38
Lichtensteiger, Frank, 85–86
lighting, 50–51, 99, 228

Lindsay, John, 53, 53–60, 68–71, 79–80,
    83, 89, 93, 160; Second Avenue subway
    groundbreaking (October 1972), 73–74,
    82, 95
lobbying, 109–110, 114–15, 149–52,
    187–88, 230, 266
London, England, 2, 97–98
Long Island, 51, 181
Long Island Rail Road, 54–55, 59–60, 131,
    142–43; 63rd Street tunnel, 120–21,
    125; extensions, 63, 82, 96, 120; Grand
    Central connection, 131–32, 138–43,
    153–55, 180–81, 186–88, 191–95, 218,
    229, 260–62; labor strikes, 105–6; Master
    Links plan, 138; Penn Station concourse,
    228; rehabilitation costs, 68; ridership, 55
Long Island Sound, 59–60, 66
Lower East Side, 64–65, 65, 106, 133, 151
Lower Manhattan, 1–2, 133, 164, 181, 265
Lower Manhattan Access Study, 138–39,
    162–63
Lower Manhattan Development
    Corporation, 1–2
Lower Manhattan Expressway, 50, 52–53, 66
Lower Manhattan Rail Link, 1, 2, 181–82,
    185–86, 191
Lunden, Glenn, 124

Madison, Tom, 190
maintenance workers, 69, 100
Maloney, Carolyn, 147–51, 154, 162, 178,
    192–93, 204–5
Manhattan, 17; central business district
    (CBD), 49–50, 64, 267; Community
    Board 8, 204–9; elevated railroads (Els),
    10; Lower Manhattan, 1–2, 133, 164,
    181, 265; manufacturing sector, 49; map,
    8; Master Links plan, 138; neighborhoods
    that would be served by a Second Avenue
    subway, 9; parking spaces, 50
Manhattan Chamber of Commerce, 212–13
*Manhattan East Side Transit Alternatives
    Study*, 132–43, 152, 161
manufacturing, 49, 71, 279n21
mass transportation, 62, 194. *See also* public
    transportation
Master Links, 138
master mechanics, 255–56
McClellan, George, 73
MCTA (Metropolitan Commuter
    Transportation Authority), 55–58. *See also*
    Metropolitan Transportation Authority
    (MTA)

media relations, 3, 6, 80, 188, 204, 208, 212, 241–42, 267
megaprojects, 58, 131–32, 180–85, *184*, 262–63. *See also* Farley Post Office; Grand Central Terminal: Long Island Rail Road connection; Hudson River Tunnel; LaGuardia Airport: subway extension to; Lower Manhattan Rail Link; Metro-North Railroad: expansion plans; PATH (Port Authority Trans-Hudson); Second Avenue subway; Seven Line extension
Melnick, Jon, 124, 128
Memorial Sloan Kettering Cancer Center, 203
Merrill Lynch, 2
Messinger, Ruth, 139–40
Metro-North Railroad, 131; expansion plans, 138, 141
MetroCards, 128–29, 142, 265
MetroLink, 146–48
Metropolitan Commuter Transportation Authority (MCTA), 55–58. *See also* Metropolitan Transportation Authority (MTA)
Metropolitan Hospital, 67–68
Metropolitan Housewives' League, 17
Metropolitan Transportation: A Program for Action, 62
Metropolitan Transportation Authority (MTA): bidding process, 259; board of directors, 59, 160–61, 226–27, 230–31, 241, 252, 310n79; bonds, 108, 114, 157–58; bureaucracy, 259; capital projects, 5, 81, 102–118, 121–24, 129–30, 139, 143, 153–58, *156*, 185–88, 195, 224–26, 230–31, 263, 274; community relations, 207–212, 214, 262, 275; creation, 58–60, 70, 73–74, 266; debt, 108, 122, 157, 185–86, 249; deficits, 69; expansion projects, 61–63, 68, 74, 86–87, 102, 195; expenses, 69, 251–52; financial health, 68–69, 79–80, 108–9, 114, 122, 142, 148, 172, 185–86; forecasts, 131–32; funding, 63–64, 74, 99, 115, 120, 130, 158, 161, 172, 185–86, 190, 192–93, 225; key dates, 274; Lower Manhattan Access Study, 138–39, 162–63; media relations, 212, 222; megaprojects, 131–32, 180; *Metropolitan Transportation: A Program for Action* (1968), 62; needs assessment, 107, 122; newsletters, 212; operating budget, 81, 91, 185–86, 223; operating costs, 98, 186, 231; organizational problems, 117; oversight, 161; pension obligations, 84;

physical network, 108; planning efforts, 60, 62, 75–79, 131–32, 137, 174, 194–95, 243, 266; priorities, 164; project labor agreements, 256; property acquisitions, 170; real estate-related expenses, 253–54; ridership, 102, 172, 231; scope of authority, 5–6, 60; transformation, 117–22
Mid-Manhattan Expressway, 50, 66
Miller, Gifford, 140
minority-owned contractors, 258
modernization, 31, 43–46, 50, 75–79, 99, 104, 228, 263, 265
Monroe, Marilyn, 168
Moody's, 82
Morgan, J. P., 22
Morgan, Stephen, 189
mortgage taxes, 68–69
Moscow, Russia, 2, 75
Moses, Robert, 21, *26*, 28–35, 41–44, 47, 50, 55–60, 82, 130, 206
Moynihan, Daniel Patrick, 120
MTA. *See* Metropolitan Transportation Authority
MTA Capital Construction Company, 180, 195–99, 207–216, 235–37
MTA Capital Program Review Board, 148, 154–55, 187
muck houses, 199, *200*, 203, 211
municipal bonds, 54, 82–85, 90, 157–58. *See also* bonds
municipal taxes, 71–72. *See also* taxes
Muniz, Vik, 245
Murdoch, Rupert, 153
Museum of Modern Art, 241

Nadler, Jerrold, 182
Nagaraja, Mysore, 118, 165–76, 180, 194–96, 199, 207, 218, 256, 259, 262
Namako, Tom, 206, 212
National Institute for Standards and Technology, 258
National Mass Transportation Assistance Act, 91
Native Americans, 177
Natural Resources Defense Council, 103
NBC, 241
New Deal, 20–21
A New Direction in Transit, 103, 107
New Haven Railroad, 49, 54
New Jersey Transit, 167, 182, 262
New Starts, 160–62, 172–76, 182, 188, 192–93, 226
New York Central Railroad, 49, 54

New York City, New York, 21; 42nd Street, 112; 63rd Street tunnel, 120–21, 125; annual budget, 80; Board of Estimate, 33–38, 64–66, 161; Board of Transportation, 16, 20, 34–36, 42, 42–43, 60–61; Budget Department, 66; bus lanes, 140; capital projects, 31, 43–45, 70–71, 81, 84, 91–92, 97; Chinatown, 274; Chrystie Street, 51; concerns for the future, 4–5; congestion pricing, 266–67, 275; construction costs, 254; contributions to MTA, 161; crime, 141; debt burden, 19–20, 41, 71, 84–85, 90; Department of Sanitation, 212–13; Department of Transportation, 66, 103, 263; East Harlem, 106, 133, 142, 151, 171, 260–62, 274; East Midtown, 133; East Side, 3, 15, 49–51, 133–34, 178–79; East Village, 93, 274; economy, 56, 81, 88–90, 93–94; federal funding, 31–32, 91; financial health, 30–32, 70, 88–90, 93–94; First Avenue, 140, 208; garment industry, 17; highways, 47, 50, 129–30; infrastructure needs, 150; labor force, 89; labor unions, 254–57; Lower East Side, 64–65, 65, 106, 133, 151; Lower Manhattan, 1–2, 133, 164, 181, 265; Manhattan, 8; manufacturing, 49, 71, 279n21; municipal bonds, 54, 82–85, 90, 157–58; municipal expenses, 31–32; municipal taxes, 71–72; O'Dwyer administration, 39–40, 45; office space, 49; operating budget, 31, 70–71, 84; Planning Commission, 30, 41, 52; Planning Department, 64, 66, 103; population, 13, 30, 49, 98, 106, 205; property crime, 141; public works, 31; regulation of fees, 13; Second Avenue, 140, 235, 243, 254, 258; skyscrapers, 13; tax burden, 89; Third Avenue, 208; Times Square, 8, 66, 81, 112, 125, 135; transit services, 55, 80, 275; transportation policy, 55; Union Square, 125; Upper East Side, 21, 47–50, 67, 106, 133, 151, 160, 179, 204–8, 211, 228, 253–54; utility maps, 78–79; violent crime, 141; vulnerability to rising sea levels, 264–65; Wall Street, 114; Water Street, 51, 61; West 4th Street, 125; West Side, 181; Whitehall Street station, 76, 77; before WWII, 10–24

New York City subway, 27–28, 31–32; accidents, 70; air-conditioning, 62, 75–76; automatic train stops, 100–101;

BMT lines, 20; cars and equipment, 168; Chambers Street station, 269; communication systems, 250–51; conditions, 27–28, 28, 67, 99, 125, 147, 228–30; construction, 11, 15–19, 73; construction costs (see construction costs); deficit, 32, 80, 98–105; delays, 101, 110, 251; depth below ground, 77; derailments, 100, 110, 251–52; description of, 27–28; design issues, 165–71; deterioration, 68–72, 80, 97, 102, 249, 251–52; Eighth Avenue line, 18, 23, 87; expansion projects, 5–7, 41–44, 62, 68, 96, 120, 188, 249; fan plants, 195; fare cards, 117–18, 128–29, 142, 265; financial health, 35, 41, 43; fires, 82, 110, 121, 251, 265; first line, 11, 73; flooding, 217, 264–65, 268; Fulton Street station, 168; funding, 11, 52, 97; groundbreaking ceremony (October 1904), 73; hours of operation, 97–98; IND trains, 20; infrastructure, 263; IRT lines, 20; J train, 163; labor strikes, 105–6; Lexington Avenue line (see Lexington Avenue subway); maintenance, 35, 43–44, 99–101, 106–7, 167, 249–52; modernization, 99, 228; MTA plan, 75–79; N line, 163; needs estimates, 97; number 1 line, 163; number 7 line, 120, 148, 181–83, 190–91, 195, 229, 236; number 9 line, 163; operating costs, 19, 43, 79; operations, 45; passenger conditions, 14–17, 27–28, 28, 36–38, 51, 70, 99–101, 125, 133–34, 145, 149, 154–55, 225–26, 251; performance, 70, 251; pricing system, 97–98 (see also fares); Queens Boulevard line, 62; R line, 163; relays, 100–101; restoration to a state of good repair, 107–110, 186–87, 195, 228–30; ridership, 14, 19, 43, 50, 69, 79, 98, 142, 145, 154, 161, 172–73, 185–86, 278n12; routes, 97–98; service interruptions, 70; signal system, 195, 263–64; Sixth Avenue line, 19, 23; South Ferry station, 265; state of emergency, 110, 249–52, 266–67; state of good repair, 107, 228, 252, 263; stations, 99; subsidies, 35, 45, 79, 83, 104, 111; subway cars and equipment, 43–45, 62, 70, 95, 96, 99–100, 108, 121, 122, 177, 216–18, 236–37, 263; suggestions for staying safe, 101; super subway, 52; support for, 46–47; Times Square station, 25; track circuits, 100–101; track conditions, 100, 117, 121; track miles, 24; track reports, 117;

New York City subway (*continued*)
track switches, 100–101; transfers
between buses and subways, 142;
travel time, 133; upgrades, 5–7, 35, 99;
ventilation system, 168; World Trade
Center station, 163, *164*; before WWII,
11–15; Z train, 163
New York City Transit Authority (now NYC
Transit), 45–47, 50–52, 56–59, 64, 70,
90–91, 96–97, 127, 131, 274. *See also*
New York City subway; NYC Transit
New York Eye and Ear Infirmary, 177
New York Hospital, 68
New York Jets, 181
New York Post, 153, 155, 179, 182, 194, 206,
212, 225, 252
New York Roadway Improvement
Coalition, 189
New York State: budget, 93, 148, 155,
226; congressional delegation, 192–93;
economy, 88–89; federal funding, 56,
68, 193; highest-priority infrastructure
projects, 193; legislation, 113–14; Office
of Transit Construction Commissioner,
15; transportation needs, 103–4
New York State Assembly, 32–33, 103–4
New York State Constitution, 39, 41–43,
42, 46
New York State Senate, 32–33
New York State Thruway, 47
New York Telephone Company, 94
New York Times, 39–40, 62, 66, 148,
152–53, 251
New York Tribune, 11
New York University, 188
New Yorker, 116
Newark Airport, 191
Newsday, 150
Ninth Avenue El, *12*, 23
Nixon, Richard, 68, 74–75, 84–86, 94, *94*, 105
noise mitigation, 79, 168–69, 199, 202–3,
205, 211, 213, 257
NYC Transit, 155; capacity problems,
134; capital improvements, 225; capital
program, 218; community relations,
207–8; coordination with MTA, 217;
Department of Subways, 250–51; design
issues, 236; funding, 223; *Manhattan East
Side Transit Alternatives Study*, 132–43,
152, 161; modernization, 228; resource
allocations for Second Avenue subway,
250–51; "Step Aside, Speed Your Ride"
program, 139; testing procedures, 233,

248, 250; vulnerable tunnels, 265. *See also*
New York City subway

O'Dwyer, William, 30–45, 59, 267, 273
oil crisis, 83–85, 87
Olivieri, Antonio, 67
Olmsted, Alan, 243
Olmsted, Bob, 60–62, 66, 92–93, 97, 125,
146, 167; death, 243; groundbreaking
ceremony (March 2007), 194; MTA
expansion plan, 137, 174, 194–95,
243, 266
Olmsted, Frederick Law, 61
Olympic Games, 181, 183, 190
operating engineers' union, 256
Our Town, 85–86

Paaswell, Robert, 149
Palace of the Soviets (Moscow), 2
Paris Metro, 97–98
parking spaces, 28, 50, 52, 56, 140
parks, 21, 29
Parsons Brinckerhoff, 196, 236
Partnership for New York City, 5, 183–85,
184
Pataki, George, 1, 135–43, 147, 152,
157–59, 162, 174, 181–82, 187, 274
Paterson, David, 195, 204, 223
PATH (Port Authority Trans-Hudson),
181, 191
Patterson, Charles, 47–48, 96
Pecora, Joe, 204
pedestrian safety, 201–4, 209, 213, 265. *See
also* New York City subway: passenger
conditions
peer pressure, 238–39
Penn Station, 17, 138, 182, 191, 228
pensions, 69–70, 84
Perkins, Roswell, 57
Phillips, Don, 197
Pickrell, Don, 130–31
plagues, 201–6
planning, 164–65; from the bottom up,
124–56; MTA efforts, 60, 62, 75–79,
131–32, 137, 174, 194–95, 243, 266
playgrounds, 21
Ploeger, Nancy, 212–13
Plotkin, Ed, 197, 204–5
plumbers, 255
Polan, Steve, 115
police corruption, 40–41
political interests, 1–2, 6, 58, 62, 86–87,
109–116, 189, 224, 267–68

political leadership, 6, 94, 268
Port Authority of New York and New Jersey, 159, 262
Port Authority Trans-Hudson (PATH), 181, 191
Porto, Michael, 211
power plants, 44
Prendergast, Tom, 223–24, 227–31, 234, 237–38, 245, 249, 264
private property, 169–70, 178–79
productivity, 118, 255–56
project labor agreements, 256
project management, 118, 166, 196, 232
property crime, 141
property takings, 170, 178–79
property values, 254
protests, 154–55
Pryor, Stefan, 1–2
public address systems, 168–69, 234
public hearings, 36–38, 57, 66–68, 145, 149–50, 153, 178
public opinion, 6, 147, 152–55, 178, 205
public relations, 42, 109–110, 117–18, 155, 188
public transportation, 54–56, 83–84, 194; false expectations about improvements, 1–3, 7, 13, 40, 59, 74, 88, 182, 267; federal funding for (see federal funding); planning efforts, 58–62, 74–80, 87–88, 96–97, 120–21, 124–56, 164–65, 174, 194–95, 241, 243, 266; votes for, 185–91. See also specific services; specific systems
public waiting and toilet rooms, 17
public works projects, 21, 28, 31
publicity, 1–2, 6
Pushkarev, Boris, 67, 93, 120

Q train, 5
quality assurance, 248
Queens, 16, 18, 22–23, 51–52, 56, 61–63, 82, 86–87, 91, 121, 127, 138, 182, 255
Queens Boulevard, 62
Quill, Michael, 34

radiator assemblies, 117
rapid transit, 31, 43. See also specific systems and lines
Ravitch, Richard, 105–117, 122, 123, 128, 143, 149–50, 158, 223, 225, 231, 266
Ravitz, John, 151–52
Reagan, Ronald, 107–8, 112, 115
real estate, 22, 71–72, 142, 190–91, 253–54
Regional Plan Association (RPA), 112, 132, 195, 266; advocacy efforts, 92–93,

144–48, 152–55, 160, 183–85, 225; projections, 66–67, 125; transportation proposals, 20, 52–53, 58, 120, 146–48, 252–53
regulations, 13, 130–31, 141, 168, 176–78, 229, 257–59, 261
Reid, William, 40
repair, good: state of, 107–110, 186–87, 195, 228–30, 252, 263
Republican Party, 40, 45, 192–93
retailers, 204, 208
Reuter, Larry, 236
Rockefeller, David, 51, 53, 60, 110
Rockefeller, Nelson, 160, 266–67; as governor of New York, 53, 53–62, 69, 73–75, 80–81, 83, 86–87, 89, 94–95; and Nixon, 74–75, 94, 94, 105; presidential campaign, 62, 72; Second Avenue subway groundbreaking (October 1972), 73–74, 95; transportation plans, 58–60, 62, 241; transportation referendums, 69, 80–81
Rockefeller University, 68
Rolling Stone, 112
Ronan, William (Bill), 54–66, 80–82, 94, 130–31, 160, 171, 218, 266; Second Avenue subway groundbreaking (October 1972), 74, 82; support for, 78, 96; transportation plan, 74, 79–80, 87–88, 96–97, 120–21
Roosevelt, Franklin D., 20, 31
Rostenkowski, Dan, 115
RPA. See Regional Plan Association
Ruppert Towers, 85
Russianoff, Gene, 145, 149, 155, 158, 186, 194, 224
Ruth, Babe, 198
Ryan, Jim, 173

safety issues, 101, 168, 205, 224, 228, 231, 234, 248, 257
safety officers, 248
salaries and wages, 35, 40, 43, 56, 69, 225, 235
sales taxes, 32–33, 113
Sam Schwartz Engineering, 209
Sander, Lee, 143–45, 160, 166, 188, 193–95, 204, 266
sandhogs (Laborers' Local Union No. 147), 215–16
Sandler, Ross, 103, 115–16
Sara D. Roosevelt Park, 177
Satterlee, Louisa Pierpont, 22
Saturday Evening Post, 27–28

Schattanek, Guido, 205, 213–14
Schneider, Barry, 204, 206–7, 209, 211, 242
Schoenbrod, David, 103
Schrag, Zachary, 102
Schumer, Chuck, 120, 181–82
Schwartz, Larry, 226–27, 237
Schwartz, Sam, 209–213
sea levels, 264–65
Second Avenue (Manhattan), 140, 235, 243, 254, 258
Second Avenue Business Association, 204
Second Avenue cough, 213–14
Second Avenue El, 3, 10, *12*, 13, 21–23, *24*, *48*, 273
Second Avenue subway: 63rd Street station, 125–26, *127*, 242; 72nd Street station, 67, *171*, *200*, 217, *219*, 239, 242, *245*; 86th Street station, *219*, 242, 249; 96th Street station, 68, 169, 196–99, 242, *244*, 248–49, 258; 116th Street station, 171; 125th Street station, 260; advocacy for, 141–55, 187, 189–91, 266; ambitions for, 49–72; approval, 155, 193, 266; artwork, 169, 236, 241–42, *245*, 257; Bronx portion, 132–33; communication systems, 233; community impacts, 262; community relations, 205–216, 262; computer model, 136–37; concern for the future, 4–5; construction (1972–76), 73–95, *95*, 274; construction (2006–14), 192–220, *199–201*, *215*, *219–20*, 275; construction (2015–16), 221–45; construction costs, 4, 6–7, 27, 42, 47, 74, 214, 247, 252–65, 274–75, 293n5; construction failure, 120–21; construction phases, 6–7, 153–54, 173–75, *175*, 218, 253–54, 274–75; construction schedule, 86–87, 160, 171, 174, 180, 186, 190, 218, 226, 235–36; cost effectiveness, 162, 173; cost estimates, 44, 61, 63, 68–69, 74, 87–88, 102, 141, 152, 171–72, 183–85, 217–18, 252–53; delays, 44, 165, 247–69; depth below ground, 77, 169–70; design issues, 165–71, 180, 190, 192–93, 196, 217, 241, 260–61; electronic signs, 233; elevators, 249; environmental impact analysis, 176–80; environmental impact statements, 141, 178, 180, 192–93; escalators, 237, 248–49; extension, 63, 66, 195, 225; first day of service, 242; first phase, 3–4, 6, 118, 140, 153–54, 229, *261*, 262, 264, 266, 275; first train, *245*; fourth phase, 262; funding, 3, 6–7, 27,
34–38, 44–46, 68–69, 74, 93, 161–62, 186, 193, 224–26, 229, 235, 241, 262, 275, 293n5; groundbreaking ceremony (March 2007), 194, 202; groundbreaking ceremony (October 1972), 73–74, 82, 95; information center, 210, 262; interim operating segments, 174; interior finishes, 239; key dates, 273–75; leaks, 248; lessons learned, 266–68; Lower East Side loop (cuphandle), 66, 86–87; Lower Manhattan stations, 165; maintenance requirements, 167; *Manhattan East Side Transit Alternatives Study* for, 132–43, 152, 161; media coverage, 241–42; near-mythical status, 2–4, 115; need for, 40, 165; neighborhoods served by, 9; O'Dwyer's promise, 38–43; plans for, 18–19, 58–62, 75–79, 124–56, *126*, *156*; problems after opening, 248–52; promises, 27–48; proposal, 128, 153; public hearings, 66–67; resurrection, 124, 155; ridership, 172, 228, 247, 277n7; route, 132–33, 153; safety officers, 248; second phase, 224–25, 229, 260, *261*, 262; signal system, 264; snob express, 65; stations, 4, 67, *76*, 140, 169–71, 179, 257, 262, 281n46; stubway, 4, 150, 153–54, *156*, 174; support for, 34, 47, 93, 135, 137, 140, 144–45, 147, 149, 151–54, 159–60, 162–63, 178, 192–93; testing procedures, 233, 236–37, 248; third phase, 262; tracks, 66–67, 217, 253; trade-offs, 5–7; tunnels, 119, 129, *269*; turning points, 266–68; twenty-first-century, 157–91; underground tours, 211–12; utility work, 78–79, 196–97, *199*; ventilation system, 168, 170; water mist system, 232; Whitehall Street station, *76*, 77; width, 66; before WWII, 18
Seven Line extension, 148, 181, 183, 190–91, 195, 229, 236
Shaw, Marc, 143, 159
Shelby, Richard, 187
signal systems, 4, 45, 62, 100, 186, 195, 217, 263–64
signs, 6, 233–34, 263
Silver, Sheldon, 140, 148, 151–57, 174–75, 181, 188, 194, 224, 266
Silverman, Norm, 97, *127*, 133, 141
Simpson, John, 100
Sixth Avenue El, *12*, 23
Sixth Avenue subway, 19, 23

small businesses, 204–6, 258–59
smells, 97, 99
Smiley, Wilson, 37–38
Smith, Al, 16
smoke detectors, 234, 265
snob express, 65
snow chains, 117
social deterioration, 121–22
social media, 251–52
South Bronx, 23
South Ferry station, 265
Spargo, George, 43–44
Spitzer, Eliot, 189, 193–95
Standard & Poor, 82
standards, 168, 217, 234, 257–59
state of emergency, 110, 249–52, 266–67
state of good repair, 107–110, 186–87, 195, 228–30, 252, 263
Staten Island, 63
Stelter, Lawrence, 23
"Step Aside, Speed Your Ride" program, 139
Straphangers Campaign, 101, 111, 142, 145–48, 151, 155, 160, 252
streetcars, 11, 19–24
Stringer, Scott, 5, 203
stubway, 4, 150, 153–54, 156
student fare discounts, 79, 135
suburbanization, 45, 47, 50, 52, 71, 89, 102
subway cars. See New York City subway: subway cars and equipment
subway tile, 169
sulfur dioxide, 214
super subway, 52
Sutton, Percy, 65, 95
Sutton Place, 22
Sydney Opera House, 262–63

The Taking of Pelham One Two Three, 80
Tappan Zee Bridge, 182, 191, 221–22, 228–29
taxes, 68–71, 84, 98, 108, 114, 117, 142; corporate, 113; efforts to avoid, 109, 157; investment credits, 108; mortgage, 68–69; municipal, 71–72; proposals to increase, 187; real estate, 71–72, 142, 190–91; sales, 32–33, 113
TBTA. See Triborough Bridge and Tunnel Authority
technology, 169, 228
Tendler, Lois, 207–210, 212, 222
terrorism, 149, 163–64, 168, 234, 265
testing procedures, 232–33, 236–37, 250
Theroux, Paul, 97–98, 101

Third Avenue (Manhattan), 208
Third Avenue El, 3, 12, 13, 21, 23, 46, 273–74
Thruway Authority, 221–23
tile(s), 169, 226
timbermen's union, 256
Times Square, 8, 66, 81, 112, 125, 135
Times Square station, 25
Tokyo, Japan, 265
tolls, 47, 68–69, 87, 98, 108, 182, 267; calls for, 186; revenues from, 91, 111, 142
Tomson, Lou, 165
tours, 211–12
transfers, 142
transit fares. See fares
transit police, 79
Transport Workers Union, 35
transportation bonds, 63, 108, 111; referendums, 56–60, 69, 73–74, 80–82, 92, 158–59, 188–91. See also bonds
trash collection, 203
trenches, 196–98, 256
Triborough Bridge and Tunnel Authority (TBTA), 29, 50–52, 56–60; bonds, 57, 60, 108, 111; toll revenues, 91, 111, 142
trolleys (streetcars), 11, 19–24
Truman, Harry, 31, 36, 40–41
Trump, Donald, 182
Trump Golf Links, 199
trunk lines, 15–16
tunnel workers, 255–56
tunnels and tunneling, 77–78, 169; abandoned tunnels, 2, 96, 106–7, 119, 127–29, 138, 269; tunnel boring, 169, 198, 200, 253, 256; vulnerable segments, 265
Turner, Daniel, 15

underground tours, 211–12
Union Square, 125
United Nations, 30
United States: Department of Commerce, 258; Department of Transportation, 130; House of Representatives, 192–93; House Transportation Committee, 182; Senate Appropriations Subcommittee on Transportation, 187; transportation laws, 130
Upper East Side, 21, 47–50, 106, 160, 204–8, 211, 228; household income, 151; population, 133, 205, 253–54; real estate, 205, 253–54; support for Second Avenue subway, 67, 179, 205
urban decay, 130. See also graffiti

Urban Development Corporation, 88
Urban Mass Transportation Act (US), 52
urban parks, 21
Urban Rail in America (Pushkarev and Zupan), 93
user fees, 70–71
utility lines, 78–79, 196–97, *199*, 203, 235, 257–58

vandalism, 119
Vanderbilt, Anne, 22
Vanterpool, Veronica, 231
ventilation, 168, 170, 257, 265
violent crime, 101, 141
Volpe, John, *94–95*
Vote Yes for Transportation, 189–91

Wagner, Robert F., Jr. (Bobby), 46, 51, 56, 89, 103, 112
Walder, Jay, 208–9, 223
Walker, Jimmy, 18
Wall Street (Manhattan), 114
Wall Street Journal, 247
War Production Board, 22–23
Washington, DC Metro, 77, 101–2
water damage, 264
Water Street, 51, 61
waterproofing, 264
Weiner, Anthony, 178
welding, 79
West 4th Street, 125

West Side, 181
Westway, 98–99, 102–3, 109–112, 120, 178
Whalen, Grover, *26*
Whitehall Street station, *76, 77*
Wi-Fi service, 6, 227, 251
Wilson, Malcolm, 86
Windels, Paul, 37
WNYC, 37
women-owned contractors, 258
Wong, Samuel, 250
Woodford, Bill, 173
Woolworth Building, 13
World Trade Center, 119, 159–65; construction of, 61; Port Authority Trans-Hudson (PATH) train station, 163; redevelopment of, 1–2; September 11, 2001 attacks, 163, *164*; subway station, *164*
World War II, 22–23, 27
Wright, Frank Lloyd, 2
Wylde, Kathryn, 183, 185

Yankee Stadium, 198
Yaro, Bob, 144–47, 152–53, 160, 183
Yoo, Young, 204
Yunich, David, 86–87, 90–91, 98, 268

Zolotow, Maurice, 27–28
Zupan, Jeff, 67, 93, 146–48, 150, 153–54, 165, 178
Z train, 163